INSIDERS' GUIDE® TO

LONG ISLAND

HELP US KEEP THIS GUIDE UP-TO-DATE

We would love to hear from you concerning your experiences with this guide and how you feel it could be improved and kept up-to-date. Please send your comments and suggestions to:

editorial@GlobePequot.com

Thanks for your input, and happy travels!

INSIDERS' GUIDE® SERIES

INSIDERS' GUIDE® TO

LONG ISLAND

JASON R. RICH

GUILFORD, CONNECTICUT
AN IMPRINT OF GLOBE PEQUOT PRESS

All the information in this guidebook is subject to change. We recommend that you call ahead to obtain current information before traveling.

INSIDERS' GUIDE®

Editor: Kevin Sirois
Project Editor: Ellen Urban
Layout artist: Kevin Mak
Text design: Sheryl Kober
Maps by Nick Trotter © Morris Book Publishing, LLC

ISBN: 978-0-7627-5674-2

Printed in the United States of America
10 9 8 7 6 5 4 3 2 1

CONTENTS

Directory of Maps

ABOUT THE AUTHOR

Jason R. Rich (www.jasonrich.com) is the best-selling author of more than 42 books, including over a dozen full-length travel guides. He also writes travel-related articles on a regular basis for the *New York Daily News* (circulation 2.5 million), as well as for several national magazines and popular Web sites (including Virgin Atlantic's new vTravelled.com and LowFares.com).

Jason maintains his own travel blog at www.jasonrichtravel.com, which is chock-full of travel advice and tips. He encourages readers to follow his day-to-day travels on Twitter (www.twitter.com/jasonrich7).

In addition to writing about travel, Jason writes books and articles covering a wide range of topics, including computers, eCommerce, blogging, pets, and personal finance. He is also an accomplished professional photographer.

While Jason visits the Long Island area often to see relatives in Nassau County, he lives with his Yorkshire terrier, named Rusty (www.mypalrusty.com), in Foxboro, Massachusetts.

ACKNOWLEDGMENTS

I would like to begin by thanking Amy Lyons at Globe Pequot Press for inviting me to write *Insiders' Guide to Long Island*. I truly appreciate her guidance, support, and understanding throughout the writing process. Thanks also to everyone else at Globe Pequot for their assistance in transforming my manuscript into the well-edited and expertly designed book you're currently holding in your hands.

Thanks also to all of the business operators, tourism specialists, publicists, restaurateurs, innkeepers, and Long Islanders who helped me conduct my research and gather the information I needed to complete this book. I could not have succeeded in writing this book without the assistance of Suzee Foster, from WordHampton Public Relations, as well as a handful of other PR professionals who shared their expertise and insight into Long Island with me.

I'd also like to thank the many hotel operators and innkeepers who offered me their hospitality during my numerous visits to Long Island as I was writing this book. I was honored to have the opportunity to stay at some of the most luxurious and comfortable inns and B&Bs on the East Coast, and to be able to share my thoughts and experiences with you, the reader.

Finally, I'd like to thank my family and friends for their never-ending love and support, and offer my gratitude to my faithful travel companion Rusty (a five-year-old Yorkshire terrier), who accompanied me on many of my Long Island trips. For fun, check out Rusty's Web site at www.MyPalRusty.com.

I would like to dedicate this book to my grandmother, who passed away as I was researching and writing this guide. She will also be loved and remembered.

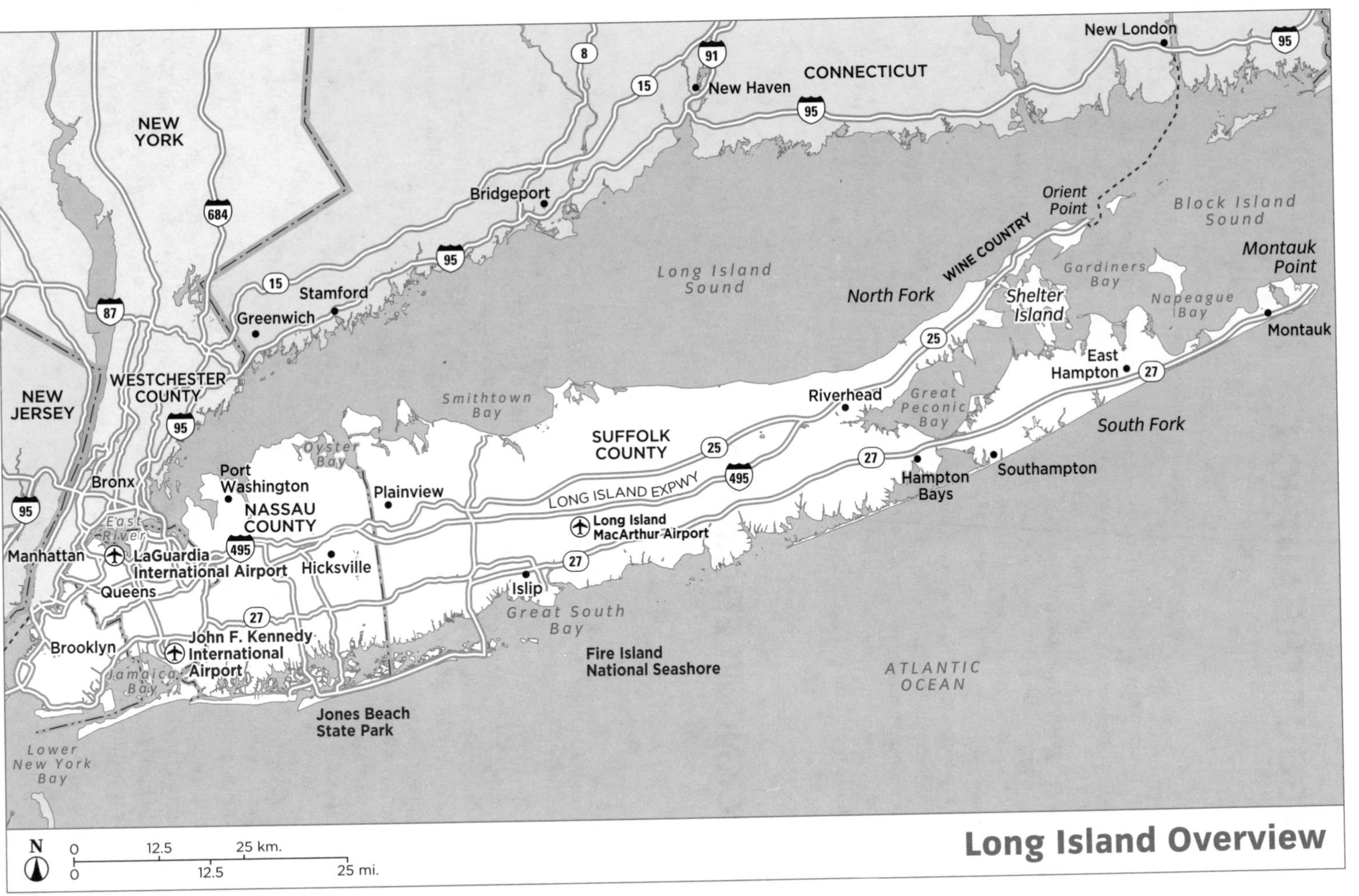
Long Island Overview
NEW YORK
CONNECTICUT
NEW JERSEY
WESTCHESTER COUNTY
NASSAU COUNTY
SUFFOLK COUNTY
New London
New Haven
Bridgeport
Stamford
Greenwich
Bronx
Manhattan
Queens
Brooklyn
Port Washington
Plainview
Hicksville
Islip
Riverhead
Hampton Bays
Southampton
East Hampton
Montauk
Montauk Point
Orient Point
Shelter Island
North Fork
South Fork
WINE COUNTRY
Long Island Sound
Block Island Sound
Gardiners Bay
Napeague Bay
Great Peconic Bay
Smithtown Bay
Oyster Bay
Great South Bay
Jamaica Bay
East River
Lower New York Bay
ATLANTIC OCEAN
LaGuardia International Airport
John F. Kennedy International Airport
Long Island MacArthur Airport
Fire Island National Seashore
Jones Beach State Park
LONG ISLAND EXPWY
95
91
8
15
684
87
25
27
495
N
0
12.5
25 km.
0
12.5
25 mi.

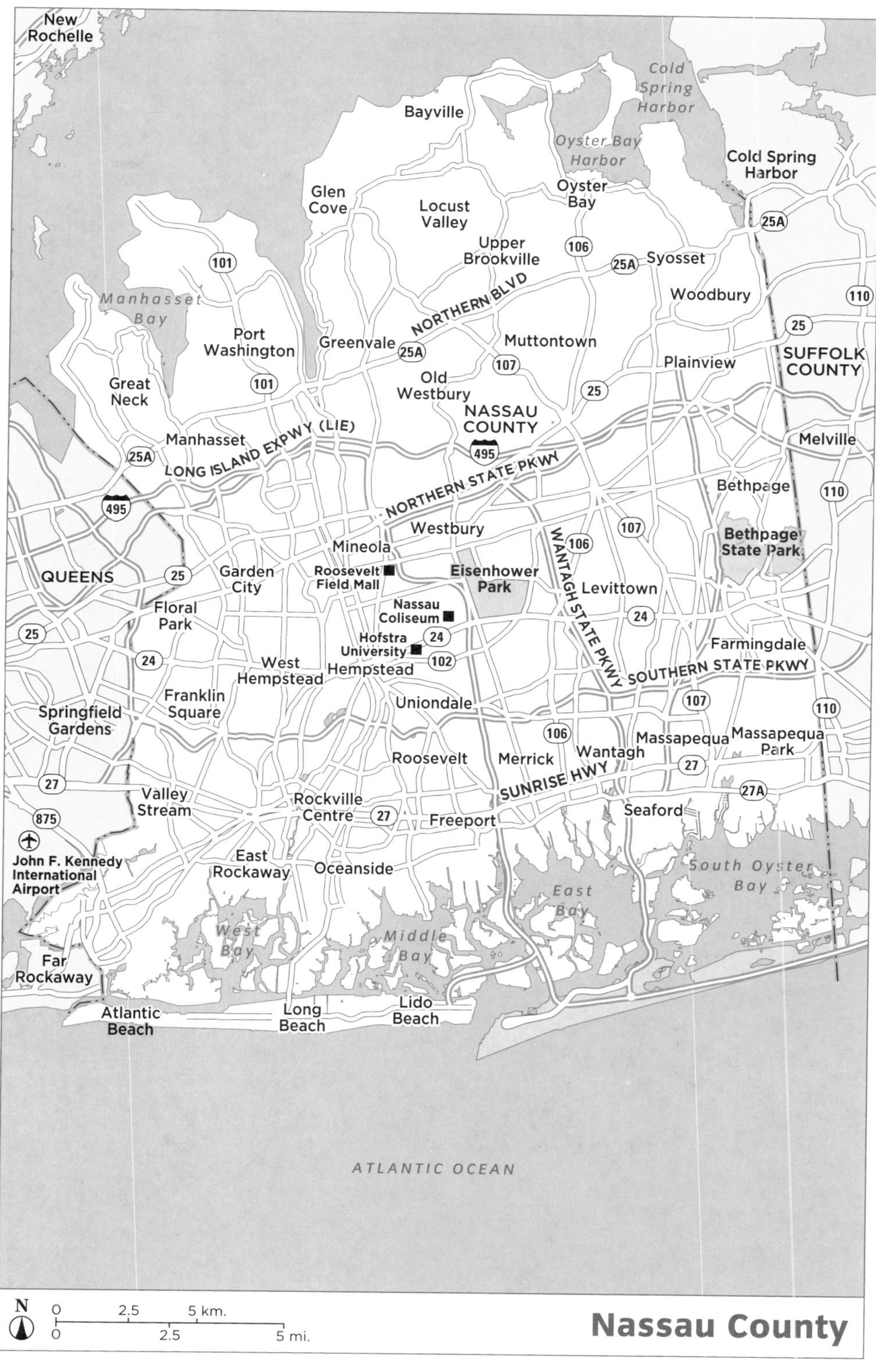
New Rochelle
Cold Spring Harbor
Bayville
Oyster Bay Harbor
Cold Spring Harbor
Glen Cove
Locust Valley
Oyster Bay
25A
Upper Brookville
106
25A
Syosset
101
Manhasset Bay
NORTHERN BLVD
Woodbury
110
Port Washington
Greenvale
25A
Muttontown
25
Great Neck
101
Old Westbury
107
Plainview
SUFFOLK COUNTY
25
NASSAU COUNTY
LONG ISLAND EXPWY (LIE)
Manhasset
25A
495
Melville
NORTHERN STATE PKWY
Bethpage
110
495
Westbury
WANTAGH STATE PKWY
107
Bethpage State Park
106
Mineola
QUEENS
25
Garden City
Roosevelt Field Mall
Eisenhower Park
Levittown
Floral Park
Nassau Coliseum
24
25
Hofstra University
24
Farmingdale
24
West Hempstead
Hempstead
102
SOUTHERN STATE PKWY
Franklin Square
Uniondale
107
110
Springfield Gardens
106
Massapequa
Massapequa Park
Wantagh
Roosevelt
Merrick
27
27
SUNRISE HWY
27A
Valley Stream
Rockville Centre
27
Freeport
Seaford
875
John F. Kennedy International Airport
East Rockaway
Oceanside
South Oyster Bay
East Bay
West Bay
Middle Bay
Far Rockaway
Atlantic Beach
Long Beach
Lido Beach
ATLANTIC OCEAN
N
0 2.5 5 km.
0 2.5 5 mi.
Nassau County

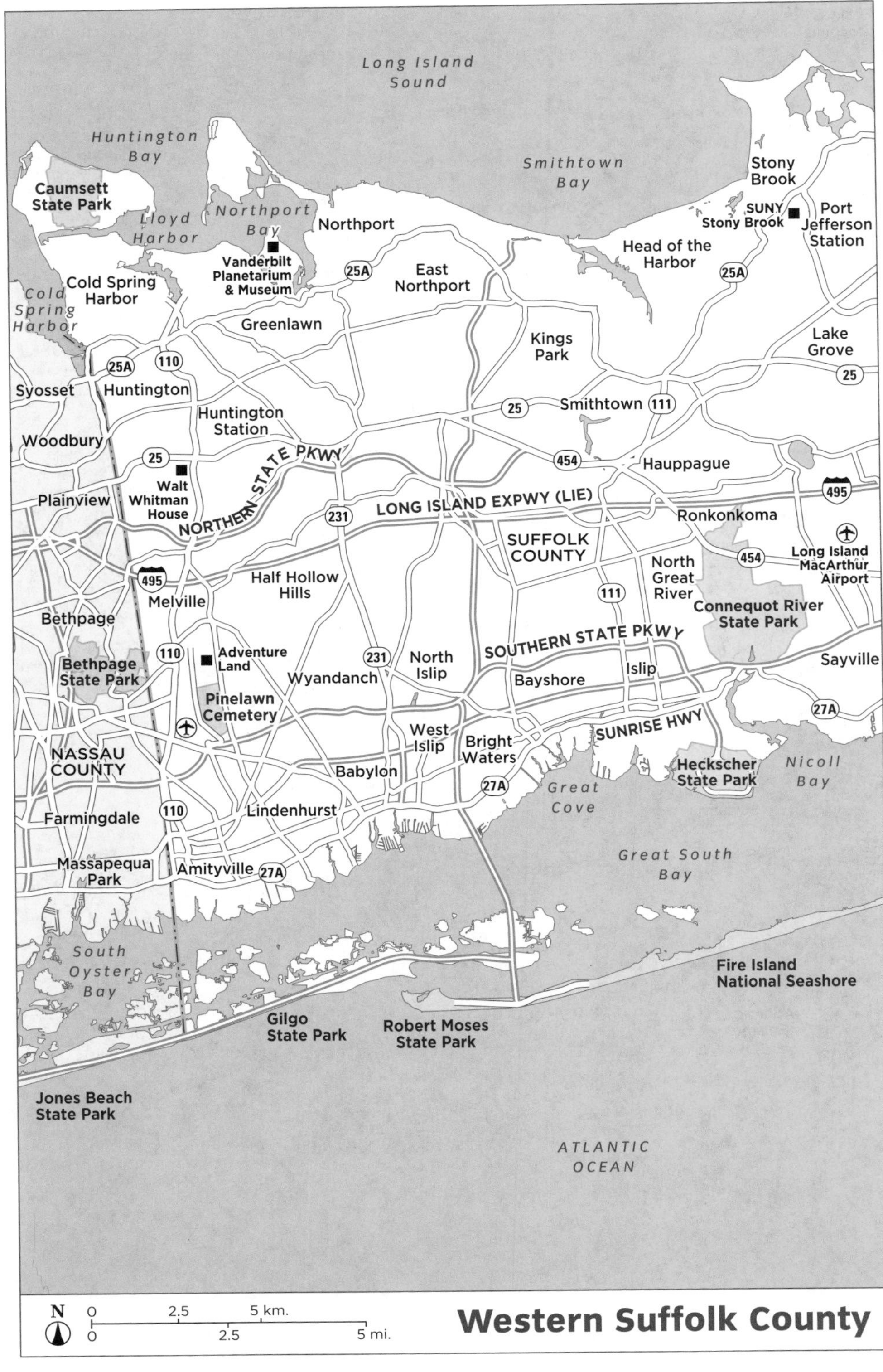

Long Island Sound
Huntington Bay
Smithtown Bay
Caumsett State Park
Lloyd Harbor
Northport Bay
Northport
Stony Brook
SUNY Stony Brook
Port Jefferson Station
Head of the Harbor
Vanderbilt Planetarium & Museum
East Northport
Cold Spring Harbor
Greenlawn
Kings Park
Lake Grove
Syosset
Huntington
Huntington Station
Smithtown
Woodbury
NORTHERN STATE PKWY
Hauppague
Walt Whitman House
Plainview
LONG ISLAND EXPWY (LIE)
Ronkonkoma
SUFFOLK COUNTY
North Great River
Long Island MacArthur Airport
Half Hollow Hills
Melville
Connequot River State Park
Bethpage
Adventure Land
SOUTHERN STATE PKWY
Sayville
Bethpage State Park
North Islip
Islip
Wyandanch
Bayshore
Pinelawn Cemetery
West Islip
Bright Waters
SUNRISE HWY
NASSAU COUNTY
Babylon
Heckscher State Park
Nicoll Bay
Great Cove
Farmingdale
Lindenhurst
Massapequa Park
Amityville
Great South Bay
South Oyster Bay
Fire Island National Seashore
Gilgo State Park
Robert Moses State Park
Jones Beach State Park
ATLANTIC OCEAN
N
0 2.5 5 km.
0 2.5 5 mi.
Western Suffolk County

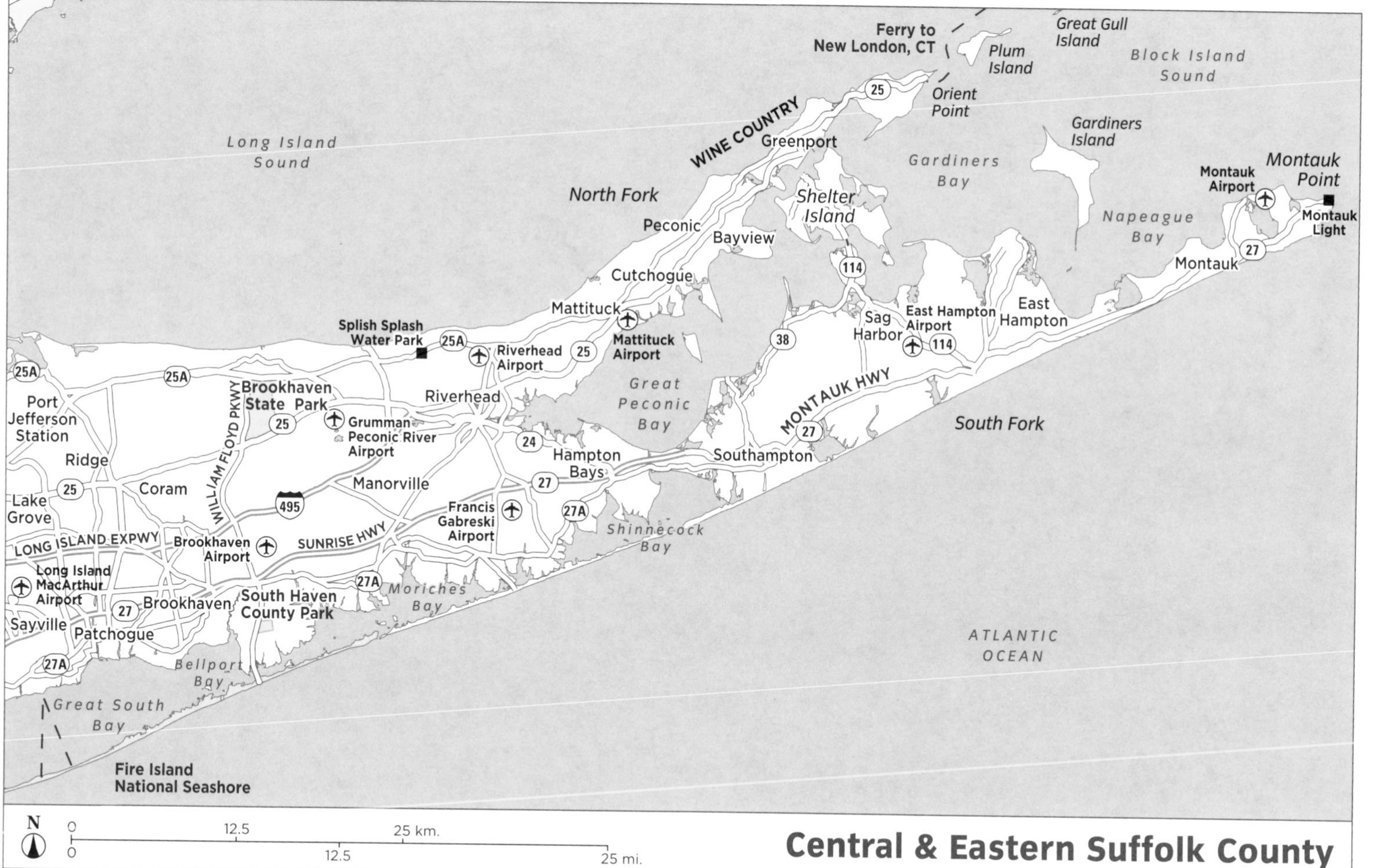
Central & Eastern Suffolk County
Long Island Sound
Block Island Sound
Great Gull Island
Plum Island
Ferry to New London, CT
Orient Point
Gardiners Island
Gardiners Bay
Napeague Bay
Montauk Point
Montauk Airport
Montauk Light
Montauk
WINE COUNTRY
Greenport
North Fork
Peconic
Bayview
Shelter Island
Cutchogue
Mattituck
Mattituck Airport
Sag Harbor
East Hampton Airport
East Hampton
Splish Splash Water Park
Riverhead Airport
Great Peconic Bay
Riverhead
MONTAUK HWY
South Fork
Southampton
Hampton Bays
Port Jefferson Station
Brookhaven State Park
WILLIAM FLOYD PKWY
Grumman Peconic River Airport
Ridge
Coram
Manorville
Lake Grove
Francis Gabreski Airport
Shinnecock Bay
LONG ISLAND EXPWY
Brookhaven Airport
SUNRISE HWY
Long Island MacArthur Airport
Brookhaven
South Haven County Park
Moriches Bay
Sayville
Patchogue
Bellport Bay
Great South Bay
Fire Island National Seashore
ATLANTIC OCEAN
25A
25
24
27
27A
38
114
495
N
0
12.5
25 km.
0
12.5
25 mi.

PREFACE

When people think about visiting New York, chances are Manhattan comes to mind, and all there is to see and experience in this incredible city. After all, no other city in the world compares to the Big Apple in terms of its culture, restaurants, hotels, tourist attractions, landmarks, and exciting activities. What far fewer people think about, however, is all that nearby Long Island, New York, has to offer for its residents and vacationers alike.

Located just a short distance from Manhattan, and on the same landmass as Queens and Brooklyn, Long Island's Nassau County and Suffolk County are fun, exciting, and interesting places to visit, whether you enjoy beaches, outdoor sports, boating/sailing, shopping, fine dining, luxurious day spas, museums, historical landmarks and sites, cultural activities, or indulging in locally produced wines.

Long Island is also where you'll find literally hundreds of gorgeous and cozy inns and B&Bs and many fancy resorts, plus everything that the world-famous Hamptons have to offer. It's true that many people love vacationing in the Hamptons during the summer, but all of Long Island is quickly becoming a popular year-round destination to live, work, and vacation.

What so many people don't realize is that while New York City and Long Island are so close together geographically, they're worlds apart in terms of what's offered and the experiences one will have. In fact, as you're about to discover, even Long Island's Nassau County and Suffolk County are vastly different—each offering a unique type of vacation or living experience.

While New York City can, without a doubt, be classified as a major metropolitan city, what you'll find within Nassau County are much smaller urban and commercial areas. Yes, you'll find some of the same world-class shopping and dining experiences in Nassau County as you'd find in New York City, but the massive skyscrapers have been replaced in many cases by stunning waterfront views from Nassau's North Shore and South Shore.

As you make your way east, toward Suffolk County, the terrain becomes more and more suburban and even rural. So, by the time you reach Suffolk County's North Fork, for example, what you'll find is acre after acre of farmland and adorable waterfront towns, villages, and communities that seem to remain timeless. Likewise, Suffolk County's South Fork is where you'll find the Hamptons (including Southampton and East Hampton) and places like Wainscott, Amagansett, and Montauk, which are well-known seasonal vacation destinations for the rich and famous.

Insiders' Guide to Long Island is about to take you on an amazing adventure through Long Island—from the most modern things to see, experience, and do, to some of the most historical places on the East Coast. You'll learn about memorable and affordable places to visit, and what some of the wealthiest people on the planet consider their summer playground.

You'll also learn about Long Island's fast-growing wine country, which is home to dozens of breathtakingly gorgeous wineries and vineyards that are currently producing locally produced wines that are as impressive and enjoyable as the wines being produced in California, Italy, Spain, and other parts of the world.

So, whether you're planning to visit Long Island for a weekend, spend a week exploring, stay for an entire summer, or relocate here, *Insiders' Guide to Long Island* will provide you with the information you want and need about this unique and exciting destination that's incredibly easy to reach by car, train, bus, ferryboat, boat, or airplane, especially if you're coming from New York City (or flying into one of New York's main airports).

What you'll discover when you visit Long Island are hundreds of affluent towns, villages, and communities, plus a few larger cities and more populated regions, that offer something that's complementary to, albeit vastly different from, anything that New York City has to offer. Yet, there truly is something for everyone on Long Island, regardless of your age or interests.

From this guide, you'll learn about Long Island's extremely interesting history, which dates back to long before America was colonized, plus discover all that there is to see, do, and experience today—whether you'll be visiting during the summer, spring, fall, or winter. In the pages that follow you'll find a timely, accurate, and comprehensive guide to the entire Long Island area (consisting of Nassau and Suffolk Counties). The goal is to put in your hands a valuable and insightful resource that will hopefully motivate you to visit or relocate to this unique and wonderful part of New York State.

As a travel writer for numerous national magazines, major daily newspapers (including the *New York Daily News*), and a handful of popular Web sites, I have the opportunity to constantly travel across the United States and visit some of the most exciting and unique countries in the world. Having grown up in New York, however, I must admit that Long Island offers a truly wonderful place to visit pretty much any time during the year, especially in the summer and fall.

I invite you to learn more about my writing by visiting www.JasonRich.com. You can also read about my ongoing travel adventures, and see photos from my travels, by reading my personal travel blog at www.JasonRichTravel.com.

Just as I have had the opportunity to experience firsthand all that Long Island has to offer, it's my sincere wish that you, too, will be able to follow in my footsteps and visit Long Island's most popular attractions and destinations, and spend some truly quality time here.

I wish you all the safest, most exciting, and memorable travels as you visit Long Island.

HOW TO USE THIS BOOK

As you're about to discover by reading this guide, Long Island is a wonderful place to visit, as well as an enjoyable place to live. This region of New York State is divided into counties that offer a vastly different experience for visitors and residents. For example, there are relatively inexpensive places to live on Long Island, as well as locations in the Hamptons that are among the most exclusive in the country. There are suburban communities that offer a very easy commute to and from New York City, and very rural areas along the water that are ideal for boaters and people who enjoy an ocean view from their home, office, or hotel room.

When people first begin exploring Long Island, they often get confused in regard to its proximity and relationship to New York City. Yes, Long Island is part of New York State, and yes, geographically it does encompass Queens and Brooklyn (which are boroughs of New York City); however, Long Island is also where you'll find Nassau and Suffolk Counties.

Because Queens and Brooklyn are, in fact, boroughs of New York City and are considered separate entities from Nassau and Suffolk Counties (although they share the same landmass surrounded by the Long Island Sound and the Atlantic Ocean), for the purposes of this guide, we'll focus almost exclusively on Nassau County and on Suffolk County's two distinct regions: the North Fork (often referred to as wine country) and the South Fork (which includes the Hamptons to Montauk, the southeastern section of the island). There's also the western region of Suffolk County, which is closest to Queens, Brooklyn, and Manhattan.

In addition to helping you understand Long Island's geography, this guide offers detailed information about planning a memorable vacation here, including where to eat and how to entertain yourself during your stay. While many people who visit Long Island take full advantage of its close proximity to Manhattan, you'll discover that various parts of the island offer their own extremely unique and memorable vacation opportunities.

If you're planning to move to or stay in the region for a while, be sure to check out the blue-tabbed pages at the back of the book, where you will find the **Living Here** appendix that offers sections on relocation, education, retirement (see "Senior Scene"), child care, and health care. However, if you're just visiting, this guide will help you plan a fun and memorable itinerary based on your unique interests, find accommodations that meet your needs and budget, choose restaurants that'll satisfy your taste buds, and discover all there is to see and do while you're here—whether you're staying for a weekend, a full week, or the entire summer. After all, there's a reason why so many people opt to "summer in the Hamptons." Plus, it discusses the many reasons why so many people who work in Manhattan opt to live on Long Island and commute to and from their city-based job on a daily basis.

We've designed this guide to be a comprehensive, portable, and easily accessible information-packed resource about Long Island. It's small enough to fit into a suitcase, briefcase, or purse, yet detailed enough to provide the information you want and need in one place.

Many of the chapters are divided by county, so you can focus on the area you'll be visiting. We've also included detailed information about, for example, hotels, resorts, restaurants, and tourist attractions. Within each listing is an address and phone number. When applicable, we've also included a Web site address, hours of operation, and a price code to help you with your budgeting, plus other quick-reference information you'll find useful.

Please be aware, however, that prices change, as do hours of operation (especially those businesses that operate in more seasonally popular areas). As a general rule, stores, some businesses, and most attractions maintain extended hours during peak travel seasons but reduce their operating hours or close entirely during non-peak seasons.

Throughout this guide you'll also find Insiders' Tips—look for the i . These tidbits of information let you in on local secrets or convey information designed to save you time and/or money. We've also included occasional Close-ups, which are informative profiles of special events and attractions worthy of extended coverage.

Finally, if you're familiar with the *Insiders' Guide* series, you know that these guides are chock-full of listings, organized by subject. For example, in the "Restaurants" chapter you'll typically find listings for every single dining establishment in the city. However, because Long Island is so large (118 miles long) and covers a lot of territory, including hundreds of separate towns, villages, and communities (some of which are over 100 miles apart), there are literally hundreds or even thousands of local listings that would be appropriate for each section. To keep things manageable, whenever possible, a sampling of what's available within each region is offered instead of a comprehensive listing of everything. When a complete list could not be included, at least one online resource for accessing a complete listing in a particular area is provided, as is a wide range of information you'll want to know about the section's subject matter. So, while you won't find literally thousands of hotel or restaurant reviews in this guide, you will find a nice sampling of what's available within a relatively short distance of where you'll be staying on Long Island.

Insiders' Guide to Long Island was designed to be a handy reference guide. To ensure this book remains accurate, timely, and comprehensive, we invite our readers to share their feedback via e-mail (Jason@jasonrich.com). If you find aspects of this guide particularly useful, or you've discovered we've missed something, please let us know so we can incorporate your feedback into the next edition.

AREA OVERVIEW

Long Island, New York, is comprised of four counties: Queens and Brooklyn (which are boroughs of New York City), Nassau, and Suffolk. As its name suggests, Long Island is, in fact, an island, surrounded by the Long Island Sound and the Atlantic Ocean.

This guide focuses almost exclusively on Nassau and Suffolk Counties, which are totally separate from New York City. (The boroughs of Brooklyn and Queens are politically part of New York City and not typically considered part of Long Island, except geographically.) Long Island is connected to several other boroughs of New York City, as well as Manhattan itself, via bridges and tunnels. Regularly scheduled ferryboat service is also offered linking Long Island to parts of Connecticut, Rhode Island, and Massachusetts. See the "Getting Here, Getting Around" chapter for details about how to reach Long Island by air, car, train, bus, or boat/ferry.

Encompassing about 1,401 square miles, Long Island is both the longest and largest island in the contiguous United States. It is 118 miles long (east to west), and at its maximum width (north to south), it is approximately 23 miles across. As of July 2008 the population of Long Island was estimated to be 7.7 million, making it the most populated island in the United States and the 17th most populated island in the world. If Long Island were its own state, it would rank 12th in terms of population.

Combined, Brooklyn and the Bronx represent 4.69 million of the island's overall population, while Nassau County's population was 1.3 million and Suffolk County's population was 1.4 million in 2008. Suffolk County has more than twice the land area than Nassau County, so it's much less congested.

While located on the same island landmass, Nassau and Suffolk Counties are vastly different. Nassau, which is located on the west side of the island, is closer to New York City and is more urbanized than Suffolk. From the 1950s to the 1970s, Nassau was the fastest growing county in the United States. Based on the 2000 Census, it was the third-richest county per capita in New York State. Suffolk County, on the other hand, is much more rural and comprised of many small towns.

The North Fork portion of Suffolk County is home to the much less populated but fast-growing wine region, while the South Fork region contains the Hamptons, Montauk, and many small, upscale beach towns. These regions are among the most affluent on the East Coast and are extremely popular vacation destinations—especially in the summer (early June through early Sept).

From a political standpoint, Long Island is part of New York State, which has a governor, as well as U.S. senators and congressmen, just like any other state. Nassau County and Suffolk County are each led by a county executive and have their own county legislature. The towns within both counties all have their own local governments. There are also two Indian reservations in Suffolk County.

THE LONG ISLAND WORKFORCE

Between the 1930s and early 1990s, the aviation industry was prominent here. These days, however, the region plays a leading role in scientific research, engineering, and the computer industry. It's also a mecca for medical and technological research, and home to the East Coast's largest industrial park—the Hauppauge Industrial Park, where you'll find more than 1,300 companies employing over 55,000 people.

Due to its close proximity to Manhattan, as much as 20 percent of Long Island's working population commutes into New York City, typically by car or train. However, the eastern side of the island still has a strong agricultural focus, while the Northport and Montauk regions maintain a prominent fishing and tourism industry.

Like everyplace else in America, starting in 2008 Long Island was affected by the turbulent economy. This has greatly impacted the job market, unemployment rates, and the real estate market, not to mention every other aspect of the local and state economy. Due to the affluence here, however, in many areas of Long Island it took a bit longer for the impact of the recession to hit the local economy and for the negative effects to be felt.

The unemployment rate on Long Island in Aug 2000 was just 3.4 percent, compared to 7.3 percent in Aug 2009. For the latest details about local job prospects, as well as the overall employment rate outlook, access the Bureau of Labor Statistics' *Occupational Outlook Handbook* Web site at www.bls.gov/OCO. The hard copy of this data, in book form, is available at libraries and career guidance offices at schools.

To quickly research job and career opportunities on Long Island, visit http://longisland.employmentguide.com or www.monster.com.

CRIME ON LONG ISLAND

The towns and communities that make up Nassau and Suffolk Counties are extremely diverse. Some areas boast extremely low crime rates, while others have rates that are more consistent with other parts of New York State. According to the FBI Crime Index, Long Island overall is one of the best places to raise children, plus it has the second-lowest crime rate in the United States.

LONG ISLAND IN THE 21ST CENTURY

Long Island's economy is greatly influenced by its proximity to New York City. As of late 2009, the United States and the world economy were undergoing massive changes. How these changes will impact the local economy in Long Island and New York State in general has yet to be seen. Thus, it's impossible to predict unemployment rates or real estate values, for example, with any precision whatsoever.

What is known for sure, however, is that many mid- to high-income professionals who work in Manhattan will continue to seek out suburban living in places like Nassau County and commute to and from work, while raising their families outside the hectic New York City environment. Meanwhile, many areas of Suffolk County will continue to attract the rich and famous and will remain a top beach-oriented tourist destination, particularly in the summer.

According to the Long Island Index (www.longislandindex.org), in 2000 62 percent of houses sold were priced less than $250,000. By 2006 that number had dropped to about 4 percent. (This was, of course, prior to the recession that began in 2008.) The Long Island Index also reports that about 88 percent of Long Islanders consider the lack of affordable housing a serious problem (based on a 2008 study by the Stony Brook University Center for Survey Research).

If you're thinking about relocating to Long Island, the Zillow Web site (www.zillow.com) is an excellent resource for learning about current real estate prices and trends for any neighborhood or city in America, including all areas of Long Island. As you explore the local real estate market, what you'll find is that Long Island has a significantly lower number of multi-unit housing options and rentals than other New York suburbs, and that more than 82 percent of its housing units are single-family dwellings.

As Long Island continues to evolve in the 21st century, a trend toward more affordable housing may arise, as local industry and businesses expand and the need for a diverse labor pool increases. The Urban Land Institute reports that "access to a large and diverse labor pool, including workers who can fill entry-level positions, is the most important factor in corporate decisions about where to locate." However, what trends actually become a reality over the next few years will, without a doubt, be directly influenced by the direction the local and national economy takes.

Bankrate.com offers a free cost-of-living calculator (www.bankrate.com/calculators/savings/moving-cost-of-living-calculator.aspx) that will help you compare and contrast two cities or neighborhoods at a time, such as where you currently live and a specific town or region of Long Island. Alternatively, BestPlaces.net offers a cost-of-living calculator (www.bestplaces.net/COL) with slightly different functionality and cost comparison options.

PROXIMITY TO NEW YORK CITY

Thanks to the Long Island Expressway and several other major roadways that lead into and out of Long Island, the ease of use of the Long Island Railroad, and the island's close proximity to New York City, many people who vacation, live, and/or work on Long Island make full use of Manhattan's vast resources in terms of cultural activities, dining options, entertainment, and shopping. From many parts of Long Island, getting to downtown Manhattan takes 60 to 90 minutes by car or train, depending on your starting location.

Likewise, New Yorkers take full advantage of Long Island's beaches and consider parts of Long Island (particularly Suffolk County) to be popular vacation destinations. For New Yorkers and other people living in the Tri-State area, activities such as weekend getaways or summering in the Hamptons, docking a boat at a marina on the Long Island Sound, or visiting Nassau Coliseum for a concert are extremely common.

While Long Island certainly offers an abundance of hotels, resorts, restaurants, shopping opportunities, day spas, golf courses, historical sites, and tourist attractions to see and experience, vacationers visiting the island would be missing out if they don't also plan to spend some time in Manhattan, even if it's just to enjoy dinner and a Broadway show.

i A resident of Long Island is referred to as a "Long Islander."

As you travel across Long Island from Manhattan (traveling east, toward Suffolk County), the more suburban your surroundings will become, until you reach some of the most beautiful and affluent beach communities on the East Coast. Visiting the Hamptons or Montauk, for example, offers a vastly different experience than a visit to most areas of Nassau County or New York City.

i Long Island is home to the largest industrial park on the East Coast. It's called the Hauppauge Industrial Park and it houses more than 1,300 companies that employ over 55,000 Long Islanders.

NASSAU COUNTY

Nassau County's population is primarily white, with a significantly smaller black and African-American population, and an even smaller Asian population. There's also a small American Indian population.

Prior to the end of World War II, Nassau County was mostly farmland. Agriculture was the primary industry, and the population was small. This all changed in 1947, when 6,500 veterans returned home from the war and responded to an ad that offered 2,000 homes for $60 a month in a new development that was built on the Hempstead plains. Almost overnight this influx of residents transformed Nassau County into the fastest-growing and largest suburb in America. The population doubled between 1950 and 1960, and continued steady growth into the 1970s. During the 1980s and 1990s, population growth slowed down dramatically, but the affluence of the residents improved as the overall economy evolved and white-collar employment opportunities (in Long Island and New York City) became more prevalent, replacing agriculture almost entirely.

While Nassau County is more urban than Suffolk County and is closer to Manhattan, you'll find a handful of very popular beaches here, including Jones Beach State Park. Shoppers will also enjoy spending time and giving their credit cards a workout at the popular Roosevelt Field Mall (one of the largest indoor malls in New York State), while those in search of more cultural activities will discover an abundant selection of unique museums and historical sites in the region.

Sports fans won't want to miss experiencing a home game at the Nassau Veterans Memorial Coliseum in Uniondale. This 18,000-plus-seat arena and 60,000-square-foot exhibition hall is home to the National Hockey League's New York Islanders and the New York Dragons indoor football team. The arena also hosts touring concerts by big-name recording artists, plus family-oriented traveling arena shows, like the *Ringling Bros. and Barnum & Bailey Circus* and *Disney on Ice.*

Nassau County also has seven public, county-operated 9- and 18-hole golf courses, along with many more privately owned and operated courses that are open to nonmembers. The Bethpage Black golf course, for example, was the site of the 2009 U.S. Open.

This county encompasses about 287 square miles and includes three dozen state and county parks that are open year-round. Many of these parks, which have free admission, are famous for their hiking and nature trails.

i **Nassau County is located just 17 miles east of downtown Manhattan. In sharp contrast to the city, you can find lovely white sandy beaches here. For information about the area's beaches, visit www.theislandnextdoor.com.**

SUFFOLK COUNTY

Suffolk County encompasses about 1,000 square miles, which translate to about two-thirds of Long Island. From the border of Nassau County to the very tip of Montauk Point is about 86 miles. The county's widest point, between the Long Island Sound and the southern shore, is about 26 miles.

This county is considered a recreational and leisure wonderland, as it offers a wide range of indoor and outdoor family-friendly activities and attractions. For nature lovers, it's here you'll find the Fire Island National Seashores (FINS), which is composed of 17 beachfront communities that encompass almost 19,600 acres of federally preserved land. For tourists, Suffolk County is home to Fire Island, the Hamptons, and Montauk, all offering a wide range of resort accommodations.

Port Jefferson and Stony Brook

While Nassau County is more commercialized and populated than Suffolk County, within Nassau, Port Jefferson and Stony Brook are just two examples of small-town tourist areas that offer unique shopping, historical sites, top-notch restaurants, and family-friendly activities and attractions, plus lovely accommodations in the form of hotels, inns, and B&Bs. These areas, in addition to a handful of other beachfront communities, are much closer to NYC than, for example, the Hamptons, but when you're visiting, it feels like you're in a different state or region of the country altogether.

Western Suffolk County

This region of Long Island is particularly popular among visitors for its beaches, shopping malls, parks, and various cultural activities, including museums, performance halls, and historic sites. It is considered the more developed section of the county, though instead of cities, you're more apt to find small and utterly charming waterfront villages. Most feature unique shops and restaurants, not national franchises or major chain operations.

Some of the tourist attractions in the region include entertainment venues, Adventureland amusement park, Long Island Game Farm Wildlife Park & Children's Zoo, Vanderbilt Planetarium, and the Fire Island Lighthouse. Western Suffolk County also boasts 18 state and county parks.

Golfers will appreciate the more than 25 public courses in Western Suffolk County, while baseball fans who don't want to trek to a major-league stadium to see the New York Yankees or New York Mets can check out a home game played by the Long Island Ducks, a minor-league team whose season is between May and Oct.

North Fork

As a family-oriented vacation destination, this region of Long Island offers an abundance of activities and popular attractions, including the Atlantis Marine World aquarium and Splish Splash water park, plus dozens of wineries. In fact, it's the wineries that have become the most popular tourist attractions in the area, in part because the wines being produced have received top reviews and awards in recent years, from virtually all of the best-known and most respected food and wine publications.

Being a farm community, the North Fork region also specializes in "agritainment," meaning that the local farms and wineries are tourist attractions unto themselves. They offer tours and pick-your-own seasonal fruit and vegetable activities, for example.

NASCAR fans can catch a race at the Riverhead Raceway, the only track in the New York metropolitan area, while shoppers can find bargains at the 165 brand-name outlet stores at the Tanger Outlet Center, also located in Riverhead.

South Fork

Known as a playground for the rich and famous, this region of Long Island includes popular beachfront resort communities, upscale small towns, and an abundance of historic sites. It's also where you'll find the famous Montauk Point Lighthouse (at the very tip of the island) and the world-famous Hamptons. It's this part of Long Island that boasts more than 50 miles of white sandy beaches.

Here you'll find the trendiest beaches on the East Coast, along with upscale accommodations, including hotels, resorts, B&Bs, inns, and rental properties; gourmet restaurants; nightclubs; and an abundance of unique boutiques and shops (most catering to the high-end market). The South Fork area is also where you'll find many historical sites and museums, a few wineries, and several world-class day spas.

Some of the most popular communities in this region are Eastport, East Quogue, Southampton, East Hampton, Bridgehampton, Montauk, and Sag Harbor. Each has its own community setting, shopping area, and activities. Because of the abundance of waterfront and beachfront property, all kinds of boating, sailing, and water sports are popular here.

Golf is also a popular pastime. Many of the best-known courses are owned and operated by private clubs, like the historic Shinnecock Hills Golf Club in Southampton, which hosted the U.S. Open in 1896, 1986, 1995, and 2004.

This region of Long Island is easily accessible by car, small airplane, boat, or ferry, as well as the Long Island Railroad.

CONVENTION AND TOURISM BUREAUS

One of the best—and free—sources of information for anyone interested in visiting or relocating to Long Island is the Long Island Convention & Visitors Bureau and Sports Commission, 330 Motor Pkwy., Suite 203, Hauppauge, NY 11788; (877) FUN-ON-LI; www.discoverlongisland.com; tourism@discoverlongisland.com.

Each region of Long Island also has its own chamber of commerce, which offers free vacation planning or relocating information for that specific town, community, city, or region. For a town-by-town listing of local chamber of commerce offices, visit www.longislandexchange.com/chambers-commerce.html.

SUGGESTED READING AND RESOURCES

When planning a trip to Long Island, be sure to request a copy of the *Long Island Travel Guide* published by the Long Island Convention & Visitors Bureau and Sports Commission. It's distributed free at many hotels, an online version is available at www.discoverlongisland.com, or you can request a printed copy by calling (877) 386-6654.

Covering the North Fork and Shelter Island regions, the *North Fork & Shelter Island Vacation Guide* is another annual information-packed, full-color resource, published by Times/Review Newspapers. This free magazine-like publication is distributed through hotels, restaurants, and tourist attractions in the region.

Many of the chambers of commerce throughout Long Island also publish their own vacation guides that focus on specific areas of the island and offer lodging, dining, attraction, and activity recommendations. For example, there's the *Montauk 2010 Vacation Guide*, which is a free publication from the Montauk Chamber of Commerce (www.montaukchamber.com), and the *Southampton Chamber of Commerce Business Directory & Visitors Guide*, a free full-color publication published by the Southampton Chamber of Commerce (www.southamptonchamber.com).

Lastly, for a comprehensive up-to-date listing of events and festivals happening throughout Long Island, visit www.discoverlongisland.com/calendar_list.cfm.

Long Island Statistics

Founded: 1683

Nassau County's county executive: Tom Suozzi

Suffolk County's county executive: Steve Levy

Population: 7,559,372 (as of 2006)

Area: 1,401 square miles (118 miles long by 23 miles across, at its widest point)

Counties and cities on Long Island: Nassau County, Suffolk County, as well as Queens and Brooklyn from a geographic but not political standpoint

Time zone: Eastern Standard Time

Major airports: LaGuardia Airport, John F. Kennedy International Airport, Long Island MacArthur Airport

Major roadways: Cross Island Expressway, Montauk Highway (27A), Sunrise Highway (27), Belt Parkway/Southern State Parkway, Hempstead Turnpike, Northern State Parkway, Long Island Expressway (495), Jericho Turnpike/Middle Country Road (25), Northern Boulevard (25A), Meadowbrook State Parkway, Wantagh State Parkway, Seaford–Oyster Bay Expressway (135), Robert Moses Causeway, Sagtikos State Parkway, Sunken Meadow State Parkway, William Floyd Parkway

Average temperatures: The temperature throughout Long Island is typically similar to Manhattan in most areas, but can be somewhat warmer or cooler in other areas based on proximity to the Long Island Sound or the Atlantic Ocean. In the winter the average temperature will typically be in the low to mid 30s (F), while in the summer it could be anywhere from the mid-60s to high 70s.

Area code: The primary telephone area code for most of Nassau County is 516. In western Suffolk County, the primary area code is 631.

Major colleges and universities: Long Island is home to more than 21 colleges and universities, including SUNY College at Old Westbury, Nassau Community College, Adelphi University, Hofstra University, Gibbs College, New York Institute of Technology, and St. John's University.

Famous sons and daughters: Billy Crystal, Billy Joel, Carol Alt, Deborah Gibson, Eddie Money, Eddie Murphy, Harvey Milk, Jennifer Capriati, John Tesh, John William, Jonathan Larson, Lindsay Lohan, LL Cool J, Lou Reed, Mariah Carey, Pat Benatar, Paul Simon, Rodney Dangerfield, Rosie O'Donnell

Public transportation: Long Island Railroad

Driving laws: Speed limits in residential and business areas throughout Long Island range from 25 to 45 mph. The speed limit on the Long Island Expressway is 55 mph, not 65 mph as it is along most expressways, highways, and thruways in New York State.

Alcohol laws: You must be 21 to purchase or consume alcoholic beverages legally. New York State drunk-driving laws are strictly enforced throughout Long Island

Major daily newspapers: *Newsday, Long Island Press,* the *New York Times,* the *New York Daily News,* the *New York Post*

Sales tax: 8.625 percent

Chambers of commerce: For a directory of chamber of commerce offices throughout Norfolk and Suffolk Counties, visit www.longislandexchange.com/chambers-commerce.html.

Weather: www.weather.com

HISTORY

Long Island has a rich, interesting, and intricate history that in some ways is tied directly to New York City, but in other ways is vastly different. Long before the Europeans arrived in 1609, Native Americans (including the Algonquin tribe) populated Long Island for more than 9,000 years.

Let's begin our look back, however, in 1609, when the first Europeans stepped foot on Long Island.

EUROPEAN DISCOVERY AND SETTLEMENT

It was Henry Hudson (for whom New York's Hudson River was named) and his crew who first visited Long Island during their quest to find a shortcut to India. While Hudson didn't stay, he was soon followed by Adriaen Block from Holland, who arrived by boat and sailed around the island. He gave Long Island its name after discovering its long length, and was the first to create a map of the island.

In the mid-1620s the Dutch established slavery on Long Island, which was a practice the English adopted soon after. As 1635 rolled around, King Charles I of England gifted Long Island to the Earl of Sterling. Soon after, the Dutch came to New York City and set up trading posts there, calling their settlement New Amsterdam. A year or so later, the Dutch West India Company created settlements on the western end of Long Island.

Around the same time as the Dutch were establishing their settlements, the English created settlements on the eastern end of the island. Some of these settlements, like Southampton (established in 1640) and East Hampton (created in 1648), have since grown and evolved substantially, and are still in existence today.

In 1650, because of vast differences between their two cultures, the English and Dutch created a formal boundary between their two settlements under an agreement known as the Treaty of Hartford. The focus of the Dutch was to establish and expand trade with the Indians, while the English's focus was on building and expanding their settlements.

In 1664 possession of Long Island changed again, when King Charles II gifted the island to the Duke of York. Around this time, the British drove the Dutch off of Long Island, allowing the English to establish an island-wide county system in 1683. The counties of Suffolk, Queens, and Kings were established.

Over the years Long Island has become known for many things. For example, the country's very first racetrack (for entertainment purposes) was built in 1668. Here, horse and mule races were held, along with a variety of other events.

18TH CENTURY: THE ERA OF EXPANSION

By 1700 Long Island's population was approximately 220,000. However, a period of tremendous growth and expansion was about to begin. During the 18th century Long Island's population doubled almost every two years. Many settlements were built close to the shore, as the sea served many purposes, such as being a primary means of communication.

In the 18th century many Long Islanders became farmers and were heavily involved with agriculture. In addition to growing crops, like tobacco and grain, these farmers also raised livestock, ranging from horses and cattle to sheep and pigs. Many of the Long Islanders who weren't farmers were accomplished fishermen, which resulted in a thriving fishing industry, including whaling. The whales were used to make oil, and oil exportation became a profitable industry on Long Island in the 18th and part of the 19th centuries.

TALKING ABOUT A REVOLUTION

Fast forwarding now to around 1760, England began demanding greater control over the colonies in America. Taxes and trade restrictions were imposed. This annoyed those living in the colonies, including the Long Islanders, resulting in the groundwork for the American Revolution to begin. By this time many Long Islanders were thriving on whale oil exporting, and didn't want their livelihood or profits tampered with by the British.

The colonists wanted more democracy, lower taxes, fewer trade restrictions, and more freedom and autonomy from England. Soon the Boston Tea Party took place (in Boston, of course) and there was fighting (during the Revolution), but by 1776 the colonists, including those living on Long Island, established their independence. At the Second Continental Congress, which met in Philadelphia to draft the Declaration of Independence, joining people like John Hancock, George Washington, Thomas Jefferson, and Ben Franklin were a few prominent Long Islanders, including William Floyd, Francis Lewis, and Philip Livingston.

During the Revolution the English utilized the harbor in New York City to deliver troops. Wanting to maintain control over the region, George Washington planted his troops on the western tip of Long Island. The Battle of Long Island took place, and was ultimately won by the British. Washington's troops were outnumbered and forced to retreat toward New Jersey. As a result, during the Revolution, the British occupied much of New York, including Long Island, which was utilized to supply food for the British troops.

i While the British occupied Long Island and forced Long Islanders to grow and provide food and lodging for their soldiers, some served as spies for George Washington. After the war, Washington visited Long Island to thank those loyal to him for their support.

19TH CENTURY: INDUSTRIALIZATION AND THE RAILROAD

After the Revolution, as America grew and New York became a thriving metropolis, Long Island directly benefitted from that growth. In the 1800s fishing and whaling continued to be major industries on the island. In fact, it wasn't until the 1970s that the fishing industry went from being a more than $100 million per year industry to a less than $40 million industry, due to pollution, lack of regulation, abuse, and a variety of other factors.

On Apr 25, 1832, one major development that would guarantee the island's long-term growth and success was the introduction of the Long Island Railroad. It took many years, however, for the railroad to reach across the island and connect to other parts of New York. Today the Long Island Railroad is used by tens of thousands of commuters each day to get to and from their Long Island homes and New York City.

In the 1890s, while people were still fishing, science and technology started to become prominent industries on Long Island, which is a trend that continues to this day. Over the years Long Islanders have won numerous Nobel Prizes in science, sometimes as a result of work done at the Cold Spring Harbor Laboratory (founded in 1890), Brookhaven National Laboratory, the Okeanos Ocean Research Foundation, and on the government's own agricultural research center located on Plum Island.

20TH CENTURY: RISE OF SUBURBIA

Along with agriculture, fishing, science, and technology, in the 1930s Long Island began to

Relive a Bit of Long Island History

Yes, you can relive history—well, sort of. Back in 1790 President George Washington visited Long Island to thank his supporters and the spy ring that helped him win the American Revolution. The route President Washington followed by riding a horse-drawn carriage was known as the "Kings Highway." Today the route is called the Long Island Heritage Trail.

Traveling mainly from west to east, Rte. 25A pretty faithfully follows the Long Island Heritage Trail along Long Island's North Shore, between Great Neck and Port Jefferson. As a modern-day tourist following the Heritage Trail, you can make numerous stops along the way and visit historical sites and landmarks, as well as 17th-century homes and farmhouses.

For example, near the start of the trail, there's the Saddle Rock Grist Mill, which dates back to 1702. The trail will also take you to Port Washington, which was settled in 1675. Here you can visit Sand-Willets House, built in 1735 (336 Port Washington Blvd.). During the American Revolution, the home was lived in by Colonel John Sands, head of the Great Neck–Cow Neck Militia. There's also the Thomas Dodge House, which was built in 1721 and ultimately occupied by seven generations of the Dodge family.

As you follow the Long Island Heritage Trail, it'll take you to Roslyn, where you can see the Roslyn Clock Tower (built in 1895), along with Cedarmere, home of William Cullen Bryan, a famous poet. The Van Nostrand–Starkins House, built in 1680, is also in Roslyn (221 Main St.). It is open to the public on weekends May through Sept.

In Old Westbury you can continue your quest along the Heritage Trail with a stop at the Old Westbury Gardens (Old Westbury Rd.), a historic 160-acre estate that was built in 1906. It features a mansion, lovely landscaped gardens, and other attractions. Throughout the year a wide range of special events are hosted here. Old Westbury Gardens is open every day except Tues Apr through Oct, as well as during the holiday season, when the entire property is decorated with festive holiday lights.

Your journey, if you choose to follow the entire Heritage Trail, will also take you through Glen Cove, Sea Cliff, and Oyster Bay. These towns also offer a few historical sites. The Raynham Hall Museum (circa 1738), located at 20 West Main St. in Oyster Bay, was where President Washington's Culper Spy Ring was located, as it also served as the British headquarters during the Revolutionary War. This museum is open year-round between Tues and Sun, from 1 to 5 p.m.

Bayville and Locust Valley, followed by Cold Spring Harbor and Huntington, will also be along your route as you follow the Heritage Trail. In Huntington you can check out the Huntington Militia Arsenal and learn about the life of soldiers who fought in the American Revolution. The arsenal is located at 425 Park Ave. and is open year-round, Sun only, between 1 and 4 p.m.

establish a more modern "suburban" lifestyle. Just before the end of World War II, in addition to building single-family houses, a developer named William Levitt began creating housing communities. In addition to providing affordable homes for the middle class, these communities contained shopping centers and recreational facilities.

Levitt's Long Island community development project really began to take off in 1947, just after World War II, when 1,200 acres of farmland were transformed into a residential community containing 17,000 homes. The community was called Levittown, and it became very popular among soldiers returning from the war who wanted to settle down with their families to establish a new

Also worth seeing in Huntington are the Joseph Lloyd Manor House (circa 1766) and the Walt Whitman Birthplace State Historic Site and Interpretive Center (246 Old Walt Whitman Rd., South Huntington), the 1819 home of poet Walt Whitman. At 41 Lloyd Harbor Rd. in Huntington, you can visit Henry Lloyd Manor (circa 1711), which is where some of the area's original settlers once lived.

As you continue along the Heritage Trail, you'll eventually reach Centerport, Northport, Smithtown, St. James, and Kings Park, along with Stony Brook and Setauket. Again, each of these towns offers a few historical sites, as well as lovely places to eat, shop, and explore.

In Stony Brook, for example, there's the Stony Brook Grist Mill (circa 1751), as well as the gorgeous Avalon Park (200 Harbor Rd.), which offers beautiful walking trails around a pond and neighboring woods. There's also the Stony Brook Village Center, where you'll find a collection of shops and restaurants in a historic colonial setting.

Your journey along the Long Island Heritage Trail will come to an end in Port Jefferson, which was where some of the country's very first shipbuilders lived and perfected their craft. Port Jefferson contains several historical sites worth visiting, along with a "downtown" area filled with lovely shops, restaurants, and several waterfront parks. It's also home to the Port Jefferson Ferry and an absolutely incredible bakery, La Bonne Boulangerie, which you should definitely visit for a homemade snack (125 West Broadway).You can learn more about Port Jefferson's history and see a variety of exhibits at the Port Jefferson Village Center (101-A East Broadway, 631-802-2660, www.pjvillagecenter.com). Here you'll also find an outdoor, seasonal ice-skating rink.

If you're a history buff, you can easily spend several full days exploring and experiencing all of the historical sites and attractions located along the Long Island Heritage Trail. If you want to expand your visit at each stop to include the modern-day shopping, dining, and other attractions, you can easily spend a full day at each one.

While you can't repeat history, you can learn all about it, at your own pace, and in a way relive it as you follow in President George Washington's steps along the Long Island Heritage Trail. You can print out a free map of the Heritage Trail by visiting www.longislandheritage trail.com, which also showcases interesting places you can stop at along the route.

In addition to visiting the official Long Island Heritage Trail Web site, be sure to pick up the free, full-color booklet *Heritage Long Island: Touring the North Shore*, which outlines all of the potential stops along the Heritage Trail and provides operating hours, phone numbers, and addresses for each site, landmark, and attraction. This highly informative brochure is available at all of the chamber of commerce offices along the trail, as well as at each of the historic attractions.

Additional details about some of these sites can also be found in the "Attractions" chapter.

life. These homes were affordable to the soldiers, as well as to the lower middle class.

Many people credit William Levitt for being the person responsible for establishing and building "modern-day" Long Island. Today much of the island, particularly Nassau County, Brooklyn, and Queens, are densely populated. The once vast areas of farmlands are gone. This fast and massive growth of Long Island in modern times led to a wide range of problems, from overpopulation in some areas to major traffic, high taxes, expensive utilities (particularly electricity and gas), and an ever-changing economy and real estate market.

While many of the top defense contractors that once dominated Long Island have either closed or have shrunk in size (causing massive layoffs), the groundwork has been laid for companies focusing on computer technology, software development, bioengineering, and other high-tech fields to grow and expand. A significant number of people who live on Long Island commute to New York City or surrounding areas to work, yet chose Long Island as their home in order to enjoy suburban living and raise their families in affluent communities that boast low crime rates, top-ranked public schools, and an abundance of local conveniences.

PRESENT DAY

Today Long Island is known as being a safe, modern, and upscale place to live. Many of the earlier problems with traffic, for example, have been worked out. Long Island is also an extremely popular tourist and vacation destination, particularly in the summer, thanks to its lovely beaches and beachfront communities. While many people call Long Island home, places like the Hamptons and Fire Island have become literal playgrounds for the rich and famous.

As you visit various parts of Long Island, it's impossible to ignore the preserved sites and landmarks that are so important to its history. Visitors who are history buffs can opt to stay in a B&B built in colonial times, for example, and visit old mansions, seaports, lighthouses, and buildings that were once crucial to the island's very existence. However, for the rest of us, it's easy to enjoy the many modern accommodations, attractions, and activities that today thrive throughout Long Island.

While parts of Long Island are extremely affluent, you don't need to be a multimillionaire to visit and vacation here. There's an abundance of things to see and do for us everyday folk who will drive, ride the train, or take a ferry to the island, as opposed to arriving in a multimillion-dollar private yacht, jet, or helicopter. Now that you have a basic understanding of Long Island's history, you'll have a much greater appreciation of your surroundings when you vacation or relocate here, which is the primary focus of the remainder of this guide.

So wake up! The history lesson is over. It's time to begin planning what is sure to be a fun, exciting, and memorable trip to Long Island!

GETTING HERE, GETTING AROUND

While Long Island has some heavily populated areas, it's primarily very suburban, composed of small to medium-size towns. So, depending on where you want to go within Long Island, driving is probably the easiest way to get to your destination, though taxi, town car, or limo services are available (but potentially costly).

From the major airports, scheduled and door-to-door shuttle buses and shared vans are available to various Long Island areas. Or, if you're coming from or going to Manhattan (New York City), train service, provided by the Long Island Railroad, is a very popular mode of transportation, particularly among daily commuters.

Mass-transit bus service can get you around Long Island, but these buses tend to be less convenient, due to the fact that they make frequent stops and have very defined routes.

To put things in perspective from a mileage standpoint, here's the distance between a few major cities and Long Island's Nassau/Suffolk border:

- Atlanta, GA: 885 miles
- Boston, MA: 240 miles
- Buffalo, NY: 400 miles
- Hartford, CT: 150 miles
- Manhattan: 30 miles
- Philadelphia, PA: 135 miles
- Washington, DC: 270 miles
- While Plains, NY: 55 miles

If you'll be traveling by air, Long Island has its own small airport, but Nassau and Suffolk Counties are near John F. Kennedy International Airport and LaGuardia Airport, which are the two major airports that service New York City and surrounding areas. Newark International Airport (in New Jersey) is also commonly used by New Yorkers; however, it's located farther away from Long Island, so it's less convenient.

Ferryboat service is offered between parts of Long Island and places like New London, Bridgeport, and Mystic, Connecticut, as well as to and from Newport, Rhode Island.

MAJOR LONG ISLAND ROADWAYS

The main road connecting New York City with Long Island is I-495, better known as the Long Island Expressway, or "LIE" This major thoroughfare, which is 71.02 miles long, runs from the Queens-Midtown Tunnel in New York City all of the way out to Riverhead, in Suffolk County, Long Island.

From the LIE, smaller roads branch off from the various exits that will take you pretty much anywhere on Long Island. This major roadway was built in stages, starting in 1939, but it didn't actually reach Riverhead until 1972.

For many years after it was built, the LIE was referred to as the world's largest parking lot, due to the heavy traffic problems that existed pretty much on a daily basis, especially during rush hour periods. In most areas, however, expansion and reconstruction of the LIE, combined with an $880 million HOV lane system (completed in 2005), have made traffic more manageable, though in some areas far from ideal, especially during rush hour.

Commuters will still experience rush hour traffic in the Queens and western Nassau sections of the LIE. The recent struggling economy, increased carpooling, higher gas prices, and the increased use of the LIRR (Long Island Railroad) commuter rail system (which was up to 276,860 riders per day in 2008) have also impacted traffic, but in a positive way. In fact, between 2007 and 2008 the New York Department of Transportation reported a 2 percent traffic decrease on the LIE. This translates to about 3,600 fewer cars per day using this popular roadway.

i According to Long Island Transportation Management, during the traditional afternoon rush hour period, 1,420 carpools and buses, carrying 3,550 people, use the eastbound HOV lane near exit 49 of the LIE. It would take more than 3,100 cars in a regular lane to carry the same number of people.

Other major east–west routes within Long Island include Northern Boulevard (Route 25A); the Jericho Turnpike (Route 25), which is located on the north shore; and Sunrise Highway (Route 27) and Merrick Road–Montauk Highway/Southern State Parkway (Route 27A), which are located on the South Shore. Southern State Parkway, as the name suggests, serves the southern portion of Long Island by connecting New York City with East Islip and Hecksher Park.

While the LIE extends out to Riverhead from the Queens-Midtown Tunnel, the Jericho Turnpike extends all of the way out to Orient Point on the easternmost tip of Suffolk County's North Fork.

The Northern State Parkway connects Hauppauge with New York City, but allows no commercial traffic whatsoever. This roadway serves the northern portion of Long Island and reaches the Bronx and Westchester via the Triboro Bridge. Once in New York City, the Northern State Parkway becomes the Grand Central Parkway.

If you're taking the Holland Tunnel or Lincoln Tunnel, or the Verrazano Bridge from Staten Island, Route 278 connects directly to the Southern State Parkway and follows Long Island's southern shore.

Meadowbrook Parkway travels north and south through Nassau Country and allows no commercial traffic. Along this major roadway are shopping malls and the Nassau Coliseum. Meanwhile, Ocean Parkway extends about 15.5 miles and runs through both Nassau and Suffolk Counties, on the South Shore of Long Island.

From these major roads, smaller roads branch off that will take you just about anywhere on Long Island. To learn more about Long Island's major roadways, visit www.longislandexchange.com/roads.html.

Invest in GPS

When it comes to navigating your way around Long Island by car, nothing comes in more handy than having a GPS system in your vehicle. These devices provide real-time, turn-by-turn directions from exactly where you are at any given moment to your intended destination.

If you're renting a car, you should request an optional GPS system for an additional $8 to $10 per day when you make your reservation or when you pick up your vehicle. Or, you can invest about $125 to purchase and own a portable GPS system that can be attached to any vehicle's dashboard using a suction cup. Many of the new cell phones, including Apple's iPhone and the various Blackberry models, have built-in GPS navigation functionality as well.

BRIDGES AND TUNNELS

Several bridges and tunnels located within New York City connect to Brooklyn and Queens on the western end of Long Island. Coming from

New York City via the Bronx to Long Island (from the west, going east), for example, you can take the Throgs Neck Bridge or the Bronx Whitestone Bridge and easily connect to the LIE.

The Queen Midtown Tunnel connects directly to the LIE, while the Holland Tunnel leads to Route 278, which will connect to either the LIE (if you go north) or Route 27A (if you travel south). From Staten Island, Route 278 connects to Route 27A and the LIE in Long Island.

TOLLS

The fastest and least expensive way to navigate your way through New York's toll booths is to acquire an E-ZPass for your vehicle (800-333-TOLL, www.ezpassny.com).

E-ZPass is an electronic toll-collection system that allows drivers to prepay for (or electronically and automatically pay for) tolls, eliminating the need to stop at toll plazas and pay with cash. The system requires that participating drivers place a special "toll tag" within their vehicle. The E-ZPass is compatible with toll booths throughout New York State, Massachusetts, New Hampshire, New Jersey, Rhode Island, and a handful of other East Coast states. Likewise, the Massachusetts Fast-Lane units, for example, work throughout New York State, including on toll roads, tunnels, and bridges when traveling to and from Long Island.

The E-ZPass also saves money. The toll fee for the Queens-Midtown Tunnel (connecting New York City to Long Island), Bronx-Whitestone Bridge, and Throgs Neck Bridge, for example, is $5.50 per vehicle if you pay using cash, or $4.57 per vehicle using an E-ZPass (as of July 2009).

The toll for the Holland Tunnel and Lincoln Tunnel (as of Mar 2008) is $8 for cars paying with cash, or $6 (during off-peak hours) and $8 (during peak hours) if using the E-ZPass. Peak hours are weekdays from 6 to 9 a.m. and 4 to 7 p.m., and weekends from noon to 8 p.m.

The Verrazano Bridge toll fee is $11 for cars paying cash, or $9.14 for cars using the E-ZPass (as of July 2009).

i If you're an iPhone user and a member of AAA, be sure to download the free AAA Roadside app from the iTunes App Store. Using this app, if you need emergency roadside assistance, instead of calling (800) AAA-HELP and having to provide your exact location, membership number, and vehicle information, the iPhone app automatically sends this information, literally with one tap of your finger. Assistance will show up at your exact location within the time frame sent to you by AAA electronically via the app.

HOV (HIGH OCCUPANCY VEHICLE) RESTRICTIONS

One of the best ways to avoid at least 20 minutes' worth of traffic each way along the LIE is to utilize the HOV lanes that exist in both directions, from exit 32 to exit 64. HOV lane restrictions are in effect Mon through Fri from 6 to 10 a.m. and 3 to 8 p.m.

During these hours the HOV lanes are reserved for buses and passenger vehicles containing at least two (human) occupants. While children are considered passengers, pets and people-shaped mannequins are not. (You'd be surprised what people try to get away with in order to utilize the HOV lane.) Minivans with two or more passengers and motorcycles with only one rider can use the HOV lanes at anytime. Most recently, hybrid vehicles, with any number of passengers, have been granted unlimited use of the HOV lanes.

At no time can trailers, commercial vans, commercial trucks, or any vehicle with a commercial license plate utilize the HOV lanes. However, all other passenger vehicles (even with just one passenger) can use these lanes outside of the specified restricted times.

For daily commuters, or when traveling on Long Island during morning or afternoon rush hours, the HOV lanes are a huge time saver, so carpool or be sure to have at least two passengers in your vehicle.

MTA'S LONG ISLAND BUS SYSTEM

The MTA Long Island Bus System—composed of more than 430 buses that cover 118 routes—offers an inexpensive link between 96 Long Island communities throughout Nassau County, western Suffolk County, and eastern Queens. Bus stops include Long Island Railroad stations, shopping malls, major corporate centers, attractions, airports, colleges, and the most popular beaches. Long Island Bus is part of the Metropolitan Transportation Authority (MTA).

Bus fares are paid using a prepaid MetroCard, available at neighborhood merchants and from vending machines at many bus and subway stations. MetroCards can also be used to travel on New York City's subway and bus system. Details about buying and using a MetroCard can be found at http://mta.info/metrocard.

Single ride, daily, weekly, and monthly passes are available, as are discounted fares for children, students, and seniors. Call (516) 228-4000 or visit www.mta.info for schedules, fares, and routes.

i **Smart phones such as the BlackBerry and iPhone can access and receive bus information via http://tripplanner.mta.info/mobile.**

TAXIS, TOWN CARS, AND LIMOS

While any New York City Yellow Cab will take passengers to Long Island destinations from Manhattan, LaGuardia, or JFK Airport, for example, using a metered fare system, there are many Long Island–based taxi companies and many private town car and limousine services that cater specifically to the Long Island area.

The following is a partial listing of taxi companies servicing all or parts of Long Island. All of these companies offer door-to-door airport service, as well as regular taxi service within the local areas or regions they serve.

Unlike NYC taxis (Yellow Cabs), which all have a fixed metered rate, Long Island taxis work on a flat-rate basis. For details, contact the Long Island Taxi & Limousine Commission at (516) 571-2564 during business hours.

Partial Listing of Long Island Taxi Companies

ALL HAMPTON TAXI
(631) 287-2121

ALL ISLAND TRANSPORTATION
East Rockaway, (516) 599-1600
Freeport, (516) 223-0000
Hempstead, (516) 481-1111
Hewlett, (516) 374-1800
Garden City, (516) 746-2500
Island Park, (516) 431-2222
Lynbrook, (516) 599-1600
Merrick, (516) 379-9999
Mineola, (516) 742-2222
Oceanside, (516) 536-3333
Rockville Centre, (516) 536-3333
Uniondale, (516) 489-3333
www.allislandtransportation.com

BAY SHORE TAXI
(631) 655-0600
www.davidbroscarservice.com

COLONIAL TAXI
(631) 588-5555
www.colonialtransportation.com

DAVID BROTHERS TAXI
(631) 655-1515
www.davidbroscarservice.com

DAWSON TAXI
(516) 223-2400
www.dawsontaxi.com

OLLIE'S TAXI & AIRPORT SERVICE
North Shore, (516) 487-3420
South Shore, (516) 437-0505
www.olliestaxi.com

OYSTER BAY TAXI
(516) 931-2929
wwwl.oysterbayli.com

QUICK TAXI OF SOUTH HAMPTON
(631) 259-8294

RELIABLE TAXI
(631) 342-1111
www.lindystaxi.com

TAXI OF THE HAMPTONS
(631) 324-9294

VILLAGE TAXI
(631) 588-1055
www.villagetaxironk.com

RENTAL CAR COMPANIES

All of the major rental car companies have pick-up and drop-off locations at the New York–area airports, as well as in communities throughout Long Island (including some hotels). While all of these companies offer daily or weekly car rentals with unlimited mileage, you will be charged extra for insurance, a GPS system, and various other vehicle upgrades you request. You're also responsible for paying for your own gas, tolls, and parking tickets.

When you add the various insurance coverage options for your rental vehicle, the quoted price will typically double or triple. Be sure to purchase at least the LDW (Loss Damage Waiver) insurance, which protects just the rental vehicle itself.

Most rental car companies require the driver to be at least 25 years old and have a major credit card in his or her name (which must be presented when picking up the vehicle). The credit card must have enough credit available to cover the cost of the entire rental. Some rental car companies will allow a debit card to be used; however, the renter must have an average or better credit rating. A temporary hold of up to three times the cost of the entire rental will also be placed on the debit card account for a period of up to a week (sometime longer) beyond when the vehicle will be dropped off.

Be sure to drop off the vehicle, with a full tank of gas (unless otherwise instructed), when and where it's stipulated in the renter's agreement. If you need to keep the car longer or change the drop-off location, be sure to call the rental car company in advance; otherwise, late fees and other charges will be applied to the rental.

Here are the main contact numbers and Web sites for the most popular rental car companies:

Alamo: (877) 222-9075, www.alamo.com
Avis: (800) 331-1212, www.avis.com
Budget: (800) 527-0700, www.budget.com
Dollar: (800) 800-3665, www.dollar.com
Enterprise: (800) 261-7331, www.enterprise.com
Hertz: (800) 654-3131, www.hertz.com
National: (877) 222-9058, www.nationalcar.com
Thrifty: (800) 847-4389, www.thrifty.com

ARRIVING BY AIR

The majority of people flying into or out of the Long Island area utilize one of New York City's primary airports. The two closest to Long Island are LaGuardia Airport and John F. Kennedy International Airport. While the majority of international flights are handled by JFK, both airports are serviced by all of the major airlines, including a majority of the "discount" airlines, like JetBlue, AirTran, Southwest Airlines, and Virgin America. These are two of the busiest airports in America.

JOHN F. KENNEDY INTERNATIONAL AIRPORT (JFK)
JFK Expwy. and South Cargo Rd., Jamaica
(718) 244-4444
www.panynj.gov/CommutingTravel/airports/html/kennedy.html

Often referred to as "Kennedy Airport" or "JFK," this is one of the major international airports that service New York City and all surrounding areas. It is located on Long Island, in the southeastern section of Queens, on Jamaica Bay. This airport handles the majority of the area's international incoming and outgoing flights, and is serviced by more than 50 major airlines. For information about ground transportation options to and from this airport, call (800) 247-7433.

LAGUARDIA AIRPORT (LGA)
Ditmars Blvd. and 94th St., Flushing
(718) 533-4000 or (718) 533-3400 (recorded Info)
www.panynj.gov/CommutingTravel/airports/html/laguardia.html

Composed of several terminals, including the Main Terminal, US Airways Terminal, Delta Terminal, and the Marine Air Terminal, this major airport is serviced by about 15 primarily domestic airlines, including Air Canada, AirTran, American, Colgan, Comair, Continental, Delta, Frontier, JetBlue, Midwest, Southwest, Spirit, United, and US Airways. LaGuardia is also located on Long Island, in the borough of Queens.

Long Island's Other Area Airports

The following airports on Long Island are available to private, small charter or executive jet and helicopter services only:

Brookhaven Calabro Airport: 135 Dawn Dr., Shirley; (631) 281-5100

East Hampton Airport: 200 Daniels Hole Rd., Wainscott; (631) 537-2202; www.soundaircraft.com

Francis S. Gabreski Airport: Westhampton Beach; (631) 852-8095; www.co.suffolk.ny.us/departments/housing/gabreskiairport.aspx

Republic Airport: 7150 Republic Airport, East Farmingdale; (631) 752-7707; www.republicairport.net

LONG ISLAND MACARTHUR AIRPORT (ISP)
100 Arrivals Ave., Ronkonkoma
(631) 467-3210
www.macarthurairport.com

Long Island MacArthur Airport (sometimes referred to as "Islip") is situated toward the center of Long Island. While conveniently located, it's very small compared to LaGuardia and JFK, and is only serviced by two major airlines, Southwest and US Airways. Long Island MacArthur Airport does, however, welcome two million visitors per year. Small regional commuter airlines, helicopter services, and private/executive charter airplanes also utilize this airport.

i You can typically save a fortune (between 20 and 60 percent off) on airfares, hotels, and rental cars by booking your travel online using a popular service such as Travelocity, Hotwire, Priceline, Kayak, Expedia, or Orbitz.

LONG ISLAND RAILROAD (LIRR)

The Long Island Railroad commuter train system connects 124 railroad stations in various communities throughout Long Island directly to Penn Station (located at Eighth Ave. and 31st St.) in the heart of New York City.

The LIRR operates more than 740 passenger trains daily on three major east–west routes, which go from New York City along the entire lengths of both Nassau and Suffolk Counties on Long Island. Because it encompasses more than 700 miles of track and carries over 250,000 passengers per day, the LIRR has become the largest commuter railroad in the United States.

i The LIRR recently celebrated its 175th anniversary. It was chartered on Apr 24, 1834, just nine years after railroads were invented. The LIRR is the busiest commuter railroad in North America, as well as the oldest railroad in the United States that's still operating under its original name.

The LIRR goes out to the tips of Port Jefferson, Greenport, and Montauk, as well as the tip of Far Rockaway Beach and Long Beach, making it easy, fast, relatively inexpensive, and convenient for travelers to get pretty much to and from anywhere within Long Island or to NYC, thanks to regularly scheduled train service that runs from early morning until late at night.

Printed, station-specific train schedules for all stops on Long Island are available from the Metropolitan Transit Authority (MTA) or can be downloaded from the Web site (516-822-LIRR or 631-231-LIRR; www.mta.info/lirr). Since train schedules change periodically, it's important to refer to the most recently published schedule.

Train fares vary for the LIRR, based on exactly where you get on the train and get off, as well as whether or not you're traveling during "peak" or "off-peak" times. For customized fare information, visit http://lirr42.mta.info/sfweb/faces/index.jspx.

Ferryboat Reservations

To/from Orient Point and New London, CT
Cross Sound Ferry, Inc.: (631) 323-2525, www.longislandferry.com; 80-minute trip one way

To/from Port Jefferson and Bridgeport, CT
Bridgeport & Port Jefferson Ferry Company: (631) 473-0286, www.bpjferry.com; 75-minute trip one way

To/from Montauk and Block Island, NY; New London, CT; and Martha's Vineyard, MA
Viking Ferry: (631) 688-5700, www.vikingfleet.com; 60-minute trip one way

To/from North Side Shelter Island and Greenport
North Ferry Company: (631) 749-0139, www.northferry.com; 7-minute trip each way

To/from South Side Shelter Island and North Haven (near Sag Harbor)
South Ferry, Inc.: (631) 749-1200, www.southferry.com; 5-minute trip each way

To/from Patchogue and Davis Park, Watch Hill, and Fire Island Seashore
Davis Park Ferry Corporation: (631) 475-1665, www.davisparkferry.com; 20-minute trip each way

To/from Fire Island and Ocean Beach, Kismet, Fair Harbor, Dunewood, Ocean Bay Park, Saltaire, Seaview, and Atlantique
Fire Island Ferries: (631) 655-3600, www.fireislandferries.com; 30-minute trip each way

Sayville to Fire Island Pines, Cherry Grove
Sayville Ferry Service: (631) 589-0810, www.sayvilleferry.com; 20-minute trip each way

Sayville to Fire Island National Seashore, Sailor's Haven/Sunken Forest
Sunken Forest Ferry Service: (631) 589-0810; 30-minute trip each way

To view and download a chart of current fares, go to http://mta.info/lirr/pubs/LIRRFares.pdf.

LIRR tickets can be purchased at all train stations, aboard the actual trains (for an added fee of up to $6.50), or directly from the Web (at a discount) at www.lirrticket.com/webticket/Cart/Welcome?id=002.

LIRR offers one-way and round-trip tickets, as well as discounted prepaid 10-trip tickets and weekly and monthly passes. Weekly passes, for example, are good for unlimited travel for a seven-day period from Sat through the following Fri, and can be purchased up to six weeks in advance. Monthly passes are valid during the calendar month that's stamped on the face of the ticket. Discounts are offered to students, children, and seniors.

i For $1.99 each, Apple iPhone users can purchase and download the iLIRR, iTransitBuddy–LIRR, or Ontime: LIRR apps from the iTunes App Store to help navigate the LIRR. These apps offer up-to-date schedules, route maps, and fares.

i The Cross Sound Ferry service between Orient Point, Long Island, and New London, Connecticut, offers up to 56 arrivals and departures daily, depending on the season.

FERRYBOAT SERVICES

Year-round ferryboat service is available on Long Island from Port Jefferson to Bridgeport, Connecticut, and from Orient Point to New London, Connecticut. There's also regular ferry service between South Fork and North Fork via the Shelter Island Ferry services.

You'll need to take a ferryboat to visit Fire Island, since private cars are not allowed there. Six different ferryboat services are available (some seasonally).

Many of the ferryboat services will transport passengers, vehicles, motorcycles, and/or small trucks. One-way and round-trip rates vary by season and are based on what's being transported.

ACCOMMODATIONS

Just as Long Island offers a vast array of vacation experiences, based on where you'll be visiting, the region also offers an abundance of accommodations options that will fit any budget. Especially in Nassau County, it's easy to find low-cost chain motels and hotels that have rates around $100 or less per night. For people not too concerned with budget, however, there is a wide range of luxurious options that are ideal for single-night, weekend, weeklong, or even longer vacation getaways.

Long Island is somewhat unique in that visitors can choose to stay at a campground, motel, traditional hotel, extended-stay hotel, full-service resort, B&B, inn, or rental property. There are also historical landmarks that have been transformed into accommodations, plus sailboat and yacht rentals are also available. Your options are limited only by your budget, vacancies, and what you're looking to get out of your Long Island vacation experience.

Since there are so many accommodations options available, it would be difficult to offer a comprehensive listing, and this guide would need to be several hundred pages longer. Thus, this section highlights an assortment of different types of accommodations, at different price points, within each county of Long Island.

Keep in mind that while your choices are plentiful, during peak travel seasons (mainly between Memorial Day and Labor Day), occupancy rates tend to be very high, so it's important to make your reservations early.

As with any popular tourist or vacation destination, the basic economic principle of supply and demand is in effect when it comes to how much you'll pay for accommodations. When demand is high and vacancies are low, prices for accommodations go up (sometimes considerably). During the "shoulder" periods (between the peak and off-peak periods), prices start to drop. However, during off-peak travel times, you can literally find bargains, even at the most luxurious resorts and historical inns.

TYPES OF ACCOMMODATIONS ON LONG ISLAND

One of the best ways to ensure a fun and memorable vacation is to select the ideal type of accommodations, based on the experience you're looking for. The following are descriptions of the various types of accommodations available throughout Long Island.

Campgrounds

The various campgrounds offer areas for tents or places to park RVs. Most offer amenities such as showers and restrooms. Camping is popular during the late spring and summer months, and it's also the least expensive option in terms of accommodations. In most cases, however, you'll need to bring all of your own camping gear and equipment. The Trails.com (www.trails.com/activity.aspx?area=15665) and Discover Long Island (www.discoverlongisland.com/sub_cats.cfm/ID/37/group_ID/1) Web sites offer detailed listings for popular campgrounds on Long Island.

Bed-and-Breakfasts

These independently owned and operated accommodations are typically housed in multi-bedroom homes and are ideal for couples. Many B&Bs don't welcome kids. Guests typically receive a private bedroom and bathroom (although some have shared bathrooms), and breakfast is always served by the innkeeper. Because they're usually privately owned, and the innkeepers live and work on the property, you can always count on highly personalized service and a cozy, homelike atmosphere. Some B&Bs are housed within historic homes, while others have a specialized theme.

Hotels

Boutique Hotels

These hotels often are independently owned and operated, offer more guestrooms than an inn or B&B, and are very unique in everything from their decor to the level of personalized service that's offered. Unlike the chain hotels, boutique hotels, especially those on Long Island, don't take a cookie-cutter approach to their design, theme, or decor. Most have under 50 guestrooms, and a theme and/or reputation that sets each apart.

Extended-Stay Hotels

Designed mainly for business travelers who need to visit a specific area for several weeks or longer at a time, an extended-stay hotel usually offers a more apartment or hotel suite–like setting. For example, guestrooms contain full kitchens or kitchenettes, plus a living room, separate bedroom, and a private bathroom. Some extended-stay hotels are more like luxury apartments in a hotel-like setting, offering maid service and room service, plus the services and amenities you'd expect from a hotel, combined with more homelike comforts. Extended-stay hotels are typically priced a bit lower than traditional hotels, but are rented by the week or month, not by the night. Rates will vary greatly based on location, time of year, and the level of luxury offered. The Homewood Suites and the Residence Inn by Marriott, both in Plainview, are perfect examples of midpriced extended-stay hotels that offer a wide range of comforts and conveniences suitable for business travelers.

Traditional Hotels

A traditional hotel is typically housed in one or more full-size buildings and offers a variety of guestroom configurations, along with on-property services, such as a restaurant, room service, gift shop, fitness center, swimming pool, and business center. The guestrooms often are more spacious, offer higher-end furnishings and decor, and provide more upscale amenities than what you'd typically find in a motel. Sheraton, Hilton, and Marriott are among the popular chains that operate traditional hotels throughout Long Island. You'll also find many one-of-a-kind, independently owned and operated hotels in the region.

Inns

An inn is a cross between a B&B and hotel. Inns are often independently owned and operated, but instead of having just a few guestrooms, they offer more rooms and more on-property services and amenities. They still maintain a homelike atmosphere, however, with highly personalized service. Inns tend to cost a bit more than B&Bs, and the guestrooms are often equivalent to what you'd find in an upscale, four- or five-star hotel or resort—complete with all of the services and amenities. Most inns have a restaurant or offer dining beyond just breakfast. Some of the most luxurious inns in the United States and Canada are members of the Select Registry of Distinguished Inns of North America (800-344-5244, www.selectregistry.com), which is an excellent resource for finding and booking this type of lodging.

Motels

Typically composed of a single one- or two-story building, motels are usually less expensive than traditional hotels and offer few on-property amenities and services. EconoLodge, Days Inn, Fairfield Inn, Best Western, and Courtyard Marriott are among the many franchised motel chains that operate throughout Long Island. These motels typically offer small, but clean and comfortable rooms, with basic furnishings such as one or two beds, nightstands, a desk, television, and private bathroom. Rates for motels tend to be between $79 and $150 per night.

Rental Properties

For people looking to spend a week or longer vacationing on Long Island, renting a full-size, multibedroom, fully furnished home is an extremely viable, popular, and cost-effective option. These properties tend to be located in the most tourist-oriented areas of Long Island (including along the beaches or waterfront), but offer all of the comforts of home. Many rental properties feature very luxurious accommodations. Rental properties are ideal for families or extended families, since they offer multiple bedrooms and bathrooms, plenty of living space, privacy, fully equipped kitchens, and other homelike comforts. The Corcoran Group in East Hampton (631-899-0215) is just one example of an agency that specializes in Long Island vacation home rentals.

Resorts

Ideal for romantic getaways, family vacations, honeymoons, or destination weddings, a full-service resort offers more luxurious accommodations than a typical hotel, plus a wide range of on-property services, amenities, and activities. A resort might offer multiple restaurants, tennis, golf, swimming pools, a day spa, fitness center, salon, business center, gift shop, banquet rooms, and a bar/lounge on property, in addition to organized activities. Especially in the Hamptons, and along Long Island's waterfront and beaches, you'll find a wide range of resorts.

Yacht/Sailboat

Instead of staying on land, some vacationers visiting Long Island opt to charter a yacht or sailboat, and then sail around the island, docking at nicely equipped marinas and yacht clubs throughout the island at night. The rates for this type of vacation experience vary greatly, based on the type and size of vessel you rent, plus your level of experience and whether or not you need to hire a crew.

Price Code

You already know that the prices for accommodations on Long Island vary dramatically based on a variety of factors, including season. However, to give you an idea of what to expect price-wise, we've provided the following scale as a general guide. It is based on the average cost for a standard, double-occupancy guestroom during peak season. Prices will fluctuate quite a bit based on season and occupancy rate, however. Plus, you can usually save money by utilizing one of the popular online travel-related services when booking your reservation. Keep in mind that any accommodations priced over $250 per night represent the most luxurious and upscale lodging you'll find on Long Island. Every motel, hotel, B&B, inn, and resort listed accepts all major credit cards, and most offer discounted off-peak season rates.

$.......... Under $125 per night
$$ .... $126 to $175 per night
$$$ ...... $176 to $250 per night
$$$$ .. More than $250 per night

CAMPGROUNDS

Nassau County

BATTLE ROW CAMPGROUND $
Claremont Rd., Old Bethpage
(516) 572-8690
www.nassaucountyny.gov/agencies/Parks/Wheretogo/campgrounds/battlerow.html

This is one of two campgrounds managed by the Nassau County Department of Parks, Recreation and Museums. To stay at this campground, an advance reservation is required. Located in the eastern part of Nassau County, Battle Row Campground is a 44-acre property that is surrounded by woodlands. The campground offers 64 campsites, each of which is between 40 and 45 feet in length. About half of the spaces are equipped with water and electric hookups for RVs and trailers. Unlike many campgrounds on Long Island, this one stays open year-round.

NICKERSON BEACH CAMPGROUND $

Lido Blvd., Lido

(516) 571-7724

www.nassaucountyny.gov/agencies/Parks/Wheretogo/campgrounds/nickerson.html

Located along the Atlantic Ocean, Nickerson Beach Campground is a popular destination for campers because it offers its own beach access. The 121-acre park also features a wide range of land- and water-based activities, including swimming and sunbathing. Plus, there's a large children's playground here. As for the campground, it offers 74 sites for RVs and trailers, along with 12 spaces for tents. Water, sewer, and electric hookups are available. Reservations must be made in advance. This campground closes in Nov for the winter season and reopens in Apr.

Suffolk County

BLYDENBURGH COUNTY PARK CAMPGROUND $

Veterans Memorial Hwy., Smithtown

(631) 854-3713

www.co.suffolk.ny.us/Home/departments/parks/Blydenburgh%20County%20Park.aspx

Located along the Nissequogue River on the North Shore of Suffolk County, this county park is known for its fishing, hiking trails, rowing, and horseback riding trails. There is also a campground with space for 50 tents or trailers within this 588-acre park. The campground, which is surrounded by wooded areas, is equipped with restrooms, showers, a dump station, and nearby grills.

CEDAR POINT COUNTY PARK $

Alewive Brook Rd., East Hampton

(631) 852-7620

www.suffolkcountyny.gov/Home/departments/parks/Cedar%20Point%20County%20Park.aspx

If you can't afford to stay at one of the pricy B&Bs or inns located in East Hampton but you still want the experience of vacationing in the Hamptons, Cedar Point County Park is for you. It offers more than 160 individual and group camping sites, along with access to restrooms, showers, and a dump station. There's also a nearby children's playground and a basketball court adjacent to the camping area. The county park itself encompasses 607 acres and offers a wide range of land- and water-based activities, including beach access, boat rentals, fishing, hiking, scuba diving, and picnicking. The park also has its own food concessions.

CUPSOGUE BEACH COUNTY PARK $

Dune Rd., Westhampton

(631) 854-4949

www.suffolkcountyny.gov/Home/departments/parks/Cupsogue%20Beach%20County%20Park.aspx

Many of the county and state parks in the Suffolk County area offer campgrounds. Most allow RVs and trailers, like this one, but some only permit tents. Cupsogue Beach County Park encompasses 296 acres and includes beach access, which is one reason why it's so popular. It's also located in the heart of the Hamptons, another major draw (particularly in the summer). Along with its white sandy beach, where people come to swim and sunbathe, fishing and scuba diving are also popular activities here. Among the park/campground amenities are a snack bar, restrooms, a first-aid center, showers, changing rooms, and a dump station.

SMITH POINT COUNTY PARK $

William Floyd Pkwy., Shirley

(631) 854-4949

www.suffolkcountyny.gov/Home/departments/parks/Smith%20Point%20County%20Park.aspx

You'll find this lovely county park on the Fire Island barrier beach. It's a popular location for surfing, swimming, scuba diving, sunbathing, and camping. The park itself encompasses 2,293 acres, which includes space for 270 tents or trailers. Smith Point County Park has its own food concessions on the premises, and during the peak summer season, lifeguards are on duty at the beach. As for the campground, you'll find both water and electric hookups, a dump station, showers, and restrooms. There are also grills available, along with a nearby children's playground. The campground's biggest perk, however, is the access to the beach.

WILDWOOD STATE PARK CAMPGROUND $
Hulse Landing Rd., Wading River
(631) 929-4314
www.nysparks.state.ny.us/parks/68/details.aspx

This beautiful state park encompasses more than 600 acres, most of which are undeveloped in any way whatsoever. A portion of the park is situated on a high bluff that offers a spectacular view of the Long Island Sound. Camping is permitted within this state park, with space for 242 tents and 89 trailers. Facilities include restrooms and showers, along with a dump station, grills, a small convenience store, and access to a beach. Activities offered within the park include hiking, cross-country skiing (in the winter), and fishing. There's also a baseball field and volleyball courts near the campground.

BED-AND-BREAKFASTS

Suffolk County

BOXFARM $$$$
78 Mecox Rd., Southampton
(814) 632-8333
www.boxfarm.com

If you're planning to spend a night, weekend, or a full week in the Hamptons, the most comfortable and lavish accommodations can be found at the local B&Bs. BoxFarm is one of several upscale establishments located in Southampton. It's housed within a colonial farmhouse that was built in the 1600s. Of course, it's been fully modernized and renovated to provide for the utmost in comfort and luxury, without compromising the historic look and setting.

BoxFarm offers an extremely romantic setting, so it's the perfect place to escape with a loved one for some quality one-on-one time. The main building includes six individual guestrooms (each with a private bathroom), plus three common rooms, a dining room, and a country kitchen. There's also a porch, which offers a spectacular view of the B&B's outdoor swimming pool.

BY THE BLUFF BED & BREAKFAST $$$
5405 Rocky Point Rd., East Marion
(631) 477-6155
www.bythebluff.com

Offering luxury accommodations, highly personalized attention, and a private beach along the Long Island Sound, By the Bluff is the perfect place to enjoy a romantic getaway on Long Island's North Fork. The guestrooms are clean, comfortable, and cozy, not to mention lavishly decorated and equipped with the finest of amenities. The B&B is located a short distance (less than 2 miles) from Greenport Village, which is a lovely, historic waterfront community that's ideal for shopping, dining, and exploring. Many of Long Island's wineries and vineyards are also just minutes away, making this the perfect place to stay if you'll be participating in wine tours and tastings.

Between May and Oct there's a minimum two-night stay for weekend guests, and on holiday weekends, a three-night minimum. These accommodations are not suitable for children or pets, and smoking is not permitted. Breakfast is served between 8:30 and 9:30 a.m. By the Bluff is known for its Annie Kate Master Suite, which is one of the most luxurious on the North Fork. It features a king-size four-post bed, a 42-inch flat-screen television, a private patio, a rainfall shower, and a wide range of deluxe amenities.

ORIENT INN $$$
25500 Main Rd., Orient
(631) 323-2300
www.orientinn-ny.com

This Dutch colonial home, which was built in 1906, has been transformed into a lovely, upscale B&B located in historic Orient. Here you'll find five nicely decorated and comfortable guestrooms, each with a private bathroom. A full breakfast is served every morning, either in the dining room or on the open-air porch that surrounds the main house.

The Orient Inn is located about 3 miles from the Cross Sound Ferry dock, so if you're coming from Connecticut or New England via the ferry, its location on the tip of Long Island is convenient. The B&B welcomes adults only. Pets are also welcome, but smoking is only permitted outside on the porch. Nearby activities include hiking, fishing, swimming, boating, golfing, and wine tasting at the nearby vineyards.

SHINN ESTATE FARMHOUSE **$$$$**
2000 Oregon Rd., Mattituck
(631) 804-0367
www.theinn.recipesfromhome.com
This historic farmhouse, built in the 1880s as a homestead and estate, is now a luxury B&B that offers four nicely decorated guestrooms, each equipped with a private bath and a view of the adjacent vineyards. Rates start at $325 per night for double occupancy, and a minimum two-night stay is required on most weekends.

Shinn Estate Farmhouse offers top-notch service and comfortable accommodations in a quiet, farm setting. Smoking, children, and pets are not permitted. Wi-Fi Internet access is available throughout the building. Surrounding much of the farmhouse is an open-air terrace, which is perfect for watching the sunset while tasting locally produced wines.

STIRLING HOUSE **$$–$$$$**
104 Bay Ave., Greenport
(631) 477-0654
www.stirlinghousebandb.com
With guestroom rates between $175 and $320 per night during the peak summer season, Stirling House offers some of the more affordable accommodations options in the North Fork region of Long Island. When you stay at Stirling House, you'll find yourself within a two-minute walk of Greenport Village, where you'll discover a historic waterfront village featuring unique shops, cafes, and galleries, in addition to several museums and historic sites.

The B&B itself is a Victorian home built in the 1880s; however, the entire building has been completely renovated and modernized. The goal of innkeepers Frank King and Clay Sauer is to provide a comfortable and luxurious "home away from home" setting for each of their guests. The property has three guestrooms, each with a private bathroom. Stirling House opened as a B&B in 2000, but was further restored and renovated in 2006. In addition to the extremely comfortable rooms, guests are treated to a lavish three-course breakfast every morning. This B&B is not open to children or pets. Smoking is permitted on the outside patio.

HOTELS

Boutique

Nassau County

THE ANDREW **$$–$$$**
75 North Station Plaza, Great Neck
(516) 482-2900
www.andrewhotel.com
Modeling itself after a New York City boutique hotel, the Andrew offers luxury, comfort, and an ultra-modern style. With 62 nicely furnished and elegant rooms, it's a relatively small hotel that's located about 12 miles from LaGuardia Airport.

The Andrew offers 24-hour concierge services, valet parking, free Wi-Fi Internet access, and a complimentary continental breakfast each morning. It prides itself on being an ideal hotel for business travelers looking for an alternative to staying in Manhattan, but who don't want to compromise on amenities, services, or luxury. The furnishings in the guestrooms are all custom-designed, using oak, marble, suede, and raw silk. The decor promotes an elegant and sophisticated style, while also offering a comfortable, homelike atmosphere. In terms of modern amenities, flat-panel LCD televisions can be found in every guestroom, along with a DVD player. Each room also has one or two beds, a full-size desk, a separate sitting area, and a nicely equipped bathroom.

Suffolk County

HARBORFRONT INN AT GREENPORT $$$
209 Front St., Greenport
(631) 477-0707
www.theharborfrontinn.com

Located in the middle of Greenport—in the heart of the shopping and dining area, right on the water—is the Harborfront Inn. This is a small, full-service boutique hotel that offers 35 spacious and luxurious rooms, most with a stunning view of the water and a private terrace. Unlike traditional chain hotels, this boutique hotel is small and very unique. In addition to comfortable accommodations, you can expect personalized and extremely friendly service. This is a wonderful place for couples or families, or for hosting a girls' getaway weekend, for example. The guestrooms are decorated in earth tones and have large windows and custom-made furnishings. Wi-Fi service is available throughout the hotel.

Greenport is a lovely village on Long Island's North Fork, and is surrounded by wineries and a few golf courses. It's also conveniently located to several ferry services and is serviced by the Long Island Railroad, so getting there from New England or Manhattan is very easy.

Extended Stay

Nassau County

HOMEWOOD SUITES BY MARRIOTT $$
1585 Round Swamp Rd., Plainview
(516) 293-4663
www.homewoodsuiteslongisland.com

Designed for extended-stay business travelers and people in the process of relocating to Long Island who need an interim place to stay, this Homewood Suites offers 147 spacious and nicely furnished studios, in addition to one- and two-bedroom suites. Each of the suites features king-size beds, a living room, a fully equipped kitchen, and complimentary high-speed Internet access. A free continental breakfast is also served daily, and guests have access to a 24-hour fitness center, indoor pool, hot tub, and business center. While this property offers affordable, three-star-quality accommodations for extended-stay guests, it's also a viable option for overnight guests looking to experience the comforts of home, as opposed to a traditional hotel room (with no kitchen or living room).

RESIDENCE INN BY MARRIOTT $$
9 Gerhard Rd., Plainview
(516) 433-6200, (800) 331-3131
www.residenceinn.com

While this Residence Inn was designed from the ground up to offer business travelers affordable extended-stay accommodations, it will also appeal to families, couples, and solo travelers looking for short-term, spacious, apartment-style lodging, including full kitchens. There's an outdoor pool, fitness center, indoor lap pool, whirlpool, sauna, and putting green on-site. Continental breakfast is included with the stay, and a full-service restaurant, Baldino's, is also located on the property. During the warm season, the hotel hosts complimentary barbeques on a weekly basis. While not a luxury hotel, this Residence Inn offers clean, comfortable, and very spacious accommodations.

Suffolk County

MARRIOTT RESIDENCE INN $–$$
850 Veterans Memorial Hwy., Hauppauge
(631) 724-4188
www.marriott.com/hotels/travel/ispri-residence-inn-long-island-hauppauge-islandia

If you'll be visiting Suffolk County and are planning to stay a while, there is a limited number of extended-stay hotels in the area that cater primarily to business travelers. With nightly rates starting at around $100 (for extended stays), this hotel offers a handful of amenities, including an indoor pool, fitness center, whirlpool, outdoor BBQ, and complimentary parking. The guestrooms themselves are more like small apartments in terms of space, and are designed for both comfort and functionality. For example, the rooms have flat-screen TVs and a living room area (with a workspace) that's totally separate from the bedroom. Free Wi-Fi is also offered throughout the property, and the hotel is pet-friendly.

MARRIOTT RESIDENCE INN $–$$
25 Middle Ave., Holtsville
(631) 475-9500
www.marriott.com/hotels/travel/isphv-residence-inn-long-island-holtsville

When it comes to extended-stay hotels on Long Island, Marriott Residence Inn pretty much has the region covered. Each of its properties is pretty consistent, in terms of what's offered to business travelers who need to stay in a specific area or region for anywhere from a week to several months, and who want to enjoy more spacious accommodations than a traditional hotel room.

The guestrooms at this Marriott Residence Inn are set up like small apartments, with kitchens and a separate living room area and bedroom. There's also a full-size desk in the living room, as well as complimentary Wi-Fi Internet access throughout the entire building. This particular property is located within the Hauppauge Industrial Park. Guests can enjoy a complimentary hot breakfast every morning, plus utilize all of the hotel's amenities, such as the indoor pool, whirlpool, and fitness center. There's also a nicely equipped business center, as well as a tennis court and basketball court on the premises.

While one-night stays are available, this hotel is more equipped for people looking to spend a week or longer. The rates start at just under $90 per night. While the accommodations are not lavish, they are clean and comfortable.

Traditional

Nassau County

GARDEN CITY HOTEL $$$
45 Seventh St., Garden City
(800) 547-0400
www.gardencityhotel.com

While the Garden City Hotel is located just 25 minutes outside of Manhattan in Nassau County, you feel as if you've been transported far away as you enjoy the luxury accommodations this hotel offers. Thanks to its award-winning hospitality and upscale accommodations, it's ideal for weekend getaways. On the property, you'll find a fine-dining restaurant, plenty of meeting and function space (for business travelers), plus 280 luxurious guestrooms, 16 suites, and 4 penthouse suites, all housed within a traditional high-rise hotel that's been in operation since 1874. Of course, everything has been fully renovated and modernized, yet the hotel's decor provides for a timeless and classic ambiance. As a full-service hotel, 24-hour in-room dining is available, though the hotel offers a wonderful restaurant. The guestrooms and suites all offer Wi-Fi Internet access, a fully stocked minibar, multiple telephones, and luxury linens and bedding. This is a pet-friendly hotel, but an additional fee applies.

The Garden City Hotel is rich in tradition and history. It offers a vastly different and more upscale experience than staying at a run-of-the-mill chain hotel. In addition, the hotel is located across the street from the Long Island Railroad's Garden City station, so getting there from NYC by train is quick (under 45 minutes) and inexpensive (less than $12 per person each way).

GLEN COVE MANSION:
A HISTORIC HOTEL $$$–$$$$
200 Dosoris Ln., Glen Cove
(516) 671-6400
www.glencovemansion.com

Situated on 55 meticulously manicured acres, this historic hotel is located just 25 miles from downtown Manhattan. It offers all of the charming, elegant, and extremely comfortable guestroom and suite accommodations that you'd expect from a premium-service hotel. The decor is posh, traditional, and sophisticated, with an emphasis on luxury. In addition to offering a gourmet restaurant and day spa, you'll find an 18-hole golf course and tennis courts located nearby. Especially on weekends throughout the year, a variety of different getaway package deals are available.

HAMPTON INN $–$$
700 North Ave., Garden City
(516) 227-2720
www.gardencity.hamptoninn.com

If you're looking for more affordable accommodations in the Garden City area, the Hampton Inn offers clean, comfortable, but no-frills accommodations that are ideal for budget-conscious leisure and business travelers alike. Included with each night's stay at this low-rise hotel is a hot breakfast, Wi-Fi Internet service, parking, local phone calls, unlimited coffee, access to a fitness center and business center, and use of an indoor pool. What's nice is that this Hampton Inn is located within walking distance to the Roosevelt Field Mall, which is the largest indoor mall on Long Island. In addition to shopping, you'll find a wide selection of restaurants and dining options nearby.

HOLIDAY INN $–$$
390 Old Country Rd., Westbury
(516) 997-5000
www.hiwestbury.com
Located in Nassau County but close to the Suffolk County border, this Holiday Inn (as well as the location at 215 Sunnyside Blvd. in Plainview; 516-349-7400) offer midpriced three-star accommodations in a traditional hotel setting. Guestrooms are available in several different one- and two-bed configurations, and multi-bedroom suites are available. This hotel offers 152 guestrooms, the Garden Court Restaurant and Lounge, an outdoor pool, and complimentary use of a nearby Bally's Fitness Center. The Westbury location is located close to Hofstra University, Nassau Coliseum, and the Roosevelt Field Mall.

MARRIOTT LONG ISLAND HOTEL & CONFERENCE CENTER $$–$$$
101 James Doolittle Blvd., Uniondale
(516) 794-3800
www.longislandmarriott.com
Having recently undergone a massive, $21 million renovation, this three-star Marriott now features newly designed and decorated guestrooms, plus plenty of available meeting space. It's been designed to be a business-friendly hotel that also offers leisure travelers the comforts and conveniences they're looking for. This hotel is located within Nassau County, close to the Nassau Coliseum, Hofstra University, Eisenhower Park, and the Roosevelt Field Mall. On the property you'll find several full-service and fine-dining restaurant options, including Champions Sports Bar & Grill, Prime Seasons Steak House & Seafood, and the Skylight Lounge. In addition to offering a great location within Nassau County, this hotel features comfort at an affordable price. The guestrooms are consistent with what you'd expect from any full-service Marriott hotel.

ROSLYN CLAREMONT HOTEL $$–$$$
1221 Old Northern Blvd., Roslyn
(516) 625-2700
www.roslynclaremonthotel.com
For someone looking for sophisticated and upscale accommodations in a traditional hotel setting, the Roslyn Claremont Hotel is an excellent choice. The guestrooms are decorated in a lavish European country style and offer comfort and luxury, plus plenty of functional living space. They feature rich imported fabrics and linens along with plenty of modern amenities, including free high-speed Internet access. Situated on Long Island's North Shore, the hotel is close to the major New York airports. On the property you'll find an upscale restaurant, called Cristina's, and a lounge. The Roslyn Claremont Hotel offers the perfect weekend getaway for New Yorkers who don't want to travel to Suffolk County but who want to enjoy what Long Island has to offer. The grand ballroom here can accommodate a wide range of private functions for up to 200 guests. Be sure to ask about the "Special Romantic Weekend Packages" offered throughout the year.

Suffolk County

COURTYARD MARRIOTT $$
5000 Expressway Dr. South, Ronkonkoma
(631) 612-5000
www.courtyard.com/ISPCY
No matter where in America you travel, you can always count on affordable but comfortable accommodations at any Courtyard Marriott hotel. This particular Courtyard Marriott offers 154 spacious guestrooms and suites, each with one or two queen- or king-size beds, a large desk, in-room coffeemaker, flat-screen TV, and a variety of other basic amenities. Guests can enjoy free high-speed Internet access, a full or continen-

tal breakfast, an on-site fine-dining restaurant called Tru North Martini Bar & Grille (plus several additional restaurants within walking distance), a free shuttle to the nearby Long Island MacArthur Airport or Long Island Railroad train station, an indoor pool and whirlpool, a nicely equipped fitness center, guest laundry service, and free parking. Each guestroom has a microwave and refrigerator, while the hotel's 20 suites contain full kitchens, spa tubs, and a spacious sitting area. This is a totally nonsmoking, midpriced hotel that is suitable for business and leisure travelers alike.

DANFORDS HOTEL & MARINA **$$$**
25 East Broadway, Port Jefferson
(631) 928-5200, (800) 332-6367
www.danfords.com

Danfords Hotel & Marina is a full-service hotel that is housed in multiple low-rise buildings right on the water. Featuring New England village–style architecture and a nautical decor, many of the rooms offer a stunning waterfront view that overlooks the ferry dock. Located in the heart of Port Jefferson, the hotel is within a very short walk to shopping, dining, and attractions. Within the hotel itself is a wonderful fine-dining restaurant, the Wave Restaurant & Lounge, as well as meeting/function space and a full-service day spa. The 86 posh guestrooms are spacious, nicely decorated, recently renovated, and extremely comfortable. While the hotel has a classic and timeless nautical theme, the amenities are all modern. Business travelers will appreciate the full-size desk and ample workspace within each guestroom, as well as the small business center and Wi-Fi Internet service. Leisure travelers will enjoy the oversize bathrooms, deck, fine amenities, and extremely comfortable beds, not to mention the location and the view. Some of the suites have fireplaces.

i **In Dec, Danfords Hotel participates in the popular Dickens Festival held in Port Jefferson. The entire property features wonderful decorations and a festive atmosphere throughout the holiday season.**

HILTON GARDEN INN **$–$$**
2038 Old Country Rd., Riverhead
(631) 727-2733
www.riverheadhgi.com

This is one of the newest hotels to open in the area. It contains 114 nicely appointed guestrooms, an indoor pool, restaurant, lounge, and fitness center. It's conveniently located close to Long Island's wine country and many of the popular vineyards, as well as the Hamptons, plus it's literally across the street from Tanger Outlet, a popular shopping destination. For kids, Splish Splash Water Park is also very close by. This is a 100 percent nonsmoking hotel that offers spacious, three-star accommodations that are affordable and comfortable. Each guestroom contains one or two queen- or king-size Sleep Number beds, a microwave, and a refrigerator, along with a desk and other basic furnishings. The on-site Great American Grill is open for breakfast and dinner.

HILTON LONG ISLAND **$$–$$$**
598 Broadhollow Rd., Melville
(631) 845-1000
www.HiltonLongIsland.com

This upscale Hilton property features 302 recently renovated guestrooms with high-speed Internet access. There's also a lovely indoor/outdoor swimming pool, lighted tennis courts, a whirlpool and sauna, a fitness center, a cocktail lounge, and a full-service restaurant called Fuse Food & Drink. The guestrooms are available in several different configurations and nicely combine comfort and luxury with affordability, which is exactly what you'd expect from a Hilton hotel.

HOLIDAY INN EXPRESS HOTEL & SUITES **$–$$**
1707 Old Country Rd. (Rte. 58), Riverhead
(631) 548-1000
www.hieeastend.com

Located near the downtown business district in Riverhead, this budget-oriented hotel is brand-new (as of 2009). It features affordable, clean, and comfortable guestrooms that are within a short drive to the Hamptons and many popular attractions. This is a three-story hotel containing

89 guestrooms and 41 suites. Guestrooms are available with a variety of bed configurations, and both smoking and nonsmoking rooms are offered. It's a pet-friendly hotel with free parking.

HYATT REGENCY **$–$$**
1717 Motor Pkwy., Hauppauge
(631) 784-1234
www.longisland.hyatt.com
This traditional Hyatt Regency offers 358 guestrooms, plus meeting and banquet rooms. During the week it caters more to business travelers, while on weekends it transforms into more of a leisure-oriented hotel. What's unique about this hotel is that it has its own private 18-hole, par-71 golf course, plus two tennis courts, a restaurant, and a health club. In terms of accommodations, this is a typical three-star hotel. It offers comfort and convenience, a nice selection of services, and a handful of on-property activities. Business travelers in particular will appreciate the concierge floor, which offers added amenities and services to guests.

MARRIOTT MELVILLE LONG ISLAND **$$–$$$**
1350 Old Walt Whitman Rd., Melville
(631) 673-4324
www.marriott.com
This full-service Marriott hotel offers three-star accommodations in its 369 guestrooms and 24 nicely furnished suites. The in-room amenities and furnishings are clean, comfortable, and very much in line with what you'd expect from a Marriott. The hotel offers complimentary parking, a gift shop, an atrium lobby bar, and a full-service restaurant called Bistro 49. There's also an indoor pool, whirlpool, and fitness center. A wide range of golf courses, beaches, and historical sites are located nearby, and special weekend packages are available. You'll find this Marriott well-suited to business travelers, as well as to couples and families planning a weekend getaway.

SHERATON LONG ISLAND **$$–$$$**
110 Motor Pkwy., Hauppauge
(631) 231-1199
www.starwoodhotels.com/sheraton/property/overview/index.html?propertyID=855
Located in the middle of Long Island, in close proximity to many of the area's beaches, golf courses, attractions, and tourist destinations, and within the massive Hauppauge Industrial Park, this full-service hotel is ideal for business travelers and vacationers alike. Featuring 209 comfortable and nicely decorated rooms, in line with what you'd expect from a Sheraton, this property also offers Sheraton's signature Sweet Sleeper beds and guestrooms with multiple bed configurations to support a solo business traveler, a couple on a weekend getaway, or even an entire family. Each guestroom, for example, contains a workspace with a large desk, high-speed Internet access, a 32-inch flat-screen LCD TV, dual-line phones, spacious bathrooms, and all of the amenities you'll need for a comfortable stay. On the property you'll find a fitness center, business center, restaurant, meeting and conference rooms, indoor heated pool, whirlpool, gift shop, laundry service, and sundeck, plus a fee shuttle to surrounding areas. Be sure to visit the hotel's Web site to view a variety of special offers and money-saving package deals.

INNS

Nassau County

THE INN AT FOX HOLLOW **$$$–$$$$**
7755 Jericho Tnpk., Woodbury
(516) 291-8090
www.theinnatfoxhollow.com
While larger than a bed-and-breakfast, the Inn at Fox Hollow presents itself as a luxury inn that offers the comforts and personalized attention of a cozy B&B, but with the conveniences, services, and amenities of a larger hotel. Each guestroom at this inn is a spacious suite by traditional hotel standards. The overall decor of the property and guestrooms is that of a European-style manor house, with furnishings that utilize a lot of mahogany, marble, and tufted rugs. Every morning a full American breakfast buffet is served, while Sun through Thurs nights, a complimentary dinner buffet is also offered.

In addition to the guestrooms, the inn offers several indoor public areas, where guests are welcome to relax and socialize. The Hearth Room, for example, resembles an oversize living room with plush couches and a big-screen TV. There's also a heated outdoor swimming pool and hot tub that's open during the summer months.

Suffolk County

THE HEDGES INN **$$$–$$$$**
74 James Ln., East Hampton
(631) 604-1550
www.thehedgesinn.com

The best way to describe the Hedges is as an upscale, relatively small inn that features top-notch modern amenities and a sophisticated decor. Here you'll find extremely friendly and attentive service, and an overall welcoming and nonpretentious attitude. The inn itself is located just a few blocks (walking distance) from the main shopping area of East Hampton. The grounds are perfectly landscaped and tranquil, and free parking is available. The Hedges Inn is housed within a homestead that dates back to 1652. The property has served as an inn since 1870; however, everything about it has been fully modernized, while maintaining a classic and traditional ambiance. Today the inn is one of the most luxurious and comfortable places to stay in the Hamptons.

The first thing you'll notice when you step through the front door is the cleanliness. You literally won't find a speck of dust anywhere, and everything will be in its proper place. You'll experience the comforts of home right away. This inn's attention to detail carries over into each of the 12 guestrooms, where the furnishings are posh and comfortable. Within the rooms are extremely comfortable beds, a bathroom with all-new fixtures and amenities from Bulgari, and a flat-screen television, along with other furnishings that contribute to the decor yet are also highly functional. Each room has its own heating/air-conditioning unit, Wi-Fi Internet access, telephones, and plush bathrobes. Upon check-in, Godiva chocolates and bottled water will be waiting in your room. As you'd expect, the breakfast offered at the Hedges Inn goes well beyond a traditional continental breakfast. You'll have plenty of options as you relax in the main dining room or outside on the large and nicely furnished deck. There are also several common indoor areas for guests to relax, watch television, and socialize.

Whether visiting for a night, a weekend, or a full week, this is the perfect place for couples to stay for a romantic getaway or when exploring Long Island's wine country. The inn is located in the heart of the Hamptons and a short drive from Montauk, so it's conveniently located to just about everything in Suffolk County.

i **When it comes to finding an inn, seek out referrals from people you know, or visit Web sites like TripAdvisor.com, where travelers review places they've stayed. To find the best inns, one excellent resource is the Select Registry of Distinguished Inns of North America (800-344-5244, www.selectregistry.com). This organization has gathered together more than 400 of the best inns in North America and requires extremely high standards for inns to maintain their affiliation.**

MILL HOUSE INN **$$$$**
31 North Main St., East Hampton
(631) 324-9766
www.millhouseinn.com

As you'd expect in East Hampton, this area has no shortage of upscale places to stay. The Mill House is another luxurious inn that's ideal for couples looking to experience a romantic getaway. This inn's focus is on offering the very best of everything—from accommodations and service to a bountiful breakfast every morning. It is located walking distance of the ocean and East Hampton Village, the area's main shopping district. Unlike many upscale inns, this one is both child- and dog-friendly. However, adults will certainly appreciate the sophistication, luxury, and comfort more than kids or teens.

Within the 10 guestrooms and suites, supreme comfort is the goal. In addition the posh furnishings, comfortable beds adorned with fine linens and down pillows and quilts, and luxury private bathroom with a walk-in shower and separate oversize whirlpool tub, you'll find a wide range of extra amenities, like a gas fireplace, wet bar, coffeemaker, iPod docking station, Wi-Fi Internet access, and flat-screen television with DVD player. Some of the guestrooms and suites also have private decks. The guestrooms in the award-winning Mill House Inn are spacious, and great attention to detail has been paid to the tasteful decor. During the peak season expect to pay top dollar to stay here, but it's worth every penny. Advance reservations are a must.

SOUNDVIEW INN **$$–$$$**
58855 North Rd. (Rte. 48), Greenport
(631) 477-1910
www.soundviewinn.com

What sets this lovely upscale inn apart is its incredible waterfront location, and the fact that it offers its own restaurant, private beach, outdoor pool, sauna, and fitness center right on the property. All guestrooms look out onto the water and offer a stunning view. Located on the North Shore, this inn is conveniently located close to the popular wineries and vineyards in the area. The one-story Soundview Inn may be less luxurious than other inns and B&Bs in the area, but it's also more affordable. Guestrooms are available with a variety of different bed configurations, and all have beachside decks, Wi-Fi Internet, a coffeemaker, and a refrigerator.

SOUTHAMPTON INN **$$$**
91 Hill St., Southampton
(631) 283-6500
www.southamptoninn.com

This charming inn is located on five acres in the lovely Southampton area. While it's considered an inn, due to its smaller size, it offers all of the services and amenities you'd expect from a full-service hotel or resort. This is a luxurious kid- and pet-friendly property that features a pool, game room, and tennis courts. It's also close to several beaches, including Cooper's Beach (which is two minutes away by car or via the inn's free shuttle van). Offering 90 guestrooms, the Southampton Inn is more like a boutique hotel, in terms of the unique design of each room. While the decor of the guestrooms is upscale, the focus is on comfort and luxury. All rooms contain refrigerators, wireless Internet, and one or two extremely comfortable Tempur-Pedic beds. Many of the rooms have spacious work areas (ideal for business travelers), though the main focus of this hotel is to offer luxury accommodations to leisure travelers.

This is an entirely nonsmoking property. The OSO restaurant within the inn is a fine-dining establishment that serves breakfast, lunch (during peak season), and dinner. As with any hotel, inn, or B&B in the Hamptons, you'll pay a premium to stay here between Memorial Day and Labor Day.

i In Southampton alone there are more than 41 independently owned and operated B&Bs, inns, hotels, and motels. For more information about these options, contact the Southampton Chamber of Commerce at (631) 283-0402 or visit www.southamptonchamber.com.

THREE VILLAGE INN HOTEL & SPA **$$$**
150 Main St., Stony Brook
(631) 537-8885
www.threevillageinn.com

The Three Village Inn has recently undergone a massive redesign and refurbishment. The inn's main historic building has a few very traditional and somewhat small but extremely cozy guestrooms. It's also home to Mirabelle, which has become one of the best fine-dining restaurants on Long Island. The majority of the 26 guestrooms at the Three Village Inn can be found in small cottages, which, as of late 2009, were in the process of being totally gutted and redesigned to offer luxurious and very romantic accommodations. (When making your reservation, be sure to request one of the newly renovated cottages.)

There is a small day spa on the premises, and the inn is within walking distance of a cluster of lovely shops, as well as a gorgeous park that offers hiking trails and a beautiful pond. In addition to

Meet Sylvia Muller, Proprietor, Mill House Inn

What you'll discover when visiting one of the many inns or B&Bs on Long Island is that the proprietors of these establishments take great pride in what they offer. Each property is unique and offers top-notch luxury accommodations and a very welcoming environment.

The Mill House Inn in East Hampton is a perfect example of the upscale inn you'll find in the Hamptons. This award-winning historic property has been called one of the top 50 small inns in America, and with very good reason. Situated close to beaches, shopping, golf courses, and Long Island's wine country, this dog-friendly inn is a member of the Select Registry of Distinguished Inns of North America (www.selectregistry.com) and features 10 extremely elegant and spacious rooms and suites. Each night's stay at the inn includes breakfast, and it's not your run-of-the-mill morning meal. The chef serves up no fewer than 30 signature items that have been featured on the Food Network. The breakfast served at the Mill House is beyond exceptional, not to mention memorable.

As an owner of the Mill House Inn, Sylvia Muller takes great pride in what she offers to guests throughout the year. "The Mill House Inn's original house was built in 1790. In 1896, a second and third floor were added. The house has been used as a boarding and guesthouse since the 1930s, and as a traditional B&B since the late-1970s. My husband and I purchased the property in 1999 and have since fully renovated it," she said.

"One of the first things we did was redesign and redecorate the house, as well as renovate and modernize it. My philosophy is that if we do a good job decorating the inn in a style we'd be comfortable in, it will attract guests whom we like, and who will be very comfortable staying here," added Muller, who explained that in the decade they've owned the Mill House, they've never stopped renovating, making improvements, and redecorating.

In 2002 the Mullers added a second house behind the main house. It contains three incredibly luxurious and well-decorated suites. In 2008 the couple purchased a gorgeous four-bedroom, four-bathroom house on the opposite end of East Hampton's village area, fully renovated it, and now offer it as a nightly, weekly, or monthly house rental property with full hotel services (something few house rentals offer in the region).

Muller explained that East Hampton is a wonderful place to live, visit, and work. She added, "Our goal is to create an experience for each of our guests that is beyond 'wow.'"

To set themselves apart from East Hampton's other inns and B&Bs, the Mullers focus on offering an extremely upscale and luxurious experience. "We are the only inn in the area that is owner occupied. We're not a major corporation, nor are we a couple renting out a few spare bedrooms in our home," said Muller.

While you won't find a Ritz-Carlton or Four Seasons hotel in the area, the Mill House Inn provides extremely posh accommodations, but in a smaller, inn environment. "During the off-season, our rates are much lower, and we attract a very different clientele than we do during the peak summer season, when our rates our significantly higher," said Muller. "Our inn appeals to couples, families with children, people traveling with their dog, honeymooners, gay couples, and single travelers. We constantly have people coming here to propose marriage, or to celebrate an anniversary or birthday. Plus, we appeal to upscale business travelers visiting the region, as well as to international clientele."

When asked to describe the Mill House, Muller stated, "It's a gracious inn in the heart of historic East Hampton village. We are cognoscente of the historic tradition of the beach cottage, as well as the colonial feel of the region. We combine the historic sensibility with modern comforts, like flat-screen TVs, iPod docking stations, and Wi-Fi. What we deliver is comfort, luxury, service, and convenience. East Hampton has been exquisitely preserved, and that keeps the entire area beautiful."

Each guestroom and suite at the Mill House Inn is uniquely and exquisitely decorated based on a theme. Muller stated, "Before we start decorating or renovating a room, we create a story upon which we base the room or suite's unique theme. A few of our six suites and four guestrooms have a more masculine design in order to appeal to guys who are visiting the area to play golf or go fishing."

According to Muller, what most people don't realize is that East Hampton has a lot going on throughout the entire year, not just during the summer season. "This region has become a year-round community," said Muller.

As you begin looking into accommodations throughout the Hamptons, you'll discover some places refer to themselves as "inns," while others are "B&Bs." Traditionally, an inn is larger in terms of the number of rooms available, plus offers food service beyond breakfast.

"*National Geographic* named East Hampton as one of the 10 most beautiful villages in America. It's no longer the quietest village in America, but East Hampton has a unique and timeless New England flair. Being surrounded by water, the natural light in the region is also uniquely beautiful, which is why so many artists are attracted to the area," explained Muller, who is an accomplished photographer. Her work is displayed throughout the Mill House and on the inn's blog (http://themillhouseinn.blogspot.com) and Web site (www.millhouseinn.com).

Between the shopping, local golf courses, beautiful beaches, wineries, farm stands, and numerous fine-dining opportunities, not to mention the luxury accommodations, museums, historical sites, and other activities, Muller believes that East Hampton offers a one-of-a-kind vacation destination that not even the other Hamptons can match.

"While there's so much to do in the region, one activity I highly recommend is simply sitting in front of the fireplace with a bottle of wine and a good book," said Muller, who added that especially during the summer, advance reservations to stay at the Mill House Inn, or any B&B or inn in the area, are an absolute must. "Some people book a year in advance. Of course, you might get lucky with a last-minute booking if someone cancels, but if there's a particular inn or a particular suite within an inn where you want to stay, make your reservations well in advance."

During the off-peak season, last-minute reservations are more readily available. Guestrooms during the off-season at the Mill House start at $275 per night, and go up considerably. For an off-season midweek stay, a suite at the inn starts at $575 for double occupancy. "Especially during the winter months, we promote specials on our Web site," said Muller.

When choosing where to stay, select an inn or B&B that offers accommodations and bedroom configurations that nicely fit your needs, wants, and personality. Some are dog- and/or kid-friendly or entirely nonsmoking establishments, for example, while others are not. Also, decide how important it is to be within a short walk to the beaches, local attractions, and/or dining establishments. Ask yourself what in-room services and amenities would you like to enjoy during your stay, such as a separate in-room dining area, a fireplace, whirlpool tub, or private balcony/deck.

First determine what you want and need, then seek out accommodations that fit that criteria, that have availability during your desired travel dates, and that are within your budget.

being close to the historic village of Stony Brook, which offers shopping, dining, and a few historical sites and museums, it's also a short drive from SUNY Stony Brook, so this inn is an ideal place for parents visiting their kids who attend this school.

MOTELS

Nassau County

BEST WESTERN $
5080 Sunrise Hwy., Massapequa Park
(516) 541-2000, (800) 528-1234
www.bestwestern.com

Located close to Jones Beach and the Nassau Coliseum, as well as shopping malls and theaters, this no-frills motel offers 51 guestrooms and 21 suites for budget-conscious travelers looking for basic but clean and comfortable accommodations. Complimentary continental breakfast is included, and business and fitness centers are available to guests. Restaurants and lounges are within walking distance. This is one of several Best Western motels on Long Island. Other locations include Woodbury (7940 Jericho Tnpk., 516-921-6900), Riverhead (1830 Rte. 25, 631-369-2200), and Rockville Centre (173 Sunrise Hwy., 516-678-1300).

COLISEUM MOTOR INN $
1650 Hempstead Tnpk., East Meadow
(516) 794-2100, (800) 540-5050

If you're planning to attend an event at the Nassau Coliseum, this motel is the closest and least expensive accommodation you'll find in the area. It's also close to Jones Beach, Eisenhower Park, and several shopping malls. The motel offers 112 newly remodeled guestrooms that are basic yet functional. As a two-star-rated property, don't expect anything extravagant. However, if you're on a budget, Coliseum Motor Inn offers the basic comforts and amenities you'll need for a good night's sleep.

i When making your reservation or checking into any chain hotel or motel, if you're a member of AAA or AARP, be sure to ask if you qualify for a discount.

FAIRFIELD INN BY MARRIOTT $$
24 Oak Dr., Syosset
(516) 921-1111, (800) 228-2800
www.marriott.com/nycsy

Offering affordable, no-frills accommodations, this Fairfield Inn by Marriott provides business travelers and budget-conscious vacationers with clean and comfortable accommodations. Guests will enjoy complimentary continental breakfast and coffee service throughout the day, as well as free high-speed Internet access and use of the in-lobby business center. The Fairfield Inn also offers free local calls, a fitness center, and a coin-operated laundry facility. The motel is conveniently located in the mid–Nassau County area, and it participates in the popular Marriot Rewards frequent traveler program.

HOLIDAY INN EXPRESS $
1 Sunrise Hwy., Lynbrook
(516) 596-3000, (800) 261-9168
www.hiexpress.com/lynbrookny

This Holiday Inn Express opened in Jan 2008 and nicely meets the needs of cost-conscious business and leisure travelers alike. It features 107 guestrooms, each with a spacious work area and complimentary high-speed Internet access. In your room you'll also find a flat-screen TV, coffeemaker, microwave, and refrigerator. While this Holiday Inn Express is located in Nassau County, it's conveniently close to the NYC-area airports, several beaches (including Long Beach and Atlantic Beach), shopping, and other attractions. Using the Long Island Railroad, New York City is just 30 minutes away.

You'll find several Holiday Inn Express locations on Long Island, including one in Riverhead (1707 Old Country Rd., Rte. 58; 631-548-1000). Many of these properties have recently undergone a total rebranding and redesign. The Riverhead location is close to Long Island's North Fork and South Fork, and the popular Tanger Outlet stores.

RED ROOF INN $–$$
699 Dibblee Dr., Westbury
(516) 794-2555, (800) RED-ROOF
www.redroof.com

This newly renovated motel offers 163 guestrooms and suites that are ideal for budget-conscious business and leisure travelers looking to stay in Nassau County. Like all of the properties in this chain, the accommodations are basic but functional. In the guestrooms you'll find one or two beds, a dresser, desk, television, chair, and perhaps some other basic furnishings. The Nassau Coliseum is only a half mile away. Free Wi-Fi is available throughout the property, and pets can stay for free.

Suffolk County

ECONOLODGE BAY SHORE $

501 East Main St., Bay Shore

(631) 666-6000

www.econolodge.com/hotel/ny267

This is one of several inexpensive, no-frills EconoLodge motels on Long Island. The rooms are basic but air-conditioned and comfortable. Free continental breakfast and a daily newspaper are included. Several different guestroom configurations are available, featuring one or two beds. Other EconoLodges on Long Island can be found in Smithtown (755 Smithtown Bypass, 631-724-9000) and Hicksville (429 Duffy Avenue, 516-433-3900).

ECONOLODGE MACARTHUR AIRPORT $–$$

3055 Veterans Memorial Hwy., Ronkonkoma

(631) 588-6800

www.econolodge.com/hotel-ronkonkoma-new_york-NY173

On the plus side, this no-frills motel is very conveniently located near the MacArthur Airport on Long Island. The average-size rooms feature one or two beds and offer free Wi-Fi, microwaves, small refrigerators, coffeemakers, and the most basic of furnishings. The motel has 59 rooms, spread out in a two-floor building. On the premises you'll find a small fitness center and a lobby area where a free continental breakfast is served. Located nearby, however, is a handful of full-service and fast-food restaurants.

TERRYVILLE MOTOR LODGE $–$$

1371 Rte. 112, Port Jefferson

(631) 928-5900

www.terryvillemotorlodge.com

Located in Port Jefferson, which is home to several extremely nice hotels and inns, the Terryville Motor Lodge offers an inexpensive, no-frills alternative. The 50 guestrooms contain basic furnishings and amenities, in configurations that include one double bed, two double beds, or a king-size bed. Each room has a color TV, telephone, small table, and dresser. A micro-fridge is available upon request at this independently owned and operated motel. Wireless Internet access is also offered. Each room has its own air-conditioning and heat controls, and free parking is available directly in front of the motel.

RESORTS

Nassau County

ALLEGRIA HOTEL & SPA $$$

80 West Broadway, Long Beach, NY

(516) 889-1300, (800) ON-BEACH

www.allegriahotel.com

Located just 25 miles from Manhattan, this full-service resort offers the perfect couples getaway, complete with a day spa and restaurant right on the premises. The Allegria is situated on the water, and the 143 guestrooms and suites offer an ultra-modern and sophisticated decor, designed for comfort and aesthetic appeal. Utilizing a color pallet of whites, beiges, creams, and sea blues, what's offered is truly a "beach chic" design that will appeal to upscale travelers looking for a comfortable and romantic getaway.

In addition to the four-star accommodations, guests enjoy a complimentary copy of the *New York Times*, *Wall Street Journal*, or *USA Today* delivered to their room each day. There's also an on-site fitness center and heated rooftop pool and deck, plus direct access to the beach. If you want to be pampered, the full-service day spa offers massages, facials, and special packages. There are private tennis courts on the property, and several popular golf courses are located nearby.

Suffolk County

DUNE RESORTS **$$$**
East Hampton and Montauk
www.duneresorts.com

Dune Resorts operates 10 unique, full-service resort properties in or very close to the Hamptons, including East Hampton and Montauk. Each is ideal for a romantic weekend getaway or a weeklong family vacation. The East Hampton House Resort (226 Pantigo Rd., 631-324-4300), for example, is located just minutes away from some of the nicest beaches on Long Island, as well as activities such as kayaking, horseback riding, and golf. This resort features 52 air-conditioned units, each with its own private sundeck or patio, along with tennis courts, a swimming pool, and a fitness center.

Operated as a small, two-story hotel, Dune Resorts' Ocean Beach property in Montauk (108 South Emerson Ave., 631-668-4000) is located right on the beach. Each nicely furnished guestroom offers its own private sundeck/patio. On the property, which is within walking distance of the downtown shops and attractions, is an atrium-enclosed swimming pool and Jacuzzi. Dune took over this resort in 1996, and it has since undergone major renovations.

Dune Resorts' other resort properties include:

Beachcomber: 727 Old Montauk Hwy., Montauk; (631) 668-2894

Driftwood: 2178 Montauk Hwy., Montauk; (800) 483-7438

Hermitage: 2148 Montauk Hwy., Amagansett; (631) 267-6151

Ocean Colony: 2004 Montauk Hwy., Amagansett; (631) 267-3130

Surf Club: 20 Surfside Ave., Montauk; (800) 527-8928

Sun 'N' Sound: 22 Soundview Dr., Montauk; (631) 668-2212

Windward Shores: 2062 Montauk Hwy., Amagansett; (631) 267-8600

A Wave Inn: 32 Elmwood Ave., Montauk; (631) 668-2700

EAST WIND **$$$**
5720 Rte. 25A, Wading River
(631) 929-3500
www.eastwindlongisland.com

Situated on 25 acres, East Wind represents one of the largest and most luxurious full-service resorts on Long Island. In addition to the posh and comfortable guestrooms, there's a full-service day spa, multiple restaurants, and plenty of function space. In fact, this is a popular place to hold weddings (with up to 200 guests) and other functions. It's also a favorite of business travelers, honeymooners, and leisure travelers.

The resort is located near the gateway to Long Island's North Fork, just a short drive from some of the region's most popular wineries and attractions. Within its 50 spacious and richly appointed rooms, guests enjoy a wide range of amenities, from Jacuzzi bathtubs in the suites to fine linens and goose down pillows and comforters on the beds. The Spa at East Wind is a 10,000-square-foot facility that offers a complete menu of world-class treatments, including massages, body wraps, and full body treatments. In fact, people often plan day trips from Manhattan and around Long Island just to visit the spa, which can easily accommodate small groups, such as bridal parties. Desmond's Restaurant and Lounge, located in the resort's main building, serves three meals a day in a fine-dining setting.

THE GURNEY'S INN RESORT & SPA **$$$**
290 Old Montauk Hwy., Montauk
(631) 668-2345
www.gurneysinn.com

Situated right on the beach in Montauk, this full-service resort offers oceanfront rooms, suites, and cottages; a full-service day spa; and several on-property restaurants, in addition to a variety of activities. Providing upscale, clean, elegant, and spacious accommodations, the guestrooms are nicely furnished and chock-full of lavish amenities. While the cottages are ideal for romantic getaways, the one- and two-bedroom suites can easily accommodate families. Located close to the very tip of Long Island, Gurney's Inn is approximately 110 miles from Manhattan (a two-and-a-half-hour drive). Montauk Downs—one of the top 50 public golf courses in the United States—is nearby, and fishing, boating, and horseback riding are also available. This is a popular destination for weddings and special events, as well as corporate functions.

MONTAUK MANOR **$$$**
Edgemere St., Montauk
(631) 668-4400
www.montaukmanor.com

While Montauk is a less expensive area to vacation in than the Hamptons, it is truly a beautiful place to visit. To ensure your stay will be a memorable one, consider staying at the historic Montauk Manor, a full-service resort that's open year-round and offers a variety of different accommodation options, including one-, two-, and three-bedroom suites, all with full kitchens. As a full-service resort, Montauk Manor offers a wide range of on-site activities, including a heated indoor/outdoor pool, Jacuzzi, sauna, fit-

Accommodations Directory

Throughout Norfolk County you'll find hundreds of chain hotels and motels to choose from, in addition to a handful of resorts, B&Bs, and inns. As you travel toward Suffolk County, the majority of accommodations available are in the form of inns, B&Bs, and resorts.

If you plan to use an online travel service to book your accommodations, such as Hotels.com, Priceline, Travelocity, Hotwire, Kayak, Expedia, or Orbitz, keep in mind that many of the independently owned B&Bs and inns do not participate in these services.

To contact the major hotel chains directly, call or visit their Web sites:

Best Western: (800) 528-1234, www.bestwestern.com

Courtyard by Marriott: (631) 612-5000, www.courtyard.com

Days Inn: (800) 329-7466, www.daysinn.com

Dune Resorts: www.duneresorts.com

EconoLodge & Choice Hotels International: (877) 424-6423, www.econolodge.com

Hilton: (631) 845-1000, www.hilton.com

Holiday Inn Express: (800) 261-9168, www.hiexpress.com

Marriott & Residence Inn: (800) 331-3131, www.marriott.com

Sheraton: (631) 231-1100, www.sheraton.com

To find listings for Long Island area inns and B&Bs, check out these Web sites:

B&B Finder: www.bnbfinder.com

B&B Travel: www.bbtravel.com

Bed and Beakfast: www.bedandbreakfast.com

Bed & Breakfast Inns Online: www.bbonline.com

The Choice Bed & Breakfast Guide: www.choicebedandbreakfast.com

Select Registry of Distinguished Inns of North America: www.selectregistry.com

Renting a House for the Summer

Many people who visit Long Island during the peak summer months choose to return year after year for a multitude of reasons. For one thing, it's close, and easy and inexpensive to reach from almost anywhere in the Tri-State area (New York, New Jersey, and Connecticut) as well as New England.

People who decide to spend a full month or the entire summer vacationing on Long Island have two main options when it comes to accommodations: They can purchase a summer home or second home, or they can avoid the hassles, maintenance costs, and responsibility of real estate ownership by renting a fully furnished home in one of the island's most popular vacation communities.

While there are certainly less expensive places to rent on Long Island, if you decide to stay in the Hamptons, chances are you'll pay a hefty premium. The East End of Suffolk County is a luxury vacation home market that attracts the rich and famous. During the peak season, it's equivalent to Aspen, for example, in terms of demand and pricing for deluxe home rentals. The difference with Long Island, however, is that the region basically only offers full-size, fully furnished rental homes. Smaller condos or short-term rental apartments are simply not available.

The East End of Suffolk County also contains very few large luxury hotels. If you want to spend more than a week or two vacationing in Suffolk County, aside from staying at an inn or B&B, your only option is to rent a home.

For almost 15 years, Gary DePersia, senior vice president of the Corcoran Group (516-380-0538, http://myhamptonhomes.com/), has been a real estate rental and sales agent in Suffolk County. He specializes in the Hamptons and surrounding areas, and has developed a top-notch reputation in the community and with his clients.

"I specialize in an area that encompasses Southampton to Montauk, and then north to Shelter Island. In other words, the East End of Long Island's Suffolk County. My business is the sale, listing, and rental of luxury properties. In terms of the sale price, a luxury property could start at $1 million and literally go as high as you want to go," explained DePersia.

"In terms of the rental market, a modest property that I'd represent in the Hamptons might go for $20,000 to $25,000 for the entire summer, which extends from Memorial Day to Labor Day. This would be for a three- or four-bedroom home with a private pool and, most likely, air-conditioning, but it would be north of the highway and not located near the water," said DePersia.

For those looking to rent anywhere on Long Island, DePersia explained that there's a catch-22 if they're also looking for great deals. "If you start working with a rental agent in September, October, or November for your summer rental property, you'll have the best selection to choose from, but you'll wind up paying top dollar. If you wait until the last minute to reserve your rental home, the selection will be much smaller, plus you run the risk of not finding a home that best suits your needs," said DePersia. "However, the property owners are often willing to accept less money for the rental, and the renter can negotiate much better deals by waiting until the last minute." Supply and demand, along with a variety of other factors, determine rental pricing and the motivation of the property owners to reduce their asking price.

Once people find the ideal home to rent for the summer, according to DePersia, they'll often rent that same property year after year. Finding that perfect property, however, can be a challenge. "Some people have visited the Hamptons many times in the past, and they know the exact area where they want to rent, and they know exactly the size and type of home they're looking for. There's not a lot of price flexibility for these people, because the options are somewhat limited. Others have a lot more flexibility, which means they won't necessarily be paying a premium for the rental property they choose," said DePersia.

As a rental agent, one of DePersia's biggest challenges is matching the perfect rental property to each of his clients. "The first question I always ask a perspective renter is whether or not they've visited the Hamptons before, and how well they know the region. The two things that need to mesh perfectly with a renter's wants and needs are the house itself and its location. Each town in Suffolk County, or anywhere on Long Island for that matter, is totally different and offers a vastly different experience for people visiting," said DePersia.

One concern many people planning to summer in the Hamptons have is traffic and their ability to commute to and from New York City for work. "Many people who summer on Long Island commute back and forth for work in Manhattan. They'll spend Thursday, Friday, Saturday, and Sunday night on Long Island, and then drive or take the train back to New York City for work on Monday morning," he added.

According to DePersia, the Hamptons and the East End of Long Island attract vacationers for the entire summer for many reasons. "We have miles and miles of wonderfully soft, sandy beaches. We also have world-class golf courses, including three or four of the very top courses in the entire world. Long Island also offers tremendous fishing and boating opportunities."

"Suffolk County has a vast selection of gourmet restaurants that are very good. For many vacationers, dining is a major activity, and we offer selection and quality when it comes to fine dining. Plenty of shopping, as well as local attractions and things to do, plus the wine country all contribute to making this region an ideal vacation destination. Of course, we're also close to Manhattan."

Another thing that makes Suffolk County unique is that it's a close-knit community and people get to know each other, especially those who return year after year. "Everyone seems to know everyone else. People who vacation here develop a strong social network," explained DePersia.

For anyone renting a home on Long Island, DePersia recommends developing a relationship with a reliable, knowledgeable, and experienced rental agent who specializes in the region you'd like to visit. Next, explain to that rental agent exactly what you're looking for in terms of the house, your ideal vacation location, and your budget. Third, spend time with the agent and visit a bunch of potential rental properties.

DePersia added, "If you're married, it's also essential that both people agree on what you're looking for in a rental home before committing to it. Everyone needs to be on the same page." Before choosing a rental property, determine what you need and want you don't really need.

As you start looking at where to rent in the Hamptons, you'll hear a lot of talk about being north or south of Montauk Highway. Many people think they want to be south of the highway, and are willing to pay a premium for this area. This demand started decades ago, when the majority of homes in the region did not have air-conditioning. Without air-conditioning, the closer you were to the ocean, the cooler it would be during the hot summer months. The more north you were situated, the hotter it would be. But because virtually all homes in the region now have air-conditioning, this is no longer a concern. "These days, unless you absolutely want to be within walking distance to the beach, you don't necessarily need to pay extra to be situated south of Montauk Highway. Many people wind up spending time by a pool or at a country club, and seldom actually go to a beach. If being close to a beach isn't a big deal for you, don't pay extra to rent south of the highway," explained DePersia.

To find the perfect rental agent to work with, try to seek a referral from someone you know. "Most of my rental business comes from referrals from past clients," said DePersia. "Allow the broker or rental agent to show you places you might not have considered. Keep an open mind as you search for a house that has the comforts, design, and amenities you like."

ness center, and tennis courts. You'll also find a shuffleboard and boccie court, a full-service day spa, and a fine-dining restaurant on the property. For the best deals, consider a midweek stay. However, money-saving weekend and weeklong vacation packages are often available.

i In Montauk and the Montauk Point area, you'll find more than 55 B&Bs, inns, hotels, and resorts to choose from. Some are targeted to adult couples looking for a romantic getaway, while others welcome families and even pets. For more information about the many accommodations options in this area, contact the Montauk Chamber of Commerce at (631) 668-2428 or visit www.montaukchamber.com.

TIPS FOR FINDING THE BEST RATES FOR ACCOMMODATIONS

Regardless of when you visit Long Island, it always helps to shop around for the best deals, particularly if you have flexibility in terms of where you want to stay or your travel dates. The following tips will help you find the lowest available rates for motels, hotels, or full-service resorts:

- Calculate your overall travel budget and determine how much you can afford to spend on accommodations. Keep in mind that in addition to your nightly accommodations, you may also need to pay for airfares, rental car, gasoline, parking, meals, activities, shopping, etc., depending on your situation.
- Select your travel dates. If you'll be visiting Long Island during a peak travel period, you'll want to make your reservations as far in advance as possible and secure it with a credit card. However, if you have some flexibility in terms of travel dates and the type of accommodations you require, you may be able to find last-minute, deeply discounted deals, even during peak periods, but there's no guarantee of this.
- Pinpoint the specific types of lodging available in the region where you'd like to stay. In and around the Hamptons, for example, there are many B&Bs and inns, plus a few full-service resorts, but very few traditional (chain) hotels and motels.
- Contact each property by telephone or visit its Web site to determine availability and rates for your desired travel dates. Be sure to ask about discounts you might be eligible for, based on AAA or AARP membership, for example.
- When you visit each property's Web site, sign up for its free online newsletter or Twitter feed (if available). Some motels, hotels, and resorts, for example, offer "online only" deals that are not advertised or available unless you receive the online newsletter or receive the Tweet.
- Once you get the "published rate" for accommodations directly from the property where you're interested in staying, utilize an online travel service to see if you can find a better deal. These services typically offer a 20 to 60 percent discount on motels, hotels, and resorts, plus they're ideal for finding last-minute travel bargains.
- If you're using an online travel service to make your travel plans, booking airfares, accommodations, and a rental car at the same time as a package will often make you eligible for a significant discount.
- If you have flexibility with your travel dates, determine if moving your arrival and departure day up or back by a few days impacts the price for accommodations.
- You can sometimes save significant money by accepting a guestroom or suite that doesn't offer a view. For waterfront properties, you typically pay a premium for an ocean view. So, if you're looking to save money, be willing to forego the view.
- On Long Island, especially in Suffolk County, hotels rates vary greatly between the peak season, shoulder season, and off-peak season. Peak season is during the last of spring and all summer (until early Sept). This is when occupancy rates are high and prices for accom-

modations will be the most expensive. As the season changes and the crowds start to dwindle, so do the prices. This is considered the shoulder season (mid-Sept through mid-Nov). Once the weather turns cold and winter hits, it's the off-season on Long Island. Especially in the tourist areas, many businesses and tourist attractions close altogether, or have greatly reduced operating hours. Few tourists visit during the off-season, so there are incredible deals to be had when it comes to accommodations. Even in the off-season, however, you'll still find plenty to see and do, plus you won't have to deal with traffic and crowds. If you can't afford to visit Long Island during the peak summer season, shop for deals during the shoulder or off-season.

i Rental properties are not listed with the popular online travel services. Finding the best deals for weeklong or monthly rentals will require a bit of extra effort. First, look for ads online and in newspapers and magazines from private home owners who rent out their property directly. Next, contact real estate agents and agencies that specialize in Long Island vacation home rentals. You may be able to negotiate for lower rates directly with the property owner or its rental agent.

RESTAURANTS

Hungry? Well, while you're visiting Long Island, your appetite will definitely be satisfied. Just as each region of Long Island offers a totally different experience for tourists and residents, though the culinary options are plentiful throughout the island, the types of restaurants vary greatly based on your location. For example, you're more apt to find all of the popular fast-food and midpriced chain restaurants in and around Nassau County and western Suffolk County than in Suffolk's North Fork and South Fork. In those regions, what you'll find are smaller cafes and restaurants, the majority of which are not part of a chain or franchise.

Since most of Long Island is fairly affluent, you'll discover an abundance of fine-dining restaurants, some of which showcase the work of celebrity or award-winning chefs. You'll also find a diverse selection of culinary specialties, ranging from classic all-American cuisine to meals influenced by regions, cultures, and countries from throughout the world.

With wine becoming such a strong focus of Long Island's tourism and industry (at least in the North Fork), many restaurants throughout the region offer vast wine selections and gourmet dishes accompanied by expertly selected wine pairings.

In 2009 and 2010, with the hard-hitting economic recession impacting just about everything and everyone, one noticeable trend among many of Long Island's top restaurants was the introduction of more affordable prix fixe menus, particularly for dinner. While guests are welcome to order whatever they'd like from the main menu, many of the more upscale restaurants also offer three-, four-, or even five-course prix fixe menu options, with far fewer choices but for a predetermined, often very affordable, flat price.

Price Code

The majority of restaurants on Long Island offer an a la carte menu. You decide whether or not you want an appetizer, soup, salad, entree, side dishes, and dessert, for example, and select from the options available for each course. Each item on the menu has its own price associated with it.

If you choose a restaurant that offers a prix fixe menu, you will pay a predetermined fixed price per person for the entire meal, which will include three, four, or five courses. For each course, you'll typically have two to five options. For an additional flat fee, you can add wine pairings to each course at some restaurants. Although a prix fixe menu offers fewer options (and most restaurants do not allow substitutions), the prices are typically lower than those you will find on the a la carte menu. At a fine-dining restaurant, a prix fixe dinner will typically cost between $25 and $50 per person. If you order from the traditional menu, you could pay a lot more.

To give you an idea of what you can expect to pay when you dine out on Long Island, we've provided the following price codes as a general guide. Price categories are for a complete a la carte dinner (appetizer, entree, side dish, and dessert), excluding alcoholic beverages (such as wine pairings) as well as tax and tip. If you opt to pair wine with each dinner course, for example, plan on adding at least $30 per person to the cost of the meal. Depending on the restaurant, mixed drinks will cost anywhere from $8 to $15 each.

$...... Less than $25 per person
$$ .... $26 to $49 per person
$$$ ......$50 and up per person

AMERICAN

Nassau County

LIBRARY CAFE $$
274 Main St., Farmingdale
(516) 752-7678
www.thelibrarycafe.com

Located in the heart of Farmingdale's main shopping district, and convenient to many areas of Nassau County, this charming restaurant and bar offers a casual but elegant setting and a library motif. Lunch and dinner are served daily. During the day Library Cafe attracts a local business clientele. People come dressed in business casual attire to enjoy a quality but affordable lunch, or after-work drinks at the full bar adjacent to the dining room. In the evening a full dinner menu is offered. The upper level of the restaurant can easily host private parties and corporate events. The lunch menu features sandwiches, wraps, salads, and burgers. The all-American fare extends to the dinner menu, which includes chicken bruschetta, grilled chicken, marinated skirt steak, bone-in short rib, and a handful of fresh seafood dishes. Locals who dine here appreciate the money-saving frequent diner loyalty program that Library Cafe offers.

PRIME: AN AMERICAN KITCHEN & BAR $$$
117 New York Ave., Huntington
(631) 385-1515
www.restaurantprime.com

Featuring an elegant, modern, and upscale setting, complete with a massive fireplace in the dining room and large windows that overlook the water, the decor is accented by glass statues and wood furnishings. As the restaurant's name suggests, Prime serves all-American cuisine that includes seafood, steak, and chicken entrees, but it also offers an impressive sushi menu. Soups and salads are among the appetizer offerings, plus there's a seafood bar that features items like lobster cocktail, king crab legs, shrimp cocktail, littleneck clams, and oysters. The Prime Plateau seasonal seafood bar tower is a popular appetizer selection for two people ($35 per person). Along with the sushi menu, house specialties include Chilean sea bass, red snapper, salmon, tuna, and lobster, along with filet mignon, roasted organic chicken, New York strip steak, a porterhouse steak for two, veal chops, and Colorado lamb rack. Sun through Thurs a $40 prix fixe menu is offered and includes a starter, an entree, and a dessert. Add selected wine pairings for $10 more per person.

REIN AT THE GARDEN CITY HOTEL $$–$$$
45 Seventh St., Garden City
(516) 877-9385
www.gardencityhotel.com

As the main restaurant within the upscale Garden City Hotel, Rein transforms throughout the day. Offering a relatively small dining room that's tastefully decorated to create a cozy, pub-like setting (complete with a full bar and multiple large-screen televisions scattered throughout the room), Rein serves breakfast, lunch, and dinner. The restaurant's design was conceived by world-renowned architect and designer Robert DiLeonardo. During the day the restaurant offers a business casual setting, which becomes somewhat more formal for dinner, although the dining room and main bar share space. The menu offers typical, all-American fare and a handful of entree choices for each meal. Hotel guests will appreciate the food quality, which is much better than a typical restaurant located in a hotel. Steak, chicken, and seafood dishes are highlights on the dinner menu.

Rein is open seven days a week and offers a special late-night bar menu. Reservations are strongly recommended for dinner. Offering a business-friendly setting, this is a wonderful place to enjoy a business lunch or dinner. It's also suitable for adult couples, but is not overly family friendly.

RUTH'S CHRIS STEAK HOUSE $$$
600 Old County Rd., Garden City
(516) 222-0200
www.ruthschris.com

Especially in Nassau County, you'll find virtually every popular restaurant chain in existence, from fast food to fine dining. In this latter category, Ruth's Chris Steak House is a top-quality chain restaurant that offers the utmost fine-dining experience. Like all of the Ruth's Chris locations, this one in Garden City serves a selection of mouthwatering "signature" steaks, including a fillet, rib eye, New York strip, porterhouse for two, and a popular T-bone. In addition to steak, Ruth's Chris offers barbecued shrimp, lamb chops, stuffed chicken breast, fresh lobster, ahi tuna steak, and at least one vegetarian entree selection. Complementing the delicious top-quality food is superior and highly personalized service, along with a sophisticated and comfortable dining room. This is definitely a business-friendly restaurant, although it is also a wonderful place for couples to enjoy a romantic dinner or for friends to gather for fine food and drinks. Full bar service is available. Especially for dinner, reservations are strongly recommended.

Suffolk County

75 MAIN **$$**
75 Main St., Southampton
(631) 283-7575
www.75main.com

Named for its address in lovely Southampton, 75 Main is open seven days a week for lunch and dinner, as well as for Sun brunch. There's a daily happy hour in the bar, and live entertainment is offered most nights. Offering both indoor and outdoor seating, 75 Main is known for its tasty "relaxed fine dining." The all-American food is expertly prepared and very nicely presented. This is a wonderful place to meet friends for lunch, dinner, and/or drinks. The menu changes seasonally.

AMERICAN ROADSIDE BURGERS **$**
80 East Main St., Smithtown
(631) 382-9500
http://americanroadsideburgers.com

If you're in the mood for quality, casual, family dining that's extremely affordable, check out American Roadside Burgers, a great alternative to traditional "fast food." Guests order at the main counter, but have their custom-prepared meals served at their table. To create the burgers, 100 percent fresh (never frozen) beef is used. In addition to traditional burgers and cheeseburgers, with a ton of extra toppings available, menu options include grilled cheese sandwiches, hot dogs, BLTs, veggie burgers, wings, and a crispy chicken sandwich. Everything on the menu is well priced. For example, with the exception of the Roadstar—which contains four cheeseburgers under one bun, includes a handful of tasty toppings, and will run you around $8—all of the burgers are priced under $6.

B. SMITH'S **$$–$$$**
Long Warf Promenade (Bay St.), Sag Harbor
(631) 725-5858
www.bsmith.com

Offering a stunning view of Sag Harbor, B. Smith's was created by television personality, best-selling cookbook author, and restaurant co-owner Barbara Smith. The prices are a bit steep—you're definitely paying a premium to enjoy the Cajun-Southern fare—but this is a popular dining establishment, so reservations are recommended. The restaurant serves lunch and dinner, as well as Sun brunch. While the menu isn't extensive, it does feature seven different and unique salads, priced between $12 and $30 each. For example, there's a classic Caesar salad, warm chicken cobb salad, and the Long Warf lobster salad. Entrees, priced in the $30 to $40 range, include Southern pit-style BBQ ribs, grilled black Angus sirloin, pan-roasted free-range chicken, grilled rack of lamb, swordfish, and fresh Maine lobster.

BAY BURGER **$**
1742 Sag Harbor Tnpk., Sag Harbor
(631) 899-3915
www.bayburger.com

Bay Burger is all about serving the highest quality and most tasty homemade "comfort food" possible. Basically, this is an affordable, family-friendly gourmet burger restaurant that takes great pride in its burger and bun recipes. Bay Burger bakes its own breads, as well as the hamburger and hot dog buns it serves. It also churns its own homemade ice cream and grinds its own hamburger meat. Even the veggie burgers are made entirely from scratch using fresh and healthy ingredients. The goal is for everything to taste like home cooking, or like it came off your own backyard barbeque. Locally grown, fresh produce is used as much as possible for all of the burger toppings, including the lettuce, thinly sliced tomatoes, onions, and pickles. While the food is truly outstanding, the prices are surprisingly low. Where else could you find a gourmet, home-cooked hamburger or veggie burger for under $7, or a delicious grilled cheese sandwich for just $5? In fact, all of the entrees are priced under $8 each.

With your meal, consider ordering an ice-cream shake, made from the homemade ice-cream flavors of the day. People of all ages will enjoy dining here, and your wallet will certainly appreciate it. The atmosphere is casual at this family-friendly restaurant, which offers both indoor and outdoor seating. One thing that sets Bay Burger apart, in addition to the delicious and affordable food, is the 50-inch plasma television that's located in the rear dining room. It's connected to an X-Box 360 video game system that guests are welcome to play. Sports are also shown on the television, making this a popular hangout during major sporting events. Local beers and wines are served.

DESMOND'S RESTAURANT & LOUNGE **$$–$$$**
5720 Rte. 25A, Wading River
(631) 846-2335
www.eastwindlongisland.com

Located within the famous East Wind resort, Desmond's is a fine-dining restaurant serving breakfast, lunch, and dinner. Even if you're not staying at the resort, it is the perfect place to enjoy intimate dinners, luncheons, rehearsal dinners, or a casual night out with friends. A traditional lunch and dinner menu is available, offering a vast selection of primarily American-influenced cuisine. A prix fixe three-course dinner is also available, as is full bar service. Reservations are highly recommended. On Sun you can enjoy a leisurely, massive, buffet-style brunch.

MICOLE'S AMERICAN CUISINE **$$–$$$**
141 Montauk Hwy., Westhampton Beach
(631) 288-6750
www.micoles.net

Serving dinner every evening, Micole's offers high-end American cuisine crafted by chef Brian Finegan. The freshest and highest quality ingredients are used to prepare each appetizer, soup, salad, entree, and dessert on the menu. Whether you're in the mood for seafood or steak, you'll find a variety of options on the menu. The dining room offers a large fireplace and a relaxed setting. This is a family-friendly restaurant that also offers takeout. If you plan to eat in, however, oversize booths and stand-alone tables are available. There's also a full bar. "Casual but neat" attire is required, and reservations are recommended.

NICOLE'S OF EAST HAMPTON **$$**
Montauk Hwy., East Hampton
(631) 324-3939

Serving breakfast, lunch, and dinner, Nicole's of East Hampton is a favorite dining establishment among locals and tourists alike. The restaurant serves up a hearty breakfast, which can include eggs Benedict, eggs Florentine, smoked salmon, a breakfast burrito, omelets, pancakes, and/or French toast. For lunch and dinner, New York strip steak, rib eye steak, homemade chicken pot pie, broiled chicken, ribs, lobster rolls, salads, and fresh fish are among the offerings. Nicole's offers a more casual dining experience.

RICK'S CRABBY COWBOY CAFE **$–$$**
435 East Lake Dr., Montauk
(631) 668-3200
www.crabbycowboy.com

Offering a relatively inexpensive, casual, family-friendly dining experience that's right on the water, Rick's Crabby Cowboy Cafe features indoor and outdoor dining, full bar service, and an expansive children's menu. Guests arrive by car or boat (free dockage is available at the restaurant), or even land their airplane across the street at the Montauk Airport. Rick's Crabby Cowboy is well-known for its steak, lobster, "crabby bakes," and crab legs; however, the menu also includes plenty of non-seafood dishes, like burgers, rib eye steak, pulled pork, and BBQ chicken. Hershey's ice cream is served for dessert. The restaurant is open seasonally for lunch and dinner.

TOWNLINE BBQ $–$$
Montauk Hwy., Sagaponack
(631) 537-2271
www.townlinebbq.com

This family-friendly restaurant serves up tasty and affordable barbeque in a casual, friendly, and upbeat setting. Texas-style cooking is the specialty here, and the portions are plentiful. Lunch and dinner is served daily. House specialties include beef short ribs, brisket, pulled pork, pulled chicken, Texas chili, California chili (vegetarian), smoked shrimp, and fried catfish, along with a variety of other smoked entrees and sandwiches. Dessert options include fried cherry pie, banana pudding, German chocolate cake, and Mexican wedding cookies.

TWEED'S RESTAURANT & BUFFALO BAR $$
17 East Main St., Riverhead
(631) 208-3151
www.tweedsrestaurant.com

Open daily for lunch and dinner, Tweed's is a classic, all-American steak house that welcomes businesspeople and leisure diners alike. What's unique about this restaurant and bar is that it's been in continuous operation since 1896, and is believed to be the oldest continuing restaurant, bar, and hotel in the entire North Fork. The restaurant is now restored to its original charm, featuring Victorian chandeliers, stained glass, the original stamped-tin ceiling, and a mantled oak fireplace. Decade after decade, the restaurant continues its reputation of offering the finest-quality food, in many cases created using locally grown ingredients.

Several of the featured menu items that have made this restaurant famous, and set it apart from other steak houses, include Tweed's bison hanger steak, grilled bison cowboy steak, and the restaurant's famous bison burgers. Rounding out the menu are more traditional items, like duck, New York strip steak, baked salmon, vegetable napoleon, roasted rack of lamb, double roast chicken, and pasta. Tweed's also features an impressive shellfish bar. If you're a steak lover but want something slightly different than your typical, run-of-the-mill steak house, give Tweed's a try. You won't be disappointed, whether you drop by for lunch or for dinner.

Book Your Restaurant Reservations Online

To quickly and easily make reservations at any of the more than 120 restaurants on Long Island (plus hundreds more throughout Manhattan and New York State), visit OpenTable.com (www.opentable.com). Using this service, you can browse restaurant descriptions and menus, plus make reservations for multiple restaurants at once.

Whenever you book a reservation using OpenTable, the reservation is entered directly into that restaurant's computerized reservation system, so your reservation will be instantly confirmed by the restaurant itself, based on real-time availability information.

The OpenTable.com service is also ideal for learning about brand-new restaurants in whatever region you select.

ASIAN

Nassau County

ASIAN MOON $$
825 Franklin Ave., Garden City
(516) 248-6161

If you're in the mood for a modern, fresh, and affordable twist on Pan-Asian cuisine that's expertly prepared and beautifully presented, look no further than Asian Moon. Entrees are offered in the $10 to $20 range, and the menu is rather extensive. The dining room's atmosphere is tastefully decorated with an Asian motif, which includes a relaxing waterfall.

YAMAGUCHI JAPANESE RESTAURANT $$
63 Main St., Port Washington
(516) 883-3500
Open for lunch and dinner every day except Mon, Yamaguchi serves up classic Japanese cuisine in a casual environment. The restaurant is known for its expertly prepared, ultra-fresh sushi and sashimi, but *shabu-shabu* and other meat dishes (such as beef or chicken teriyaki skewers) are also available. If you enjoy sushi, you won't be disappointed. Take-out service is available.

Suffolk County

PHAO THAI KITCHEN $$
29 Main St., Sag Harbor
(631) 725-0101
www.phaorestaurant.com
This is an authentic, upscale Thai restaurant that serves dinner only every night (until 10 p.m. weekdays, 11 p.m. Fri and weekends) in an elegant setting. Appetizers include Thai BBQ ribs, chicken satay, beef satay, fresh shrimp and vegetable summer rolls, wok-charred squid, Thai mussels, and fried vegetable spring rolls. In addition to soups such as *tom yum goong* and *tom kha gai*, several unique salads appear on the menu. Entrees include red curry with shrimp, green curry with chicken and eggplant, massaman curry with beef and potatoes, vegetarian green curry, and eggplant *kra prow*. One of the house specialties is grilled tofu steak. You'll also find crispy tamarind duck, pineapple fried rice with chicken and shrimp, and *phao* drunken noodles with shrimp on the main dinner menu.

CAFES

Suffolk County

LA BONNE BOULANGERIE $–$$
125 West Broadway, Port Jefferson
(631) 473-7900
www.labonneboulangerie.com
While La Bonne Boulangerie isn't a restaurant per se, it is a full-service bakery and catering service that offers tables and chairs for dining in. In terms of baked goods, everything is created on the premises, including the more than 25 varieties of breads. This is the place to come for truly delicious baked goods and mouthwatering desserts, including cookies, cakes, and pastries. There are literally dozens of freshly baked goods to choose from each and every day. La Bonne Boulangerie is also a gourmet coffee shop, so you get a cup of coffee, hot cocoa, or tea to go with your Danish, apple strudel, cupcake, or muffin. The bakery also creates amazingly detailed, fully customized cakes, edible party favors, and party platters for all types of special occasions.

The bakery has been in existence for more than 35 years and has developed a reputation for being one of the most high-quality, delicious sources for baked goods, cakes, and breads anywhere on Long Island. It is located across the street from the Port Jefferson ferry dock, at the edge of Port Jefferson's tourist-oriented shopping district.

POST STOP CAFE $$
144 Main St., Westhampton Beach
(631) 288-9777
Homemade soups, salads, pasta dishes, steaks, burgers, chicken, and seafood are among the diverse options available at this midpriced, cozy, and casual restaurant. Dinner is served nightly, and lunch and brunch are offered on weekends. Compared to other restaurants in the area, the prices here are more affordable, yet the food quality and service is impressive. Because the menu is so diverse, Post Stop Cafe caters to a broad audience, including families.

i During your visit to Long Island, if you tour some of the wineries and purchase locally produced bottles of wine, you can often bring them to a fine-dining restaurant in the area and enjoy them with your meal. However, you may be charged a corking fee by the restaurant. If this is something you might want to do, inquire about the restaurant's policies when you call to make your reservation.

CARIBBEAN

Suffolk County

FLYNN'S **$$**
Ocean Bay Park, Fire Island
(631) 583-9300
www.flynnsfireisland.com
Whether you're visiting Fire Island for a day or the weekend, or enjoying the island for the entire season, Flynn's offers an upbeat, Caribbean-style dining and drinking experience right on the waterfront. Especially on the weekends, you can expect this restaurant and bar to be packed. Flynn's is known for its king crab leg and steak buffet. Featured starters include jumbo shrimp cocktail, chips and dip, buffalo shrimp, and crab cakes, plus a selection of salads. You can enjoy a selection of burgers for lunch or dinner, or one of the restaurant's entrees, including grilled sea scallops, crispy tuna loin, pan-seared salmon fillet, barbequed baby back ribs, organic chicken, grilled baby lamb chops, and Black Angus steak. Flynn's offers indoor and outdoor dining and full bar service. Especially at night, it's more suitable for adults than families. Happy hour is daily, from 5 to 7 p.m.

DELI

Suffolk County

VILLAGE GOURMET CHEESE SHOPPE **$**
11 Main St., Southampton
(631) 283-6949
Serving sandwiches, soups, and other light fare, this is primarily a cheese shop that offers a very diverse selection of locally produced, domestic, and imported cheeses. If you're planning a picnic at one of the local wineries or at a nearby park, for example, drop by the Village Gourmet Cheese Shoppe for a take-out meal and cheese that will go perfectly with your wine.

ECLECTIC AND EVER-CHANGING MENUS

Suffolk County

1770 HOUSE RESTAURANT & INN **$$$**
143 Main St., East Hampton
(631) 324-1770
www.1770house.com
The 1770 House is a famous inn, located in the heart of East Hampton. Especially during the peak summer season, reservations are an absolute must. For dinner, there's a three-course prix fixe menu, offered between 5:30 and 6:30 p.m., which is affordably priced at $32 per person. Ordering the expertly prepared, award-winning cuisine from the traditional menu will be significantly more expensive, but the dining experience is well worth it. For a flat fee of $75, the restaurant also offers a five-course chef's selection "market menu," which is prepared for the entire table. The meals are prepared by award-winning chef Kevin Penner, who specializes in contemporary American cuisine. Connected to the fine-dining restaurant is a separate, less fancy tavern/pub area. In addition to the fine food and extensive wine list, guests receive superior service and highly personalized attention.

The building that houses the 1770 House Restaurant & Inn was originally built in 1663. However, it was in 1770 that the home became an inn. The building retains much of its original architecture, and the decor creates a lovely and timeless dining atmosphere. This is a wonderful place to celebrate a special occasion or a romantic meal with a loved one. In addition to a variety of appetizers, guests can choose from a selection of fine cheeses from around the world, while enjoying perfectly paired wines. House specialties include roasted organic baby chicken,

Copper River rib eye steak, roasted Iowa pork loin, roasted breast of Long Island duck, pan-roasted organic Scottish salmon, and poached lobster. Just like the inn itself, the 1770 House Restaurant is one of the nicest and most upscale establishments in the Hamptons.

BEACON **$$$**
8 West Water St., Sag Harbor
(631) 725-7088
www.beaconsagharbor.com

Serving both lunch and dinner, this restaurant offers waterfront dining. What's unique about this fine-dining restaurant is that the menu changes weekly. While it's open year-round, a more limited menu is offered during non-peak seasons. Typical appetizers served at Beacon include lobster bisque, tuna carpaccio, roasted pear salad, and a classic Caesar salad. For entrees, you might find pan-roasted blackfish, grilled halibut, pork chops, grilled baby rack of lamb, or New York strip steak on the main dinner menu, though executive chef Sam McCleland is also known to offer pasta dishes and vegetarian entrees on his menus as well. The dining room is elegant, and reservations are definitely recommended, especially for dinner during the peak season.

FRESNO **$$$**
8 Fresno Pl., East Hampton
(631) 324-8700
www.fresnorestaurant.com

Offering dinner only, Wed through Sun, Fresno was created by veteran restaurateurs David Loewenberg and Michael Nolan and opened its doors in 2004. The menu features New American cuisine with a focus on local fare. The dining atmosphere is sophisticated, yet semicasual. An affordable ($28 per person) three-course prix fixe dinner is available until 6:32 p.m. in the dining room, and at the bar throughout the evening. On Wed nights a three-course specialty dinner (with selections from the entire menu) is offered for $30 per person. From the traditional menu, entrees include roasted natural chicken breast, mezze rigatoni, cazuela-roasted halibut, pan-seared Scottish salmon, grilled center-cut pork chop, pan-seared loin of lamb, and a grilled hanger steak. As you'd expect, the restaurant offers full bar service, and expertly selected wine pairings are available with the meal.

HARBOR BISTRO **$$–$$$**
313 Three Mile Rd., East Hampton
(631) 324-7300
www.harborbistro.net

Located on the waterfront, Harbor Bistro is the ideal place to experience a "before the sunset" three-course prix fixe dinner, affordably priced at between $19 and $29 per person. Like many of the restaurants in the Hamptons, the atmosphere is upscale, yet casual. On the main menu over a dozen appetizers are offered, including lobster bisque, yellowfin tuna poke, flash-fried calamari, crab cakes, and slow-cooked duck and mushroom crepes. The Fuji apple and blue cheese salad is also a popular option on the menu, as is the Mediterranean shrimp-quinoa. When you're ready for your entree, you'll have an extensive choice among the pasta, fish, and meat dishes, including rigatoni Bolognese, shichimi shrimp linguine, pistachio-crusted tilapia, hibachi salmon, sesame seared yellowfin tuna, line-grilled local "catch," rib eye steak, pork tenderloin, pan-roasted Crescent Farms duck breast, and filet mignon. A full wine and alcohol selection, including tequilas and cognac, are offered, as is an impressive homemade dessert selection.

LEGENDS **$$**
835 First St., New Suffolk
(631) 734-5123
www.legends-restaurant.com

Utilizing culinary influences from around the world, Legends is open daily for lunch and dinner. Located in the North Fork, and surrounded by local wineries and vineyards, Legends serves New American cuisine, featuring fresh local seafood and produce, and premium steaks and chops, all prepared with culinary artistry. You can end your meal with a homemade dessert, and throughout your meal enjoy expertly selected local wine pairings. The menu selections are eclectic, ranging from shell steak and rib eye steak to rigatoni, Egyptian-style pecan-dukkah-crusted shrimp, penne con gamberi, Alaskan king crab legs, fried oysters, pad thai with vegetables, and Chilean sea bass. The wine and champagne list is extensive.

MIRABELLE RESTAURANT AT THREE VILLAGE INN $$$

Three Village Inn, 150 Main St., Stony Brook
(631) 751-0555
www.threevillageinn.com

When the Three Village Inn was taken over by new owners, everything, including the restaurant and tavern, was completely renovated, refurbished, or redesigned. The inn's main restaurant, called Mirabelle, was transformed into a stunning, extremely upscale, award-winning establishment that offers one of the best fine-dining experiences on Long Island. Chef Guy Reuge relocated from the St. James in New York City to re-create Mirabelle and provide a truly memorable dining experience. The restaurant is open for dinner only and is closed Mon. A more casual dining option can be found at the adjoining Mirabelle Tavern, which also offers a full bar.

The main dining room, however, features an extremely well-designed, contemporary, elegant setting. The service is top-notch and incredibly personalized, and the food is delicious. The menu changes regularly and features a variety of steak, seafood, chicken, and vegetarian dishes. Yes, Mirabelle is housed within the Three Village Inn, however, this is nothing like a traditional hotel restaurant. People literally drive from all over, including Manhattan, just to experience dinner here—it's that good! Business attire is appropriate for dinner.

OSO AT SOUTHAMPTON INN $$–$$$

91 Hill St., Southampton
(631) 283-1166
www.southamptoninn.com

Located in the Southampton Inn, this award-winning restaurant serves steaks, chops, local fish, seafood, and a variety of vegetarian dishes created by chef Bryan Naylor. As you'd expect, the freshest organic ingredients are used to prepare each and every meal, many of them locally grown and seasonal. Thus, the menu changes regularly. To accompany your meal, wine pairings, featuring local Long Island wines, are available. In fact, on weekdays between 5 and 7 p.m., all Long Island wines that are served by the glass are offered at half-price. Between 5:30 and 7 p.m., a three-course prix fixe ($29 per person) menu is served, and at OSO Thurs night is lady's night in the both the dining room and bar area. This is a wonderful place to meet friends for drinks and a delicious meal, or to enjoy a romantic dinner for two.

RUGOSA $$$

290 Montauk Hwy., Wainscott
(631) 604-1550
www.rugosarestaurant.com

Open for dinner only, at Rugosa guests will find modern American cuisine in a relaxed, yet refined atmosphere. Chef and owner Bill Mammes has a broad background in European flavors and classic French cooking techniques. The menu doesn't offer a lot of selections, but what is offered are top-quality, expertly prepared dishes. Entrees include pan-roasted monkfish, seared local scallops, roasted cod, seared Long Island duck breast, pan-roasted chicken breast, roasted lamb loin, and grilled New York strip steak. Choose from the a la carte menu, or opt for the three-course prix fixe menu, which is available between 5:30 and 7 p.m. Fri and Sat, and all night Sun through Thurs.

FRENCH

Nassau County

BRASSERIE CASSIS $$

387 South Oyster Bay Rd., Plainview
(516) 653-0090
www.reststarinc.com

Voted one of Long Island's top 10 new restaurants by *Newsday* readers in 2007, Brasserie Cassis is a traditional French bistro that offers a casually elegant setting. The decor is very much influenced by Paris and includes globe chandeliers, colorful artwork, and marble-topped tables. Brasserie Cassis is one of several restaurants on Long

Island owned and operated by RestStar Hospitality. Entrees include steak *frites*, steak *au poivre vert*, *onglet de boeuf bordelaise*, *jarret d' agneau*, and *saumon aux lentilles*. In English, selections include New York strip steak, grilled hanger steak, pecan-crusted chicken breast, walnut-crusted rack of lamb, duck breast, fillet of trout, black cod, Dijon-crusted salmon, and fillet of sole. Every day of the week a different house special is offered, priced between $22 and $28 each. Brasserie Cassis is a family-friendly restaurant that's also suitable for business people. Reservations are recommended for dinner.

ITALIAN

Nassau County

BASIL LEAF CAFE $$
Plaza Shops, 7B Birch Hill Rd., Locust Valley
(516) 676-6252
www.thebasilleafrestaurant.com

Open daily for lunch and dinner, this midpriced Italian restaurant may be located in a shopping center, but once you step into the dining room, you'll discover there's nothing run-of-the-mill about the dining experience offered. Complete with a wood-burning stove, Basil Leaf Cafe offers a vast menu of classic Italian favorites in a family-friendly setting that's elegant but not too formal. Executive chef Marco Divina trained in northern Italy, so you can be sure that every meal served will have true authentic flavor. The menu features 8 appetizers, 6 different salads, 3 soups, plus a nice selection of pasta dishes, chicken and steak entrees, and more than 10 different homemade pizzas. The Caprina pizza, for example, features goat cheese, sun-dried tomatoes, zucchini, and basil, while the Margherita is topped with mozzarella cheese, basil, and tomatoes.

BENNY'S RISTORANTE $$$
199 Post Ave., Westbury
(516) 997-8111
www.bennysristorante.com

Benny's Ristorante is an upscale, fine Italian restaurant that's family-friendly. In addition to a full lunch and dinner menu, a prix fixe dinner menu ($24.95 per person) is offered. It includes a choice of four appetizers and four entrees, dessert, and coffee or tea. Early bird specials are also offered between 5 and 7 p.m. for $29.95 per person. The traditional menu has a strong seafood influence and features a vast selection of appetizers, including prosciutto di Parma, shrimp cocktail, cold seafood salad, a seafood crepe, and golden fried calamari. Along with the appetizers, no fewer than six salads are featured on the menu, including Benny's house salad and more unique offerings such as *insalata tre colori* and baby string bean salad. In terms of entrees, nine different pasta dishes are offered, each prepared using classic Italian recipes. You'll also find veal, lamb, wild king salmon, filet mignon, Angus steak, and several chicken dishes, in addition to an extensive wine list.

BOCCACCIO $$
275 West Old Country Rd., Hicksville
(516) 433-6262
www.boccacciony.com

Authentic Italian cuisine, served "family style" with massive portions, is what you'll find at this casual but elegant restaurant. Since it opened in 1977, Boccaccio has been serving lunch and dinner daily. A new owner took over the restaurant in July 2009, but the chef and main kitchen staff remain the same. On the dinner menu you'll find a wide range of specialties, such as the shrimp cocktail and oysters oreganata appetizers, along with the veal osso buco and veal chop entrees. The menu is well-rounded and includes soups, salads, and pasta dishes, as well as chicken, veal, steak, chops, fish, and shellfish entrees. Almost all of the desserts, including the signature Italian cheesecake and tiramisu, are homemade.

Suffolk County

CITTANUOVA $$$
29 Newtown Ln., East Hampton
(631) 324-6300
www.cittanuova.com

While vacationing in the Hamptons, you can enjoy an authentic Italian lunch or dinner seven

Meet Robert Ornato, Owner of Jonathan's Ristorante

For more than 15 years, Robert Ornato has been the owner of Jonathan's Ristorante (15 Wall St., Huntington; 631-549-0055; www.jonathansristorante.com), a casual but elegant, authentic Italian restaurant in Nassau County.

"Over the years the restaurant has become famous for a handful of dishes, but at least every two to three months, I try to introduce new items to the menu. Some of our perennial favorites include Fritto di Carciofini, which is sautéed baby artichokes with basil oil, and Tartare di Tonno, which is yellowfin tuna tartare served over avocado salad with fresh wasabi drizzle," said Ornato.

The restaurant is also known for its freshly made pasta and sauces. "Everything we serve is extremely fresh, because I believe food tastes its best right after it's prepared," added Ornato.

Jonathan's Ristorante is open daily for lunch and dinner, except Sun, when the restaurant opens just for dinner. "I used to live in New York City, where everything is very compartmentalized, including the restaurants. For example, a restaurant that served lunch to businesspeople would not also appeal to families for dinner. Being on Long Island, for a restaurant like mine to be successful, it needs to cater to a wide range of customers, from businesspeople to singles, families, couples, and seniors. Our most loyal customers are the people who travel often. I have had numerous customers visit Venice and then return to Jonathan's Ristorante and report that one or more of our dishes was as good, if not better than, what they experienced in Italy. For me, that's the highest praise I can receive," said Ornato, who in addition to serving the finest-quality foods, prides himself on the wine selection his restaurant offers.

Just a few years ago, less than 30 percent of Ornato's customers ordered wine with their dinner. These days, however, consuming wine with a meal has become much more popular in America, particularly among people living and vacationing in or near Long Island's wine country. "More than 80 percent of our customers will order either a bottle of wine or wine by the glass with their dinner," he explained.

days a week at CittaNuova. Modeled after the traditional trattoria and located in the heart of East Hampton, the dining room's decor has a strong Italian influence, as does the expertly prepared food that's served here. The main menu changes throughout the year, but house specialties include pasta, seafood, chicken, and steak dishes. In addition to the fine food, CittaNuova is known for its extensive and impressive wine list, as well as its desserts.

SEA GRILLE $$$
290 Old Montauk Hwy., Montauk
(631) 668-2345
www.gurneysinn.com

As part of Gurney's Inn Resort & Spa, this upscale restaurant has been around more than 80 years and specializes in seafood and pasta dishes. The restaurant overlooks the water and features superior and highly personalized service. With a strong Italian influence, house specialties include stuffed local flounder, mid-Atlantic salmon, baked shrimp, lobster, linguini, penne primavera, chicken parmigiana, chicken marsala, and roasted duck. Reservations are strongly recommended.

A TOUCH OF VENICE $$
2255 Wickham Ave., Mattituck
(631) 298-5851
www.touchofvenice.com

The majority of the wines Jonathan's Ristorante offers come from Long Island, California, and Italy, but the restaurant's extensive wine list also includes vintages from Portugal, France, Spain, Australia, and Argentina. "At any given time, we'll offer at least 100 wine selections, plus an assortment of 15 to 20 wines served by the glass. Especially now, some people can't readily afford a full bottle of wine with dinner, or they don't want to consume the whole bottle because they plan on driving home. Therefore, I believe offering a large selection of quality wines served by the glass is important," said Ornato, who appreciates it when customers turn to him for advice about which wine to order with their meal.

One of Ornato's biggest challenges is constantly updating his menu and wine list, while maintaining the quality his customers have come to expect. "I like to keep the menu changing. There are over 1,000 different types of pasta, for example, that I could potentially offer on the menu. I believe that a good restaurant should allow its customers to always try something new," he said.

To gather new ideas for his authentic Italian menu, Ornato travels to Italy at least once a year. "Over there, I visit lots of different restaurants, and to tell the truth, I occasionally borrow some ideas. In the Huntington area alone, for example, there are more than 60 restaurants. My ongoing goal is to offer the highest-quality and freshest foods, while being able to maintain affordable prices," said Ornato, who believes in offering superior hospitality in addition to excellent food.

In addition to the keeping the menu fresh with new options every few months, several years ago Ornato totally renovated the entire restaurant and added a full bar. "We discovered that some people enjoy sitting at the bar, so we also introduced a separate, less-expensive bar menu. Even if people don't want to dine at the bar, they can stop by to enjoy a glass of wine," he added.

Long Islanders and visitors alike certainly have many restaurants to choose from throughout Nassau County. However, if you're in the mood for authentic Italian cuisine, a visit to Jonathan's Ristorante is well worth the trip.

Like many upscale regions of Long Island, Mattituck features a wonderful, authentic Italian restaurant. A Touch of Venice offers a lovely waterfront view, patio dining, and expertly prepared cuisine. The restaurant has been a hallmark in the region for more than 20 years. Live music is presented during dinner on Fri, Sat, and Sun nights, and an affordable prix fixe menu is offered nightly ($20 per person). Classic Italian selections are showcased on the menu, along with steak, chicken, and seafood entrees. House specialties include five pasta dishes, such as rigatoni and linguine, as well as grilled swordfish, grilled tuna Capri, and veal parmigiana.

MEDITERRANEAN

Nassau County

AYHAN'S FISH KEBAB **$$**
286 Main St., Port Washington
(516) 883-1515
www.ayhans.com

This seafood restaurant is known for its grilled whole-fish dishes that are prepared in a Turkish style (basted in extra virgin olive oil and then cooked on an open flame). It's a family-friendly restaurant that's open for lunch and dinner daily. Just about everything on the menu is seafood-related, from the shrimp cocktail and baked clams appetizers, to the broiled flounder fillet and sesame-crusted salmon entrees. There's also a popular two-pound lobster on the menu, along with entrees prepared using more than 22 different types of freshly caught fish, from flounder to red snapper. Of course, for non–seafood lovers, there are a few steak and chicken options, but most people come here for the fresh seafood, most of which is authentically prepared on an open flame, using cooking techniques perfected in the Mediterranean over thousands of years.

Long Island Restaurant Reviews and Listings

For additional Long Island–area restaurant recommendations, reviews, and descriptions, visit any of the following Web sites. Many of these sites allow you to search by region, cuisine type, and/or price range, plus allow you to read a restaurant's entire menu online.

Dining Out Long Island: www.diningoutli.com

Eat Out Long island: www.eatoutlongisland.com

Explore Long Island: www.exploreli.com/restaurants

Great Restaurants of Long Island: www.greatrestaurantsmag.com/LI

Long Island Convention & Visitors Bureau: www.discoverlongisland.com (Click on "What to Do," followed by "Restaurants.")

Long Island Exchange Restaurant Directory: www.longislandexchange.com/restaurants

Menu Frog: www.menufrog.com

Zagat Long Island: www.zagat.com/longisland

LIMANI $$$
1043 Northern Blvd., Roslyn
(516) 869-8989
www.limaniny.com

Offering an upscale but relaxed dining environment, Limani is primarily a Greek/Mediterranean seafood restaurant that also serves steaks. The chef boasts that only the freshest and highest-quality ingredients are used to prepare each dish. In addition to the quality food, Limani puts a strong emphasis on offering superior service. The dining room serves lunch and dinner, along with brunch on Sun, and the restaurant also features a separate wine-tasting room.

For dinner, there are 4 salads and almost 20 appetizers to choose from, including mussels, octopus, and scallops. Whole fresh fish, including black sea bass, fagri, pompano, yellowfin tuna, swordfish, halibut, red snapper, and Dover sole are available, as are lobster and other types of shellfish. Rounding out the dinner menu are chicken, veal, and steak entrees, including filet mignon, rib eye, and a porterhouse for two. Limani offers a perfect setting for a business lunch, and is a great place to dine with a loved one or friends.

Suffolk County

BLUE SKY MEDITERRANEAN LOUNGE $$
63 Main St., Sag Harbor
(631) 725-1810
http://blueskysagharbor.com

Serving lunch and dinner daily, Blue Sky's menu has a strong Mediterranean influence, although all-American cuisine, including classic burgers, lobster rolls, and clams on the half shell, is also served. Lunch entrees include fish-and-chips, pizza, grilled steak, fresh fruit yogurt, spaghetti, and a delicious tropical grilled salmon salad. There's also a vegetarian panini on the menu. The dinner menu is a bit more formal, but overall this is a midpriced, casual restaurant with booth seating. Dinner entrees include pan-seared baccalà, black pepper tuna, roast chicken limone, seared baby lamb chops, shrimp scampi, braised pork tenderloin, and sirloin steak. A full bar, complete with extensive wine list, can also be found here. On weekend nights the restaurant and bar remain open until 11:45 p.m. Takeout is also available.

MEXICAN

Nassau County

BESITO **$–$$**
1516 Old Northern Blvd., Roslyn
(516) 484-3001
www.besitomex.com
Located in a strip mall, from the outside Besito doesn't look like much. However, once you step through the front door, you're transported into an elegant and spacious dining room that is highlighted by an entire wall lined from floor to ceiling with flickering candles. This is a midpriced dining establishment that specializes in Mexican cuisine, some of which can be spicy. Open daily for lunch and dinner, the food is expertly prepared using fresh ingredients. Entrees include gourmet tacos, enchiladas, and a handful of other Mexican classic dishes. This is a wonderful and elegant, yet casual and family-friendly restaurant that caters primarily to people who enjoy good Mexican food. An additional location can be found at 402 New York Ave., Huntington (631-549-0100).

Suffolk County

GOLDMINE MEXICAN GRILL **$–$$**
99 Broadway, Greenlawn
(631) 262-1775
Offering a casual atmosphere with limited seating, Goldmine Mexican Grill specializes in burritos and tacos, and is known for its fresh salsa bar. All of the entrees are served with saffron-basmati rice, black beans, sour cream, pico de gallo, and shredded lettuce, along with flour tortillas. The restaurant offers counter service and takeout. The utensils and plates are plastic, and the dining room is small, but what's served here is authentic and tasty Tex-Mex cuisine.

ORGANIC AND FRESH

Nassau County

THYME RESTAURANT & CAFE BAR **$$**
8 Tower Place, Roslyn
(516) 625-2566
Serving lunch and dinner daily, plus brunch on weekends, Thyme Restaurant & Cafe Bar takes what it calls a "harmonious approach" to food. This means the chef embraces wholesome ingredients, diligence, and care in preparation. Presentation of the food is also an essential element of the whole dining experience. Combined with a sophisticated dining room atmosphere and top-notch service, the experience guests have at Thyme is typically memorable. To accomplish its task of using only the finest and freshest ingredients, the restaurant works closely with local farms and purveyors, whenever seasonally possible.

In addition to a traditional menu, like many upscale restaurants on Long Island, Thyme offers an affordable prix fixe dinner menu ($24.95 per person), which includes an appetizer, entree, and dessert. Some of the dinner entrees on the traditional menu include braised short ribs of beef, sesame-crusted yellowfin tuna, seafood bouillabaisse, wood-fired double-cut pork chops, pan-seared diver sea scallops, brick-roasted chicken, pan-seared fillet of salmon, and grilled swordfish. Burgers, duck, homemade cavatelli, and filet mignon also appear on the dinner menu. Reservations are strongly recommended, especially for dinner and Sun brunch.

Suffolk County

BACKYARD RESTAURANT **$$**
90 Second House Rd., Montauk
(631) 668-2105
www.soleeast.com
Serving breakfast, lunch, and dinner, Backyard Restaurant prides itself on offering an upscale, country club setting. A three-course prix fixe menu is served nightly between 5:30 and 7:30 p.m. Instead of leaving the kids at home with a babysitter, what's unique about Backyard Restaurant is that it offers its "drop and dine" service for

a flat fee of $20 per child on weekends. This is an on-site babysitting service that allows the adults to enjoy a quiet and elegant dinner, while their kids are fed, supervised, and entertained. Backyard Restaurant is part of Sole East, an upscale boutique hotel in Montauk. The restaurant itself is inspired by a healthy approach to diet and lifestyle. Thus, the chef focuses on using good, wholesome, fresh, and natural ingredients, and sources those ingredients from local farmers and fishermen. Reservations are recommended for lunch and dinner.

CITARELLA **$–$$**
2 Pantigo Rd., East Hampton
(631) 324-9190, (631) 726-3636 (Main Number)
www.citarella.com
Citarella offers a selection of prepared meals for takeout, plus a few tables within the storefront location. However, this is primarily an upscale, gourmet supermarket that offers a wide range of ultra-fresh and organic foods. It's basically East Hampton's answer to the Whole Foods Market, only a bit smaller and nicer. This is the place to shop for fresh seafood, prime meats, fine cheeses, caviar, and other gourmet foods. The selection of prepared foods includes steamed lobster and other dishes that are made fresh daily. Additional locations can be found at 670 Montauk Hwy., Watermill, and 2209 Montauk Hwy., Bridgehampton.

ON THE GO

Suffolk County

PANERA BREAD **$**
Rte. 24 and Montauk Hwy., next to Macy's
(631) 728-3101
www.panerabread.com
Panera Bread is a high-quality fast-food alternative. Featuring freshly baked goods, gourmet coffees, unique salads, and tasty sandwiches, everything is prepared to order at this popular chain restaurant. Dine in, or order takeout for breakfast, lunch, or dinner. Other locations are Bridgehampton Commons, Bridgehampton (631-537-2855), and Old Country Rd. (Rte. 58), Riverhead (631-727-0277).

PUB FARE

Suffolk County

TOM MCBRIEN'S RESTAURANT & PUB **$–$$**
174 East Montauk Hwy., Hampton Bays
(631) 728-7137
www.tommcbrienspub.com
You're probably familiar with the concept of a genuine Irish pub—an upbeat and fun place to socialize and drink. Well, in addition to offering this type of authentic Irish pub atmosphere, Tom McBrien's serves up genuine Irish cuisine. During the week, a prix fixe dinner menu is offered for just $19.95 per person (Mon through Thurs). On Sat between 4 and 10 p.m., the restaurant offers its popular Chef's $25.95 Prix Fixe, which includes an appetizer, entree, and dessert. Sun brunch is served from noon to 3 p.m.

Open for lunch and dinner, Tom McBrien's features Throw Back Thursdays, where $5 burgers, $10 shepherd's pie, and $13 fish-and-chips are offered throughout the day and night. The dining room is casual, but well decorated. In terms of American fare, salads, burgers, and sandwiches are featured menu items. Entrees include penne pasta with garden vegetables, spice-rubbed pork tenderloin, Gorgonzola-crusted filet mignon, USDA Prime New York strip steak, roasted chicken breast, and stuffed flounder. Fish-and-chips, shepherd's pie, Gaelic chicken curry, bangers and mash, and chicken pot pie are among the Irish-influenced dishes.

SEAFOOD

Nassau County

LEGAL SEA FOODS **$$–$$$**
Roosevelt Field Mall, 630 Old Country Rd., Garden City
(516) 248-4600
www.legalseafoods.com
This popular, upscale chain seafood restaurant started in New England, but now has locations

throughout the East Coast, including Long Island. While it is a chain restaurant, it has a stellar reputation for serving only the freshest seafood available (along with a few non-seafood entrees), prepared using authentic New England styles. Legal Sea Foods is formal enough to host an important business lunch or dinner, yet welcomes families dining with kids (and offers a decent children's menu). In addition to its tasty New England clam chowder, some of the restaurant's signature dishes include a lobster roll, a shrimp and garlic entree, jumbo shrimp cocktail, New England lobster bake, and baked stuffed lobster. The signature crab cakes and wood-grilled mahi mahi are also favorites.

OTTO'S SEA GRILL **$$**
271 Woodeleft Ave., Freeport
(516) 378-9480
www.ottosseagrill.net
Offering indoor and seasonal outdoor waterside dining, this casual seafood restaurant serves lunch and dinner, as well as late-night snacks (until 1 a.m.). The atmosphere is family-friendly, although Otto's also features a full-service bar and lounge area. In terms of dining, older people will appreciate the "early bird specials" offered daily, while seafood lovers will enjoy the extensive raw bar. Located along Freeport's "Nautical Mile," Otto's Sea Grill offers a handful of non-seafood entrees; however, it's primarily an affordable seafood establishment.

Otto's has been in business since 1926, and is a popular dining destination among price-conscious residents and tourists alike. Only the freshest seafood and ingredients are used. House specialties include clams, oysters, fried calamari, a selection of salads, sandwiches, burgers, lobster, stuffed lobster tail, Alaskan king crab legs, shrimp, and a seafood posillipo (combo platter). To accompany your meal, a selection of wine, beer, and mixed drinks is offered.

PADDY MCGEES **$$–$$$**
6 Waterview Rd., Island Park
(516) 431-8700
www.paddymcgees.com
This is a popular seafood restaurant in Nassau County that closes for the winter, reopening in Mar. Paddy McGees offers a traditional fish house/bar atmosphere, making it the ideal stop for dinner after spending a day at Lido Beach, for example. The house specialty is lobster, but the menu features a wide range of mouth-watering seafood dishes. American oysters and littleneck clams, lobster bisque, and New England clam chowder are among the appetizers offered, while some of the entrees include a pan-roasted jumbo lump crab cake, BBQ shrimp, grilled Northern Atlantic salmon, and a catch of the day. Paddy McGees serves lunch and dinner during the spring and summer months, but is open for private parties only in the fall and winter.

RED FISH GRILLE **$$$**
430 Woodbuy Rd., Plainview
(516) 932-8460
www.redfishgrille.com
Serving lunch and dinner daily in a casual but tasteful dining room, Red Fish Grille serves up all-American cuisine with a heavy emphasis on ultra-fresh seafood dishes. In addition to the diverse menu, there's a full bar and an extensive wine list, making this the perfect place to dine for a business lunch or a dinner with friends. Kick off your meal with crispy fried calamari, jumbo lump crab cakes, baked clams, or spicy lobster egg rolls, for example, and then move on to a jumbo shrimp cocktail, littleneck clams, or a half chilled lobster. Among the entrees you'll find are horseradish-potato-crusted salmon, sesame seared yellowfin tuna, crispy cod fish-and-chips, Key West mahi mahi, and baked stuffed fillet of sole. The wok-fried whole fish and seafood risotto are also featured specialties. While the menu is extensive, it does change a bit daily, based on the freshest seafood available at any given time.

RIVERBAY SEAFOOD BAR & GRILL **$$–$$$**
700 Willis Ave., Williston Park
(516) 742-9191
www.riverbayrestaurant.com
This classic seafood house offers traditional ocean fare, plus a full bar. It's a great place to enjoy a

meal with friends or loved ones, particularly if you're all seafood lovers. The menu is diverse, but a strong emphasis is placed on freshness. On any given day, for example, you're apt to find at least 10 kinds of oysters featured on the menu. In addition to regular seafood, Riverbay serves sushi throughout the week, and presents a memorable Sun brunch. House specialties include Atlantic swordfish Milanese, sesame seared tuna, crisp salmon in phyllo, pan-crusted Chatham cod, and seared sea scallops. The prices are reasonable, and the food, atmosphere, and service are top-notch.

Suffolk County

AQUA $$

17 South Edison, Montauk
(631) 668-4147
www.aquaeastmontauk.com

This family-friendly seafood restaurant is popular among locals and tourists alike. It's open nightly for dinner and features specially priced appetizers and desserts for just $6 each. Between 5:30 and 6:30 p.m., a prix fixe dinner is also available. The dining room features a bright and open setting, and the menu has a strong Italian influence. In addition to numerous pasta dishes—such as spaghetti marinara, fettuccine Alfredo, risotto, and classic spaghetti and meatballs—roasted half chicken, tuna alla Siciliana, Atlantic salmon steak, and grilled pork chops round out the menu.

COAST GRILL $$$

1109 Noyac Rd., Southampton
(631) 283-2277

Open daily starting at 5 p.m. for dinner, Coast Grill features the culinary creations of chef Brian Cheewing. To begin your meal, a nice selection of hot and cold appetizers are available, ranging from local littleneck clams, oysters, and shrimp cocktail to New England clam chowder, jumbo lump crab cakes, and wild mushroom strudel. The homemade lobster ravioli is a house specialty. Entrees include linguine with littleneck clams, crispy roasted free-range chicken, Thai-spiced bouillabaisse, seasonal vegetable fricassee, New York steak, and Atlantic salmon. Located right on the water, this "rustic" restaurant has been a popular dining option in Southampton for more than two decades.

INLET SEAFOOD RESTAURANT & SUSHI BAR $$

At the end of East Lake Dr., Montauk
(631) 668-4272
www.inletseafood.com

Offering a vast menu composed primarily of ultra-fresh seafood, including lobster and sushi, Inlet Seafood promotes that its staff actually catches some of its own seafood daily. This waterfront restaurant features a gorgeous sunset view and offers indoor or outdoor dining. If you're not a seafood lover, steaks, pastas, burgers, and salads also appear on the lunch and dinner menus. The restaurant is open daily starting at noon, and also serves a lovely Sun brunch. The full bar serves wines, margaritas, martinis, and a variety of other specialty drinks.

LOBSTER INN $$$

162 Inlet Rd., Southampton
(631) 283-1525

Even after recently celebrating its 40th year in business, the Lobster Inn continues to offer a fine-dining experience on the waterfront for both lunch and dinner daily. On the menu you'll find local seafood. One of the house specialties is a steamed shellfish platter for two. While the food is top-notch, the atmosphere is casual. Arrive by car or boat (free docking is available). If you're a seafood lover, you'll definitely enjoy dining here.

SALTWATER GRILL $$

379 Dune Rd., Westhampton Beach
(631) 288-1485

Located within the Dune Deck Beach Resort, this is a casual, family-friendly restaurant that is open daily from noon to 11 p.m. On Fri, Sat, and Sun evenings, live music is presented on the outdoor deck (seasonally). Reservations are required, but there's a very casual dress code. The restaurant offers a waterfront view, delicious food, and a large assortment of drinks. There's a "light menu," which includes a handful of appetizers and smaller entrees, plus a selection of sandwiches, salads, and chowders. Entrees include fish-and-chips, sirloin steak, grilled chicken, Baja fish tacos, Alaskan halibut, and seared ahi tuna. The prices aren't cheap, but they're reasonable. For example, you'll pay about $14 for a basic burger, and $18 for the lobster roll. The petite sirloin is priced at $24. Wines are available by the glass, plus full bar service is offered.

SOUNDVIEW RESTAURANT $$–$$$
North Rd. (Rte. 48), Greenport
(631) 477-0666
www.soundviewrestaurant.com

Primarily an upscale seafood restaurant, Soundview is located right on the water and offers an incredible view, especially at sunset. Indoor and outdoor seating and full bar service is available. The wine list contains a vast selection of locally produced wines. Featuring expertly prepared, all-American cuisine, with a strong seafood influence, a lot of emphasis is placed on utilizing ultra-fresh and local ingredients, including farm-fresh produce. Appetizers include calamari, clams on the half shell, chicken quesadillas, baked clams, and baked Brie, along with soups and several salads. The goat cheese salad is a house specialty. For your main course, choose from over a dozen choices, including grilled shrimp, stuffed flounder, seared sea scallops, New York shell steak, grilled pork chops, and lamb chops. Like many restaurants in the area, the atmosphere is sophisticated, yet casual. After spending an afternoon on the North Fork visiting the wineries and vineyards, dinner at Soundview Restaurant offers a great way to wind down the day.

STONEWALLS RESTAURANT $$
967 Reeves Ave., Riverhead
(631) 506-0777
www.stonewalls-restaurant.com

Open for lunch and dinner and overlooking the Woods Golf Course, Stonewalls Restaurant is a fine-dining establishment on eastern Long Island. The restaurant is open seven days a week for lunch. Dinner is served daily, except Tues. On Sun, brunch is served between 11:30 a.m. and 3:30 p.m. In addition to a traditional menu, a seasonal prix fixe dinner menu is available on Sun, Mon, Wed, and Thurs nights. Much of the produce used to prepare the meals is homegrown. This is primarily a seafood restaurant that boasts that it serves the freshest fish available, so offerings change daily, based on availability. The dining room is simply decorated, open, spacious, and features plenty of windows.

TIDE RUNNERS $$
7 North Rd., Hampton Bays
(631) 728-7373
www.tiderunners.com

Featuring an elegant indoor and outdoor dining experience right on the water, overlooking Shinnecock Canal, Tide Runners is a popular, family-friendly restaurant and bar that offers a wide range of daily specials. It's primarily a seafood restaurant that specializes in lobster, snow crab legs, and clams. On Sun, happy hour lasts from 4 until 7 p.m., and deeply discounted drink specials are in abundance. For Sun brunch, Tide Runners is famous for its twin one-pound lobster meal, which includes corn and a baked potato, for just $29.95 per person. The Sun brunch special is served between noon and 3 p.m. only. With docks located right outside the restaurant, people come here by car or boat, for lunch or dinner, seven days a week.

WAVE RESTAURANT & LOUNGE AT DANFORDS $$–$$$
25 East Broadway Rd., Port Jefferson
(631) 928-5200
www.danfords.com/restaurant.cfm

Featuring massive windows on two sides that overlook the Long Island Sound and the Port Jefferson Ferry dock, Wave Restaurant is located in the famous Danfords Hotel, and serves lunch and dinner. Designed to appeal to just about everyone, the American-influenced menu offers a sampling of seafood, steaks, chicken, soups, and salads. Fresh seafood favorites, such as salmon, sea bass, and tuna, along with more unique options, like hamachi and black cod char siu and sushi, are typically on the menu. A variety of seasonal specials are offered throughout the year. The dining room is spacious and tastefully decorated with a nautical theme. It offers a romantic setting for couples, yet an environment that's also perfectly suitable for an important business lunch or dinner. The service is friendly, professional, and highly attentive. While most hotel restaurants cater primarily to the guests of that hotel, Wave attracts local residents as well as passengers disembarking from the ferry and tourists visiting the area. Reservations are strongly recommended, especially for dinner.

i Especially between Memorial Day and Labor Day (Long Island's peak tourism season), you'll want to make your dinner dining reservations as far in advance as possible, especially on Fri and Sat nights.

SOUTH AMERICAN

Nassau County

CAFE BUENOS AIRES **$$**
23 Wall St., Huntington
(631) 603-3600
www.reststarinc.com

Serving fine Argentinean cuisine, Cafe Buenos Aires offers a unique and semicasual dining experience in Huntington. The menu includes a full tapas bar and traditional bar service. In the sandwich category, house specialties include the *Lomito* (sliced hanger steak with lettuce, tomato, onions, and melted Swiss cheese), *Pollo* (herb-seasoned chicken breast with lettuce, tomato, onions, and provolone cheese), and *Hamburguesa de Atun* (fresh yellowfin tuna with lettuce, tomato, and onions). Specially prepared New York strip steak, grilled lamb chops, Cornish hen, roasted pork chops, grilled skirt steak, grilled flap steak, stuffed chicken breast, and a handful of pasta and seafood dishes round out the menu. All of the entrees are prepared in an Argentinean or European cooking style, using fresh ingredients.

While Cafe Buenos Aires has the laid-back but classy atmosphere of a privately owned, one-of-a-kind restaurant, it's operated by RestStar Hospitality, which owns a handful of unique restaurants in New York City and on Long Island. Reservations are suggested, but typically not required. The restaurant does, however, tend to get busy on weekends.

SPANISH

Suffolk County

COPA **$$**
95 School St., Bridgehampton
(631) 613-6469

This is a small, casual dining establishment that specializes mainly in offering full bar service, along with tapas. There's a strong Spanish influence in the food offerings. It's a great option for late-night dining (until 3 a.m.) in the Hamptons, where most restaurants, and even many of the bars, close early. While the Hamptons are chock-full of dining establishments that have been around for decades, Copa opened in 2009, so it's one of the newer places to dine in the region.

WINE AND DINE

Nassau County

HONU: KITCHEN & COCKTAILS **$$–$$$**
363 New York Ave., Huntington
(631) 421-6900
www.honukitchen.com

Open exclusively for dinner, Honu: Kitchen & Cocktails offers a classy and sophisticated dining experience. While the menu isn't extensive, the food is top-notch and tastes delicious. The focus is on pairing the food with fine wines. The restaurant offers an extensive wine list, including at least a dozen wines served by the glass and a half-dozen selections served by the half-bottle. Appetizers include pumpkin soup, lobster bisque, seared ahi tuna, Caesar salad, shrimp, and wings. Entrees include swordfish, shrimp, tuna, Chilean sea bass, mahi mahi, pork tenderloin, French chicken breast, and short ribs, along with a cheeseburger, rib eye steak, New York strip steak, and filet mignon. Without the wine pairings, the food prices are affordable (in the $15 to $30 range for the entrees); however, the meal price goes up somewhat considerably when you start pairing the fine wines with each course. Reservations are strongly recommended.

VITTORIO'S RESTAURANT & WINE BAR **$$–$$$**
184 Broadway (Rte. 110), Amityville
(631) 264-3333
www.vittorios.biz

Located in Amityville, a Nassau County village most people know from *The Amityville Horror* movies, is this lovely, family-friendly restaurant and wine bar. The menu has a strong Italian influence, though featured menu items also include steak and seafood entrees. In addition to the award-winning food, Vittorio's is known for its extensive wine list. House specialties include fried calamari, Maryland crab cakes, baked clams, tri-color salad, and shrimp for appetizers. For entrees, guests can choose from a selection of pasta dishes or marinated skirt steak, lamb chops, New York sirloin steak, veal chops, duck, chicken Vittorio, or Hawaiian lobster tail, for example. Seafood lovers will enjoy the raw bar. Like many restaurants on Long Island, this one caters to businesspeople, couples, and families, plus it can host group events. Lunch and dinner are served daily. Reservations are strongly recommended for dinner, and can be made by calling the restaurant directly or using the popular OpenTable.com online reservation service.

CHAIN RESTAURANTS

Chain restaurants can be found throughout Long Island, especially in Nassau Country and central Suffolk County. If you're looking for a mid- to high-priced, fine-dining experience that's familiar and consistent, no matter which location around the country you are visiting, here are a few options to consider:

- **Benihana** (Japanese and sushi, $$): 920 Merchants Concourse, Westbury; (516) 222-6019; www.benihana.com. Meals are prepared tableside teppanyaki style, in a festive dining environment. Groups of 8 to 10 are seated together. Entrees include steak, chicken, and seafood, plus sushi. This is a great place to celebrate a birthday or special occasion.
- **Blackstone Steak** (American steak house, $$$): 10 Pinelawn Rd., Melville; (631) 271-7780; www.blackstonesteakhouse.com. A traditional, upscale, all-American steak house. Ideal for families, couples, and businesspeople alike.
- **Houston's** (American, $$): Roosevelt Field Mall, 630 Old Country Rd., Garden City; (516) 873-1454; www.hillstone.com/#/restaurants/houstons. Offers a midpriced, diverse menu, featuring contemporary American cuisine, including steak, chicken, and seafood entrees. Great for families and couples.
- **Il Mulino** (Italian, $$$): 1042 Northern Blvd., Roslyn; (516) 621-1870; www.ilmulino.com/longisland.html. This is an extremely upscale and exclusive, authentic Italian restaurant. It's more suitable for adults than families, and is a wonderful place to celebrate a special occasion. For dinner, formal attire is recommended, and reservations are a must.
- **Melting Pot** (fondue, $$): 2377 Broadhollow Rd. (Rte. 110), Farmingdale; (631) 752-4242; www.meltingpot.com. This midpriced restaurant serves fondue entrees and desserts. It's a slightly different dining style than what's typically offered at an American restaurant.
- **Morton's Steak House** (American steak house, $$$): 777 Northern Blvd., Great Neck; (516) 498-2950; www.mortons.com. Enjoy a mouthwatering steak at this high-end, fine-dining restaurant. It caters to couples and businesspeople alike for both lunch and dinner. The atmosphere is upscale. Reservations are recommended, especially for dinner.
- **P.F. Chang's** (Chinese, $$): Mall at the Source, 1504 Old Country Rd., Westbury; (516) 222-9200; www.pfchangs.com. Contemporary Asian dishes that are expertly prepared and nicely presented are what's offered at this popular chain. Steak, chicken, noodles, seafood, salads, and vegetarian dishes are featured. Expect a wait on weekends. Takeout is also available.

- **The Palm Restaurant** (steak and seafood, $$$): 94 Main St., East Hampton; (631) 324-0411; www.thepalm.com. Whether you're in New York, Los Angeles, Las Vegas, or any other city that features one of the Palm Restaurant locations, you'll experience consistently superior service as you dine on delicious steaks that are cooked to perfection. Other popular menu options include jumbo Nova Scotia lobster, premium fish, and heritage Italian entrees—all prepared to perfection using only the highest-quality ingredients and served in generous portions. This is a wonderful place to celebrate a special occasion or to host an important business lunch or dinner. Full bar service is available. What makes the Palm truly unique is the genuine old-world atmosphere. The dining rooms are decorated with rich wood furnishings and display a panorama of the classic cartoons and caricatures of local regulars, businesspeople, politicians, and celebrities who have dined at the restaurant.

DINING OPTIONS IN MANHATTAN

Depending on where on Long Island you're staying, getting to Manhattan by car, bus, or train will take between 30 and 120 minutes (two hours from the easternmost end of Long Island, near Montauk, for example). If, however, you're looking to celebrate a special occasion or experience a truly memorable night out, consider visiting Manhattan and enjoying one of the fine-dining restaurants the city has to offer.

The drawback to visiting Manhattan from Long Island by car is that in addition to the commute time, you'll need to pay tolls, plus an extra $30 to $50 to park your car once you reach the city. However, if you combine dinner at an upscale restaurant with a Broadway show or an afternoon of shopping or sightseeing, for example, the added expense and commute time is well worth it. Getting to Manhattan using the Long Island Railroad is a time- and money-saving option from many parts of Long Island.

Manhattan is known for its world-class dining. Many of the world's best-known chefs have restaurants here, and you can easily find just about any type of cuisine your taste buds are craving. In fact, there are more than 20,000 restaurants in Manhattan, offering everything from fast food to ultra-fine-dining experiences. For New York City restaurant recommendations, reviews, and descriptions, visit any of these Web sites:

CitySearch: http://newyork.citysearch.com
Menu Pages: www.menupages.com
***New York Magazine* Restaurant Reviews:** http://nymag.com/restaurants
***New York Times* Restaurant Reviews:** http://travel.nytimes.com/travel/guides/north-america/united-states/new-york/new-york-city/restaurant-listings.html
NYC.com: www.nyc.com/restaurants
NYCGo.com: www.nycgo.com/dining

NIGHTLIFE

Long Island is a wonderful vacation destination. However, much of what people do while visiting the island involves early-morning activities, like golfing or fishing, or daytime activities, like touring wineries, boating, sailing, shopping, visiting day spas, sightseeing, or experiencing the beaches. Dining is also a popular pastime for vacationers, and many of the restaurants offer expertly prepared, three- to five-course gourmet dinners, which when accompanied by the right wines, for example, can take two to three hours to properly consume and enjoy.

Thus, by the time 9 or 10 p.m. rolls around, many vacationers are ready to wind down their day. As a result, the nightlife on Long Island, especially in Suffolk County, is very limited. Sure, some restaurants, bars, and lounges remain open until 4 a.m. in Nassau County and until 11 p.m. (sometimes later) in Suffolk County, but, especially in Suffolk County, even many of the movie theaters don't bother with late-night showings (except possibly Fri and Sat nights during the peak season), so if you do see a movie, you'll be done by 11 p.m. at the latest.

If you're planning to see a show or concert, those too typically end sometime between 10 and 11 p.m., and the majority of wineries and vineyards close in the early evening, unless a special event is taking place. Scattered throughout Long Island, mainly in Nassau County, are a few traditional nightclubs and dance clubs that remain open until the wee hours of the morning, but the majority of people who truly want to experience an exciting nightlife wind up traveling into Manhattan.

This section offers a sampling of places to go, things to do, and experiences to have on Long Island once the sun sets.

NASSAU COUNTY

After dark you'll discover a handful of bars, lounges, nightclubs, and dance clubs throughout Nassau County, some of which are listed here. Be sure to check with each venue for operating hours or to learn about special events being hosted at each location. While some of these nightspots are traditional bars, others offer live music, or a live DJ, and a dance floor equipped with lights and an awesome sound system.

Keep in mind that most of these venues are open nightly, but hours of operation will vary based on the day of the week, season, and local laws. As in any region, the trendy "hot spots" where you can experience the best nightlife change every few months. Check with your hotel's concierge or ask friends for referrals and recommendations, based on what type of nighttime entertainment you're seeking.

i For a complete, up-to-date listing of dance clubs, bars, and nightclubs on Long Island, visit http://nightlife.longisland.com/nightspots. For detailed reviews of newly opened nighttime hot spots, visit www.exploreli.com/going-out/bars-clubs.

BACKSTAGE SPORTS BAR & GRILL
948 Broadway, Woodmere
(516) 374-5252
http://thebackstageonline.com

Located within the Woodmere Lanes bowling alley, Backstage Sports Bar & Grill offers a traditional sports bar atmosphere, serving food and drinks. Karaoke is also available on many nights. Happy hour is hosted weekdays between 6 and 8 p.m. This lounge recently celebrated its 50th anniversary.

BLACK FOREST BREW HAUS
2015 New Hwy., Farmingdale
(631) 291-9500

Three bars are offered here, including one that's outside. In addition to a traditional bar menu, the finest malts from their own maltery in the Black Forest region of Germany is served here, along with a variety of beers.

BOLD O'DONOGHUE
2 Ocean Ave., East Rockaway
(516) 887-8969

This is a popular nightspot and dance club that stays open until 3 to 4 a.m. nightly. In addition to music, full bar service is offered. Special events are held throughout the week.

CHARACTER'S BAR & GRILL
677 Hempstead Tnpk., Franklin Square
(516) 485-2320

This is a traditional bar that serves up a nice selection of drinks. To entertain visitors, karaoke is offered multiple nights a week. The bar typically stays open until at least 3 a.m.

CHUCKY'S BAR & DANCE CLUB
267 Mineola Blvd., Mineola
(516) 739-3009

This gay bar offers full bar service along with its dance floor. Every night there's a different theme, and a cover charge applies. You'll enjoy a live DJ who plays techno, club, and pop music. There's also an outdoor patio and indoor pool tables, plus free parking.

CJ MCALE'S
509 Great Neck Rd., Great Neck
(516) 482-9154

Enjoy drinks and karaoke at this traditional bar that stays open until the wee hours of the morning. Great drinks and friendly service, plus a predominately local crowd is what you'll find here.

CLUB MANOR
432 North Wantagh Ave., Bethpage
(516) 932-3333
www.couplesnightclub.com

This is a popular dance club and edgy nightspot that's definitely for adults only. It's mainly targeted to couples; however, single men are welcome to join the festivities on Fri nights, while single women can visit on Fri or Sat nights. Check the Web site for special events. A cover charge applies.

CROXLEY ALE HOUSE
190 Main St., Farmingdale
(516) 293-7700
www.croxley.com

With three locations in addition to Farmingdale—Franklin Square (516-326-9542), Rockville Centre (516-764-0470), and Manhattan (212-253-6140)—this is a popular place to watch sports, dine, and drink. Live music is also presented here, with local bands appearing on Wed nights. This chain is famous for its beer and wings. Happy hour extends throughout much of the day on weekdays, between 11 a.m. and 7 p.m. The kitchen remains open until 1 a.m. nightly.

DAVE & BUSTER'S
1504 Old Country Rd., Westbury
(516) 542-8501
www.daveandbusters.com

Enjoy a full meal, hang out at the bar, watch your favorite sports, shoot pool, or challenge yourself by playing one of the latest video arcade games. This is a complete, indoor entertainment complex that is suitable for families by day. However, at night, guests must be over the age of 21. The atmosphere tends to be a bit loud, as the bar and entertainment areas are usually crowded at night.

DUBLIN PUB
2002 Jericho Tnpk., New Hyde Park
(516) 352-9131
www.thedublinpub.com

Sporting events are shown here on big-screen TVs in an Irish pub setting. Live music is presented several nights a week (usually starting at 9 p.m.), and on other nights a live DJ is featured. Dance lessons and a wide range of special events are held on an ongoing basis.

GOVERNOR'S OF LEVITTOWN
90 Division Ave., Levittown
(516) 731-3358
www.govs.com

For more than 15 years, this venue has hosted some of the country's best stand-up comics, as well as local favorites. The theater has a 220-person capacity, and the lineup of performers and show-times change daily. A pub menu and dinner menu are also available, as is full bar service. Nobody under the age of 18 is admitted. This is one of the most successful and well-known comedy clubs in Nassau County.

GUIDO'S IRISH PUB
1923 Wantagh Ave., Wantagh
(516) 826-7623
http://guidospub.com

Enjoy drinks and karaoke at this cozy, traditional Irish pub. Live entertainment is periodically featured, and there's a pool table towards the back of the bar area. The bar typically stays open until at least 2 a.m., usually later.

GUYS & DOLLS BILLIARD LOUNGE
175 East Merrick Rd., Valley Stream
(516) 825-8822
www.guysanddollsbilliards.com

This traditional pool hall, with full bar service, was established in 1961. The pool area features 17 original Gold Crown pool tables and a Gold Crown heated billiards table. You'll also find a large video arcade room, as well as Ping-Pong and foosball tables. Pool tournaments and other special events are held throughout the week, free pool lessons are offered every Sat between 10 a.m. and noon.

HAVANA CIGAR PUB @ THE CARLTUN
Eisenhower Park, East Meadow
(516) 542-0700
www.thecarltun.com, www.HavanasCigarClub.com

This private club is ideal for Long Island residents who enjoy smoking cigars. Havana Cigar Pub is located within the elegant Carltun Hotel, where you'll find several upscale restaurants, bars, and lounges in addition to Havana. Enjoy smoking cigars in a posh, private-club setting. The club itself has its own dining room, which accommodates up to 80 guests, plus a walk-in cedar humidor where you'll find 250 individually personalized cigar storage boxes within a glass-enclosed room. On Fri and Sat the club stays open until 1 a.m. Members are required to pay an annual membership fee and can bring an unlimited number of guests. Other dining areas and lounges within the hotel, however, are open to the general public.

LEISURE TIME BILLIARDS & CAFE
2953 Hempstead Tnpk., Levittown
(516) 796-4600
www.leisuretimebilliards.com

This is a traditional pool hall that stays open until at least 1 a.m. nightly. Leisure Time invites families to enjoy the festive atmosphere during the day, but only adults are allowed at night. The bar and pool hall area features six large-screen TVs that show sporting events on an ongoing basis. Unlike other pool halls, this one offers a clean environment and a snack bar, as well as full bar service.

MULCAHY'S
3232 Railroad Ave., Wantagh
(516) 826-MULS
http://muls.com/index_mulcahys.html

Mulcahy's has been a landmark nightspot and music venue on Long Island since 1965. It offers live music every Sat night, starting at 8 p.m. On other nights, live DJs host dance parties with a different theme almost every day. It is also a popular sports bar.

OZ NIGHTCLUB
514 Hempstead Tnpk., West Hempstead
(516) 481-8915

DJs spin the latest club music at this large, popular dance club. To get in, you'll need to "dress to impress." Guys must be over the age of 25, while ladies over the age of 23 are always welcome. To keep things fresh for the locals and tourists alike, different themed events are hosted here, typically on the weekends. This is one of the few true dance clubs still in existence in Nassau County.

RAILZ
115 Audrey Ave., Oyster Bay
(516) 624-6911
This is a great place to watch sporting events, drink beer, and enjoy great wings. There's also a full-service restaurant that serves food in the daytime and evenings. At night, Railz is primarily a bar/lounge that stays open late. Special events are held in conjunction with major sporting events.

R.J. DANIELS: CONTEMPORARY AMERICAN GRILL
279A Sunrise Hwy., Rockville Centre
(516) 536-6258
www.rjdaniels.com
Open for lunch and dinner, this restaurant and bar transforms into a happening nightspot after dark. A live DJ or cover bands perform every Fri and Sat night. This is the place to enjoy drinks and dancing until 4 a.m. daily. Special events are hosted here in conjunction with holidays and major sporting events. There's also an outdoor patio.

SAMBUCA NIGHTCLUB
272 Post Ave., Westbury
(516) 876-0393
http://clubsambuca.com
DJs, dancing, upbeat music, and full bar service combine for a night of fun. Special themed events are held here almost every Sat night. Doors typically open at 7 p.m., and a cover charge of at least $10 applies. Happy hour runs from 7 to 8 p.m. Sambuca periodically transforms into a festive comedy club, when headline entertainers and comedians are brought in to perform. The club remains open until around 4 a.m.

STEAMBOAT LANDING
76 Shore Rd., Glen Cove
(516) 759-3921
This is a midpriced restaurant and bar that also has a dance floor. It's located right on the water, and an outdoor patio is available for dining, drinking, and socializing. If you're looking to enjoy casual, late-night drinks with a loved one or friends, check out Steamboat Landing.

WINNER'S CIRCLE NITE CLUB
39 Post Ave., Westbury
(516) 997-4050
www.clubwc.com/schedule.htm
This is the place to go for Latin music and dancing, as well as Latin dance lessons on Sun evenings. Live music and DJs are presented nightly. This club has been around since 1996, but it continues to attract crowds, thanks to its festive but friendly and safe atmosphere. Live DJs play salsa, merengue, cumbia, bachata, reggaeton, tipico, and punta, as well as Latino pop and rock. Special events are hosted here throughout the week.

ZACHARY'S
1916 Hempstead Tnpk., East Meadow
(516) 794-9770
www.zacharysny.com
This large club offers a disco atmosphere, complete with dance floor, state-of-the-art lighting, and a great sound system. Live DJs play a wide range of music, and special events are hosted here several nights per week. You can always find something exciting happening here on Fri and Sat nights.

SUFFOLK COUNTY

50 YARD LINE
371 Little East Neck Rd., West Babylon
(631) 661-9778
www.myspace.com/50yardlinebar
This is a traditional sports bar where special events take place around virtually every sporting event. Thus, there's a party atmosphere almost every night as sports fans gather to cheer on their favorite teams and enjoy drinks and a pub menu. Karaoke is also offered.

ARIZONA BAR
6106 Jericho Tnpk., Commack
(631) 462-9382
http://www.myspace.com/60146204
This is a traditional bar, where every night a different drink special is offered. For example, on Sun, Buds are $3 and a pitcher of any on tap beer is just $8. Live bands perform every Sat night. In existence for almost 30 years, Arizona Bar recently remodeled and is now under new ownership.

BEACH BAR
58 Foster Ave., Hampton Bays
(631) 723-3100
www.beachbar.net
At this club you'll find dancing and full bar service almost every night of the week, with special themed events most Tues, Fri, and Sat nights. This is a popular destination for bachelorette parties. It's also a place where local college students come to party, so the crowd tends to be younger. Hours are from noon until 4 a.m.

BRICKYARD BAR & GRILL
Veterans Memorial Hwy., Ronkonkoma
(631) 585-9500
Brickyard Bar & Grill is located within a Holiday Inn; however, the bar attracts locals and tourists alike. It tends to stay open late. The main bar area has a handful of TVs showcasing sporting events and headline news, and you'll also find karaoke here. Full menu service is available until 10 p.m., and a pub menu is offered during the late-night hours until closing.

BUNKHOUSE
192 Montauk Hwy., Sayville
(631) 567-2865
www.myspace.com/bunkhousesayville
Bunkhouse is one of the area's few gay bars that offers drinking and dancing in a festive environment. Special themed events are held several nights a week. For example, there's "Skin Fridays," and one recent special event had a pajama party theme. Live DJs play the latest dance and pop music nightly. This club has been around for more than 30 years. While it's not located on Fire Island, during the summer season it does attract the Fire Island crowd due to its close proximity to the ferry.

CLUB 56
7160 Rte. 110, East Farmingdale
(631) 694-8280
This is a full-service restaurant, but on Fri nights during the summer season, Club 56 transforms into one of the area's hottest nightclubs. Enjoy dancing, drinking, and socializing in a casual setting.

CRAZY DONKEY BAR & GRILL
1058 Rte. 110, Farmingdale
(631) 753-1975
www.thecrazydonkey.com
The Crazy Donkey is one of the most popular dance/nightclubs in the area. Eat, drink, and socialize at this local watering hole where, of course, full bar service is offered nightly. Special themed events, like Latin Night, are hosted throughout the week. The dance club area is more than 6,000 square feet, and there's a large outdoor deck area (open seasonally).

FATTY MCGEES BAR & GRILL
138 Connetquot Ave., East Islip
(631) 581-9868
This is a small but popular sports bar where like-minded sports fans gather to eat, drink, cheer on their favorite team, and socialize, particularly when major sporting events are being held. However, it's a fun place to go for drinks anytime. Karaoke is also offered on certain nights.

FINS PUB
4608 Sunrise Hwy., Oakdale
(631) 589-9525
www.myspace.com/finspub
Drink, socialize, and challenge friends to a game of pool at Fins. Happy hour is offered weekdays between 4 and 7 p.m. There's a free buffet on Fri, and live entertainment is showcased periodically. Each night a variety of different drink specials are offered. Sun nights there's usually a live DJ and karaoke, while on Mon nights you'll often find

a comedy show presented here. On Fri there's dancing and karaoke, while on Sat live metal bands perform.

GOVERNOR'S OF MEDFORD
2320 Rte. 112, Medford
(631) 207-9212
www.govs.com

For more than 15 years this venue has hosted some of the country's best stand-up comics, as well as local favorites. Showtimes and cover charge vary by night, depending on the lineup. This is one of the few comedy clubs in the area that attracts high-profile comedians.

HURRICANE HUT
Montauk Hwy. at Beach Ln., Westhampton Beach
(631) 288-5828

This small club is open seasonally and for special events; full bar service is offered. For more than 30 years it was formally known as Casey's Dance Hall and Saloon. Each event here has a different theme, so be sure to call to find out what's happening on the night you plan to visit.

LILY FLANAGAN'S OF WANTAGH
528 Main St., Islip
(631) 581-1550
www.lilyflanaganspub.com

This is a popular local hangout with a traditional pub atmosphere. During the day and evening the restaurant offers a full menu; at night, however, live music is presented. Happy hour is held weekdays between 4 and 7 p.m. There are 10 large-screen televisions in the bar area, and things tend to get really festive during major sporting events. In addition, there's dancing and sing-alongs almost nightly. Last call is typically around 4 a.m.

NAPPER TANDY'S
229 Laurel Ave., Northport
(631) 757-4141
http://nappertandysirishpub.com/northport/northport.html

Combining sports with a traditional Irish pub, this is a great place to drink, watch sporting events, and socialize year-round. On Mon beer and a burger are just $6 between 7 and 11 p.m.; however, there's always some type of drink special being offered. All of the major sporting events are shown on high-definition, big-screen TVs. Live music is presented on weekends.

NICK'S
148 South Emerson Rd., Montauk
(631) 668-4800
www.nicksmontauk.com

This full-service restaurant offers indoor and outdoor dining until 10 p.m., as well as full bar service. At night, Nick's takes on more of a lounge vibe, with live music and karaoke. The festivities continue nightly until at least 2 a.m. The atmosphere is always casual, and it's a favorite nighttime destination for locals and tourists alike, particularly in the summertime.

PORT JAZZ
201 Main St., Port Jefferson
(631) 476-7600
www.portjazz.com

This is the place to go on Long Island to experience live jazz performances, as well as DJs, dancing, and traditional bar service. The atmosphere is upbeat, yet sophisticated. In addition to jazz, the venue hosts a wide range of tribute bands throughout the week, so regardless of your musical taste, if you're looking for an elegant way to spend an evening that involves live music, drop by Port Jazz.

PORT JEFFERSON BILLIARDS
4747 Nesconset Hwy., Port Jefferson
(631) 928-7104

Offering nothing fancy, this is a basic billiards club featuring a handful of pool and billiard tables. It's open late. A variety of beers and other beverages are served; however, there are several full-service bars within walking distance. This is definitely an adults-only nightspot.

RACHEL'S
Lewis and Ocean Walk, Cherry Grove, Fire Island
(631) 583-9552

During the day and evening, Rachel's is a full-service restaurant and a great place to meet and socialize. At night during the summer season, however, it transforms into a hangout as a bakery (not a bar), located in one of the more gay-friendly hotspots on Fire Island. On weekends, Rachel's is open until 4 a.m. This is a great place to enjoy a late-night snack, a sobering cup of coffee, or even an early breakfast after hitting the nearby clubs.

i By day, Fire Island is a popular beach destination. However, at night, there are more than two dozen straight, gay, and mixed bars and nightclubs that remain open for drinking, dancing, and partying until the wee hours of the morning. For a complete listing of Fire Island's nightclubs and bars, visit www.clublongisland.com/FireIslandClubs.aspx. The clubs are mostly open seasonally.

RARE OLIVE
400 West Jericho Tnpk., Huntington
(631) 423-3444
www.rareolivelounge.com
If you're looking for a sophisticated and elegant lounge where you can enjoy late-night drinks, drop by Rare Olive. The lounge is open on Thurs, Fri, and Sat nights, typically between 8 p.m. and 4 a.m. On Fri, Rare Olive hosts a dance party (sometimes with live music), while on Sat, a live DJ plays popular music.

SOUTHAMPTON PUBLICK HOUSE
40 Bowden Sq., Southampton
(631) 283-2800
www.publick.com
While Long Island is a place people go to experience the local wines, thanks to Southampton Publick House, it's also a destination for enjoying local brews. This microbrewery offers a wide range of events and entertainment night after night, not to mention an impressive menu of beers. Lunch and dinner menus, as well as a pub menu, are offered within a classic pub atmosphere.

STEPHEN TALKHOUSE
161 Main St., Amagansett
(631) 267-3117
www.stephentalkhouse.com
Local bands, as well as nationally known recording artists, perform almost nightly in an intimate setting at this local nightspot. Shows often sell out. It's a friendly and somewhat cozy venue that stays open very late. No food is served, but full bar service is offered. Guests must be at least 21 years old. Ticket prices for concerts range from $35 to $75, depending on the artist or lineup.

VITTORIO'S RESTAURANT & WINE BAR
184 Broadway, Amityville
(631) 264-3333
While this is the place to dine if you're looking for an upscale Italian dinner, it's also the ideal destination to enjoy drinks at the elegant wine bar that stays open until 10 p.m. Sun through Thurs, and until 11 p.m. Fri and Sat. The wine list, featuring Long Island and other domestic and imported wines, is extensive, whether you're ordering by the glass or bottle. Wine-tasting events are also hosted here.

SHOPPING

If you're looking for discount, midpriced, and high-end department stores, designer boutiques, a choice of mass-market superstores, and massive and very impressive indoor malls—all within a few miles radius—Nassau County is definitely the place to shop. The Roosevelt Field Mall in Garden City, for example, is one of the largest malls on the East Coast, and it's surrounded by mile after mile of smaller strip malls, stand-alone retail stores, and mass-market superstores within shopping complexes. Thus, no matter what you're looking for, you'll find it shopping in and around Garden City, which is why people travel from all over the region to shop here.

Some of the more affluent areas of Nassau County are also home to extremely upscale shopping plazas, where you'll find high-end, designer stores clustered together; for example, Americana at Manhasset. For more budget-conscious shoppers, it's not difficult at all to find a local Wal-Mart, Target, Sam's Club, or BJ's Wholesale Club, for example. Virtually all of the malls in the area are also anchored by affordable department stores, like Sears, JCPenney, and Macy's.

The majority of shopping opportunities, with a few exceptions, in Nassau County consist of chain stores. While the shopping experiences available are certainly plentiful, they're not unique, though one thing that sets the Roosevelt Field Mall apart from most other malls across America is that this one attracts chains that open concept stores here, so while the brand names will be familiar, the appearance of the stores and what's offered will be a bit unique.

The indoor and outdoor shopping centers and malls throughout the region have pretty much replaced "Main Street" in most Nassau County towns and communities. It's here that franchises and chain store retail shopping dominates, having long ago replaced independent, mom-and-pop boutiques, shops, and stores for the most part.

In terms of shopping, much of Suffolk Country is vastly different than what's offered in Nassau Country for a number of reasons. First, as you know, Suffolk County contains many waterfront towns, villages, and communities that cater to affluent tourists visiting seasonally. Second, the zoning laws in these communities are extremely strict in terms of what types of stores and shopping complexes are allowed to open, what operating hours they can maintain, and the external appearance of the retail locations. Third, because the visitors to this region have money and demand designer boutiques over discount stores, the economic law of supply and demand definitely plays a role in the types of stores that open in this region and their success.

As a result, what shoppers will discover in many parts of Suffolk County, including the Hamptons, Greenport Village, Port Jefferson, Stony Brook, and Montauk, for example, are very few mass-market superstores and indoor malls. Even outdoor strip malls are few and far between. Instead, you'll find an abundance of one-of-a-kind, independently owned boutiques, gift shops, and retail stores located on the Main Street of each community.

Along these Main Streets (which go by different names in each town), you'll also find boutiques from top designers and some upscale chain stores, though their appearance will be vastly different from anything you'd find in even the most upscale indoor shopping malls, or along

Fifth Ave. or Madison Ave. in Manhattan. It's for this reason that people who enjoy unique shopping experiences love to visit the communities in Suffolk Country and spend literally days at a time exploring the unique shops in each community. Of course, your credit card will most likely receive a workout as well, unless you're able to show restraint or seek out sales.

Because even extremely wealthy people (not to mention middle-income folks) enjoy shopping for bargains occasionally, two of the most popular shopping opportunities in Suffolk County are the Tanger Outlet outdoor shopping complexes in Deer Park and Riverhead. At the Deer Park location, you'll find 70 brand-name outlet stores, including Neiman Marcus Last Call, Saks Fifth Avenue Off 5th, Calvin Klein, Juicy Couture, and many more designers offering significant discounts on close-out merchandise, overstocked merchandise, and last season's fashions and household goods. The more popular Riverhead location is significantly larger, with more than 165 brand-name outlet stores in one location. Both Tanger Outlet locations are open year-round. Keep in mind that while the prices are already low, most of the outlets also have sales throughout the year, during which time even bigger discounts and price cuts are offered. People come from all over Long Island to shop at the two Tanger Outlet locations. More details about Tanger Outlet is offered later in this section.

For shoppers looking for unusual or unique gifts, artwork, home goods, or jewelry, many of the popular museums on Long Island feature lovely, one-of-a-kind gift shops that offer themed merchandise based around the focus of that museum. So, while visiting the area's museums will provide an enjoyable cultural experience, it'll also provide for memorable shopping.

SHOPPING IN NASSAU COUNTY

The following is just a sampling of the shopping opportunities that await you throughout Nassau County. Most are situated in indoor malls, within outdoor shopping centers, or in commercial districts that feature franchise after franchise along a main thoroughfare. The hours of operation of the stores vary greatly in this region. However, most remain open seven days a week, until 9 p.m. or even 10 p.m., except on Sun, when hours are reduced. You can expect most stores to offer extended hours between the day after Thanksgiving (aka Black Friday) and the day before Christmas.

AMERICANA AT MANHASSET

2060 Northern Blvd., Manhasset
(516) 627-2277, (800) 818-6767
www.americanamanhasset.com

Featuring more than 60 shops and boutiques, this is an upscale shopping center. Stores include Ann Taylor, Anne Fontaine, Burberry, Cartier, Coach, Cole Haan, David Yurman, Dior, Escada, Gucci, Hermes, Jimmy Choo, Lacoste, Louis Vuitton, Max Mara, Prada, Ralph Lauren, Tiffany & Co, and Versace. Several fine-dining restaurants are also in the immediate area. If you need assistance, personal shoppers are at your disposal (for an additional fee). Normal business hours are Mon through Sat, 10 a.m. to 6 p.m., and Sun, noon to 6 p.m.

BROADWAY MALL

Rte. 106/107, Hicksville
(516) 822-6336
www.broadwaymall.com

This mall features 130 shops, including Target, H&M, Old Navy, and a massive IKEA. There's also a multiplex movie theater located within the mall, which is open Mon through Sat, 10 a.m. to 9:30 p.m., and Sun, 11 a.m. to 7 p.m.

GREEN ACRES MALL

2034 Green Acres Mall, Sunrise Hwy., Valley Stream
(516) 516-1157
www.greenacresmallonline.com

At this 1.8-million-square-foot indoor mall, you'll discover more than 200 stores. Anchor department stores include Sears, Macy's, and JCPenney. Normal hours of operation are Mon through Sat, 10 a.m. to 9:30 p.m., and Sun, 11 a.m. to 7 p.m. This mall has been in existence for more than 50 years.

MALL AT THE SOURCE
Old Country Rd., Westbury
(516) 228-0303
www.simon.com/mall/default.aspx?id=104
Combining both affordable and expensive shopping with entertainment, some of the shops and restaurants offered at the Mall at the Source include As Seen On TV, Ayhan's Mediterranean Restaurant, the Cheesecake Factory, Dave & Busters, Famous Footwear, Foot Locker, Gap, Gap Kids, H&M, Nordstrom Rack, Off 5th–Saks Fifth Avenue Outlet, Old Navy, and P.F. Chang's China Bistro. Normal operating hours are Mon through Sat, 10 a.m. to 9:30 p.m., and Sun, 11 a.m. to 7 p.m.

ROOSEVELT FIELD MALL
630 Old Country Rd., Garden City
(516) 742-8000
www.simon.com/mall/?id=102
When it comes to shopping in Nassau County, you won't want to skip a visit to the Roosevelt Field Mall. It's by far the largest and one of the most upscale indoor malls on the entire East Coast (and the fifth largest in America). The mall itself encompasses 2.2 million square feet. In addition to offering a handful of major department stores as anchors, including Bloomingdale's, Dick's Sporting Goods, JCPenney, Macy's, and Nordstrom, this massive mall features 270 specialty stores, including virtually every chain store in existence that you'd find in malls elsewhere in America, such as Abercrombie & Fitch, Aeropostale, the Apple Store, Banana Republic, Brookstone, the Disney Store, Gap, the Limited, and Victoria's Secret.

The Roosevelt Field Mall is also home to a handful of upscale designer boutiques, including Ann Taylor, bebe, Coach, Diesel, Mont Blanc, Movado, Timberland, and Tumi. The mall's offerings also include unique "concept" stores and one-of-a-kind shops not found in any other mall or shopping center. Within the mall you'll also find multiple full-service restaurants and a massive food court, plus a state-of-the-art movie theater. Special events, including designer fashion shows, are held at the mall throughout the year.

Regular (non-holiday) mall hours are Mon through Sat, 10 a.m. to 9:30 p.m., and Sun, 11 a.m. to 7 p.m. When you visit the Roosevelt Field Mall, plan on doing a lot of walking, as this mall is massive. And don't forget where you park your car (write down the location).

i Just like everywhere else in America, particularly with the struggling economy, retail stores use virtually every holiday as an excuse to host a sale. When it comes to shopping for clothing, for example, you'll also discover tremendous savings if you shop during "after season" or holiday-themed sales.

WESTFIELD SUNRISE MALL
1 Sunrise Mall, Sunrise Hwy., Massapequa
(516) 795-3225
http://westfield.com/sunrise
More than 160 stores and restaurants are offered at this large indoor mall, including Macy's, Sears, H&M, and JCPenney. Hours of operation are Mon through Fri, 10:30 a.m. to 9 p.m.; Sat, 10 a.m. to 9 p.m.; and Sun, 11 a.m. to 6 p.m.

Shopping beyond the Malls in Nassau County

In addition to the massive indoor malls scattered throughout Nassau County, you'll find an abundance of stand-alone mass-market superstars, including Wal-Mart (www.walmart.com), Target (www.target.com), BJ's Wholesale Club (www.bjs.com), and Sam's Club (www.samsclub.com). You'll also find consumer electronics superstores, like Best Buy (www.bestbuy.com) and P.C. Richard & Sons (www.pcrichard.com), throughout the region. Check the company Web sites for specific locations.

Within a few of Nassau Country's villages and communities, you'll discover unique shopping opportunities along their various Main Streets. Here, you'll find one-of-a-kind shops and independently owned and operated boutiques, as well as familiar chain stores. Cafes and restaurants, along with small local parks, can also be found in these areas, which provide for a more casual and laid-back shopping experience. If, however, this is the type of shopping experience you're looking for, you'll also find it within many communities in Suffolk County.

Some of the more popular communities in Nassau Country that offer a timeless, small town, Main Street experience, or at least a shopping district or region, include:

- **Freeport:** Located along what's referred to as the "Nautical Mile" on Woodcleft Avenue, you'll discover shops, restaurants, a few museums, open-air fish markets, and a variety of other tourist attractions. Visit www.freeportny.com.
- **Garden City:** In addition to being home to the Roosevelt Field Mall and a handful of major superstores, throughout Garden City you'll also find a few smaller, stand-alone shops, restaurants, and boutiques, although they're few and far between.
- **Glen Cove:** This small Gold Coast village features a handful of upscale shops, several dozen boutiques and gift shops, plus museums and other tourist attractions.
- **Great Neck:** On Long Island's North Shore, Great Neck offers a nice selection of trendy, upscale shops and restaurants. For example, you'll find more than 250 shops, boutiques, and restaurants within the one-third-square-mile area known as the Village of Great Neck Plaza (www.greatneckplaza.net).
- **Locust Valley:** Within this village, particularly along Birch Hill Road and Forest Avenue, you'll find locally owned boutiques and shops, plus a lot of antiques shops.
- **Manhasset:** The main shopping area here is the Americana at Manhasset. It's an upscale, outdoor shopping center that contains 60 designer shops and boutiques, as well as fine-dining restaurants. This is not a Main Street shopping experience, but it is a beautiful shopping plaza.
- **Oyster Bay:** This village is known for its sheltered harbor and a handful of historic landmarks. There is also a lovely shopping area that offers unique shops and restaurants.
- **Port Washington:** Particularly along the Main Street area near the harbor, you'll discover many antiques shops, boutiques, and art galleries.
- **Roslyn:** This historic town offers a wonderful shopping area, particularly along Main Street. The buildings date back to between 1690 and 1865, but have been fully restored. You'll find a nice selection of shops and restaurants here.
- **Sea Cliff:** This village has a strong New England vibe, and is where you'll find a vibrant arts community, along with lovely shops and restaurants.

i For more than 20 years the Tri-County Flea Market has been a popular destination for bargain hunters. It's located at 3041 Hempstead Tnpk. in Levittown, and it's a massive, indoor flea market with hundreds of dealers. Hours are Thurs and Fri, noon to 9 p.m., and Sat and Sun, 10 a.m. to 5 p.m. Call (516) 579-4500 or visit http://fleaman.com.

SHOPPING IN SUFFOLK COUNTY

The following is just a sampling of the shopping opportunities that await you throughout Suffolk Country. Being a seasonal tourist destination, some of the shops close altogether during off-peak seasons (particularly the winter), while others have vastly reduced hours of operation. Also, unlike most malls that stay open at least until 9:30 or 10 p.m., you'll discover that the independent shops located along the Main Streets in the various communities sometimes close much earlier, even during the peak tourist season.

While Suffolk County doesn't have an indoor mall equivalent to the Roosevelt Field Mall, there are three decent-size malls in the county that have at least 100 stores each.

SMITH HAVEN MALL

Nesconset Hwy., Lake Grove
(631) 724-1433
www.simon.com/mall/default.aspx?id=103

This is the largest indoor mall in Suffolk County. In addition to a Macy's, Sears, and JCPenney, it contains about 140 stores and a handful of restaurants, plus a food court. Stores include Abercrombie & Fitch, Aerie, Ann Taylor, the Apple Store, Banana Republic, bebe, Brookstone, Coach, Coldwater Creek, Gilly Hicks, Godiva, Guess, Hollister, Lucky Brand Jeans, Sephora, Swarovski, and Williams-Sonoma. Restaurants include Bobby's Burger Palace, California Pizza Kitchen, the Cheesecake Factory, and T.G.I. Friday's. Normal mall hours are Mon through Sat, 10 a.m. to 9:30 p.m., and Sun, 11 a.m. to 6 p.m.

WALT WHITMAN MALL
Rte. 110, Huntington
(631) 271-1741
www.simon.com/mall/default.aspx?id=103

This indoor mall has Macy's, JCPenney, and Sears as its anchor department stores, along with about 150 retail stores and restaurants, including Abercrombie & Fitch, Aerie, Ann Taylor, the Apple Store, Banana Republic, bebe, Brookstone, California Pizza Kitchen, the Cheesecake Factory, Coach, Coldwater Creek, Gilly Hicks, Godiva, Guess, Hollister, Lucky Brand Jeans, Sephora, Swarovski, T.G.I. Friday's, and Williams-Sonoma. Regular mall hours are Mon through Sat, 10 a.m. to 9:30 p.m., and Sun, 11 a.m. to 6 p.m.

WESTFIELD SOUTH SHORE
1701 Sunrise Hwy., Bay Shore
(631) 665-8600
http://westfield.com/southshore

Featuring more than 100 retail stores, including American Eagle, Forever 21, G By Guess, Gap, Kay Jewelers, Lids, New York & Company, Pacific Sunwear, and Victoria's Secret, the anchor department stores at this mall include Macy's, JCPenney, Sears, and Lord & Taylor. Normal mall hours are Mon through Fri, 10:30 a.m. to 9 p.m.; Sat, 10 a.m. to 9 p.m.; and Sun, 11 a.m. to 6 p.m.

Tanger Outlet Centers

Open year-round, though particularly busy during the peak summer season, the two Tanger Outlet shopping center locations are major tourist shopping attractions. Both locations attract visitors from throughout Long Island.

Tanger Outlet at the Arches in Deer Park (152 The Arches Circle, 631-242-2939, www.tangeroutlet.com) is open Mon through Sat from 9 a.m. to 9 p.m., and Sun from 10 a.m. to 8 p.m. This outdoor shopping complex features 70 brand-name designer outlets. The Tanger Outlet in Riverhead (1770 West Main St., 631-369-2732, www.tangeroutlet.com) is open year-round, but has different hours of operation throughout the year. Between Jan 1 and Mar 8, the outlet's normal business hours are Sun through Fri from 10 a.m. to 7 p.m., and Sat from 9 a.m. to 9 p.m. Between Mar 9 and Dec 31, hours of operation are Mon through Sat from 9 a.m. to 9 p.m., and Sun from 10 a.m. to 8 p.m. This location offers 165 brand-name and designer outlet shops.

Major designers and chain stores with outlet stores at the Tanger center in Riverhead include Aeropostale, Ann Taylor, Anne Klein, Barney's New York, Bass, Bose, Calvin Klein, Champion, Coach, DKNY, Epic Jeans, Esprit, Gap, Guess, Hugo Boss, Izod, J. Crew, Jockey, Jones New York, Juicy Couture, Kenneth Cole, Lacoste, Levi's, Liz Claiborne, Maidenform, Nautica, Nine West, Oakley, Old Navy, Perry Ellis, Polo, Puma, Ralph Lauren, Saks Fifth Avenue, Sketchers, Sony, Sunglass Hut, Timberland, Tommy Hilfiger, True Religion, Tumi, Wilson Leather, Yankee Candle, and Zoo York. Many of the stores at the Deer Park location are the same. The main appeal of the outlets is that regardless of when you shop, you're virtually guaranteed to find discounts of 20 to 70 percent off suggested retail prices. Sometimes, during sale periods, the savings can be even greater.

i **Be sure to visit the customer service counter at either Tanger Outlet Center location and present your AAA membership card to receive a money-saving coupon book that offers discounts at many of the outlets.**

Many shoppers manage to transform a visit to either Tanger Outlet Center into a full day's activity. Conveniently, many of the buses, as well as the Long Island Railroad, have stops close to both outlet locations, so even without a car, getting to the outlets is a relatively easy process from almost anywhere in Suffolk County.

Shopping beyond the Malls and Outlets in Suffolk County

Suffolk County attracts tourists for many reasons, including the beaches, wineries, fine-dining options, historical sites, beaches, day spas, and the unique golf and fishing opportunities. The county boasts many small, often waterfront villages and communities that offer a beautiful, small-town atmosphere, often with historic significance. Within many of these villages and communities are classic Main Street areas (although the actual streets go by different names). Here you'll find unique boutiques, shops, restaurants, cafes, galleries, and other attractions for avid shoppers.

Nowhere is this more evident than in the Hamptons. Hampton Bays, Southampton, Westhampton Beach Village, East Hampton, and Bridgehampton, along with Amagansett, Water Mill, Wainscott, Sag Harbor, and Montauk, for example, all offer a uniquely charming, beautiful, and very upscale shopping district. The shopping in East Hampton is probably the most upscale and expensive overall, while the other villages and communities offer more diverse shopping opportunities from a pricing and selection standpoint.

i In addition to the independently owned shops and boutiques, among the popular designer shops you'll discover in Southampton Village (on or near Main Street) are Brooks Brothers, Saks Fifth Avenue, and Theory.

Especially during the peak summer season and well into the fall, it's easy to spend a full day exploring each of these areas, shopping, dining, and experiencing the sites and attractions that make each of them unique. Of course, in the process, your credit cards will get a lot of use. Many of the shops in these towns and villages cater to an affluent clientele. You'll find a nice mix of one-of-a-kind shops and stores operated by top designers.

Since shops and boutiques in these areas come and go with each new season, if you want an overview of which specific stores can be found where, drop by the local chamber of commerce in each town or village and pick up a free *Southampton Chamber of Commerce Business Directory & Visitors Guide*. Store and business directories are also typically available on the chamber of commerce Web site for each town or village. For example, for Southampton, visit www.southamptonchamber.com (631-283-0402). For Montauk, visit www.montaukchamber.com (631-668-2428).

In the western Suffolk County area, some of the communities that offer beautiful shopping districts include:

- **Bellport:** This small seaside village features a nice selection of boutiques, shops, and restaurants.
- **Cold Spring Harbor:** In addition to an assortment of antiques shops, this historic community has a genuine Main Street, where you'll find shops, boutiques, cafes, and fine-dining restaurants.
- **Huntington Village:** Restaurants, cafes, unique retail shops, upscale boutiques, and even a few popular nightspots can be found in this lovely village.
- **Northport:** Like so many towns in the area, this seafront village offers a quaint and unique shopping experience, plus a handful of fine-dining options.
- **Patchogue:** Situated along Montauk Hwy., the downtown area features a vast assortment of shops, boutiques, galleries, and restaurants.
- **Port Jefferson:** This historic village is larger than most in the area and offers a greater mix of one-of-a-kind shops and galleries, plus a few chain stores that have a home-town feel. It's easy to spend an entire day roaming around the various stores and small shopping complexes that are all within walking distance

Meet Jill Lynn Brody, Southampton Shop Owner and Jewelry Designer

Southampton is one of the most pleasant and beautiful towns on Long Island to spend a day shopping. Within a several-block radius, you'll discover a wonderful mix of one-of-a-kind boutiques, upscale designer shops, cafes, restaurants, and a few galleries—all within a historic village setting. Sure, some of the stores are pricey and cater primarily to affluent customers, but unlike East Hampton, for example, the main retail streets in Southampton offer a wide range of shopping opportunities that everyday people, not just the rich and/or famous, can afford.

Jill Lynn Brody is a jewelry maker and store owner in Southampton. Her small but extremely elegant jewelry store, called Jill Lynn & Co., is located at 66 Jobs Ln. in the heart of Southampton's shopping district (631-287-1001, www.jilllynnandco.com).

For years Brody has been designing handcrafted 14k and 18k gold, silver, and platinum jewelry, often incorporating precious and semiprecious gemstones, including diamonds that have been custom cut to her personal specifications. Until 2008 she sold her creations through a showroom and at various art shows and craft festivals held throughout Long Island. In June 2008, however, she decided it was time to open her own boutique, and thought Southampton would be the perfect location to showcase and sell her one-of-a-kind jewelry that's typically priced anywhere from $35 to $80,000 (or more) per piece.

While her work is extraordinary, Brody has developed popularity in Southampton because of the highly personalized attention she gives to each and every one of her customers. "A lot of my jewelry designs are for everyday wear; however, I also have developed many pieces that are more appropriate to be worn in conjunction with dressed-up occasions. I have also designed a lot of bridal jewelry. For example, I'll be commissioned to create custom earrings for a bride-to-be that matches her wedding dress," said Brody.

She added, "I am more of a personal jeweler than anything. I tend to get to know my clients and develop personal relationships with them." And, being based in Southampton, some of her clients are among the richest and most famous people who spend time in the Hamptons.

When Brody decided it was time to open her own store, she knew it had to be located somewhere in the Hamptons. "I chose Southampton because I believe it has the most variety in terms of the overall shopping experience it offers. I really enjoy spending time here. The shopping district features a bunch of mom-and-pop shops, and the location is, in my opinion, both convenient and absolutely perfect," said Brody, who keeps her shop open year-round.

Brody compares the charm and quaintness of Southampton's shopping district with that of Sag Harbor. The biggest misconception about shopping in Southampton, however, is that all of the stores only offer extremely expensive, designer merchandise that only the wealthy can afford. "Nothing could be further from the truth," said Brody. "Normal people can shop here and find extremely nice merchandise at very affordable prices. It's not hard, for example, to find a sweater for $35 as easily as you can find one for $300. I think of East Hampton as offering all of the extremely upscale stores, while Southampton offers much more of a mix."

"If you come into my store, for example, you might see a beautiful pair of sterling silver handmade earrings for $35. However, those same earrings can also be custom-fabricated in 18k gold for $200 or $300. The merchandise offered at the mom-and-pop stores in Southampton, for example, is extremely high-quality," added Brody. "Offering a mix of merchandise is a goal of many Southampton shop owners."

Southampton offers a lot of options and variety for shoppers. "If I really want to shop, as opposed to browse, Southampton is definitely one of the villages I'd visit. When you're shopping in this region, I always tell people to go into the stores you've never heard of before. Those are usually the stores that'll offer the most unique merchandise, as opposed to the shops that have a bunch of locations."

Brody explained that between 70 and 80 percent of the shops in Southampton remain open year-round. "If you're a savvy shopper, you can find great deals throughout the year. A lot of stores have sales at the end of each season to clear out older merchandise. Holiday sales are also common. If you're truly looking for the best sales, wait until the very end of each season. In late August, stores will hold sales in order to make room for new fall merchandise, for example," she said.

Aside from staying close to home and doing her own shopping in Southampton, she enjoys going places that are quaint and that don't offer a lot of generic chain stores, like Greenport and the other towns situated on the North Fork. "If I'm going to spend the day shopping, I like to take myself somewhere. The drive from Southampton through the North Fork is absolutely beautiful. I am not a fan of malls that only offer the same old stuff, whether you're on Long Island or anywhere else in America," added Brody.

Recently Brody attended a meeting with a bunch of other Southampton store owners and business operators. She explained, "Together we're making a huge effort to ensure our town doesn't turn into another East Hampton. To differentiate ourselves, we're striving to offer a really nice mix of upscale and expensive as well as extremely affordable merchandise. We are also taking extra steps to create a warm and friendly shopping environment for our customers by really focusing on providing top-notch customer service and a welcoming environment. We really want people to come in and enjoy shopping in our stores and feel like we, the shopkeepers, have taken the time to get to know them, whether or not they actually buy something. People need to ignore the stereotype about the Hamptons and know there's a variety of shopping experiences to be had here."

One of the jewelry collections that Jill Lynn Brody is known for throughout the Hamptons is called "Best Friend." It's a collection of dog bone and dog paw–themed jewelry, created in memory of her dog Scout. A portion of all sales from this beautiful collection are donated to ARF, an animal charity. The pieces can be seen in her store or ordered online at www.jilllynnandco.com/bfrco.html.

Unlike many jewelry stores in the Hamptons, when you come into Jill Lynn & Co., you'll almost always actually meet Jill Lynn Brody, the owner and jewelry designer. Her selection of merchandise truly offers something for everyone, from Hollywood's biggest stars (who often shop in her store) to everyday tourists looking to take home an affordable, handmade piece of jewelry that they can wear proudly and cherish for decades to come.

from the waterfront and the Port Jefferson Ferry dock. Within Port Jefferson, you'll find no shortage of cafes, ice-cream shops, candy stores, and fine-dining restaurants. Because of the ferry traffic, this village stays pretty busy throughout the year. It's a great place to do some holiday shopping in the winter.

- **Sayville:** This South Shore community also has a small Main Street area that offers a nice collection of shops, boutiques, cafes, and restaurants.
- **Stony Brook:** The Stony Brook Village Center (631-751-2244, www.stonybrookvillage.com) offers a relatively small but very nice collection of upscale boutiques and shops within an outdoor shopping complex that's not a Main Street–type environment. Some of the stores here include Ann Taylor Loft, Blue Dove Spa, Christopher Gallery, Crabtree & Evelyn, Stony Brook Gift Ship, Talbots, and Van Heusen. You can spend a few hours exploring this quaint, colonial village–style shopping center and then take a short walk to the Three Village Inn, where you can enjoy an amazing fine-dining restaurant called Mirabelle. Reservations are definitely required. Within the Stony Brook Village Center, however, is a very casual sandwich shop/ice-cream parlor that's well worth visiting for a lunch or a snack. The Stony Brook Village Center is located on Main St. on the Harbor in the heart of Stony Brook. The shops are open Mon through Sat from 10 a.m. to 6 p.m., and Sun from noon to 5 p.m.

On Long Island's North Fork, you'll also find a handful of small villages, many of which offer adorable Main Streets and town centers where you'll find unique shops, restaurants, cafes, and galleries. There are very few chain stores or franchised stores in this region, so most of the shopping opportunities are truly unique.

Local Artists, Craftspeople, and Artisans

Another type of unique shopping opportunity on Long Island, particularly in Suffolk County during the peak summer tourist season, are the galleries, shops, and events hosted by the local artisans, craftspeople, and artists, who are in abundance throughout the area. These people showcase their crafts and creations, and offer them for sale. Thus, you're apt to find beautiful gifts, handmade clothing, one-of-a-kind jewelry, and all sorts of fine art, for example, sometimes created by local artists and artisans who have received worldwide recognition and fame.

Many communities also host craft fairs and other events where artists and craftspeople from throughout the region gather for a day or two to showcase their work and sell it to the public. Check local event directories and listings to learn when and where these craft shows will be taking place. For example, there's the Rockville Centre Arts and Crafts Show held in late Apr at the Rockville Centre (631-724-5965), the Montauk Fine Arts Festival on the Green held in late May (631-668-2428), and the Fine Arts and Crafts Festival at the Nassau County Museum of Art in Roslyn Harbor held in late May (516-484-9337).

i Antiques collectors will also enjoy shopping on Long Island, as independent antiques shops are located in almost every community. Throughout the year many communities also host antiques fairs, such as Huntington's Antiques in the Park, which is held in Apr (631-868-2751); the Smithtown Antiques and Garden Fair in early May (516-868-2751); and the Great Neck Antique Show in mid-May (516-868-2751).

Farm Stands

Suffolk County, particularly the North Fork and South Fork, is also famous for its seasonal farm stands. This is where you can purchase ultra-fresh fruits and vegetables and farm-fresh eggs directly from the farms that grew them. What's offered at each independently operated farm stand will depend on a specific farm's specialty and season, but if you're looking for freshly grown, sometimes certified organic produce, it's abundantly available throughout the summer and fall at the various roadside farm stands you'll encounter as you explore the region.

You'll find more than 50 farm stands throughout Suffolk County, particularly in places like Calverton, Wading River, Riverhead, Greenport, East Marion, Orient, Shelter Island, Laurel, Mattituck, Jamesport, Aquebogue, Peconic, and Cutchogue, where family-owned-and-operated farms are in abundance.

i As you explore the North Fork and tour the region's wineries and vineyards, you'll find that many offer gift shops that sell their locally produced wines by the bottle or case, as well as wine accessories, exotic cheeses, homemade gourmet foods, gift baskets, and other home goods and specialty items.

Greenport Village

On the North Fork, Greenport Village (www.greenportvillage.com) is the most popular shopping destination for tourists. This is a midsize historic village that offers several blocks' worth of one-of-a-kind boutiques, galleries, antiques shops, restaurants, and cafes. Most are located on or near the waterfront and are open year-round. The majority of shops here are unique (and independently owned and operated) but affordable. Plus, they offer a nice selection of merchandise that goes well beyond souvenir shops.

Interspersed between the stores and restaurants are historic landmarks and buildings, a few museums, and a town park that contains a historic working carousel and a re-created blacksmith shop. Many local artists have set up small galleries here, and you'll find a wide range of restaurants open for breakfast, lunch, and dinner.

Greenport Village is in the heart of Long Island's wine county, so it's a great place to stop during or after your tour of the various wineries and vineyards. Within walking distance of the village are several inns and B&Bs, making this a picturesque place to spend a weekend or week, particularly during the peak summer season.

i As you're driving around touring some of the wineries, consider stops in places like Aquebogue, Jamesport, Laurel, Southold, Greenport, East Marion, and Orient, where you'll find charming shopping opportunities.

If you have time to explore just one shopping area during your visit to the North Fork area, you'll definitely enjoy your experience at Greenport Village.

DAY SPAS

When you're exhausted after a long day of shopping, your feet hurt from all of the walking, and your shoulders are stiff from carrying your purchases, you can unwind, relax, and be pampered at the many world-class day spas that operate throughout Long Island. You'll find a handful of stand-alone day spas, as well as spas within many of the upscale hotels, resorts, and country clubs throughout Long Island. For example, people travel from all over the region to visit the amazing spa located in the East Wind resort in Wading River (see Accommodations chapter).

In addition to offering full-service hair and nail salons, these day spas feature a comprehensive menu of massages, body wraps, facials, and full-body treatments. You can enjoy one of these spas for an hour or two and experience a single treatment, or transform a typical day into a day of decadence by signing up for a complete spa package. The day spas throughout Long Island also offer specials for "girls-only weekends," bachelorette parties, and bridal parties, for example. The spa experience isn't exclusively for women, however. Most offer specialty treatments and packages designed just for men.

Since many couples visit Long Island to experience a romantic getaway weekend, many of the region's day spas offer special couples massages and treatments in specially designed, ultra-private treatment rooms.

i When choosing a spa to experience, don't just concentrate on the menu of treatments offered—consider the spa's other services and amenities. For example, are the locker room facilities equipped with a steam room, sauna, hot tub, and relaxation lounge? Can you order a healthy meal or snack, and enjoy it in the spa between treatments? If you're participating in a romantic getaway weekend, can you sign up for a couples massage and experience it in a specially designed treatment room?

A-STUDIO SPA
10 Main St., East Hampton
(631) 324-6996
www.astudiospa.com

This is a full-service day spa and hair salon, offering a complete menu of massages, full-body treatments, body wraps, facials, and other procedures designed to relax and pamper you. The spa offers a couples treatment room (for his and her massages), as well as a small shop where you can buy the skin-care products used in conjunction with the treatments. A-Studio Spa is upscale and elegant, and charges accordingly.

ALLEGRIA HOTEL & SPA
80 West Broadway, Long Beach
(516) 889-1300
www.allegriahotel.com

Within this upscale hotel is a small, full-service day spa. Starting in summer 2010, however, a new, state-of-the-art, upscale spa called Joseph Christopher for Beauty & Wellness Spa (www.josephchristopher.com) is being introduced. This spa chain has several locations, all within luxury hotels and resorts across America. A full menu of spa treatments is offered, but at premium prices. For example, a standard 50-minute massage will cost around $100, plus tip, while a Sea Holistic massage will run $140 for 50 minutes. A variety of different half-day and full-day spa packages are offered.

ATLANTIS SPA
650 Hawkins Ave., Suite 11, Ronkonkoma
(631) 467-2770
www.atlantishn.com

Each Atlantis Spa is a therapist-owned-and-operated business that offers a decent selection of treatments, ranging from therapeutic massages to body wraps and facials. Here a basic 30-minute massage will cost about $45 (plus tip), while a 60-minute massage will run $74 (plus tip). To enjoy four full hours of pampering, consider the Atlantis Deluxe treatment package ($299), which includes a 90-minute aromatherapy massage, a one-hour facial, a one-hour body treatment, a paraffin hand and foot treatment, and a spa lunch. Additional Atlantis Spa locations can be found at 99-11 Rte. 25A, Shoreham (631-744-3661) and 466 Moriches Road, St. James (631-584-2323).

DANFORDS HOTEL & MARINA (ATLANTIS SPA)
25 East Broadway, Port Jefferson
(631) 928-5200
www.atlantishn.com

This is a small day spa located in the historic Danfords Hotel & Marina. Like the four other Atlantis Spa locations on Long Island, it offers a nice selection of treatments. For details, visit the Web site or see the Atlantis Spa entry above.

EPIPHANY DAY SPA
285 Fulton Ave., Hempstead
(516) 647-0873
www.epiphanydayspany.com

Epiphany Day Spa is a midpriced, full-service spa and hair salon, offering a wide range of massages, full-body treatments, facials, body wraps, and skin-care treatments. A standard 30-minute massage will cost around $45 (plus tip), while a 60-minute massage is priced around $80 (plus tip). If you visit the spa's Web site, you can learn about monthly specials and money-saving packages, including party and wedding packages.

GURNEY'S INN RESORT & SPA

290 Old Montauk Hwy., Montauk
(631) 668-2345
www.gurneysinn.com

Located in the famous Gurney's Inn Resort, which is situated along a beach on the very tip of Long Island, is an upscale, full-service spa. This spa has an oceanfront "seawater" theme, and many of the treatments somehow utilize sea salts or seaweed. Seawater baths, including an algae slimming bath and a seawater herbal bath; an algae body polish; and a seaweed body wrap are among the signature treatments offered here. The menu of available treatments and services is extensive, much larger than most spas.

Beyond lavish spa treatments, this spa also offers fitness and wellness services, ranging from biofeedback to a body composition analysis, comprehensive fitness evaluation, nutrition consultation, and personal fitness training. A full hair salon, makeup services, and tanning beds are available, as is a wide range of spa day packages and wedding packages. Treatments at Gurney's Inn Resort & Spa aren't cheap, but they'll certainly be relaxing and memorable. A 60-minute aromatherapy massage will cost about $105 (plus tip), and a 90-minute active green argillite mud therapy is priced art $220 (plus tip).

LA CAREZZA

43-45 Windmilla Ln., Southampton
(631) 283-1483
www.lacarezza.com

A trip to the Hamptons, particularly East Hampton or Southampton, where La Carezza is located, is usually about extravagance—whether you're shopping, dining, enjoying the local entertainment, or sailing around in a luxury yacht. Your lavish vacation experience can continue with a top-notch spa treatment, or a full day of spa pampering, at this lovely day spa. Here you'll find a full-service beauty salon, offering hair, makeup, and nail services, along with a comprehensive spa treatment menu. At this upscale spa, a signature G. M. Collin's Collagen Facial is priced at $160, while the La Carezza Signature Body Treatment "The Worx" is priced at $150. A 50-minute Swedish massage will cost you $105, while a 50-minute deep-tissue massage is priced at $120. As with most upscale day spas, this one focuses on offering highly personalized attention in an ultra-relaxing environment.

NATUROPATHICA HOLISTIC HEALTH SPA AND PURE BEAUTY LOUNGE

Red Horse Plaza, 74 Montauk Hwy., East Hampton
(631) 329-2525
www.naturopathica.com/ourspa.html

As the name suggests, Naturopathica Holistic Health Spa and Pure Beauty Lounge is a full-service, extremely posh day spa and beauty salon located in the heart of East Hampton. On the menu is a wide range of therapeutic and luxurious treatments, designed for people looking to relax, indulge, and promote personal wellness within themselves. Featured on the spa menu are 11 different facials, such as the Pure Touch Facial (90 minutes), which is priced at $175. A handful of different full-body treatments are also offered, including the Body Drench (60 minutes), which utilizes aromatic cocoa butter and is priced at $150. Over a dozen different massage treatments are also offered, ranging in price from $125 to $180 for a 60-minute treatment.

ORANGE SKYE BODY & BEAUTY BAR

50 Rockaway Ave., Valley Stream
(516) 284-6378
www.longislandorangeskye.com

Orange Skye Body & Beauty Bar is an elegant, but not overly pretentious, full-service day spa and salon. Many of the treatments are designed to promote wellness and health maintenance, not just relaxation. The spa facility itself is cozy and charming, and the service is personalized and top-notch. While the treatment menu isn't extensive, it is comprehensive and includes a variety of massages, facials, and body detox treatments, including full-body wraps and scrubs. Orange Skye regularly hosts private spa parties, which can be customized to meet a group's unique interests and budget.

RANI SPA
1582 Hillside Ave, New Hyde Park
(516) 437-RANI
www.ranispa.com

Offering their own skin- and hair-care product line, Rani Spa is a full-service, midpriced day spa and beauty salon with three locations on Long Island. In addition to traditional spa treatments, like massages and facials, Rani Spa also offers waxing, threading, cellulite treatments, makeup services, and henna tattoos, along with ayurvedic services. The spa specializes in bridal services, but is also a wonderful place to visit if you're looking to kick back, relax, and get pampered for a few hours. Other locations are at 247-38 Jericho Tnpk., Bellrose (516-354-5412), and 473 Old Country Rd., Westbury (516-333-3783).

RED DOOR SPAS BY ELIZABETH ARDEN
1399 Franklin Ave., Garden City
(516) 747-7474
www.reddoorspas.com/RedDoorLocations/day-spa-in-long-island.aspx

Red Door Spas is one of the more prestigious chains of day spas, offering locations throughout the United States. All are full-service spas and beauty salons that combine luxury facilities with both traditional and more exotic spa treatments and services. The goal of all Elizabeth Arden spas is to enhance life through "beauty, harmony and well-being," which is the focus of most of the treatments offered here.

In addition to individual treatments, which are all top-notch, this Red Door Spa is known for its half-day and full-day spa packages, which range in price from $99 to $482. As you'd expect, a variety of different massages, facials, and full-body treatments are offered. For example, a 50-minute Red Door Signature Massage is priced at $120, while an Ultimate Arden Facial is priced at $180. Like many full-service spas, Red Door caters primarily to women, but also offers a handful of treatments designed specifically for men, including a Gentlemen's Facial ($110), Gentlemen's Manicure ($27), Gentlemen's Pedicure ($65), and a Deep Tissue Massage (starting at $145).

THREE VILLAGE INN HOTEL & SPA
150 Main St., Stony Brook
(631) 751-0555
www.threevillageinn.com

As part of the ongoing renovation and expansion of the Three Village Inn Hotel & Spa, plans are under way to build a large and elegant day spa facility, which will fit nicely into this prestigious hotel. Currently, however, what's offered is a small selection of spa treatments, including massages, in a cozy private area of the hotel's main historic building. In-room massages are also available upon request. The spa treatments offered are mainly European in origin, and include massages, body wraps, facials, and body scrubs. This hotel hosts many weddings, and thus offers a wide range of spa services for brides and bridal parties.

VILLAGE SPA
17 Main St., Roslyn
(516) 625-0019
www.the-village-spa.com

Village Spa is a midpriced, full-service day spa that can best be described as whimsical. Sure, it offers a wide range of treatments designed to pamper its clientele, but it also offers a complete couples massage menu (including massage services for two . . . or three), four-handed massages for one, and a range of more exotic spa treatments, such as the Yummy Chocolate Body Wrap and the Not Your Usual Milk & Honey Wrap. The massage suites look like luxury hotel rooms, complete with a Jacuzzi jet shower, sauna, and TV. Here you can spend the day being pampered if you sign up for one of the spa's elaborate spa packages—designed to de-stress, deep clean, and relax you.

Village Spa is conveniently located in historic Roslyn Village and is a wonderful place to enjoy a single treatment or a full day's worth of pampering and indulgences.

SHOPPING IN NYC

While Long Island offers some pretty amazing shopping experiences, nothing compares to the shopping available in New York City, along Fifth

Avenue and Madison Avenue, for example. Out-of-towners visiting Long Island for several days or the entire season would be remiss if they didn't travel into Manhattan by car, bus, or train in order to experience the shopping that the city is world-famous for. Along with the dozens upon dozens of stand-alone designer shops, the world's largest Macy's department store can be found in New York's Herald Square, for example. In terms of major department stores, here are some of NYC's top shopping choices:

BARNEY'S NEW YORK
660 Madison Ave. (between 60th St. and 61st St.)
(212) 965-9964
www.barneys.com
This upscale department store features top fashion and accessories, plus casual clothing for men and women.

BERGDORF GOODMAN
754 Fifth Ave.
(212) 753-7300
www.bergdorfgoodman.com
Located within 2 blocks of the Pierre, Essex House, the Ritz-Carlton, and several other upscale hotels located along Central Park, you'll find one of NYC's most famous and most upscale department stores. It features everything from designer apparel to handbags, cosmetics, jewelry, and fragrances. Located across the street is the Bergdorf Goodman men's store (745 Fifth Ave., 212-339-3311).

BLOOMINGDALE'S
1000 Third Ave. (between 59th St. and 60th St.)
(212) 705-2000
www.bloomingdales.com
This upscale department store offers a wide range of designer clothing, household items, and gifts. Spend more than $100 and receive a free signature tote bag by bringing your receipts to the visitor center located on the first-floor balcony (59th St. and Lexington Ave.).

MACY'S HERALD SQUARE
151 West 34th St. (between Broadway and Seventh Ave.)
(212)-695-4400
www.macys.com
This is the largest and most famous department store in America. You can easily spend an entire day here and not see everything. Hours are Mon through Sat, 10 a.m. to 9:30 p.m., and Sun, 11 a.m. to 8:30 p.m. Be sure to stop by the visitor center on the 34th St. balcony to receive a Macy's Savings Pass. This pass entitles you to an 11 percent savings on your purchases. Also, for a fee of between $18 and $50, Macy's offers same-day delivery of purchases made before 6 p.m. to anywhere in NYC, so you don't have to carry around heavy parcels.

i Macy's is the world's largest store, offering 2.1 million square feet of unique shopping. The massive store stocks over 500,000 different items.

MANHATTAN MALL
Sixth Ave. and 33rd St.
(212) 465-0500
www.manhattanmallny.com
This indoor mall features more than 50 stores, as well as New York City's largest food court. Containing mostly traditional mall chain stores (as opposed to designer boutiques), it's one of the few indoor malls in the Big Apple, and also one of the most affordable.

SHOPS AT COLUMBUS CIRCLE
10 Columbus Circle (Time Warner Center–Broadway, between 58th St. and 60th St.)
(212) 823-6300
www.shopsatcolumbuscircle.com
This is an upscale, indoor mall featuring dozens of designer shops and boutiques.

SOUTH STREET SEAPORT
Fulton St. and South St.
(212) 732-7678
www.southstreetseaport.com

This indoor mall features over 100 stores, cafes, and restaurants. It's located on the water, and it's also a historic landmark attraction with several museums and exhibits in the area. It's an exciting place to walk around, dine, or shop. During warmer months, you'll also find outdoor cart vendors and street performers here. From the South Street Seaport, you can get a nice view of the Statue of Liberty on a clear day.

i If you're looking for a bargain on close-out and overstock designer fashions, you'll want to plan on spending several hours exploring the Century 21 Department Store (22 Cortlandt St., 212-227-9092, www.c21stores.com). Taking up more than one full square block in Manhattan, this department store offers nothing but well-known, brand-new, designer brands at up to 80 percent off retail prices. The Manhattan location is located directly across the street from Ground Zero, the World Trade Center's location prior to Sept 11, 2001, and where the future Freedom Tower will eventually be located.

ANNUAL EVENTS

No matter where on Long Island you live or visit, there are all sorts of special events that take place throughout the year. Some are related to a particular season or holiday, while others celebrate a historical event or commemorate some other type of special happening.

This section highlights just some of the more popular annual events that are worth experiencing. In fact, some people plan their vacations or visits to the region around these specific events or happenings. You'll discover that every town, tourist attraction, museum, vineyard, and historical landmark on the island hosts a wide range of special events and activities throughout the year, particularly in the summer and fall, when most of the tourists are in town. You'll also find a wide range of harvest-related events in Oct (particularly in the North Fork region), as well as holiday events throughout Nov and Dec across the island.

JANUARY

WINTER SEAL WALKS AT JONES BEACH

Theodore Roosevelt Nature Center at Jones Beach, Wantaugh
(516) 679-7254
http://nysparks.state.ny.us/events/event.aspx?e=590.0

Seal Walks on Jones Beach are held between early Jan and mid-Mar. The Nature Center, which is part of Jones Beach, is located on a barrier island, and is a popular spot for viewing a wide range of marine life, including seals. These guided tours take about 90 minutes and are hosted by marine wildlife experts. The price is just $4 per person.

SEAL WALKS IN WESTHMAPTON AND MONTAUK

Cupsogue Beach County Park, Westhampton
Montauk Point State Park, Montauk
(516) 244-3352
www.cresli.org/cresli/seals/sealwalk.html

Seal Walk in Cupsogue Beach County Park and at Montauk Point State Park are held early Jan through mid-May (weather permitting). Join a marine wildlife expert on a walking tour during which you'll see seals up close. The fee is $5 per adult and $3 per child. During a typical excursion, participants will see upwards of 40 or more harbor seals in the wild.

FEBRUARY

LONG ISLAND WINTERFEST

(631) 951-3900
www.liwinterfest.com/liwinterfest

This event runs mid-Feb through late Mar and includes six consecutive weekends of free jazz concerts held at various venues throughout the island, including at several Long Island wineries and vineyards. During the performances, wine tastings are held. This annual event is sponsored by the Long Island Wine Council, East End Arts Council, Suffolk County Department of Economic Development and Workforce Housing, and Long Island Convention & Visitors Bureau. Check out the festival's Web site for a schedule of featured events and free concerts.

VALENTINE'S DAY DINNER DANCE

East Wind Inn & Spa, Wading River
(631) 929-6585
www.eastwindlongisland.com/upcoming_events.html

Get in the Valentine's Day spirit and enjoy a romantic evening at the famous East Wind Inn &

Spa in Wading River. For adults only, the Valentine's Day Dinner Dance is held on Feb 13 and is a formal and elegant dinner and dancing opportunity that offers an extremely fun and romantic way to enjoy the evening with someone you love. Reservations are a must, especially if you plan to also book a room for the evening. The dinner dance, however, is open to non-guests as well. Special events are also held here on Easter Sunday and Mother's Day.

LONG ISLAND SPRING HOME SHOW

Suffolk County Community College, Sports & Exhibition Complex
Brentwood
(888) 560-3976
www.biztradeshows.com/travel-events/spring-home-longisland.html

With spring on the horizon, the Long Island Spring Home show comes to town in mid-Feb. This three-day-long event is ideal for local home owners or people looking to relocate to the Long Island area. The show features workshops, exhibits, lectures, and demonstrations related to remodeling, landscaping, and home decorating. Admission for adults is $9. The Long Island Spring Home Show also comes to the Nassau Veterans Memorial Coliseum in Uniondale in mid-Apr each year.

WINTER BIRDING AT THE LIGHTHOUSE

Fire Island Lighthouse, Captree Island
(631) 321-7028
www.fireislandlighthouse.com

If you enjoy bird-watching and nature, you won't want to miss the Winter Birding at the Lighthouse event held in late Feb. Hosted by the Fire Island Lighthouse Preservation Society, you'll be joined by a guide as you identify and observe some of Fire Island's various bird species. This event lasts about two hours (starting at 9 a.m.), during which you'll probably see waterfowl, shorebirds, hawks, and songbirds. Call or visit the Web site for details about this and other events held at the landmark lighthouse throughout the year.

MARCH

WINE CAMP

Various locations in wine country
(631) 495-9744
www.winecamp.org

Held in early Mar, as well as several other times throughout the year, including dates in Apr and June, Wine Camp is an adults-only, three-day-long experience that includes wine tastings, classes, tours, and the opportunity to learn from and interact with the region's top wine experts. Fine-dining and upscale accommodations are included as part of the experience. The price starts at $899 per person, based on double occupancy, for this unique event.

i For a listing of special events taking place at Long Island's wineries and vineyards throughout the year, visit www.liwines.com/default.ihtml?page=events or www.longislandwinecountry.com/events.html.

LONG ISLAND GOLF EXPO

Suffolk Community College, Brentwood
(631) 851-6900
www.longislandgolfexpo.com

This three-day event is a must for golfers of all ages. In addition to exhibits and hands-on equipment demonstrations, attendees can experience two driving ranges set up for the event, or try out several different golf simulators. Get your swing analyzed, or participate in a putting challenge. Somewhere between 15,000 and 20,000 golfers attend this event annually.

IRISH FESTIVAL

Hofstra University, Hempstead
(516) 463-6671
www.hofstra.edu/Community/Fest/Fest_irish.html

You don't need to be Irish to enjoy the fun and activities offered at this annual, daylong event that takes place at Hofstra University in mid-Mar. Ethnic food is served, and live music and dance performances are showcased. If you're feeling more Italian than Irish, you'll have to wait until Sept for the annual Italian Festival, which is also held at Hofstra (www.hofstra.edu/Community/Fest/Fest_italian.html).

ST. PATRICK'S DAY PARADE

Main St. in Montauk
(631) 475-0121, (631) 688-1578
www.montaukchamber.com

Held along Main St. in Montauk on St. Patrick's Day, this annual event focuses around a town-wide parade, but culminates with a handful of other activities hosted by local restaurants, hotels, and venues.

APRIL

ARBOR DAY FESTIVAL

Planting Fields Arboretum State Historic Park
Oyster Bay
(631) 321-3510
www.plantingfields.org

This is a family-oriented and kid-friendly event featuring activities, performances, exhibits, and a petting zoo. Learn about nature while enjoying the outdoors, and expect an appearance by Smokey Bear.

LONG ISLAND GUITAR FESTIVAL

C. W. Post Campus of Long Island University
School of Visual and Performing Arts—Department of Music
Brookville
(516) 299-2475

The Long Island Guitar Festival has been a much-anticipated annual event for 20 years running, especially among musicians. The event is also for music lovers in general, and features workshops, master classes, and performances. In 2010, for example, over a dozen guitarists, composers, and arrangers are slated to appear, teach, and perform. The all-events pass is priced at $125; however, admission to individual performances and workshops is priced starting at $10 each.

i Contact the local chamber of commerce for the area you'll be visiting to determine what special events will be taking place during your stay on Long Island. For a listing of chambers of commerce on the island, visit www.longislandexchange.com/chambers-commerce.html.

MAY

AIR SHOW

Jones Beach State Park, Wantagh
(516) 785-1600
www.jonesbeachairshow.com

Experience some high-flying fun at the popular Air Show at Jones Beach. This family-friendly event is held every Memorial Day weekend, and is the largest air show in the region. On the final day of the 2009 show, 186,000 people attended the event. Performances by the U.S. Air Force Thunderbirds, U.S. Army Golden Knights, New York Air National Guide, Canadian Forces Snowbirds, and over a dozen legendary pilots are on the annual roster. Plus, dozens of authentic and historic aircrafts are displayed.

LONG ISLAND MARATHON

East Meadow
(516) 986-5537
www.thelimarathon.com

For almost 40 years the Long Island Marathon has been the premier competitive running event on Long Island. The main event is a grueling 26.2-mile run. In the 1980s, however, a second Half Marathon race was added, along with a 10K, 5K, 1-mile, and Kidz Fun Run, which collectively have become known as the RXR Long Island Marathon Festival of Races. Spectators are encouraged to watch the marathon and sister races from the start or finish line areas, as well as from various view points along the route. There is no charge for spectators.

BIG CARRIAGE SHOW

Stony Brook
(631) 751-0066
www.longislandmuseum.org

The Big Carriage Show offers a chance to see a vast collection of historic horse-drawn carriages in Stony Brook. The event is sponsored by the Long Island Museum of American Art, History and Carriages. Each year the museum showcases some of its collection of 200 horse-drawn carriages, allowing visitors to actually see them in operation. Encompassing nine acres, it is one of the most comprehensive displays in the world.

OLD VILLAGE OF GREAT NECK STREET FAIR
Middle Neck Rd. and Fairview Ave., Great Neck
(631) 724-5966

Looking for unique gifts or unusual handcrafted items for your home? If so, you'll enjoy experiencing the annual Old Village of Great Neck Street Fair in Great Neck. Admission to this well-attended, daylong arts and crafts fair is free. The outdoor event has become a 30-plus-year tradition. Call for directions, as well as exact dates and times.

NORTHEAST EQUINE EXPO
Belmont Park Racetrack, Elmont
(877) 778-3976
www.neequineexpo.com

The Northeast Equine Expo is one of the region's largest and most popular equestrian events. Held at the Belmont Park Racetrack in Elmont for two days every May, this is a premier trade show and exhibition related to the equestrian lifestyle. The show features hundreds of exhibitors and vendors, as well as demonstrations and workshops. Call or check out the Web site for show details and dates.

JUNE

U.S. OPEN GOLF TOURNAMENT

The U.S. Open is held each year in a different city; however, during this popular event's history, it has returned to Long Island on several occasions, most recently in mid-June 2009, when it was held at the Bethpage State Park Black Course in Farmingdale. Even when the main USGA U.S. Open tournament isn't being held on Long Island, between June and Oct, weekly PGA, USGA, and locally sponsored tournaments and matches are held at Bethpage State Park's golf courses every Sun, as well as at many other Long Island–area courses. Explore Long Island (www.exploreli.com/recreation/golf) and Golf on Long Island (www.golfonlongisland.com) are great resources for learning about tournaments and matches, whether you're a competitor or spectator.

i **Throughout the summer, one of the biggest reasons to visit Long Island, especially for city dwellers, is to experience the many gorgeous beaches. Most are open daily, from sunrise to sunset, and have lifeguards on duty between Memorial Day and Labor Day. At many of the beaches, special events, concerts, and activities are held throughout the peak tourist season. For a complete listing of public Long Island beaches and parks, visit www.longisland.com/parks.**

JULY

JULY 4 FIREWORKS
Various locations

Fireworks celebrations are held throughout Long Island in places like Jones Beach (516-785-1600), Oyster Bay (516-922-4447), Farmingville (631-888-9000), and Montauk (631-668-2428). Many of these events are family-oriented and feature carnival-like atmospheres, complete with live musical performances, prior to the actual fireworks displays, which take place just after sunset.

LONG ISLAND INTERNATIONAL FILM EXPO
Bellmore
(516) 783-3199
http://liifilmexpo.org

Movie buffs will enjoy the annual Long Island International Film Expo, held in Bellmore in early to mid-July. Throughout the festival, between 70 and 180 short and feature-length films are presented by independent filmmakers from around the world. Those who attend can often spot celebrities, sit in on panel discussions, attend award ceremonies, enjoy parties, and, of course, watch films. Call or visit the Web site for details about this popular and highly successful nine-day-long event.

CLASSIC CAR SHOW CHARITY FUNDRAISER

Capital One Operations Center, Mattituck
www.cutchoguelions.org

Held each year in Mattituck, this charity fund-raiser draws more than 250 classic car owners and their award-winning classic automobiles. The event is held in mid-July at the Capital One Operations Center, and is presented by the Cutchogue Lions Club. Admission is $5 per adult for this event, which has taken place for more than 40 consecutive years.

AUGUST

LIGHTHOUSE WEEKEND

Montauk Point Lighthouse, East Hampton
(631) 668-2544
www.montauklighthouse.com

Over a dozen unique activities, exhibits, and attractions take place during this weekend-long event. For example, there's a showcase of colonial toys and games, plus a boat safety and knot-tying exhibition by the U.S. Coast Guard. Several local authors are on hand to sign their books, while local artists showcase and sell their work. Admission is $8 per adult, plus $6 for parking.

HAMPTON CLASSIC HORSE SHOW

Bridgehampton
(631) 537-3177
www.hamptonclassic.com

This is a massive annual event where competitors compete in a handful of competitions for hundreds of thousands of dollars in prizes. It takes place over eight days from 8:30 a.m. until 5 p.m. In addition to competitions, various workshops and exhibitions are held. For example, the ASPCA hosts an animal behavior clinic called Learn to Think Like a Horse. Admission is $10 per person or $20 per car. Admission to the Grand Prix event on the final day costs extra.

U.S. OPEN TENNIS CHAMPIONSHIP

USTA Billie Jean King National Tennis Center and Arthur Ashe Stadium, Flushing
(718) 760-6200

The U.S. Open Tennis Championships are held between late Aug and mid-Sept, and attract more than 720,000 spectators. The event technically takes place in Flushing (part of Queens); however, due to the close proximity to Long Island's Nassau County, many spectators and visitors opt to stay on Long Island throughout the two-week-long sporting event, which features the biggest names in tennis.

SEPTEMBER

LONG ISLAND GARLIC FESTIVAL

Aquebogue
(631) 680-1699
www.gardenofevefarm.com/garlic-festival.htm

Whether you enjoy cooking, eating, or simply participating in fun and festive events, the Long Island Garlic Festival is worth experiencing. Enjoy two days of garlic-themed events, cooking demonstrations, and dining opportunities in late Sept.

OCTOBER

OYSTER FESTIVAL

Oyster Bay
(516) 628-1625
www.theoysterfestival.org

Seafood lovers won't want to miss the annual Oyster Festival, which is one of Oyster Bay's most popular annual events. The festival, which is held in mid-Oct, features more than 25 booths that showcase hundreds of items. Participants also have an opportunity to see the USS *Growler* and USS *Liberator* tall ships sailing around the harbor. Musical entertainment is showcased throughout the weekend-long event, which has been taking place for over 25 years.

HAMPTONS INTERNATIONAL FILM FESTIVAL
East Hampton
(631) 324-4600
www.hamptonsfilmfest.org
Be one of the first to see what could become an award-winning, blockbuster film by attending the Hamptons International Film Festival in East Hampton. The goal of this festival, according to the organizers, is to introduce independent film from all genres to the general public. The festival is also open to international filmmakers, and offers guests the chance to meet and interact with the filmmakers themselves, in addition to viewing the films. Call or visit the Web site for movie descriptions, showtimes, and event schedules.

Long Island Events Web Sites

- For a detailed listing of annual events on Long Island, visit www.discoverlongisland.com/calendar_list.cfm.
- For a full listing of events broken up by category, such as sporting events, charity events, festivals, and cultural events, visit http://events.longisland.com.
- Broken down by month, category, and community, the Life on Long Island site, www.lifeonlongisland.com/index.cfm?fuseaction=events.bymonth, also maintains a comprehensive listing of annual and special events in the region.
- Operated by the *Long Island Newsday* newspaper, the Explore Long Island site, www.exploreli.com/events/search, provides a detailed listing of events occurring throughout the island.

NOVEMBER

LONG ISLAND RESTAURANT WEEK
Various restaurants
www.longislandrestaurantweek.com
Anyone who enjoys dining out and experiencing the fine cuisine of award-winning chefs will want to participate in Long Island Restaurant Week. During the first week of Nov each year, many of the island's most upscale and exclusive restaurants open their doors and offer a three-course, prix fixe menu for dinner. While dinner at these restaurants might typically cost $50 to $100 per person, during Restaurant Week in Nov 2009, the per-person cost for dinner was just $24.95 at all participating restaurants. Long Island Restaurant Week is an incredible opportunity to experience the cuisine of award-winning chefs. Make your reservations at participating restaurants early. Visit the Web site for dates and a list of participating restaurants for 2010 and beyond.

HOLIDAY GIFT & CRAFT FAIR
Ward Melville High School
380 Old Town Rd., East Setauket
(631) 675-1615
www.bgcsuffolk.org
Start your holiday shopping early at the annual Holiday Gift & Craft Fair that's presented by the Boys & Girls Club of Suffolk County. This daylong event in mid-Nov attracts more than 100 vendors and artisans who showcase and sell a wide range of holiday items, gifts, apparel, and homemade gourmet foods. Call or visit the Web site for additional information, including the exact date of this annual event. Admission is free.

LIGHTING THE LIGHTHOUSE
Montauk Point Lighthouse, East Hampton
(631) 668-2544
www.montauklighthouse.com
This is an annual pre-holiday event held in late-Nov during which the entire Montauk Point Lighthouse is lit up with holiday lights. Live musical performances and other events take place leading up to the lighting. While New Yorkers enjoy the lighting of the Christmas tree in Rock-

efeller Center, Long Islanders have transformed the Lighting of the Lighthouse into an annual tradition.

1863 THANKSGIVING CELEBRATION
Old Bethpage
(516) 572-8400
As Thanksgiving comes around, so does Old Bethpage's annual 1863 Thanksgiving Celebration. Travel back in time as a 19th-century village is re-created and a Thanksgiving feast is prepared. Family-friendly events are held on two consecutive weekends around the Thanksgiving holiday.

GRAPE EXPECTATIONS!
Wolffer Estate Vineyards, Saqaponack
(631) 283-2494
www.wolffer.com
Held in late Nov, just before Thanksgiving, Grape Expectations! is just one of many popular special events that take place throughout Long Island's wine country each year. At this event, well-known winemakers speak and conduct wine tastings, and live entertainment is featured. The admission fee is between $40 and $50. Call or visit the Web site for information about this and other special events at Wolffer Estate Vineyards, one of the very first vineyards in the region.

DECEMBER

DICKENS FESTIVAL
Port Jefferson
(631) 473-0286
http://gpjac.org
Don't just read or watch movies about classic holiday villages and experiences—partake in the popular Dickens Festival, which is held in Port Jefferson in early Dec. The entire town transforms into a village from Charles Dickens's classic holiday story. Townspeople dress in period attire, and a wide range of activities, performances, and events are held throughout Port Jefferson.

ANNUAL VICTORIAN CHRISTMAS
Hallockville Museum Farm & Folklife Center
Riverhead
(631) 298-5297
www.hallockville.com/events_calendar.html
At the Hallockville Museum Farm & Folklife Center in Riverhead, visitors can experience the Annual Victorian Christmas. Throughout the day, visitors can take guided tours of the fully decorated 18th-century homesteads and interact with costumed guides and interpreters as part of this entertaining and educational experience. Musical entertainment, children's activities, and appearances by Santa are held throughout the day. No matter what time of year you visit the area, you'll find a wide range of other events, like Civil War reenactments, nature walks, fall festivals, tractor pulls, and gardening classes, taking place at this popular, family-friendly attraction. This particular daylong annual event is typically in early Dec; call or visit the Web site for details.

ANNUAL HOLIDAY LIGHT SHOW
600 Lakeview Ave., Bayport
(631) 472-1625
Throughout much of Dec, the Annual Holiday Light Show takes place in Bayport between 5 and 9 p.m.. It's an impressive fund-raising event presented by the Girl Scouts of Suffolk County. Visitors drive through a wooded trail filled with incredible holiday light displays and vignettes. On Thurs, Fri, and Sat nights, guests can visit the Holiday Village and have a photo taken with Santa, plus enjoy snacks and beverages.

i In conjunction with these and other annual events held throughout Long Island, many local inns and B&Bs typically offer specially priced accommodations or package deals. Be sure to check with the local chamber of commerce for information about special offers.

ATTRACTIONS

As you know, there's a huge difference between Nassau and Suffolk Counties. While Nassau County is more of a year-around destination, as well as where the majority of the island's residents live, Suffolk County is more of a seasonal place to visit (though that's slowly changing). When late Oct rolls around, it's well into the off-peak season in Suffolk County, so many of the area's attractions close until the spring. Those that remain open throughout the year have greatly reduced hours, or only operate on weekends and holidays.

Throughout Long Island there are literally hundreds of historical places to visit, as well as museums, attractions, cultural centers, and parks that offer organized activities and events. This chapter highlights just a sampling of the more popular tourist attractions in Nassau and Suffolk Counties. If you're traveling with kids, you'll definitely want to check out this guide's "Kidstuff" chapter to learn about children's museums, aquariums, zoos, and other kid-oriented attractions and activities on the island.

Price Code

Many popular attractions on Long Island have some type of ticket or admission charge associated with them. In some cases, admission is free but you'll be required to pay for nearby parking, or for specific activities you choose to participate in at an attraction that offers free admission. For example, you can visit the grounds of the famous lighthouse on Montauk Point for free, but there's a $6 parking fee on weekends, plus an admission fee if you choose to climb to the top of the lighthouse.

The following price code provides a general guideline for what you can expect to pay per person to experience the specific attractions highlighted in this chapter. When purchasing tickets for any attraction, be sure to ask about discounted rates for kids, students, seniors, and military personnel.

$. . . . . Under $5 per person
$$ . . . . $5 to $8 per person
$$$ . . . . $9 to $15 per person
$$$$ . . . . . More than $15 per person

NASSAU COUNTY

AFRICAN AMERICAN MUSEUM OF NASSAU COUNTY FREE
110 North Franklin St., Hempstead
(516) 572-0730
http://aamoflongisland.org

This 6,000-square foot museum, which opened in 1970, traces the history of African Americans on Long Island, and is the only one of its kind in the area. Some of the exhibits come from the Smithsonian Institute. One of the more recent exhibits showcased prominent living or recently deceased African Americans who have earned national or international fame or recognition for their accomplishments in a wide range of areas—from sports and music to art and industry.

The goal of this museum is to foster a better understanding of the contribution and influence the local African-American population has had, and continues to have, on American culture. In addition to its exhibits, the African-American Museum regularly hosts lectures and workshops covering a wide range of topics. It is open Tues through Sat from 10 a.m. until 5 p.m.

AMERICAN MERCHANT MARINE MUSEUM AT THE UNITED STATES MERCHANT MARINE ACADEMY $$
300 Steamboat Rd., Kings Point
(516) 773-5515
www.usmma.edu/about/museum/default.htm

Housed within the campus of the U.S. Merchant Marine Academy, this museum features 14 galleries that showcase the evolution of American shipping since the Civil War. On display here are a wide range of scale ship models and nautical artifacts, along with marine-related artwork that tell the story of how the U.S. Merchant Marine has contributed and continues to contribute to America's entire shipping industry, as well as to the military.

A few of the artifacts on permanent display here include the ship's wheel from the USS *Constitution,* a collection of ancient navigational tools used aboard ships prior to the computer and digital age, a collection of fine china used aboard famous ships, and the Japanese surrender sword from World War II that was given to the museum by General Douglas MacArthur. There's also a display created in memory of the 142 U.S. Merchant Marine Academy cadets who died in the line of duty during World War II. The museum is closed in July, on holidays, and on weekends during semester breaks.

BAYVILLE ADVENTURE PARK $$$
8 Bayville Ave., Bayville
(516) 624-RIDE
www.bayvilleadventurepark.com

Open throughout the summer and on select dates in the spring and fall, this family-friendly amusement park features a minigolf course, bumper boats, rock climbing, and an arcade, plus a fun house, ice-cream parlor, skating, and a train ride. It's a great place to bring kids, but also a fun date activity for teens and adults. This park is famous for its Halloween activities and events in Oct, when the park transforms into "Bayville Scream Park."

CAPITAL ONE BANK THEATRE
960 Brush Hollow Rd., Westbury
(516) 334-0800
www.capitalonetheatre.com

This large theater, with a 3,000-seat capacity, hosts a wide range of concerts and shows throughout the year. The theater attracts big-name recording artists and comedians. In 2010, for example, some of the events taking place here include performances by Bill Maher, Kevin Hart, America, Jackie Mason, Kenny Loggins, Don Rickles, Joan Rivers, Gladys Knight, and Ringo Star. The theater is also host to the annual Long Island Comedy Fest in Apr. Visit the Web site for a complete, up-to-date listing of shows and events held here.

CLARK BOTANIC GARDEN FREE
193 I. U. Willets Rd., Alberton
(516) 484-8600
www.clarkbotanic.org

People of all ages will enjoy this 12-acre "living museum," which features lush gardens showcasing more than 1,000 kinds of trees, shrubs, plants, and flowers. There's a gorgeous rose garden, wildflower garden, dwarf evergreen exhibit, and many other outdoor exhibits which evolve throughout the seasons. The gardens are open year-round, 10 a.m. to 4 p.m., seven days a week during the spring, summer, and fall months. In the winter, it's closed on weekends. Within the garden's complex, you'll find a lovely gift shop. Admission is free, but donations are appreciated.

COLD SPRING HARBOR FISH HATCHERY & AQUARIUM $
Rte. 25A and Rte. 108, Cold Spring Harbor (on the Nassau/Suffolk border)
(516) 692-6768
www.cshfha.org

This fish hatchery opened in 1883, when the very first brown trout were imported to the United States. Today it serves as a museum and environmental education complex which offers demonstrations of how hatcheries operate. The aquarium houses the largest collection of native freshwater fish, reptiles, and amphibians in the region. The admission fee is very reasonable.

Open year-round, this is a fun place for kids and teens to visit, as well as an educational attraction for adults. During June, July, and Aug, the hatchery and aquarium is open weekdays from 10 a.m. to 5 p.m. and on weekends from 10 a.m. to 6 p.m. Throughout the rest of the year, hours of operation are reduced.

CRADLE OF AVIATION MUSEUM $$$
Charles Lindbergh Blvd., Garden City
(516) 572-4111
www.cradleofaviation.org

Visitors to this museum will see more than 70 different aircraft and spacecraft from throughout aviation history on display, including Charles Lindbergh's "Jenny." In addition to the airplanes themselves, you'll find one of the largest and most technologically advanced IMAX theaters here. The museum is open Tues through Sun from 9:30 a.m. to 5 p.m. The on-site snack shop, called the Red Planet Cafe, is open from 10 a.m. to 4 p.m., while the IMAX theater is open seven days a week. Showtimes vary throughout the day, but most movies run between 40 and 50 minutes. Admission to the museum is $9 per adult and $8 per child. For IMAX movies, the admission is $8.50 per adult and $6.50 per child for a "classic" movie, and $13.50 per adult and $11.50 per child for a "Hollywood blockbuster."

HOLOCAUST MEMORIAL & TOLERANCE CENTER OF NASSAU COUNTY FREE
100 Crescent Beach Rd., Glen Cove
(516) 571-8040
www.holocaust-nassau.org

This impressive museum offers an emotional and educational look at World War II and the Holocaust, and invites visitors to participate in age-appropriate seminars, lectures, and workshops that are designed to help develop a true understanding related to the causes and results of these tragic events. The exhibits are housed within the 20-acre Welwyn Preserve, which also showcases art and photo exhibits that change throughout the year.

NASSAU COUNTY FIREFIGHTERS MUSEUM & EDUCATION CENTER $
1 Davis Ave., Garden City
(516) 572-4177
www.ncfiremuseum.com

Within this museum you'll find firefighting equipment from throughout the history of Long Island's fire departments. The objective of the museum is to provide interactive displays that will interest people of all ages about the proud traditions upheld by Long Island's local fire departments and their accomplishments when it comes to saving lives. Some of the exhibits are also educational and focus on the importance of testing and using smoke alarms, and what someone should do if he or she is caught in an actual fire. Visitors can also learn about the volunteer opportunities that may be open to them at their local fire department.

The museum is open Tues through Sun from 10 a.m. until 5 p.m., except for July to mid-Aug, when it's open seven days a week. The Firefighters Museum is part of Long Island's "Museum Row," which also includes the Cradle of Aviation Museum, an IMAX theater, and the Long Island Children's Museum.

NASSAU COUNTY MUSEUM OF ART $$–$$$
1 Museum Dr., Roslyn Harbor
(516) 484-9773
www.nassaumuseum.com

Here you'll find several museums in this one 145-acre complex. Within the restored neoclassical-style mansion are 10 unique galleries featuring exhibits that change throughout the year. There's also the MiniArt Museum for Children offering family-friendly interactive exhibits. Outside the museum is an extensive and lovely sculpture gallery, featuring more than 50 sculptures set in nicely landscaped surroundings. The main museum within the Arnold & Joan Saltzman Fine Art Building is open Tues through Sun from 11 a.m. to 4:45 p.m. The children's MiniArt Museum is open Tues through Sun from noon to 4:30 p.m. Daily docent-led tours are available at specific times throughout the afternoon at no extra cost. The museum's cafe is open from noon until 4 p.m. on days the museum is open.

NASSAU COUNTY NATURE PRESERVES FREE

Located throughout Nassau County are a handful of nature preserves that are open to the public. Some are ideal for taking nature walks or bike rides along predefined paths, while others host a wide range of free concerts, programs, and special events throughout the year. The following is a partial listing of these nature preserves:

Barbara Johnson Park & Preserve: Shore Rd. and Central Dr., Port Washington (5 acres)

Brookside Preserve: Brookside Ave., Freeport (22 acres)

Leeds Pond Preserve: Plandome Manor (35 acres), (516) 627-9400

Massapequa Preserve: Massapequa (423 acres), (516) 571-7443

Meroke Preserve: Orange St. and Farmers Ave., Bellmore (25 acres)

Mill Pond Preserve: Merrick Rd., Wantagh (54 acres)

Muttontown Preserve: East Norwich (550 acres), (516) 571-8500

Stillwell Woods Preserve: South Woods Rd., Syosset (270 acres)

Tackapausha Preserve: Seaford (84 acres), (516) 571-7443

Tanglewood Park & Preserve: Lakeview (11 acres), (516) 764-0045

Tiffany Creek Preserve: Oyster Bay (197 acres), (516) 571-8500

Welwyn Preserve: Crescent Beach Rd. and New Woods Rd., Glen Cove (204 acres)

William Cullen Bryant Preserve: Roslyn Harbor (141 acres), (516) 484-9337

i Within Nassau County alone there are more than 36 state and county parks, most of which are open throughout the year. The state parks offer free admission; however, a parking fee may apply.

OLD WESTBURY GARDENS $$

71 Old Westbury Rd., Old Westbury

(516) 333-0048

www.oldwestburygardens.org

Old Westbury Gardens is situated on the former Georgian mansion estate of financier-sportsman John S. Phipps. While the mansion, built in 1906, is filled with English antiques, the 160 acres of grounds include formal gardens, woodlands, and ponds that visitors can explore. Hours and days of operation vary throughout the year. If the weather is nice, plan on spending several hours exploring the mansion and grounds. There's a gift shop and cafe on the premises.

SADDLE ROCK GRIST MILL FREE

Grist Mill Ln., Saddle Rock

(516) 571-7900

www.saddlerock.org/gristmillbig.html

This historic gristmill, built in 1702, is one of the few that still operate, and one of the oldest in America. Free tours are offered on Sun between May and Oct from 1 to 5 p.m. You'll find several gristmills available for touring throughout Long Island, including the Roslyn Grist Mill (1384 Old Northern Blvd., Roslyn), which dates back to 1735.

SCIENCE MUSEUM OF LONG ISLAND $$–$$$

1526 North Plandome Rd., Manhasset

(516) 627-9400

www.smli.org

This is a family-friendly "hands-on workshop museum" and activity center that features an ongoing series of events throughout the year. Many of the special events are kid-oriented, though there's plenty for parents to experience here as well. Instead of focusing on exhibits, guests participate in seminars, workshops, and activities that focus on various aspects of science. Some are educational, while other activities are purely entertainment-oriented, but with a science-related twist.

For preschoolers, there's an ongoing year-round nursery program, while special activities are hosted here almost daily for older kids during school vacation periods and throughout the summer. During the school year, for elementary school–age students, there's an afterschool workshop on weekdays from 4 to 5 p.m.

WANTAGH RAILROAD MUSEUM **FREE**
1700 Wantagh Ave., Wantagh
(516) 826-8767
www.wantagh.li/museum
Open between Apr and Oct, this seasonal museum is housed within the old Wantagh post office and features a fully restored, early 20th-century Long Island Railroad station and parlor car, along with other historic train memorabilia. The railroad station that this museum focuses around was originally built in 1885. In 1966 it was moved to its current location and restored to how it looked in 1904. Historical photographs showcasing life in turn-of-the-century Wantagh, along with a handful of railroad artifacts, are on display. This is a relatively small museum that most people can fully experience within a one- or two-hour visit.

SUFFOLK COUNTY

Suffolk County is home to exciting and popular places like the Hamptons, Montauk, and Fire Island, as well as Long Island's wine country (see the "Wine Country" chapter). With so much to see, do, and experience in this region, it's no wonder people opt to spend their summers here year after year.

Following are some of the more popular or unique tourist attractions worth experiencing when visiting Suffolk County. Keep in mind that some of these attractions are seasonal or have reduced hours of operation during off-peak travel periods.

ADVENTURELAND AMUSEMENT PARK **$$$**
2245 Broadhollow Rd. (Rte. 110), Farmingdale
(631) 694-6868
www.adventureland.us/themepark
Since 1962 Adventureland has been one of the island's most popular family-friendly attractions. It combines theme park rides with shops and dining to create a fun-filled, carnival-like atmosphere. Some of the major rides include a roller coaster, log flume, Ferris wheel, bumper cars, and a haunted house. There are also plenty of kiddy rides, plus arcade games and classic pinball. Adventureland is open between Apr and Nov; hours vary throughout the seasons. Guests can pay per ride or purchase one of two "Pay One Price" packages: One offers unlimited rides during a single day from the park's opening until 7 p.m., and the other is offered from 4 p.m. until closing.

ATLANTIS MARINE WORLD **$$$**
431 East Main St., Riverhead
(631) 208-9200
www.atlantismarineworld.com
Open all year long, this is Long Island's largest and most impressive indoor/outdoor aquarium. Plan on spending between a half day and a full day here, especially if you're visiting with kids. On display are hundreds of animals, ranging from penguins to sharks, which are showcased in more than a dozen impressive exhibits. Some of the other animals you'll see within the indoor displays are electric eels, jellyfish, puffer fish, sea horses, and a giant pacific octopus. Some of the outdoor exhibits include a massive koi pond, a sea lion exhibit, and seals. For kids, there are also a handful of interactive exhibits.

Beyond the experience you can have here as a basic guest, the aquarium hosts a variety of separate programs for kids, teens, and adults (for an additional fee) that offer a behind-the-scenes look at the aquarium and the animals that live here. For example, guests can participate in a shark dive in the aquarium's impressive 120,000-gallon shark tank, or go snorkeling with the stingrays.

With the purchase of a full-price adult ticket, a child can receive a 50 percent discount if you download a coupon from the aquarium's Web site.

BAYARD CUTTING ARBORETUM **$**
Montauk Hwy., Oakdale
(631) 581-1002
http://bayardcuttingarboretum.com
This 690-acre estate includes an English Tudor–style mansion that is open to the public, and a lovely arboretum that was started in 1887. It

features many original plantings, as well as some of the largest and oldest trees in the region. On the premises is a cafe and gift shop. Throughout the year a variety of special programs are hosted at the Arboretum, most conducted by the Bayard Cutting Arboretum Horticultural Society, a volunteer organization based at the Arboretum. Visit www.bcahs.net for a schedule of activities and events. The annual Sunday Concert Series is also hosted here, which is organized by the Islip Arts Council (www.islipartscouncil.org).

From Nov 1 through Apr 3, hours of operation are 10 a.m. to 4 p.m.; Apr 4 through Oct 31, hours are 10 a.m. to 5 p.m. The entrance fee is $6 per vehicle, but this fee is only collected Apr 4 through Oct 31.

DOLAN DNA LEARNING CENTER $
334 Main St. (Rte. 25A), Cold Spring Harbor
(631) 367-5170
www.dnalc.org

Get the inside scoop on Long Island's history in just 28 minutes at the Dolan DNA Learning Center. Here you can experience a multimedia, surround-sound presentation that offers a look at Long Island from the Ice Age to the late 20th century. Another presentation hosted here on an ongoing basis is *DNA: The Secret of Life,* a 32-minute movie that combines animation and special effects to educate viewers about how DNA was discovered, and how its discovery has changed medicine as well as our understanding of biology and genetics.

These presentations are just two of the many exhibits, programs, and hands-on activities offered at this unique science center, which was designed mainly to teach visitors about molecular genetics research and the work being done at the Cold Spring Harbor Laboratory. In addition to the exhibits, the learning center hosts ongoing hands-on workshops for people of all ages. Many of the rotating exhibits displayed at the Donal DNA Learning Center were created in conjunction with, or supplied by, the Smithsonian Institute.

The Dolan DNA Learning Center is open to the public Mon through Fri from 10 a.m. to 4 p.m. With a few exceptions throughout the year, it is closed on Sat and Sun. A visit to this center is more suitable for teens and adults, rather than children.

FIRE ISLAND LIGHTHOUSE $–$$
4640 Captree Island, Captree Island
(631) 661-4876
www.fireislandlighthouse.com

Built in 1826, the Fire Island Lighthouse is one of the handful of extremely popular lighthouses on Long Island that thousands of tourists visit each year. This one was built to guide ships into New York Harbor. It now has an automated beacon that shines brightly some 74 feet above sea level. Tours of the lighthouse are available Apr to mid-Dec. Plus, guests are welcome to climb the 192 steps to the observation deck at the top. Hours of operation vary by season, but from July 1 to Labor Day, they are 9:30 a.m. to 6 p.m. daily.

i Special sunset and private tours of the Fire Island Lighthouse can be arranged for a minimum fee of $125 (for up to 10 people). Call (631) 661-4876 for reservations.

HALLOCKVILLE MUSEUM FARM $
6038 South Ave., Riverhead
(631) 298-5292
www.hallockville.com

This historic farm is on the National Register of Historic Places, and has been fully restored to replicate farm life in the period from 1880 to 1910. On display are period rooms, restored barns, a farmhouse and workshop from the 1930s, plus dozens of farm tools. The 28-acre farm preserves a total of 18 historic houses, barns, and outbuildings. Visitors are invited to tour the museum's buildings, gardens, and collections; experience real farming in the museum's fields; and see live farm animals, including cows, sheep, and chickens. Tours are offered Fri through Sun from 11 a.m. to 4 p.m. On the premises is a small gift shop that sells unique, handcrafted items, like birdhouses, pottery, and knitted and crocheted items. This is the site where the Annual Hal-

Fire Island

This island is a seasonal tourist and vacation destination unto itself that can only be reached by boat or ferry. However, if you're already staying on another part of Long Island, a visit to Fire Island makes for a fun and fascinating day trip.

On Fire Island you'll discover 17 unique waterfront communities, including Ocean Beach, which is the main shopping and commercial area of the island. Between Memorial Day and Labor Day, this island is packed with tourists and vacationers alike, who come to experience the beaches, historical sites, resorts, nightclubs, and bars that the island has become famous for.

In addition to the Fire Island Lighthouse (see the attraction listing on the previous page), another site you won't want to miss is the Sunken Forest (631-687-4750, www.nps.gov/fiis/planyourvisit/sunken-forest.htm). This lovely park and forest appears as if it's below sea level. As you explore the forest by following the trails, they'll drop down the back side of the secondary dune into a canopy of trees, which creates a very unusual and beautiful effect.

While people from all walks of life visit Fire Island, the Cherry Grove and the Pines areas, for example, are known as popular gay-friendly vacation destinations, although everyone is welcome.

What's unique about Fire Island is that no passenger vehicles are allowed. So, you'll need to rely on your feet, a bicycle, a scooter, or public transportation to navigate your way around. Once you reach the island, anything you might need can be purchased at the independently owned stores and boutiques. There's no Wal-Mart here.

If you're planning to stay for a night, weekend, or a week, you'll find a wide range of small inns and B&Bs available. For longer stays, consider renting a house through an agency or broker, such as Fire Island Real Estate (631-583-5100, www.fireislandrealestate.com).

To reach Fire Island, you'll need to take a private boat or hop aboard one of the ferry services that operate throughout the year, such as Fire Island Ferries (631-655-3600, www.fireisland ferries.com), Sayville Ferry Service, Inc. (631-589-0810, www.sayvilleferry.com), or Fire Island Davis Park Ferry (631-475-1665, www.davisparkferry.com).

lockville Fall Festival and Craft Fair is held in early Oct. Visit www.hallockville.com/fall_festival.html for details.

i When visiting Long Island's South Fork, don't miss Montauk, definitely a wonderful and unique place to explore—for a day, week, month, or the entire summer. To learn more about Montauk, contact the Montauk Chamber of Commerce at (631) 668-2428 or go to www.montaukchamber .com.

MONTAUK POINT LIGHTHOUSE $–$$
2000 Montauk Hwy., Montauk
(631) 668-2544
www.montauklighthouse.com

The Montauk Point Lighthouse, located at the extreme tip of Long Island, was built in 1796 and is the oldest lighthouse in New York State. It was built at the request of President George Washington, and to this day is one of the most spectacular sights on Long Island. Visitors can climb to the top of this lighthouse by trekking up a 137-step spiral staircase in order to experience a breathtaking 360-degree view from the observation tower. Tours are offered between Mar and Dec. Adjacent to the lighthouse is a cafe and gift shop. There is an admission fee to enter the lighthouse, as well as a parking charge on weekends, but visitors can roam the grounds for free. During the holiday season the lighthouse is illuminated with thousands of lights, and special events are held on the premises.

i Another historic lighthouse in Suffolk County is the Huntington Harbor Lighthouse, built in 1912. It's located at the entrance to Lloyd Harbor and Huntington Harbor, several hundred feet offshore. The 42-foot-tall lighthouse is open to the public between May and Oct. For details, call (631) 421-1985 or visit www.huntingtonlighthouse.org.

OLD HOOK MILL $

North Main St., East Hampton
(631) 324-0713

The mill itself is open to the public during the summer, but the grounds are accessible throughout the year. The mill, which is a large windmill design constructed primarily of wood, was built in 1806 and is still in working condition. This particular mill remained in full use until 1908. Using wind energy, it was used to grind grain into flour. The windmill technology, however, became obsolete in the 20th century. The Old Hook Mill is located within a park near the center of East Hampton (at the intersection between Rte. 27 and East Main St.). This is one of 11 historic mills still standing on Long Island, and just one of several free historic sites that visitors can experience during a visit to East Hampton.

For the locations of other mills still standing on Long Island, visit www.discoverlongisland.com/pr_detail.cfm/ID/65/group_ID/6. Many of these mills offer incredible photo opportunities, as the structures themselves are massive and expertly constructed works of art (that also happened to be extremely useful in their day).

SECOND HOUSE MUSEUM $

Montauk Hwy., 0.5 mile west of Montauk
(631) 668-5340

Operated by the Montauk Historical Society, this house was built for the East Hampton shepherds in 1746 and is the most historic building in Montauk. It was literally the second house built in this region, hence its name. These days, in addition to being a museum, a variety of events are held here throughout the summer, including craft fairs. Also in the area and open to the public are the First House and Third House, both offering a look into Montauk's past.

i To reach Shelter Island, you'll need to take the Shelter Island Ferry. For the South Ferry, call (631) 749-1200 or visit www.southferry.com. For the North Ferry, call (631) 749-0139 or visit www.northferry.com. The one-way fare is under $10 per car with a single driver, and a same-day round-trip ticket is under $15. (There is an additional fee for extra passengers within each vehicle beyond the driver.)

SKY DIVE LONG ISLAND $$$

4062 Grumman Blvd. (LIE exit 69 North), Calverton
(631) 208-3900
www.skydivelongisland.com

If you're looking for the thrill of a lifetime, or just want to get your head out of the clouds for a bit, experience a 13,500-foot skydive. This company offers all the equipment and instruction needed for first-timers over the age of 18. Sky Dive Long Island operates seven days a week; reservations are required. For a first-time jumper, plan on spending $225 for the complete tandem skydive experience.

SPLISH SPLASH ISLAND $$$

2549 Splish Splash Dr., Calverton
(631) 727-3600
www.splishsplashlongisland.com

Encompassing 96 acres, this is one of the region's largest and most exciting water parks. It's open seasonally (late May through early Sept) and

Shelter Island

Located between Long Island's North and South Forks, Shelter Island is only accessible by taking a short (10-minute) ferryboat ride from either Greenport (on North Fork) or North Haven (on South Fork). This historic island provides a traditional, New England maritime atmosphere and offers some of the nicest beaches on or near Long Island. As Shelter Island is very much a summer resort community, some people opt to vacation here for a weekend, week, month, or the entire summer. However, it's also a popular destination for a day trip.

On the island you'll find lovely inns and lodges, plus unique boutiques and one-of-a-kind shops and fine-dining restaurants. Plenty of land- and water-based sports and activities are also offered—from golf and tennis to swimming and boating in the island's protected harbors. One highlight of this island is that it's not overly commercialized or developed. In fact, more than 2,039 acres are home to the Mashomack Nature Preserve (631-749-1001), which offers tours, hiking, and a wide range of other outdoor activities.

While Shelter Island is busiest during the summer season, even at its peak it offers a laid-back, quiet, and unhurried atmosphere that many tourists appreciate. For more information about Shelter Island as a day trip or as a vacation destination unto itself, contact the Shelter Island Chamber of Commerce at (631) 749-0399 or visit www.shelter-island.org.

Numerous special events are held on Shelter Island throughout the year, including a fireworks celebration in July at Crescent Beach, an Oktoberfest celebration in mid-Oct, and a holiday tree lighting in early Dec.

offers over a dozen water-based "thrill" rides and slides suitable for teens and adults. One of the park's most recent additions is Dr. VonDark's Tunnel of Terror, which features a scary 40-foot drop. Land-based attractions at Splish Splash Island include the *Close Encounters of the Bird Kind* tropical parrot show, which is presented several times daily (11 a.m., 1 p.m., 3 p.m., and 5 p.m.) between mid-June and early Sept. Daily ticket prices are $36.99 per adult and $27.99 per child; however, if you'll be staying in the area, an annual pass, priced at $69.99 per person, offers a much better deal. Tickets can be purchased online or at the park's ticket counter. Especially on a hot and sunny day, this is an exciting alternative to the beach that kids, teens, and adults alike will enjoy.

ST. JAMES GENERAL STORE **FREE**
Moriches Rd., St. James
(631) 854-3740

Open to the public as a retail establishment since 1857, this general store is a National Historic Landmark and a fun place to shop. Here you'll find a wide range of 19th-century-style goods, from candies and preserves to crafts, gifts, and home goods. The store is open year-round and offers ongoing interpretive programs, including craft demonstrations and special events every weekend. The store also hosts quarterly festivals and holiday celebrations—all focusing on the turn-of-the-century period.

i In Suffolk County alone, between Huntington and Montauk, there are more than 46,000 acres of parks, campgrounds, golf courses, historic sites, marinas, and beaches. Many of these locations offer activities, special events, and unique programs for visitors. To learn more, visit www.suffolkcountyny.gov or call (631) 854-4949.

Suffolk County Getaways

For New Yorkers and New Englanders, Suffolk County is an extremely popular place to experience a weekend getaway. While Suffolk County is part of New York State, its atmosphere and surroundings are vastly different from Manhattan, making it feel like you're in another part of the country altogether. The activities and attractions highlighted within this chapter are just a small sampling of what's offered, particularly in the spring, summer, and fall.

Many vacationers visit Long Island for its beaches. Some of the public beaches within Suffolk County include:

- **Crescent Beach:** This lovely beach is situated on Shire Rd., off of West Neck Rd. on Southold Bay. It offers swimming, sunbathing, a snack shop, restrooms (open 8:30 a.m. to 8:30 p.m.), and picnic tables.
- **Goldsmith Inlet Beach:** Situated at the end of Mill Rd. in Peconic, this beach offers swimming and sunbathing, but no lifeguards.
- **Goose Creek Beach:** Located off of North Bayview Rd. in Southold, this beach offers swimming, a playground, restrooms, and seasonal lifeguards.
- **Iron Pier Beach:** This is a full-service beach on Pier Rd. in Jamesport, offering swimming, a boat ramp, restrooms, a playground, a snack shop, and plenty of space to sunbathe.
- **Kenney's Beach:** Also located in Southold, on Kenney Rd., this beach offers swimming, sunbathing, restrooms, and seasonal lifeguards. McCabe's Beach (located on North Sea Rd.) and Southold Town Beach (located along Rte. 48) are two other popular Southold beaches.
- **Montauk Town Beach:** Located at the end of South Edison St., this is one of two town beaches and one of six public beaches in Montauk. Restaurants and shops are within walking distance, and nearby parking is available. Lifeguards are on duty during the peak season.
- **New Suffolk Beach:** In New Suffolk, this beach can be found on Jackson St. It offers lifeguards and beach attendants, plus a boat-launching ramp.
- **Reeves Beach:** Located off Park Rd. in Riverhead, this beach offers swimming, a boat ramp, and restrooms.
- **Riverhead Town Beach:** Open sunrise to 10 p.m. Call (631) 727-5744 for details.
- **Shelter Island Beach:** Lifeguards are stationed at this popular beach from mid-June to early Sept. Call (631) 749-1166 for details about what's offered here and how to obtain a visitor's permit.
- **South Jamesport Beach:** Located off of Peconic Bay Blvd. in South Jamesport, this beach offers a 3,000-foot shallow-water bay beach, outdoor showers, a playground, a picnic area, restrooms, tennis courts, and basketball courts.
- **Wades Beach:** Located on Shelter Island, this popular beach offers swimming, sunbathing, picnic tables, and restrooms.
- **Wading River Beach:** You'll find this beach at the end of Creek Rd. in Wading River. It offers restrooms, a playground, ample parking, and a gazebo.

SUFFOLK COUNTY VANDERBILT MUSEUM $$

180 Little Neck Rd., Centerport
(631) 854-5555
www.vanderbiltmuseum.org

The Vanderbilt Museum offers a unique combination of activities, attractions, and exhibits in one complex. There's a mansion, a marine and natural history museum, a state-of-the-art planetarium, and a gorgeous park. Exhibition and program themes focus on Long Island's Gold Coast era, and upon William K. Vanderbilt II's desire that his marine, natural history, and ethnographic collections promote appreciation and understanding of the marvelous diversity of life, other cultures, and scientific knowledge. The planetarium, for example, is one of the largest and most impressive in the country. It's housed within a 60-foot-tall sky theater and contains a projector that can display more than 11,300 stars.

The Vanderbilt Museum is open throughout the year, and can provide a half day or full day's worth of entertainment that's suitable for older children, teens, and adults.

TANGER OUTLET CENTER FREE

1770 West Main St., Riverhead
(631) 369-2732
www.tangeroutlets.com

This outdoor outlet mall features more than 70 brand-name shops—all offering excellent discounts on designer merchandise and clothing. Some of the stores you'll find here include Kate Spade, Calvin Klein, Juicy Couture, Giorgio Armani, Williams-Sonoma, J. Crew, and Nike. From Jan 1 to Mar 8, hours of operation are 10 a.m. to 7 p.m. Sun through Fri, and 9 a.m. to 9 p.m. on Sat. Between Mar 9 and Dec 31, hours are 9 a.m. to 9 p.m. Mon through Sat, and 10 a.m. to 8 p.m. on Sun. A second Tanger Outlet location is located at 152 The Arches Circle in Deer Park (631-242-0239). Parking at both locations is free.

VILLAGE BLACKSMITH SHOP FREE

Mitchell Park, Greenport
(631) 477-2100
www.eastendseaport.org

Built to replicate a traditional blacksmith shop, this attraction offers live demonstrations on weekends from 11 a.m. to 5 p.m., June through mid-Sept. While exploring the lovely village of Greenport, which features unique shops and restaurants right on the waterfront, be sure to visit the Greenport Carousel (631-477-2200), especially if you're visiting with kids. This is a historic carousel that operates between 10 a.m. and 9 p.m. throughout the summer.

WINE COUNTRY

Long Island's wine country is probably one of the best-kept secrets of this region. Many New Yorkers (the city dwellers, that is) don't even know about it. In recent years, however, a lot of emphasis has been put on literally growing the region and expanding the offerings. While some world-renowned wine experts have declared that Long Island wines are comparable or superior to anything you'll find in California, or even parts of Europe, others believe the wines produced on Long Island are still in need of refinement.

That being said, there is a large assortment of wineries and vineyards located in Long Island's wine country. Some are well-established and are producing top-quality and award-winning wines that are well worth experiencing. Other wineries and vineyards are still developing their niche. What few people realize about Long Island is that in recent years, it has become a leading source of fine wines. In fact, there are more than 50 wineries throughout the North Fork and South Fork regions of Long Island. Some of these wineries are very small and exclusive, but some have grown not just in size, but also in terms of worldwide recognition for producing the finest-quality wines. Since 1973, the area's vineyards have expanded to occupy more than 3,000 acres, and together they currently grow 38 different varieties of grapes.

For tourists visiting Long Island, taking wine tours and participating in the many year-round events that take place at the various wineries has become an extremely popular activity. Many wineries offer tastings and wine education and food-pairing classes, conduct free tours of their vineyards and manufacturing facilities, and feature live musical entertainment. In fact, a complete tourism industry has been born based on visits to these wineries.

Over a dozen bus and limo companies offer guided, daylong tours of the top wineries (which include wine tastings). Meanwhile, plenty of visitors opt to explore Long Island's wine country on their own, at their own pace. These self-guided tours can easily include an enjoyable picnic lunch on or near the various vineyards. It's also common to transform an interest or passion for wine into a weekend or weeklong vacation, which includes staying at one of the many upscale and cozy inns or B&Bs in the region.

In addition to being a weekend getaway destination for people from New York City, Nassau County, and throughout the Tri-State area, Long Island's wine country is also a popular location for honeymoons and a lovely place to host weddings due to the beautiful surroundings. Like the Hamptons, Long Island's wine country is mainly a seasonal destination, with the majority of people visiting and spending time here in the summer. However, the North Fork and South Fork region offers wine connoisseurs plenty of reasons to visit all year long.

i In this area of Long Island, there are very few traditional chain hotels. Most of the accommodations are small to midsize, one-of-a-kind, independently owned and operated inns, B&Bs, hotels, and resorts. Combining a tour of the wineries with a romantic stay at any of these establishments makes for a wonderful weekend getaway—especially if you're just driving in from New York City or taking a ferry from New England.

Wine Tours on Wheels

Because visiting the wineries typically involves wine tasting, one of the best ways to experience this region is to hire a chauffeured limousine, or take a group bus tour, so you can leave the driving to someone else.

Limo and tour companies that offer private or group guided tours of Long Island's wineries and vineyards include:

Hampton Jitney: (631) 283-4600, www.hamptonjitney.com

LI Vineyard Tours: (718) WINE-TOURS, www.LIVinyardTours.com

Long Island Wine Tours: (631) 924-3475, www.LongIslandWineTours.com

Metro Limousine Services: (516) 946-3868, www.metrolimousineservice.com

Red Carpet Limousine Ltd.: (631) 828-8464

Regal Limousines: (516) 596-6620, www.RegalNYLimo.com

Regency Tours of the Vineyards: (631) 543-2500, www.regencylimos.com

RJ's Limousines: (516) 221-3040, www.RJLimos.com

Vintage Tours: (631) 765-4689, www.vintagetour.com

As you explore Long Island's wine country, you will discover a nice selection of fine wines. However, in addition to the wine-tasting experience, simply visiting the various vineyards and wineries is a fun activity in and of itself, especially for adults. Participating in an organized wine tour will ensure you get to experience the best wineries and wines offered in the region. However, if you choose to venture off on your own, you can create your wine-tasting tour itinerary by contacting the area's wineries directly. Especially if the weather is nice, plan on spending at least 60 to 90 minutes or more per winery in order to explore the vineyards and grounds, participate in a tasting, and tour the production facilities. If special events or classes are taking place, or if you choose to relax and enjoy a picnic lunch or live entertainment on the premises, you can easily spend several hours at a single winery.

Keep in mind that the hours these wineries are open to the public vary by season. Hours are typically extended on weekends throughout the year. Also, some wineries are only open on weekends, particularly during off-peak seasons. In the summer months, many of the wineries are open seven days a week and offer ongoing activities, tastings, special events, and the opportunity to enjoy the grounds. Outdoor concerts, picnicking, and other events are commonplace at the mid-size to large wineries. The fall is harvest season, and a wide range of related activities are hosted at the wineries at that time. During the winter the crowds are greatly reduced, making it the perfect time for more serious wine connoisseurs to visit. In addition to participating in indoor wine tastings, you can enjoy more one-on-one time with the winery operators. In the springtime you'll be able to see the grape vines budding, which make the properties extra beautiful. No matter when you visit, if you find wines you enjoy, you'll have the opportunity to purchase and take home individual bottles, gift baskets, or cases.

i If you're visiting from Connecticut, Rhode Island, or Massachusetts, you can easily take the Cross Sound Ferry (631-323-2525, www.longislandferry.com) from New London, Connecticut, and in 80 minutes find yourself docking in Orient Point, which is at the edge of Long Island's wine country and the perfect place to start a wine-tasting tour.

> **A Note to Parents**
>
> During the warm-weather months, visiting a winery can be a fun family activity, as visitors are invited to enjoy the grounds and have picnics, while listening to live entertainment. However, the wineries themselves don't offer kid-oriented activities or supervision for children while parents are participating in wine tastings. In other words, for adults (over the legal drinking age of 21) to get the most out of the experience, leave the kids at home.

WINERIES AND VINEYARDS

All of the wineries on Long Island that are open to the public offer free parking and free access to their grounds, and do not charge an admission fee to visit. However, if you want to participate in a wine tasting, tour, class, or special event being hosted at the winery, a fee may apply. Likewise, if you participate in an organized private or group wine tour operated by a third party, such as a local charter bus or limousine company, a fee will apply. For first-time visitors to the wine country, this is the best way to experience the area for several reasons. For example, the tour operators choose a nice selection of vineyards to visit that offer various types of wines to enjoy. Plus, they do all of the driving, so you're free to consume all the alcohol you'd like. Each of the wineries sell their wine by the bottle or case to take home, in addition to gift baskets and/or other wine-themed gift items. Obviously, additional fees apply for your wine purchases.

Navigating your way between wineries and vineyards is very easy, since most of them are located close together, mainly in the North Fork area. However, there are a few wineries and vineyards in the South Fork area (close to the Hamptons) that are well worth visiting as well.

The following is a brief summary of what's offered at some of Long Island's most popular vineyards and wineries. Keep in mind that each winery and vineyard has its own specialty in terms of what's produced there. So, if you're planning your own tour and choosing which wineries and vineyards to visit, base your decision on the types of wines you enjoy drinking, as well as the activities offered at each location.

ACKERLY POND VINEYARDS

1375 Peconic Ln., Peconic
(631) 765-6861
www.ackerlypondvineyards.com

Founded in 1999, this vineyard offers a wine-tasting room and group tours of the production facilities (by appointment only). It consists of 81 planted acres and produces Chardonnay, Cabernet Franc, Cabernet Sauvignon, and Merlot.

BAITING HOLLOW FARM VINEYARD

2114 South Ave. (Rte. 48), Baiting Hollow
(631) 369-0100
www.baitinghollowfarmvineyard.com

Founded in 1997, this vineyard has 11 planted acres and offers a wine-tasting room, tours of its production facilities, and a lovely outdoor area. It also regularly hosts special events as well as private functions. Cabernet Franc, Cabernet Sauvignon, Merlot, and Riesling are produced here.

BEDELL CELLARS

36225 Main Rd. (Rte. 25), Cutchogue
(631) 734-7537
www.bedellcellars.com

This is one of the larger and more tourist-oriented vineyards in the region. It was founded in 1980 and is composed of 57 planted acres. In addition to beautifully landscaped public outdoor areas, you'll find a large wine-tasting room. Tours of the production facilities are also available. Chardonnay, Gewürztraminer, Riesling, Viognier, Cabernet Franc, Cabernet Sauvignon, Merlot, Petit Verdot, Syrah, and Malbec are among the wine varieties produced here.

A Visit to Bedell Cellars

There are many well-established wineries and vineyards on Long Island that create award-winning wines that are comparable to wines from California or Europe. However, not all of the wineries and vineyards on the island are open to the public or have tasting rooms, immaculately landscaped properties, and ongoing activities and events of interest to visitors. Bedell Cellars is one of the most popular vineyards in the region in terms of the wines it creates, and the tasting rooms and events offered on the property that are open to the public throughout the year.

Michael Lynne is the founder of Bedell Cellars. He is the former co-chairman and co-CEO of New Line Cinema and served as executive producer of the *Lord of the Rings* trilogy. When he took over the vineyard, Lynne hired a world-class winemaking team, led by consulting oenologist Pascal Marty (formerly of Chateau Mouton Rothschild), founding winemaker Kip Bedell, winemaker Kelly Urbanik, and industry veteran Dave Thompson, who serves as vineyard manager.

According to Amy Finno, a representative from Bedell Cellars, "Our facility is unmatched regionally for its sophistication. The new state-of-the-art winery was completed in 2005 and boasts custom-designed open-top fermenting tanks and a gravity-driven regime to minimize pumping and filtering. The tasting room is housed in a renovated potato barn that was originally built in 1919. It showcases an impressive collection of contemporary art on display for the public. An outdoor grand tasting pavilion was constructed from nearly 4,000 square feet of mahogany and offers visitors a sweeping view of hundreds of acres of vineyards and open farmland."

The tasting room at Bedell Cellars is open to the public year-around, seven days a week, from 11 a.m. until 5 p.m. Memorial Day through Halloween, the tasting room remains open until 6 p.m. It is closed on New Year's Day, Easter, Thanksgiving, and Christmas. While there is no admission charge to visit the vineyards or to explore or picnic on the grounds, like all local vineyards and wineries on Long Island, there is a small fee of between $8 and $12 per person to participate in wine tastings.

On weekends at noon and 3 p.m., a special two-hour VIP Tour and Tasting is offered at Bedell Cellars for $35 per person. This tour is limited to groups of 15 people, so it's important to register early. On weekdays, this tour is available to private groups of at least eight people by appointment only. Also on weekends at noon and 3 p.m., the winery offers a more exclusive Proprietor's Garden VIP Tour and Tasting, which is limited to six people and costs $50 per person. Tastings are hosted in a private garden, which is closed to the general public. Reservations for the VIP Tour and Tasting or Proprietor's Garden VIP Tour and Tasting should be made at least five days in advance by calling (631) 734-7537.

"One of the highlights we offer throughout the summer is free live musical entertainment on weekends. At no cost, people can relax, enjoy our property, and listen to music. At the same time, for a small fee, they can taste our wines," explained Finno.

In addition to the tasting rooms, Bedell Cellars sells snacks and gourmet food items that nicely complement the wines. "All of the wine we offer are made and bottled entirely on the premises. We are well-known for our blended Merlot, but offer at least 16 different vintages," added Finno.

"I think the wineries on Long Island continue to be a well-kept secret in terms of the wines we offer, as well as the experience we offer to our guests. The best resource for learning about the wines being made in this region, and how the maritime climate positively impacts our ability to create world-class wines, is to contact the Long Island Wine Counsel [631-369-5887, www.liwines.com]," said Finno.

While many of the Long Island wineries and vineyards are open throughout the year, Finno believes the best time to visit is the summer or fall months. She added, "Between June and October there is a lot happening on Long Island, and the wineries and vineyards are busy with all sorts of special events, in addition to our day-to-day activities."

There are many different ways to experience Long Island's wineries and vineyards, from driving your own car and stopping at the vineyards of your choice, to participating in organized bus or group tours. To add a bit of luxury and extravagance to the experience, many people opt to hire a chauffeured limousine for an afternoon or full day (or two) in order to tour the various vineyards at their own pace, without having to drive. Especially on the weekends, the parking lots of each winery and vineyard will often contain more limos than a Hollywood red carpet event.

"The best way to experience Long Island's wine country is to visit several different wineries that make the type of wine you personally enjoy the most. I recommend participating in one of the popular group tours. This is a cost-effective way to visit multiple wineries and vineyards, but not have to worry about driving after having sampled the delicious wines," said Finno, who is also a fan of the popular, multiday wine camps that are held throughout the year.

"Before getting to the wine country, I recommend doing research on the Web to learn about the area's different vineyards. Preselect a handful of vineyards you'd like to visit, and then figure out whether you want to drive yourself, rent a limo, or participate in an organized group tour," explained Finno. "Choose the places you'll visit based on your personal taste in wines. Not all of the vineyards offer the same types or quality of wine. Look at what each vineyard offers. For example, at Bedell Cellars, we specialize in blended wines."

If you'll be spending one or more days sampling wines, Finno recommends pairing wines with food and cheeses. This helps to clear your pallet between tastings, and depending on the food, will help heighten each wine's unique taste.

While most of the vineyards allow children on their properties, few are set up to entertain young people while their parents are participating in wine tastings. A picnic, for example, might be a suitable family activity; however, for parents looking to indulge in the wine tastings, classes, and tours, it's best to find alternate activities for your children.

"I don't think people realize how beautiful it is to spend the day visiting wineries. People are welcome to walk around the vineyards, and enjoy the grounds at many of the wineries and vineyards, which are especially breathtaking when the weather is nice.

"If you want to do more than just sip some wine and move on, the experience takes a lot longer than most people anticipate. Allow ample time to enjoy your surroundings. Plan a picnic lunch, for example. You can bring your own food and blanket, or purchase food and snacks at some of the wineries, and don't forget your camera," concluded Finno.

CASTELLO DI BORGHESE VINEYARD & WINERY
17150 Sound Ave. (Rte. 48) at Alvah's Ln., Cutchogue
(631) 734-5111
www.borghesevineyard.com
Since 1973 this vineyard has been producing Chardonnay, Riesling, Sauvignon Blanc, Cabernet Franc, Merlot, and Pinot Noir from its production facility and 85 planted acres of vines. It's one of the oldest wineries in the region. A wine-tasting room, tours, and public outdoor areas are available, and special events are held here throughout the year.

CHANNING DAUGHTERS WINERY
1927 Scuttlehole Rd., Bridgehampton
(631) 537-7224
www.channingdaughters.com
On its 25 planted acres, grapes used to produce Chardonnay, Gewürztraminer, Pinot Bianco, Pinot Grigio, Sauvignon Blanc, Semillon, Tocai Friulano, Viognier, Blaufrankisch, Cabernet Franc, Cabernet Sauvignon, Merlot, Pinot Noir, and Syrah are grown. This vineyard was founded in 1997. A wine-tasting room, public outdoor areas, and tours are offered.

CLOVIS POINT WINES
1935 Main Rd. (Rte. 25), Jamesport
(631) 722-4222
www.clovispointwines.com
On its 20 planted acres, Clovis Point Wines produces Chardonnay, Cabernet Franc, Merlot, and Syrah. It was founded in 2001 and offers a wine-tasting room, public outdoor areas, tours, and special events.

COMTESSE THERESE
Union Ave./Rte. 25, Southhold
(631) 871-9194
www.comtessetherese.com
Established in 2000, this is a small vineyard that's open to the public by appointment only. On its 10 planted acres, grapes used to produce Pinot Grigio, Sauvignon Blanc, Cabernet Sauvignon, and Merlot are grown. Your best bet is to visit the Tasting Room (2885 Peconic Ln., Peconic; 631-765-6404; www.tastingroomli.com) to experience the wines produced here, unless you're visiting with a group and prearrange your visit.

Long Island Wine Press

Published twice a year, *Long Island Wine Press* is a free, full-color magazine that covers the entire Long Island wine region. The magazine includes a complete list of area wineries, plus details about each one, including how large each is and the type(s) of grapes that are grown on the premises. You'll also find a comprehensive price list for local wines and a list of local, national, and international awards the wines produced on Long Island have won. This is the official publication of the Long Island Wine Council. Copies are distributed at all of the wineries, hotels, inns, and visitor information centers in the area.

COREY CREEK VINEYARDS
45470 Main Rd. (Rte. 25), Southhold
(631) 765-4168
www.coreycreek.com
Established in 1993, this vineyard features 30 planted acres, plus a tasting room and outdoor public area. Chardonnay, Gewürztraminer, Cabernet Franc, Merlot, Sauvignon Blanc, and Viognier are produced here. Like many of the vineyards in the area, it's open daily year-round, but hours of operation vary by season.

CROTEAUX VINEYARD
1450 South Harbor Rd., Southhold
(631) 765-6099
www.croteaux.com
This too is a relatively small vineyard, utilizing just 10.5 planted acres. From the grapes grown here,

Sauvignon Blanc, Cabernet Franc, and Merlot are produced. A wine-tasting room and public outdoor area are available. This vineyard was established in 2003.

DILIBERTO WINERY
250 Manor Ln., Jamesport
(631) 722-3416
www.dilibertowinery.com
Operating on just four planted acres, Diliberto Winery was established in 1998 and produces Chardonnay, Cabernet Franc, Cabernet Sauvignon, and Merlot. A wine-tasting room, tours of its production facilities, and an outdoor public area are offered here.

DUCK WALK VINEYARDS NORTH
44535 Main Rd. (Rte. 25), Southhold
(631) 765-3500

DUCK WALK VINEYARDS SOUTH
231 Montauk Hwy. (Rte. 27), Water Mill
(631) 726-7555
www.duckwalk.com
Between its North and South locations, Duck Walk Vineyards is composed of 150 planted acres. Here you'll find lovely wine-tasting rooms, beautiful outdoor public areas, and tours of the production facilities. Chardonnay, Gewürztraminer, Pinot Grigio, Sauvignon Blanc, Semillon, Cabernet Sauvignon, Malbec, Merlot, Pinot Meunier, and Pinot Noir are among the wine varieties produced here.

THE GRAPES OF ROTH
Sag Harbor (call for address)
(631) 725-7999
www.thegrapesofroth.com
This is a small vineyard that was founded in 2001. It is open to the public by appointment only. Many of its wines, however, can be purchased from local wine merchants and are served at area restaurants.

HARBES FAMILY VINEYARD
715 South Ave. (Rte. 48), Mattituck
(631) 298-0700
www.harbesfamilyfarm.com
As another one of Long Island's smaller, family-owned-and-operated vineyards, this one encompasses just five planted acres and was established in 2003. It's known for its Chardonnay and Merlot. A wine-tasting room, tours, and outdoor public areas are offered here.

JAMESPORT VINEYARDS
1216 Main Rd. (Rte. 25), Jamesport
(631) 722-5256
www.jamresportwines.com
Chardonnay, Pinot Blanc, Riesling, Sauvignon Blanc, Semillon, Cabernet Franc, Cabernet Sauvignon, Malbec, Merlot, and Pinot Noir are among the varieties produced on this vineyard's 60 planted acres. It was established in 1981 and offers a wine-tasting room, tours, and public outdoor areas.

JASON'S VINEYARD
1785 Main Rd. (Rte. 25), Jamesport
(631) 926-8486
www.jasonsvineyard.com
Since 1997 Jason's Vineyard has been producing Chardonnay, Cabernet Franc, Cabernet Sauvignon, Malbec, and Merlot on its 20 planted acres. Here you'll find a cozy and elegant wine-tasting room and public outdoor areas. As with many of the region's wineries and vineyards, live entertainment and special events are hosted here throughout the year.

LAUREL LAKE VINEYARDS
3165 Main Rd. (Rte. 25), Laurel
(631) 298-1420
www.llwines.com
When visiting this vineyard's wine-tasting room or enjoying its outdoor public areas, you can taste the Chardonnay, Sauvignon Blanc, Merlot, Shiraz/Syrah, or Sangiovese produced on the vineyard's 24 planted acres. Laurel Lake Vineyards was founded in 1980.

LIEB FAMILY CELLARS
35 Cox Neck Rd., Mattituck
(631) 298-1942
www.liebcellars.com

Founded in 1992, the grapes used to produce Chardonnay, Pinot Blanc, Cabernet Franc, Cabernet Sauvignon, Malbec, Merlot, and Petit Verdot are grown here on the 50 planted acres. A wine-tasting room, tours, and outdoor public areas are among this family-owned-and-operated vineyard's offerings.

LOUGHLIN VINEYARDS

South Main St., Sayville
(631) 589-0027
www.loughlinvineyard.com

If you're coming from New York City, Loughlin Vineyards is the first vineyard you'll encounter as you enter Long Island's wine country. Occupying just six planted acres, it was founded in 1982 and yields about 1,000 cases of dry and sweet wines per year. A tasting room and outdoor public areas are offered. Cabernet, Chardonnay, and Merlot are among the wine varieties produced here.

i The majority of wineries on the North Fork can be found along Rte. 48 or Rte. 25. While the vineyards are technically located in different towns, they are really very close together, so you'll often find several vineyards by driving just a few miles along Rte. 48 or Rte. 25. The wineries on the South Fork, however, are spread out much more and are much fewer in number.

MACARI VINEYARDS & WINERY

150 Bergen Ave., Mattituck
(631) 734-7070
www.macariwines.com

Occupying more than 200 planted acres, Macari Vineyards & Winery is one of the largest in the region. It was established in 1994 and produces Chardonnay, Sauvignon Blanc, Viognier, Cabernet Franc, Cabernet Sauvignon, Malbec, Merlot, Petit Verdot, Pinot Noir, and Syrah. There's a lovely wine-tasting room and beautiful outdoor areas that visitors can explore.

MARTHA CLARA VINEYARDS

6025 South Ave. (Rt. 48), Riverhead
(631) 734-7070
www.macariwines.com

Also encompassing about 200 planted acres, Martha Clara Vineyards specializes in producing Chardonnay, Gewürztraminer, Riesling, Semillon, Viognier, Cabernet Franc, Cabernet Sauvignon, Merlot, and Syrah. Here you'll find a wine-tasting room, gorgeous outdoor areas, tours of the production facilities, and a wide range of special events.

MATTEBELLA VINEYARDS

46005 Main Rd. (Rte. 25), Southold
(888) 628-8329
www.mattebellavineyards.com

This vineyard is open to the public by appointment only, but you can taste the wines produced here at the Tasting Room (2885 Peconic Lane, Peconic; 631-765-6404; www.tastingroomli.com), plus order the wines at many local restaurants.

OLD FIELD VINEYARDS

59600 Main Rd. (Rte. 25), Southhold
(631) 765-0004
www.theoldfield.com

Located on 12 planted acres, Old Field Vineyards has limited hours when it's open to the public, particularly during the off-season. Chardonnay, Cabernet Franc, Merlot, and Pinot Noir are produced here. There's a small but lovely wine-tasting room and outdoor areas that are open to the public, plus visitors can participate in tours of the production facilities. Old Field Vineyards, like many of the smaller vineyards in the region, can be rented for private parties, wine tastings, or events.

ONE WOMAN WINES & VINEYARD

5195 Old North Rd., Southhold
(631) 765-1200
www.onewomanwines.com

Chardonnay, Gewürztraminer, Sauvignon Blanc, and Merlot are among the wines produced from the grapes grown on this vineyard's 16 planted acres. This vineyard is open to the public throughout the year Thurs through Mon only, usually between 9 a.m. and 6 p.m., but hours vary by season. Tours are available by appointment, but during business hours, there's a wine-tasting room and public outdoor areas for guests to enjoy.

OSPREY'S DOMINION VINEYARD
44075 Main Rd. (Rte. 25), Peconic
(631) 765-6188
www.ospreysdominion.com

Operating from its 90 planted acres since 1983, Osprey's Dominion Vineyard is known for its Chardonnay, Gewürztraminer, Pinot Gris, Riesling, Sauvignon Blanc, Cabernet Franc, Cabernet Sauvignon, Carmenere, Merlot, Petit Verdot, Pinot Noir Merlot, and Pinot Noir. Here you'll find a wine-tasting room, public outdoor areas, and production-facility tours. As with the majority of the larger vineyards in the region, special events and live entertainment are also presented on an ongoing basis. This winery is open year-round seven days a week, usually between 11 a.m. and 5 p.m.

PALMER VINEYARDS
5120 South Ave. (Rte. 48), Riverhead
(631) 722-9463
www.palmervineyards.com

Established in 1986 and occupying more than 125 planted acres, Palmer Vineyards has developed a reputation for its Chardonnay, Gewürztraminer, Pinot Blanc, Riesling, Sauvignon Blanc, Cabernet Franc, Cabernet Sauvignon, and Merlot. Guests can experience the wines for themselves in the tasting room, enjoy a picnic (and often live entertainment) on the public grounds, or partake in a tour of the production facilities. This is a family-owned-and-operated vineyard.

i Aside from participating in wine tastings at the actual vineyards, you can often order local wines by the glass or bottle from the many restaurants on Long Island, particularly those in Suffolk County.

PECONIC BAY WINERY
31320 Main Rd. (Rte. 25), Cutchogue
(631) 734-7361
www.peconicbaywinery.com

Situated on 200 planted acres, Peconic Bay Winery is one of the largest in the region. It was established in 1979. Among its offerings are Chardonnay, Riesling, Cabernet Franc, Cabernet Sauvignon, and Merlot. Enjoy a tour of the production facilities, relax and experience the wines in the tasting room, or explore the gorgeous outdoor areas. As you'd expect, if you visit on a weekend during the summer, this winery (along with most of the others) will be crowded.

PELLEGRINI VINEYARDS
23005 Main Rd. (Rte. 25), Cutchogue
(631) 734-4111
www.pellegrinivineyards.com

Chardonnay, Gewürztraminer, Sauvignon Blanc, Cabernet Franc, Cabernet Sauvignon, Merlot, and Petit Verdot are among the varieties produced using the grapes from the 70 planted acres at this vineyard. It was established in 1991 by Bob and Joyce Pellegrini, and offers a wine-tasting room, public outdoor areas, and tours of the production facilities. Special events and live music are presented here on a regular basis.

PINDAR VINEYARDS
37645 Main Rd. (Rte. 25), Peconic
(631) 734-6200
www.pindar.net

This is one of the largest and most established vineyards in the region. It opened in 1979, when Long Island's wine country was first becoming established, and now occupies more than 667 planted acres. Over 17 varieties of grapes are grown here, and the vineyard annually produces 70,000 cases of wine. More than a dozen different varieties are produced here, including Chardonnay, Riesling, and Gamay Beaujolais. You'll find a wine-tasting room, beautiful outdoor areas, and tours of the production facilities offered here, along with an extensive lineup of special events and live entertainment throughout the year. This vineyard has won numerous awards and medals for its wines.

PUGLIESE VINEYARDS
34515 Main Rd. (Rte. 25), Cutchogue
(631) 734-4957
www.pugliesevineyards.com

Utilizing 53 planted acres, Pugliese Vineyards produces Chardonnay, Gewürztraminer, Niagara, Pinot Grigio, Riesling, and Cabernet Franc in addition to a few other varieties. It was established in 1980 and is a family-owned-and-operated business. The wines produced here have won numerous awards. The wine-tasting room and outdoor public areas are open year-around, seven days a week, usually between 11 a.m. and 6 p.m. Tours of the production facilities are offered, as is live entertainment. If you purchase wines by the bottle here, you can have a special message hand painted on the bottle for an additional fee.

In addition to offering samples of the wines produced at each vineyard (served by the glass), many of the wineries sell cheese and crackers or other gourmet foods you can enjoy with the wines.

RAPHAEL WINE
29290 Main Rd. (Rte. 25), Peconic
(631) 765-1100
www.raphaelwine.com

Since 1996 Raphael Wine has been producing Sauvignon Blanc, Cabernet Franc, Cabernet Sauvignon, Malbec, Merlot, and Petit Verdot from the grapes grown on its 60 planted acres. Like all of the midsize wineries in the region, this one offers a wine-tasting room, beautiful outdoor areas that are open to the public, tours of the wine-production facilities, and live entertainment. Special events are also hosted here throughout the year. Reservations are required for the tours.

ROANOKE VINEYARDS
3543 Sound Ave. (Rte. 48), Riverhead
(631) 727-4161
www.roanokevineyards.com

Roanoke Vineyards is a smaller property that occupies just 10 planted acres in Long Island's wine country. It was founded in 2000 and specializes in Cabernet Franc, Cabernet Sauvignon, and Merlot. A wine-tasting room and public grounds are among the offerings for visitors. Roanoke Vineyards is one of the many vineyards and wineries in the region that sponsor a wine club. Members receive a variety of perks, including discounts on purchases and the opportunity to preview new wines before the general public.

SCAROLA VINEYARDS
56995 Main Rd. (Rte. 25), Southold
(631) 335-4199
www.scarolavineyards.com

Focusing mainly on producing Chardonnay and Merlot, this small vineyard operates on six planted acres and is only open to groups by appointment.

SHERWOOD HOUSE VINEYARDS
2600 Oregon Rd., Mattituck
(631) 298-1396
www.sherwoodhousevineyards.com

Operating from its 38 planted acres since 1996, Sherwood House Vineyards specializes in Chardonnay, Cabernet Franc, Cabernet Sauvignon, Merlot, and Petit Verdot. The small wine-tasting room and outdoor area is open to the public seven days a week year-round, usually between noon and 6 p.m.

No GPS? You can plot your wine-tasting route using a free downloadable and printable map of Long Island's wine country by visiting www.liwines.com/default.ihtml?page=mapanddirections.

SHINN ESTATE VINEYARDS
2000 Oregon Rd., Mattituck
(631) 804-0367
www.shinnestatevineyards.com

Another of the smaller vineyards in the region, Shinn Estate produces Pinot Blanc, Sauvignon Blanc, Cabernet Franc, Cabernet Sauvignon, Malbec, Merlot, and Petit Verdot from the grapes grown on its 22 planted acres. For $8.50 per person, the vineyard's owners host 20- to 30-minute walking tours of the vineyards and winemaking facilities, which end with a short wine-tasting. Reservations are required.

SPARKLING POINTE
39750 Country Road 48, Southhold
(631) 765-0200
www.sparklingpointe.com

Pinot Noir, Pinot Meunier, and Chardonnay are among the offerings of this relatively small winery

Adults Can Go to Camp, Too

While it's common for parents to ship their kids off to camp for part or all of the summer, the Long Island Wine Country Bed & Breakfast Group offers a different sort of camp experience—for adults only.

Each year, for three days per session, people over the age of 21 are invited to participate in Wine Camp. This camplike experience is nothing like a typical kids' camp, however. For starts, the package includes luxury accommodations at one of the area's premier B&Bs or inns, in addition to transportation between activities, extravagant breakfasts each morning, gourmet dining opportunities, and the chance to learn about and experience Long Island wines while interacting with some of the region's foremost wine experts and producers. Oh, and as a parting gift, participants take home a case of Long Island wines.

Participation in Wine Camp costs $899 per person, based on double occupancy. In 2010, for example, the four-day, three-night camp sessions are slated to be held Mar 4 through 7, Apr 15 through 18, June 3 through 6, and July 17 through 22.

On day one, participants in Wine Camp learn about the history of Long Island wine and discover why this region is ideal for growing wine grapes. The day of education ends with a gourmet dinner and wine tasting. (You'll experience wine tastings throughout each day of the camp.)

During day two, campers learn about the chemistry of winemaking, tour local wineries, and are taught about the differences between wood and steel in the winemaking process. A session about the art of blending and the opportunity for participants to create their own vintage is included.

As day three rolls around, participants will have the core knowledge needed to actually work on a vineyard for a few hours. During this experience, campers learn about sustainable vineyard management and how to maintain the perfect vineyard. The day ends with a workshop on food and wine pairing, plus a gourmet dinner. All lunches throughout the experience are served alfresco at the various vineyards, while breakfasts are enjoyed at the inn or B&B where you'll be staying.

For adults looking for a fun and educational way to enjoy a romantic weekend getaway on Long Island, or who want to quickly improve their knowledge of fine wine, participating in Wine Camp offers a unique and memorable experience.

For more details about Wine Camp, or to register, call (631) 495-9744. Groups are kept reasonable small, so it's important to register well in advance to reserve a spot during your desired camp dates.

and vineyard located on 12 planted acres in the heart of Long Island's wine country. This vineyard was established in 2003 and offers a wine-tasting room, outdoor areas, tours, and other activities for its visitors. Approximately 3,000 cases per year are produced here. The wine-tasting room is spacious, bright, and comfortable, and like most of the wineries in the region, the outdoor landscaping is immaculate and breathtakingly beautiful.

THE TASTING ROOM
2885 Peconic Ln., Peconic
(631) 765-6404
www.tastingroomli.com

Featuring many wines from about nine smaller vineyards and wineries, many of which are not open to the public, this is the place to visit to sample and purchase a wide range of Long Island wines. A wine-tasting room if offered here, but no vineyard. The Tasting Room is open year-round, typically Fri through Sun, from 11 a.m. to 6 p.m. Private tastings for groups can also be scheduled.

VINEYARD 48

18910 South Ave. (Rte. 48), Cutchogue
(631) 734-5200
www.vineyard48winery.com

Established in 1982, Vineyard 48 is situated on 28 planted acres and produces Chardonnay, Riesling, Sauvignon Blanc, Cabernet Franc, Cabernet Sauvignon, and Merlot. The vineyard is known for hosting live entertainment and family-friendly outdoor events during the spring, summer, and fall months. (Not all events, however, are open to young people.) People also come to play chess in the game room while enjoying fine wine. You'll also find a cigar lounge and, of course, a wine-tasting room. Approximately 10,500 cases of wine are produced here annually.

WOLFFER ESTATE VINEYARD

139 Sagg Rd., Sagaponack
(631) 537-5106
www.wolffer.com

Chardonnay, Pinot Grigio, Cabernet Franc, Merlot, and Pinot Noir are among the offerings at this midsize vineyard located in Long Island's wine country. Situated on 50 planted acres, the vineyard has been in existence since 1988 and offers a wide range of activities for its visitors, including a wine-tasting room and outdoor public space. Tours, live music, and special events are also offered.

i For more information about Long Island wines, contact the Long Island Wine Council at (631) 722-2220 or visit www.LIWines.com.

THE ARTS

When it comes to experiencing culture and the arts on Long Island, there's a lot more than just the "liquid culture" (in the form of wine tastings at the various wineries and vineyards) offered throughout Long Island's wine country. While it's not New York City, within Nassau and Suffolk Counties you'll find a wide range of theaters, concert halls, and outdoor amphitheaters, not to mention many interesting, thought-provoking, and entertaining museums, as well as several independent galleries showcasing and selling all styles of art. Long Island is also known for hosting numerous prestigious film festivals, and movie theater multiplexes showing the latest Hollywood blockbusters are never more than a few miles from any of the popular tourist destinations and more densely populated residential areas.

In many ways, however, New York City defines culture and sets standards for what people should expect from theaters, museums, and the arts. And, with the city being just a short trip away, it makes perfect sense to experience it while staying on Long Island. Taking a day trip or weekend trip to Manhattan will allow you to go sightseeing, see a Broadway show, or attend a performance at Carnegie Hall, Lincoln Center, the New York City Ballet, or the Metropolitan Opera, for example. You can also experience some of New York City's incredible museums, like the Museum of Modern Art, the Metropolitan Museum of Art, the Guggenheim Museum, or the American Museum of Natural History.

This section focuses on the cultural experiences available on Long Island, plus offers a preview of what you'll find just one or two hours away in New York City when it comes to theater, art, museums, and cinema.

BALLET

Numerous ballet schools throughout Long Island hold showcases and fully staged performances. There are, however, only a few professional ballet companies in the area.

BALLET LONG ISLAND

1863 Pond Rd., Ronkonkoma
(631) 737-1964
www.balletlongisland.com

Established in 1985, Ballet Long Island is a professional ballet company that offers performances, arts-in-education programs, an apprentice program, and a trainee program, along with choreography, master classes and workshops. The ballet company's repertoire includes *The Nutcracker, Cinderella, Snow White, Sleeping Beauty, The Fantastic Toyshop, Beauty and the Beast, The Little Mermaid, Swan Lake Act II,* and *Don Quixote pas de deux,* as well as original ballets choreographed for the company. Ticket prices are kept affordable at under $20 per adult and under $10 per child and senior citizen. Most performances are held at the Islip Town Hall West in Islip.

LONG ISLAND BALLET THEATRE

310 New York Ave., Huntington
(631) 271-4626, (866) 811-4111
www.liballettheatre.com

The Huntington Center for the Performing Arts was established in 2005 by Joan Albright and Susan Alessi. The goal was to create a conservatory environment that would allow Long Islanders to learn about and experience the performing arts without having to travel to New York City. The Huntington Ballet Academy was then created to support the work of the Long

Island Ballet Theatre, an organization that was established in 2000. The Long Island Ballet Theatre is a not-for-profit ballet company that was created to allow up-and-coming ballet students to perform side by side with professional dancers. This is a community-based ballet troupe that holds open auditions for every production, plus recruits professional dancers from throughout the region. The Long Island Ballet Theatre is a permanent resident of the Huntington Center for the Performing Arts.

CINEMA

Film Festivals

HAMPTONS INTERNATIONAL FILM FESTIVAL
East Hampton
(631) 747-7978
http://hamptonsfilmfest.org

Held in the fall, typically in mid-Oct, the Hamptons International Film Festival was founded with the goal of celebrating independent film in all genres. The festival selects films that express fresh voices and different global perspectives. For almost 20 years, this five-day festival has attracted some of Hollywood's biggest names, both as participants and attendees.

In a typical year more than 100 films, from more than 20 countries, are screened as part of the festival. Awards worth over $200,000 are presented. The Hamptons International Film Festival is an Academy-qualifying festival for short films, but also accepts documentaries, narratives, and other film genres. Being one of the most prestigious film festivals in the area, the Hamptons International Film Festival often has the honor of being the regional or world premier venue for major independent films. For example, the festival hosted the East Coast premier of the eight-time Academy Award–winning film *Slum Dog Millionaire* in 2008.

THE LONG ISLAND FILM FESTIVAL
(516) 238-1325
www.lifilm.org

The Long Island Film Festival is the first, annual, island-wide competitive film festival of its kind. It was established in 1984 and annually showcases works by professional and student filmmakers alike. The Long Island Film Festival is not anchored to any one particular venue, movie house, or specific town, making it a truly island-wide event. Any village, town, or city in the region can be a host location for Long Island Film Festival screenings, receptions, and special events.

During the festival, tickets are available for $10 per screening "block" of films. Tickets can be purchased via cash or personal check (credit cards are not accepted) on the day of the screenings at the box office, starting one hour prior to that day's starting schedule. A day pass is available for $25 and entitles the holder admission to all films and presentations on that day. Venue, date, and ticket price for the closing awards, screenings, cocktail receptions, awards presentation, and after-party change each year. Visit the Web site for screening and event dates and times.

The Cinema Arts Centre, Parrish Art Museum in Southampton, Inter-Media Arts Center, Guild Hall/John Drew Theater in East Hampton, various venues on Shelter Island, Vail-Levitt Music Hall in Riverhead, Theater 3 Cinema Village in Port Jefferson, and the Patchogue Theater for the Performing Arts in Glen Cove, as well as several area colleges, host screenings and events during the Long Island Film Festival.

LONG ISLAND GAY AND LESBIAN FILM FESTIVAL
Huntington
www.liglff.org, http://cinemaartscentre.org

Held each year in Nov, the Long Island Gay and Lesbian Film Festival is a nonprofit organization that showcases gay, lesbian, bisexual, and transgender experiences in movies. The organization is supported by a grant from the New York State Council of the Arts, as well as a handful of sponsors. Visit the organization's Web site for a full listing of events and screenings.

LONG ISLAND INTERNATIONAL FILM EXPO

Bellmore

(516) 783-3199

http://liifilmexpo.org

This annual, weeklong film festival is held every July and is sponsored by the Long Island Film/TV Foundation and the Nassau County Film Commission. The festival hosts between 70 and 180 short and feature-length independent films from throughout the world. It starts with an opening night party that is by invitation only and open to participating filmmakers, sponsors, dignitaries, board members, and the press. Winners of the Long Island International Film Expo are selected by a combination of audience ballot and judging committee. Each winning film is then honored at the festival's closing night party and awards ceremony, where the filmmakers receive their trophies and prizes

Some of the categories awarded include Best Director, Best Story, Best Feature Film (in 35 mm, 16 mm, and video), Best Short Film (in 35 mm, 16 mm, and video), Best Long Island Film, Best Student Film, Best Animation, and Best Foreign Film, among others. There are also several technical categories judged before the film festival by special entry, including Best Actor, Best Actress, Best Cinematography, Best Art Direction, and Best Lighting. Every film genre is typically represented in the festival. A schedule of screenings and a synopsis of each film can be found on the organization's Web site starting several months prior to the event.

LONG ISLAND LATINO INTERNATIONAL FILM FESTIVAL

Stony Brook University, Stony Brook

http://liliff.com

Held annually in early Nov, the Long Island Latino International Film Festival celebrates and showcases the finest in Latino filmmaking. For more than five years, this festival has screened world premiers of several films, including *Stereo Types,* which was produced on Long Island. In addition to locally produced independent films, the festival showcases international films that offer top-quality programming and compelling storytelling through all genres.

Each year the festival showcases films ranging from narrative features, short films, and animation, to experimental and documentary-style films. Following each screening is a question-and-answer session with the filmmakers that is open to the public. Admission to the three-day festival is $40; however, tickets for individual blocks of screenings can be purchased for $10 each.

Seeing the Latest Movies on Long Island

Locating a theater near you that's playing the latest movie you want to see is easy, regardless of where you're staying on Long Island. Check the local newspaper; ask your hotel's concierge; visit Yahoo! Movies (http://movies.yahoo.com/showtimes-tickets/), Fandango (www.fandango.com), or Moviefone (www.moviefone.com); or download the free Movies OneTap application for your iPhone (from the Apple iTunes App Store). In Nassau County, you can also call (516) 777-FILM for theater listings and movie showtimes.

There are also several independent movie theaters that show films aside from current Hollywood releases throughout Long Island, particularly in the small towns and communities in Suffolk County. For example, there's GuildHall (158 Main St., East Hampton; 631-324-0806; www.guildhall.org/home.ihtml), which shows primarily foreign and independent films. The Cinema Arts Centre (423 Park Ave., Huntington; 631-423-2696) presents independent and foreign films, and often hosts film festivals.

MUSEUMS

The "Attractions" chapter also offers details about many of the major museums on Long Island, as well as historical sites, lighthouses, and landmarks that are open to the public. If you enjoy visiting museums, be sure to block out at least one full day in your schedule (more, if possible) to explore Museum Row, which is a complex in Garden City (in Nassau County) that features multiple museums.

Nassau County

AFRICAN AMERICAN MUSEUM OF NASSAU COUNTY

110 North Franklin St., Hempstead
(516) 572-0730
http://aamoflongisland.org

This museum examines the history of African Americans on Long Island. Some of the exhibits come from the Smithsonian Institute, while others have a strong focus on African-American Long Islanders who have had a strong impact on the region's arts, music, entertainment, sports, and politics. Educational and informative lectures and workshops are housed here throughout the year. Open year-round, hours vary by season.

AMERICAN MERCHANT MARINE MUSEUM AT THE UNITED STATES MERCHANT MARINE ACADEMY

300 Steamboat Rd., Kings Point
(516) 773-5515
www.usmma.edu/about/Museum/default.htm

Closed in July and on holidays and weekends during semester breaks, this museum features 14 galleries that trace the evolution of American shipping since the Civil War. Here you'll find a handful of maritime artifacts, along with an impressive collection of model ships and maritime artwork. There's also a memorial dedicated to the merchant marines who have lost their lives in the line of duty while serving their country.

CRADLE OF AVIATION MUSEUM

Charles Lindbergh Blvd., Garden City
(516) 572-4111
www.cradleofaviation.org

Located in an old airplane factory, this museum displays more than 70 legendary aircraft from throughout the history of aviation and also features exhibits dedicated to space travel. One of the region's only IMAX theaters can also be found at this popular museum. The theater shows a combination of educational IMAX-only films and Hollywood blockbusters shown in IMAX format, with the incredibly large movie screen and state-of-the-art sound system. Open year-round, hours vary by season.

HOFSTRA UNIVERSITY MUSEUM

Hofstra University Campus
(516) 463-6600
www.hofstra.edu/Community/museum/index.html

Located on the Hofstra University campus, this museum contains five galleries showcasing a wide range of paintings, sculptures, photographs, and other pieces of art. There are also more than 75 outdoor sculptures on display, making it the largest collection of public art in the New York metropolitan area. In addition to its permanent collection, the museum features changing exhibits. Open year-round, hours vary by season.

HOLOCAUST MEMORIAL & TOLERANCE CENTER OF NASSAU COUNTY

100 Crescent Beach Rd., Glen Cove
(516) 571-8040
www.holocaust-nassau.org

This museum is located on the 20-acre Welwyn Preserve and offers permanent and changing exhibits that focus on understanding the cause and results of the Holocaust. These exhibits, along with the lectures and special events programs held here, are designed to foster tolerance. Many of the lectures and workshops cater to specific age groups. In 2009 and early 2010, the museum underwent a significant renovation. It now offers a state-of-the-art experience featuring multimedia displays, as well as exhibits that combine artifacts with photos and archival video footage.

NASSAU COUNTY MUSEUM OF ART

1 Museum Dr., Roslyn Harbor
(516) 484-9337
www.nassaumuseum.com

Within the historic mansion that houses this museum you'll find 10 unique galleries that showcase at least four major exhibits per year. The works of internationally acclaimed artists are presented. The 145 acres of land on which the museum is situated also features outdoor sculptures. Open year-round, hours vary by season.

i Be sure to visit each museum's Web site to learn about special events happening throughout the year, as well as new and upcoming exhibits.

RAYNHAM HALL MUSEUM
20 West Main St., Oyster Bay
(516) 922-6808
www.raynhamhallmuseum.org

Within this historic 22-room mansion you'll discover exhibits that depict the lives of two generations of people who lived in Oyster Bay between the 1770s and 1870s. Visitors will learn about life during the American Revolution, as well as how the quality of life improved for people living in the region during the Victorian period (in the late 1800s). More than 5,000 pieces of furniture, household accessories, clothing, and artwork are on display, including a handwritten letter from General George Washington dated Aug 2, 1777.

SCIENCE MUSEUM OF LONG ISLAND
1526 North Plandome Rd., Manhasset
(516) 627-9400
www.smli.org

Open throughout the year, this museum features an array of hands-on activities and exhibits designed to educate visitors about the physical sciences. In the summer several different camp-like programs are offered to children in different age groups. Throughout the year a variety of parent and infant activities are offered. This is considered a "workshop museum" that takes a hands-on approach to learning, as opposed to showcasing passive exhibits and displays. Hours vary by season.

WANTAGH RAILROAD MUSEUM
1700 Wantagh Ave., Wantagh
(516) 826-8767
www.wantagh.li/museum

Open seasonally (Apr through Oct), this small museum focuses on the early 20th-century Long Island Railroad and has on display some original train cars and equipment. The museum itself is housed in three structures, including an actual old railroad car (circa 1912), the original Wantagh Post Office, and a train station that was built in 1885 and has been refurbished and moved to its current location. Within the historic train station is a small exhibit that pays homage to Emma Whitmore, the first woman to serve as a ticket agent at this railroad station.

Suffolk County

AMERICAN AIRPOWER MUSEUM
1300 New Hwy. at Republic Airport, Farmingdale
(631) 293-6398
www.americanairpowermuseum.com

This museum showcases an impressive collection of operational World War II aircraft housed in a former airport hangar. The site where this museum is now located was the former home of Republic Aviation, a company that produced more than 9,000 P-47 Thunderbolt aircraft used during WWII. The museum is open throughout the year, but hours vary by season. An aviation-themed gift shop is also on the premises.

COLD SPRING HARBOR WHALING MUSEUM
279 Main St. (Rte. 25A), Cold Spring Harbor
(631) 367-3418
www.cshwhalingmuseum.org

Explore the history of whaling and view a former 19th-century American whaleboat containing its original gear. Also on display is an impressive scrimshaw collection, as well as artwork, ship models, and artifacts from the whaling industry. The museum is open year-round, but hours vary by season.

HALLOCKVILLE MUSEUM FARM
6038 Sound Ave., Riverhead
(631) 298-5292
www.hallockville.com

This 1765 homestead offers an authentic peek at the past—between 1880 and 1910, to be exact. Learn what life was like through photos, exhibits, and genuine artifacts. The 28-acre property has 18 historic buildings, including houses and barns, that can be visited. This is also a working farm, so live animals, including cows, sheep, and chickens, can be seen. One of the goals of this museum is to showcase and teach about eastern Long Island's agricultural history. Open year-round, hours vary by season. Throughout the year, private parties, festivals, and craft fairs are held here.

HECKSCHER MUSEUM OF ART
2 Prime Ave., Huntington
(631) 351-3250
www.heckscher.org

This museum showcases works from local and national collections throughout the year. Within the permanent collection are European and American paintings, drawings, prints, and sculptures. Between Jan and Apr 2010, an exhibit titled "Arcadia/Suburbia: Architecture on Long Island, 1930–2010" was on display. This exhibit utilized photos, paintings, and other media to showcase well-known architects, their works, and how they have been incorporated on Long Island.

HUNTINGTON HISTORICAL SOCIETY MUSEUMS
209 Main St., Huntington
(631) 427-7045
www.huntingtonhistoricalsociety.org

Located within four historic buildings, the Huntington Historical Society presents museums that showcase life from the late 1700s through the early 1900s. The museums are open year-round, but hours vary by season. Visitors see firsthand how life has evolved from farming and country living within the region. The museum's genealogy workshop has been in existence since 1975 and continues to help people from all over the country research and trace their family's roots.

ISLIP ART MUSEUM
50 Irish Ln., East Islip
(631) 224-5402
www.islipartmuseum.org

The Islip Art Museum showcases the work of contemporary Long Island– and New York State–based artists. Five unique exhibitions are presented each year, and most somehow reflect or relate to issues or concerns in the current art world. This museum offers the opportunity to see the work of up-and-coming local artists and well-established artists who have received international recognition. The museum also offers art classes for both adults and children throughout the year. The on-site store sells unique, handcrafted items, artwork, jewelry, and gifts, often created by the artists whose work is showcased within the museum's galleries. Open year-round, hours vary by season.

LONG ISLAND MARITIME MUSEUM
86 West Ave., West Sayville
(631) 854-4974
www.limaritime.org

This museum focuses on the history of boating and features a variety of historical small boats, including a 19th-century oystering vessel. There's also a small diving exhibit. The museum is open year-round. Hours are 10 a.m. to 4 p.m. Mon through Sat, and noon to 4 p.m. on Sun. Throughout the year the museum hosts a wide range of family-friendly activities, including a seafood and music festival (which also includes a crafts show) in Aug, a kite festival in Sept, and a Halloween boat burning in late Oct.

LONG ISLAND MUSEUM OF AMERICAN ART, HISTORY & CARRIAGES
1208 Rte. 25A, Stony Brook
(631) 751-0066
www.longislandmuseum.org

This impressive art museum showcases works from the 19th and 20th centuries, along with a collection of horse-drawn carriages, maritime artifacts, and a blacksmith shop. The museum has a charming gift shop on the premises. Open year-round, hours vary by season. There's a charming collection of shops nearby.

MUSEUM OF LONG ISLAND NATURAL SCIENCES
State University of New York
Nicholls Rd., Stony Brook
(631) 632-8230
www.geosciences.stonybrook.edu/museum

With the goal of teaching about nature and natural history, this museum features a collection of rocks and minerals, fossils, and exhibits that teach about the geological history of Long Island. Some of the exhibits also focus on dinosaurs and astronomy. Open year-round, but hours vary by season.

SCIENCE MUSEUM AT BROOKHAVEN NATIONAL LABORATORY
William Floyd Pkwy., Upton
(631) 344-4049
www.bnl.gov/bnlweb/Museum/Science_museum.html
Get a behind-the-scenes look at Brookhaven National Laboratory while learning about science. This museum utilizes an array of interactive exhibits combined with audiovisual presentations. The museum is open during the summer months only. One of 10 national laboratories overseen and primarily funded by the Office of Science of the U.S. Department of Energy (DOE), Brookhaven National Laboratory conducts research in the physical, biomedical, and environmental sciences, as well as in energy technologies and national security.

SOUTHOLD INDIAN MUSEUM
Main Bayview Rd., Southold
(631) 765-5577
www.southoldindianmuseum.org
Learn about the history of Long Island's Native Americans. The museum boasts the largest collection of Algonquin ceramic pottery that exists anywhere, as well as an impressive collection of pots and bowls carved out of soapstone. Many arrowheads are also on display. A separate interactive children's area is featured. Open year-round, hours vary by season.

SUFFOLK COUNTY HISTORICAL SOCIETY MUSEUM
300 West Main St., Riverhead
(631) 727-2881
www.suffolkcountyhistoricalsociety.org
As you explore this museum, you'll delve into the past and see a wide range of artifacts, crafts, furniture, and exhibits that relate directly to Long Island's history. The museum regularly hosts lectures and workshops that cover a wide range of topics, from a Civil War symposium to lectures about ghosts and haunted locations hosted by the Long Island Paranormal Society. There's also a gift shop on the premises. The museum was founded in 1886 with the goal of collecting, preserving, and interpreting the ongoing history of the region. Open year-round, hours vary by season.

i As you explore Suffolk Country, particularly the many small, historic villages and towns, you'll discover a huge number of historical sites and landmarks that are open to the public.

SUFFOLK COUNTY VANDERBILT MUSEUM
180 Little Neck Rd., Centerport
(631) 854-5555
www.vanderbiltmuseum.org
Located on the former 43-acre estate of William Kissam Vanderbilt II, this complex now houses several different museums and outdoor exhibits. A wide range of special events, concerts, workshops, and lectures are hosted here throughout the year, including children's theater performances. The planetarium, for example, runs a variety of shows targeted to either adults, kids, or families. Mansion tours are offered on an ongoing basis. For the holidays, the entire property displays festive lights and decorations. The on-site museum store offers a unique collection of gifts and merchandise. Open year-round, hours vary by season.

WALT WHITMAN BIRTHPLACE STATE HISTORIC SITE AND INTERPRETIVE CENTER
240 Old Walt Whitman Rd., South Huntington
(631) 427-5240
www.waltwhitman.org
See the actual birthplace of world-renowned poet Walt Whitman. The museum showcases authentic furnishings, letters, manuscripts, and artifacts of the poet. Plan on spending at least an hour or two here. Throughout the year the museum hosts a variety of unique events, from

a "Make a Corn Husk Figure" activity for kids to a Victorian tea party that's more suitable for adults. Poetry readings, contests, and workshops are also held throughout the year for established, up-and-coming, and amateur poets. A museum shop and bookstore can also be found here. Open year-round, hours vary by season.

MUSIC

Local music lovers can enjoy live philharmonic performances of classical compositions and hear professional orchestras perform without having to travel into Manhattan, thanks to the Long Island Philharmonic and other regional orchestras.

LONG ISLAND PHILHARMONIC

Melville
(631) 293-2222
www.liphilharmonic.org

The Long Island Philharmonic performs throughout the year at concert venues across Long Island and beyond, such as the Tilles Center for the Performing Arts (Brookville), Cathedral of the Incarnation (Garden City), Staller Center for the Arts (Stony Brook), Heckscher Park (Huntington Village), Eisenhower Park (East Meadow), Brookhaven Amphitheater (Farmingville), and Riverhead High School (Southampton).

Under David Wiley, the Long Island Philharmonic's music director and conductor, the 28th-season schedule consisted of eight subscription classics concerts, six youth concerts, a New Year's Eve concert, two free outdoor park concerts, two candlelight concerts, and a handful of other contracted engagements. The musicians who are part of this popular philharmonic come from throughout the New York area. The Long Island Philharmonic Chorus is a 150-member adjunct ensemble under the direction of Frances C. Roberts. The philharmonic was founded in 1979 by folk singer Harry Chapin, who worked in collaboration with Maestro Christopher Keene and a handful of local businesses. Today the Long Island Philharmonic is considered one of the most professional and respected regional orchestras in the United States.

A typical performance of the Long Island Philharmonic lasts about two hours, including an intermission. Anyone over the age of eight is welcome to attend a performance. The family- and kid-oriented concerts tend to last no more than 90 minutes, including an intermission, and are open to people of all ages. The dress code for attending a performance of the Long Island Philharmonic is "business" or "business casual." To insure prompt seating, be sure to arrive at the venue at least 15 minutes before showtime. If you arrive late, you may have to wait in the lobby until the ushers deem it's appropriate to seat you without disrupting the performance.

i **It's common for the Long Island Philharmonic to perform long Beethoven symphonies or Mozart concertos, which have three or more movements. In between each movement there will be a short pause; however, it's not appropriate to applaud until the very end of the piece. Check the concert program to determine how many movements a piece contains, so you'll know when it ends and it's appropriate to clap.**

WEST ISLIP SYMPHONY ORCHESTRA

West Islip
(631) 968-7575
http://wisymphony.org

Throughout the year this well-established symphony orchestra performs at local and regional venues, including West Islip High School, Beach Street Middle School, and the West Islip Library Field. In 2004 Murray R. Kahn was named permanent conductor of the West Islip Symphony. The organization, which recently celebrated its 30th anniversary, welcomes locally based musicians to audition for the symphony.

OPERA

Maintaining its reputation for offering a broad selection of ways Long Islanders and visitors alike can experience culture, the Long Island Opera, as well as several other opera companies, offer fully staged productions of famous operas throughout the year.

GILBERT & SULLIVAN LIGHT OPERA COMPANY OF LONG ISLAND
Performances held throughout Long Island
(516) 877-2802
www.gaslocoli.snickersnee.com

This is a traveling company that performs all over Long Island, from Brooklyn to Montauk, and from Glen Cove to Long Beach. It was founded in 1954 and is one of America's oldest organizations devoted almost exclusively to performing the works of Gilbert and Sullivan. While the performances are highly professional, the performers are all volunteers and come from all walks of life. Since its inception, the Gilbert & Sullivan Light Opera Company has performed the entire series of Gilbert and Sullivan operas. The performances are all accompanied by an 18-piece ensemble orchestra.

LONG ISLAND OPERA
(212) 722-1482
www.longislandoperaco.org

The Long Island Opera began in 1958, when it was established by Nino Luciano, the leading tenor of the New York City Opera and a resident of Long Island. The organization started as an adult education program in opera, offered in Floral Park, and slowly evolved into an opera workshop that presented fully staged productions. It was during the 1960–61 season that the Long Island Opera Showcase was incorporated in New York State. During the 1970s, under artistic director Benard Hart (another singer from the New York City Opera), the organization became known simply as the Long Island Opera, and over the next 27 years, under Hart's leadership, it transformed from an opera workshop into a full company.

In 1992 the Long Island Opera became affiliated with the State University of New York at Old Westbury, and during the 1990s the company performed at least three operas a year, fully staged at the Maguire Theater. During this period the company also performed outside at the Chapin Rainbow Stage in Hecksher Park, and at the Morgan Park in Glen Cove.

The Long Island Opera is now the oldest and most substantial professional opera company on Long Island. Performances are held throughout the year at a handful of different venues, including the Southampton Cultural Center in Southampton.

OUTDOOR STAGES AND AMPHITHEATERS

During the summer, when the evenings are warm and mild and there's not a cloud in the sky, you can enjoy music and live performances under the stars at several different outdoor amphitheaters, including the world-famous Jones Beach in Wantagh.

BROOKHAVEN AMPHITHEATER
Brookhaven Amphitheater Arts & Cultural Center at Bald Hill
South Bicycle Path, Farmingville
(631) 451-8010,
(631) 888-9000 (Ticketmaster)
www.brookhavenamphitheater.com

Throughout the summer and fall, the Brookhaven Amphitheater in Farmville presents an ongoing lineup of concerts and special events. Some of the major acts that have performed here include Pat Benatar, Tony Orlando, Twisted Sister, The Temptations, Alice Cooper, Cheap Trick, the B.B. King Blues Festival featuring B.B. King, and Kenny Wayne Shepard. Visit the Web site for a current schedule. Free parking is available near the venue.

JONES BEACH AMPHITHEATER AND THEATERS
1 Ocean Pkwy., Wantagh
(516) 221-1000
www.jonesbeach.com

For the past 80 years, Jones Beach has provided a wide assortment of outdoor entertainment throughout the summer. At this world-famous beach, there are currently three main stages, including the 5,000-seat Bay Stage, which opened in 2009.

THE BAY STAGE

Throughout the summer the Bay Stage offers a series of outdoor concerts with the intimate feel of a small music club. All shows have a general admission policy. This new stage is located on the opposite side of the concession area from the main amphitheater. For a schedule of concerts, visit http://baystage.jonesbeach.com. People of all ages are invited to attend Bay Stage concerts and shows; however, everyone over the age of two must have their own ticket. Seating is available around the Bay Stage, which does not offer open space for blankets or folding chairs. Not all shows presented at this venue, particularly the rock shows, are suitable for kids.

JONES BEACH AMPHITHEATER (AKA NIKON AT JONES BEACH THEATER)

This is definitely the largest and most famous outdoor amphitheater on Long Island, which makes sense, since it's located within Jones Beach State Park, the most popular of Long Island's state parks. In 2009 Jones Beach celebrated its 80th anniversary. While swimming and sunbathing at the beach continue to be this park's biggest draw, attending concerts and events at the Jones Beach Amphitheater has become synonymous with summering on Long Island. In its 80-year history, more than a half-billion people have visited this state park.

The Jones Beach Amphitheater attracts big-name recording artists and music groups who perform here almost nightly throughout the summer. It's common for shows to sell out weeks in advance. Commonly known as the Jones Beach Amphitheater, although its official name is now Nikon at Jones Beach Theater, this outdoor venue opened in 1952. It currently has a seating capacity of 15,000. The theater announces its concert lineup for the upcoming summer in early May. Advance tickets can be ordered online at www.tickets.jonesbeach.com or www.livenation.com/venue/nikon-at-jones-beach-theater-tickets. All performances offer general seating. The venue maintains a strict no alcohol policy, except in a few VIP areas.

JONES BEACH BOARDWALK BANDSHELL AND WEST POOL BANDSHELL

The Jones Beach Boardwalk Bandshell presents a lineup of concerts and performances that are held almost nightly throughout the summer. Certain nights of the week have themes. For example, Sun is Latin night, while Tues is Kids Nite and Wed offers line dancing. On Fri tribute bands typically perform, and on Sat you'll find concerts featuring "greatest hits." The West Pool Bandshell also hosts an ongoing lineup of concerts and special events throughout the summer.

PERFORMING ARTS VENUES AND THEATERS

Nassau County

If you're interested in seeing a performance, play, or musical, the following are a few of the theater groups and playhouses in the area. In some cases, these theater troupes attract Broadway-caliber talent, especially in the summertime.

BROADHOLLOW THEATRE COMPANY
700 Hempstead Tnpk., Elmont
(516) 775-4420
www.broadhollow.org

Located near the border between Nassau and Suffolk Counties, this repertory theater offers an ongoing schedule of shows and musicals throughout the year, plus has a children's theater and an academy of musical theater. *Fame, Annie,* and *Sweeney Todd* were among the musicals presented in early 2010.

CAPITAL ONE BANK THEATRE AT WESTBURY
960 Brush Hollow Rd., Westbury
(516) 334-0800
www.northforktheatre.com

This 2,742-seat theater hosts a variety of concerts and musicals throughout the year, including special children's shows. Ticket prices vary by performance, but generally are in the $40 to $60 range. In 2010, some of the music, comedy, and variety acts slated to perform here include: Kevin Hart, Train, America, Jackie Mason, Kenny Loggins, Don Rickles, Joan Rivers, Gladys Knight, and Ringo Star. Many performances are held in a theatre-in-the-round setting. See the venue's website for a 3-D seating chart for each performance.

JEANNE RIMSKY THEATER, LANDMARK ON MAIN STREET
232 Main St., Port Washington
(516) 767-6444
www.landmarkonmainstreet.org

The historic building in which this theater is housed was built in 1916 as an elementary school. Today the 425-seat theater offers world-class music, theater, and dance performances to residents and tourists visiting the North Shore. The theater has been fully restored since the early 1900s, and now boasts a state-of-the-art sound system. Big-name recording artists and musicians often appear here.

NASSAU VETERANS MEMORIAL COLISEUM
1255 Hempstead Tnpk., Uniondale
(516) 794-9303
http://nassaucoliseum.com

With its 17,500-seat capacity, this is the largest concert, show, and sporting event venue on Long Island, attracting a wide range of high-profile shows and concerts featuring big-name acts throughout the year. A few of the family-friendly shows that appear here annually are *Disney on Ice*, the Harlem Globetrotters, and the *Ringling Bros. and Barnum & Bailey Circus*. See the Web site for a complete list of events and shows. This venue, also known simply as Nassau Coliseum, is home to the New York Islanders NHL hockey team. For Islanders ticket information, call (800) 882-4753 or visit www.newyorkislanders.com.

SHOWPLACE AT THE BELLMORE MOVIES AND THE BELLMORE THEATRE
222 Pettit Ave., Bellmore
(516) 599-6870
http://plazatheatrical.com

The Showplace at the Bellmore Movies and the Bellmore Theatre are the permanent homes of Plaza Theatrical Productions, a professional theater company that presents Broadway shows and plays within these historic theaters. Recent productions have included *Godspell, Annie Get Your Gun, Camelot, The Wizard of Oz, Anything Goes, A Christmas Carol, Guys and Dolls,* and *Gypsy*. Throughout the year the company also offers kid- and family-friendly shows, like *Sleeping Beauty, Charlotte's Web, Willy Wonka, Blue's Clues—Live!* and *Pinocchio*.

STAGE THEATRE
222 Hewlett Ave., Merrick
(516) 868-6400
www.thestageinmerrick.com

People travel from around Long Island throughout the year to see the musicals, comedies, dramas, and original plays that are presented at this rather small and intimate theater. Children's musicals are also presented. All tickets are reasonably priced, typically under $20.

TILLES CENTER FOR THE PERFORMING ARTS
720 Northern Blvd., Greenvale
(516) 299-3100
www.tillescenter.org

This is primarily a world-renowned concert hall, where music, dance, and theatrical performances are presented. For example, performances by the Long Island Philharmonic and New York Philharmonic are held periodically throughout the year. In addition, shows like *Hairspray* are presented, as are major concerts by popular recording artists like Bryan Adams. In 2010 *An Evening with Garrison Keillor* could also be found on the theater's schedule.

Suffolk County

AIRPORT PLAYHOUSE
218 Knickerbocker Ave., Bohemia
(631) 589-7588
www.airportplayhouse.com

At least 10 different productions are staged every year at this midsize theater that seats 264 people. Plays and musicals are among the offerings, as are special children's theater performances in the summer. Some of the recent shows presented here have included: *A Chorus Line, Dirty Rotten Scoundrels, Aladdin, Sweet Charity,* and *Children of Eden.* Tickets range in price based on the performance but average around $20 each for adult tickets. Children's shows start as low as $8 per ticket.

ARENA PLAYERS THEATER
296 Rte. 109, East Farmingdale
(516) 293-0674
www.arenaplayers.org

This is a local repertory theater company that produces a lineup of shows and musicals year-round. The theater has a main stage, a second stage, and a popular children's theater. In addition to regularly scheduled shows and performances, the theater hosts many special events throughout the year. Visit the Web site for a schedule of performances. Arena Players has been in existence for more than 60 years.

BAY STREET THEATRE
Bay St. (Long Wharf), Sag Harbor
(631) 725-9500
www.baystreet.org

This not-for-profit theater is located on the Long Wharf in Sag Harbor and is known for presenting classic and contemporary works. Between late May and the end of Aug, the theater typically presents at least four different shows. This venue is also home to Kidstreet, which offers programming for children, as well as the Comedy Club, which is where you can see top stand-up comics perform.

BAYWAY ARTS CENTER
265 East Main St., East Islip
(631) 581-2700
www.broadhollow.org

From kid- and family-friendly productions, such as *Robin Hood and Maid Marian, The Wizard of Oz, Alice in Wonderland, Disney's High School Musical 2,* and *Rudolph the Red-Nosed Reindeer,* to mainstream Broadway productions like *Fame, The Producers, The Wedding Singer,* and *Evita,* BayWay Arts Center offers an ongoing lineup of professional and highly enjoyable live theatrical entertainment.

BOULTON CENTER FOR THE PERFORMING ARTS
37 West Main St., Bay Shore
(631) 969-1101
www.boultoncenter.org

Housed in a historic movie theater that was built in the late 1920s, this venue now presents a full lineup of shows, concerts, films, poetry readings, lectures, and seminars throughout the year. Children's entertainment is also offered, as is a summer performing arts camp for kids.

GATEWAY PLAYHOUSE
215 South Country Rd., Bellport
(631) 286-1133
www.gatewayplayhouse.com

For more than 55 seasons the Gateway Playhouse has presented professional musical theater productions between May and Sept. In Dec the venue also offers holiday shows. Tickets are typically less than $40 each.

JOHN E. ENGEMAN THEATER AT NORTHPORT
250 Main St., Northport
(631) 261-2900
www.engemantheater.com

Often by tapping Broadway's talent pool, the professional quality of the stage productions offered at this theater is outstanding. Shows are presented throughout the year in a theater that offers a full-size orchestra pit and stadium-style seating. Some of the recent productions staged at this theater include *Miracle on 34th Street, Run for Your Wife, Dial M for Murder, Rent, Crazy for You, The Odd Couple, Little Women, The Little Shop of Horrors, Man of La Mancha, Lend Me a Tenor, Smokey Joe's Cafe, Oliver!*, and *Jekyll & Hyde*.

STUDIO THEATRE
141 South Wellwood Ave., Lindenhurst
(631) 226-8400
www.broadhollow.org

This theater offers plays, musicals, concerts, and performances targeted to adults, kids, and families throughout the year. Around the holidays you can catch a stunning performance of *The Nutcracker*, for example. Shows like *Aladdin, The Legend of Sleepy Hollow, Cinderella, A Gentleman and a Scoundrel, The Wizard of Oz, I Love You Because*, and *Suddenly Last Summer* can be seen during the rest of the year.

THEATRE THREE BROADWAY ON MAIN STREET
412 Main St., Port Jefferson
(631) 928-9100
www.theatrethree.com

For more than 40 years this small but nicely designed theater has brought highly professional Broadway productions, including plays and musicals, directly to residents and tourists in Port Jefferson. Throughout the year the theater presents several different Broadway shows, such as *The Wedding Singer, Little Shop of Horrors, The Producers, The Graduate, Smokey Joe's Cafe*, and *Jewtopica*, all of which were part of the 2009 lineup.

In the evening, Theatre Three presents Broadway musicals and shows, but during the day it supports a very active children's theater program and presents a wide range of kid-friendly performances and special events. In 2009, for example, some of the kid-oriented shows included *Barnaby Saves Christmas, Starship Imagination: Sheep in Space, The Three Little Kittens, The Golden Goose, The Adventures of Peter Rabbit*, and *Little Red Riding Hood*. This is a perfect place to host a child's birthday party. Having developed an annual tradition, Theatre Three also presents a wonderful, family-friendly rendition of Charles Dickens's classic *A Christmas Carol* between mid-Nov and late Dec.

WESTHAMPTON BEACH PERFORMING ARTS CENTER
76 Main St., Westhampton Beach
(631) 288-1500
www.whbpac.org

This venue offers several different performances, as well as special events and concerts, throughout the summer. In 2010, for example, Michael Bolton, Los Lonely Boys, George Clinton, Dan Zanes, and Little Feat were among the musical acts slated to perform live. At this theater, independent films are also shown throughout the year, and performing arts "camp" sessions are offered for kids. Each camp ends with a performance. Check the Web site for a listing of performances and events.

NEW YORK CITY ARTS, MUSEUMS, AND THEATER

New York City is a world-renowned destination for museums, performing arts, theater, and culture. For example, Manhattan offers a vast array of performing arts entertainment, including the New York Philharmonic (212-721-6500, http://nyphil.org), the Metropolitan Opera (212-262-6000, www.metopera.org), Alvin Ailey American Dance Theater (212-405-9000, www.alvinailey.org), the New York City Center (212-581-1212, www.nycitycenter.org), and the New York City Ballet (212-870-5570, www.nycballet.com), each providing world-class entertainment throughout the year.

On any given day you'll also find the biggest names in music, along with other types of shows, appearing at major venues like Madison Square Garden (212-465-6741, www.thegarden.com), Carnegie Hall (212-247-7800, www.carnegiehall.org), Lincoln Center (212-875-5456, www.lincolncenter.org), and Radio City Music Hall (212-247-4777, www.radiocity.com), along with hundreds of smaller, more intimate venues located in and around the Manhattan.

In terms of museums, New York City also has a lot to offer. In fact, it's easy to spend entire days, not just a few hours, exploring each of New York's most famous museums.

AMERICAN MUSEUM OF NATURAL HISTORY
Central Park West at 79th St.
(212) 769-5100
www.amnh.org

This museum features more than 40 permanent exhibits, a variety of temporary exhibitions (in five separate, massive exhibit halls), and an IMAX theater. It's known among young people in particular for its spectacular dinosaur exhibit. Kids will also enjoy the Butterfly Conservatory, a seasonal exhibit that features more than 500 colorful, live butterflies. The new Journey to the Stars space show is narrated by Whoopi Goldberg and takes viewers 13 billion years into the past, when the first stars were formed. Adults will appreciate the New Diamonds exhibit, which showcases 25 breathtaking diamonds within the museum's Hall of Gems. Visitors can easily spend at least a full day (or much more) exploring this unique and popular museum located in the heart of Manhattan.

GUGGENHEIM MUSEUM
Fifth Ave. at 89th St.
(212) 423-3500
www.guggenheim.org

This is the home of one of the world's finest collections of modern and contemporary art. The museum's building was designed by Frank Lloyd Wright and completed in 1959. It's now a New York City landmark. Special exhibits are held throughout the year. Also in the museum is the Guggenheim Cafe, an excellent choice for breakfast, lunch, or a light dinner, and the Guggenheim Store, which features limited-edition items, plus a wide range of more affordable souvenirs. Open Sat through Wed from 10 a.m. to 5:45 p.m., and Fri from 10 a.m. to 7:45 p.m. (closed Thurs). To purchase tickets in advance online, go to www.ticketweb.com.

Golden Tickets

For a predetermined number of days (one, two, three, or seven), the New York Pass (877-714-1999, www.newyorkpass.com) allows tourists to enjoy unlimited admission to over 40 of NYC's best museums and attractions, plus receive dining and shopping discounts. Participating attractions include the Empire State Building, Statue of Liberty and Ellis Island, Museum of Modern Art, American Museum of Natural History, Guggenheim Museum, Madame Tussaud's Wax Museum, Brooklyn Museum of Art, NBC Studio Tour, Circle Line Sightseeing, Radio City Music Hall Stage Door Tour, United Nations Tour, and Madison Square Garden All Access Tour. Pass prices start at $65 per person.

For a flat fee of $53, the New York CityPass (888-330-5008, www.citypass.com) offers admission to the Empire State Building Observatory, a two-hour Circle Line harbor cruise, and admission to the American Museum of Natural History, Guggenheim Museum, Museum of Modern Art, and Intrepid Sea Air and Space Museum—it's a $122.50 value. Each CityPass is valid for nine consecutive days from the day it's first used.

METROPOLITAN MUSEUM OF ART (THE MET)
1000 Fifth Ave. at 82nd St.
(212) 923-3700
www.metmuseum.org

The Met is known for many of its exhibits, including its collection of Impressionist art. There are also new Greek and Roman galleries that take you back some 5,000 years. See a sampling of the splendor of ancient Egypt, for example, along with some of the most provocative works by contemporary artists—all under one roof. Open Sun, Tues, Wed, and Thurs from 9:30 a.m. to 5:30 p.m., and Fri and Sat from 9:30 a.m. to 9 p.m. (closed Mon).

Close-up

Discounted Off-Broadway and Broadway Show Tickets

If you look at the box office ticket prices for any off-Broadway or Broadway show, you might think that seeing a show as part of your NYC trip is simply too expensive. Well, this isn't the case at all! For starters, in the heart of Times Square is the TKTS Booth, which sells same-day show tickets at up to 50 percent off. In addition, surrounding the TKTS Booth are people distributing discount coupons for individual Broadway and off-Broadway shows. On any given day (regardless of the weather), there are at least a dozen individuals giving out coupons offering $25 tickets for various plays and musicals.

There are a bunch of amazing shows currently playing on Broadway. While you probably won't find half-off tickets for the Broadway shows that sell out night after night, like *Wicked*, these shows have daily lotteries at their respective box offices, during which a limited number of $25 seats are offered to those who attend the seat lottery in person. To participate in the *Wicked* ticket lottery, for example, show up at the box office (Gershwin Theater, 222 West 51st St.) at least 2.5 hours prior to showtime and add your name to the list. Two hours before each performance, the lottery is held. There's a two-ticket-per-winner limit, and you must be present for the actual lottery to purchase your $25 ticket(s) if you win. For more info about the *Wicked* ticket lottery, visit www.gershwin-theater.com/help.html.

Instead of waiting in potentially long lines at the TKTS Booth, you can also go online and visit www.broadwaybox.com and/or www.playbill.com/club (if you're a member of *Playbill*'s club) and receive special codes that you can use at a theater's box office to obtain a significant discount on New York–based show tickets (up to 50 percent). If a show is sold out but you still want to get your hands on tickets, you can work directly with an independent ticket broker; however, you may wind up paying up to three times the face value of the ticket, plus processing charges. You can work with a licensed ticket broker online, or ask your hotel's concierge or innkeeper for a local referral. A few Web-based ticket brokers include:

Razorgator Tickets: (800) 542-4466, www.razorgator.com

Sold Out Tickets: (800) 316-5733, www.soldoutbroadwaytickets.com

StubHub: www.stubhub.com

Ticket Center: (800) 838-9292, www.ticketcenter.com

Ticket City: (800) 880-8886, www.ticketcity.com

Ticket Liquidator: (800) 456-8499, www.ticketliquidator.com

Tickets of America: (800) 736-2300, www.ticketsofamerica.com

To purchase full-price tickets for any Broadway or most Off-Broadway shows, you can visit the theater's box office in person and pay the full ticket price. Or, if you want to buy tickets by phone or online, you can utilize the Ticketmaster service; however, a variety of extra charges will apply. Ticketmaster also has various ticket sales locations on Long Island and throughout New York City. To purchase tickets via Ticketmaster by phone, call (866) 448-7849 or (212) 307-4100. To order Broadway or off-Broadway tickets through Ticketmaster's Web site, visit www.ticketmaster.com. In addition to offering information about all of the current shows, Broadway.com (800-BROADWAY, www.broadway.com) allows you to order tickets online for any Broadway or off-Broadway production.

MUSEUM OF MODERN ART (MOMA)
11 West 53rd St.
(212) 708-9400
www.moma.org

MOMA's rotating exhibitions feature works from some of the most well-known artists in the world. People who appreciate fine modern and contemporary art should not miss visiting this world-famous museum. It's easy to spend an entire day (or longer) here. Open every day except Tues from 10:30 a.m. to 5:30 p.m., with extended hours on Fri to 8 p.m.

STATUE OF LIBERTY AND ELLIS ISLAND
(212) 363-3200
www.statuereservations.com

Visiting the Statue of Liberty and/or Ellis Island is at least a half-day activity. Both offer museum exhibits and the chance to visit and explore these historic landmarks. A variety of ferries and boats offer transportation to the Statue of Liberty and Ellis Island, both of which are open to the public but only if you sign up for a tour. Tours must be booked in advance, and they are free. There is a charge for ferry service, however.

i For information on 15 additional museums located in lower Manhattan, check out www.museumsoflowermanhattan.org. These museums include the Museum of Jewish Heritage—A Living Memorial to the Holocaust (36 Battery Pl., at First Pl., 646-437-4200), New York City Police Museum (100 Old Slip, between Water St. and South St., 212-480-3100), New York City Fire Museum (278 Spring St., between Varick St. and Hudson St., 212-691-1303) and Skyscraper Museum (39 Battery Pl., at First Pl., 212-968-1961).

KIDSTUFF

Kids have a lot of reasons to love Long Island, especially in the summer. Like so many popular tourist destinations, the island offers a wide range of indoor and outdoor activities that kids and teens enjoy.

First and foremost, Long Island's beaches are a huge draw for young people. Plus, many of the hotels and resorts also have swimming pools and organized, camplike activities for kids to keep them entertained.

Long Island also has several museums, aquariums, theme parks, zoos, water parks, and other attractions that are extremely popular with the younger crowd. This section highlights some of the kid-, teen-, and family-friendly activities and attractions throughout Long Island.

NASSAU COUNTY

As you'll discover, Nassau County offers many kid- and family-friendly activities that are open year-round, unlike Suffolk County, where many of the kid-oriented attractions are open seasonally, often between Memorial Day and Labor Day.

BAYVILLE ADVENTURE PARK

8 Bayville Ave., Bayville
(516) 624-RIDE
www.bayvilleadventurepark.com

Open seasonally, this popular local theme park features a handful of rides, a miniature golf course, bumper boats, a rock-climbing wall, an arcade, a funhouse, and a variety of other family-friendly activities. In Oct the park transforms into "Bayville Scream Park" for Halloween. Guests can pay separately for each ride and attraction, or purchase a one-day ticket for unlimited use of all rides and attractions. This is a fun-filled, outdoor amusement park where you can easily spend an entire day (weather permitting). It's also an ideal place to celebrate a child's birthday or other special occasion.

CANTIAGUE PARK

West John St., Hicksville
(516) 571-7056
www.nassaucountyny.gov/agencies/Parks/Wheretogo/active/cantiague.html

This park has been part of the county's public park system since 1961. Within its 127-acres are an indoor ice-skating rink (open year-round), a swimming pool complex, and an 18-hole miniature golf course. A large athletic field, five tennis courts, six handball/paddleball courts, and three basketball courts—all lighted—are also situated in the park. The park also has a lighted, artificial turf field that accommodates football, soccer, and lacrosse.

Families with young kids will also appreciate the impressive playground and massive picnic areas, which can be reserved in advance. At the ice-skating rink, separate skating lessons are available for kids, teens, and adults, while swimming lessons are offered at the pool. Hours for each of the park's facilities vary by season. To utilize many of the county parks, you can pay a per-day fee or purchase an annual Leisure Pass for $25, which offers unlimited admission and use of all county park facilities. For details, visit www.nassaucountyny.gov/agencies/Parks/leisure.html.

CHRISTOPHER MORLEY PARK

Roslyn
(516) 571-8113
www.nassaucountyny.gov/agencies/parks/WhereToGo/active/morley.html

In addition to offering full park amenities, during the winter Christopher Morley Park features an outdoor ice-skating rink that's open to the public. In the summer the park offers a large, outdoor swimming pool. Also offered at this park are five tennis courts, four lighted handball/paddleball courts, four basketball courts, two paddle-tennis courts, and a large athletic field. There's also a playground for young kids, plus a 9-hole, par-30 golf course and a mile-long fitness trail.

A small fee applies for use of some park amenities and facilities, including the ice-skating rink, which is open from early Dec to mid-Mar. There's also a fee for use of the swimming pool and kiddie pool; lockers are available. Located on the north side of the park is a dog run. In all, Christopher Morley Park offers more than 30 acres of wooded nature trails and other outdoor activity areas suitable for the entire family.

i Grant Park in Hewlett also offers an outdoor ice-skating rink. Visit www.nassaucountyny.gov/agencies/Parks/WhereToGo/active/grant.html for details.

CRADLE OF AVIATION MUSEUM
Charles Lindbergh Blvd., Garden City
(516) 572-4111
www.cradleofaviation.org

Kids and teens will enjoy this firsthand look at the history of aviation and space flight. The museum is part of Museum Row and is housed within a former aircraft construction facility used during World War II. These days, you'll find dozens of genuine, full-size aircraft on display, as well as artifacts and interactive exhibits related to space travel. It's here that you'll also find one of the region's only IMAX theaters. Open daily, this theater showcases an ongoing selection of IMAX-specific movies, like *Space Station, Under the Sea,* and *Grand Canyon*, along with some of Hollywood's latest blockbuster releases, which are presented on the massive IMAX screen and utilize the theater's state-of-the-art sound system.

During the summer months the museum is open daily from 9:30 a.m. to 5 p.m. Throughout the rest of the year, it's open Tues through Sun, except for the IMAX theater, which is open daily year-round. Admission to the museum is $9 for adults and $8 for children. IMAX theater admission is extra; however, package deals are available.

DAVE & BUSTER'S
1504 Old County Rd., Westbury
(516) 542-8501
www.daveandbusters.com

By day this is a family-friendly restaurant that also boasts a massive arcade that features the latest video arcade games, shuffleboard, and virtual reality simulators. There's also a 20-screen video dome. This is a great place to spend a rainy day, enjoy a few hours of fun after lunch, or celebrate a child's birthday party. The restaurant features a vast menu, offering affordable burgers, sandwiches, and other goodies that kids love. It's open year-round. Special dining and gaming discounts are available, or you can pay for each arcade game separately. At night Dave & Busters transforms into more of a sports bar that caters to the 21-plus crowd. There are additional locations in Farmingdale and Islandia, Suffolk County.

LONG ISLAND CHILDREN'S MUSEUM
11 Davis Ave., Garden City
(516) 224-5800
www.licm.org

Designed to appeal to kids between the ages of 2 and 12 (and their families), the Long Island Children's Museum offers a wide range of fun and interactive activities. Back in 1993 it originally opened as a private, not-for-profit institution, within a 5,400-square-foot site donated by KeySpan Energy (formerly Long Island Lighting Company). After receiving more than 25,000 visitors during its first four months of operation, it was obvious that the community's response to the museum was overwhelming. It wasn't long before expansion plans were under way for this innovative and highly popular museum. Within a short time, Nassau County approached the museum's board with the idea of moving the Long Island Children's Museum to Museum Row, a 15-acre cultural site at Long Island's historic Mitchel Field. To facilitate the move, the county offered a 60-year, rent-free lease to a

Long Beach

This is one of Nassau County's most popular beaches. Here you'll find a gorgeous 3.5-mile stretch of white sand. It's located on the South Shore and offers a variety of seasonal activities, with swimming, surfing, and sunbathing being the most popular. Along this beach is a famous 2.5 mile-long boardwalk, which is accessible year-round. It's ideal for walking, bicycling, jogging, and rollerblading, for example. Adjacent to some of Long Beach is Park Ave., which is lined with shops and restaurants. Long Beach is actually one of the older communities on Long Island, having been founded in 1880.

One reason for this beach's appeal is that Long Beach averages 10 degrees warmer in the winter and 10 degrees cooler in the summer than other communities on Long Island. The ocean is on one side, and the bay is on the other. This geography, in addition to the beach, has allowed Long Beach to develop into a thriving seaside community. A wide range of kid-friendly activities are hosted at the beach throughout the year, particularly in the summer. For beach information, call (516) 431-3890.

40,000-square-foot former aircraft hangar, which has since become the new and permanent home for the museum.

The Long Island Children's Museum opened in Feb 2002 in its current location. It houses 14 hands-on, interactive exhibit galleries, a 145-seat state-of-the-art theater, and 3 classroom-size learning studios. In addition to providing opportunities to have fun and learn through exhibit exploration and participation in performing arts programming, the museum offers a wide range of educational and culturally diverse public programs, including the annual "From Generation to Generation" folk arts series; daily early-childhood programs; art-, music-, and science-based workshops; and parenting workshops. A family membership to the museum offers unlimited admission for up to four people, as well as participation in various special events. Nonmembers pay a daily admission fee. The museum is open year-round.

i In addition to housing the Long Island Children's Museum, Mitchel Field is where you'll find the Cradle of Aviation Museum and IMAX theater. The Nassau County Firefighters Museum & Education Center (1 Davis Ave., 516-572-4177, www.ncfiremuseum.com) is also located on Museum Row in Garden City. This museum pays tribute to local fire departments and showcases their historical memorabilia and equipment.

MICHAEL MANCUSO AIR SHOWS
Mid-Island Air Service, Inc.,
Brookhaven Airport
139 Dawn Dr., Shirley
(516) 359-9948
www.mmairshows.com, www.midislandair.com

For wealthy families who are vacationing on Long Island and looking for a truly unique and over-the-top way to entertain their teenager, consider scheduling an aerobatic ride with world-famous stunt pilot Michael Mancuso. Riders will experience midair loops, rolls, and inverted flight. In addition to trips in a stunt airplane, rides in a biplane and Beech 18 war bird are also available. Exhilarating 20-minute flights start at $275 per person, and are guaranteed to be memorable and more exciting than a thrill ride offered at any amusement park.

NASSAU COUNTY AQUATIC CENTER
Eisenhower Park, East Meadow
(516) 572-0501
www.nassaucountyny.gov/agencies/Parks/WheretoGo/recreation/NC_aqua_ctr.html

Operated by the Nassau County Parks Department, this indoor public swimming pool is massive. Swimming lessons are offered for toddlers, kids, and teens, and water exercise classes and other events are hosted here year-round. The 80,000-square-foot center regularly hosts swimming and diving competitions, and is considered one of the most impressive public aquatic centers in America.

The building's main attraction is a unique "stretch" swimming pool that is 68 meters long and utilizes three movable bulkheads. Thus, the pool's setup varies from day to day, with 50-meter, 25-yard, and/or 25-meter lap lanes. There's also a diving well with a 10-meter competition diving tower, as well as 1- and 3-meter springboards. Admission and use of the pool is free; however, the Aquatic Center also features a recently renovated health club, for which a paid membership is required. Overlooking the pool, the health club includes a selection of professional fitness and exercise equipment, including treadmills, arc trainers, stationary bikes, stair machines, free weights, and an assortment of Cybex weight machines.

i **The Nassau County Aquatic Center was built in 1998 to host the International Goodwill Games.**

NEW YORK ISLANDERS
Nassau Veterans Memorial Coliseum
1255 Hempstead Tnpk., Uniondale
(800) 882-ISLES, (516) 794-9300
www.newyorkislanders.com, http://nassaucoliseum.com

For young hockey fans, experiencing a New York Islanders home game can be a thrilling experience, not to mention a great way for parents to spend quality time with their kids (assuming, of course, they're hockey fans). The NHL season typically runs between Oct and Apr. Visit the team's Web site for a schedule of home games and to purchase tickets online. Single-game tickets range from $19 to $140 through the box office. However, there's also the TicketExchange (available through the Islanders' Web site) that allows ticket holders to resell their unwanted tickets. Prices for these tickets are set by the ticket holders and will sometimes be offered at a significant discount (or sold at a premium, if a game is sold out and tickets are in demand).

At the Broadway Mall in Hicksville (516-935-2213) and the Westfield Sunrise Mall in Massapequa (516-795-0131), you'll find official New York Islanders Stores, where merchandise and other items of interest to fans are sold.

i **For kids and teens that enjoy the outdoors, in addition to the beaches, Nassau County has more than 36 state and county parks, most of which are open throughout the year. Some offer organized, kid-friendly activities and programs, while others simply offer beautiful places to enjoy nature. In the winter, for example, some of these parks contain awesome sledding hills, while during the warmer months, kids and teens (and their parents) can enjoy the bike and hiking paths, playgrounds, and picnic areas.**

RINGLING BROS. AND BARNUM & BAILEY CIRCUS
Nassau Veterans Memorial Coliseum
1255 Hempstead Tnpk., Uniondale
(516) 794-9300
http://nassaucoliseum.com

Throughout the year a variety of kid-friendly touring shows and concerts are presented at the Nassau Veterans Memorial Coliseum (also known simply as the Nassau Coliseum). For example, in Mar the *Ringling Bros. and Barnum & Bailey Circus* (www.ringling.com) comes to town. Other touring, kid-oriented shows that visit the coliseum include *Disney on Ice, Smucker's Stars on Ice,* and the Harlem Globetrotters. Visit the coliseum's Web site for a complete listing of events. Ticket prices vary, but the kid-oriented shows seldom sell-out, so same-day tickets are often available.

To keep up to date on the latest shows and events happening at the Nassau Coliseum so you can reserve your tickets in advance, sign up for the free electronic newsletter by visiting the coliseum's Web site (http://nassaucoliseum.com).

THE WATERFRONT CENTER
1 West End Ave., Oyster Bay
(516) 922-SAIL
www.thewaterfrontcenter.org

When the weather is warm, consider signing your kids up for sailing lessons. The WaterFront Center is a not-for-profit organization with a mission to serve the public by encouraging students of all ages to become actively involved in the preservation of the environment, and to promote the safe, enjoyable use of marine resources. The WaterFront Center is a U.S. Sailing Association–accredited facility, as well as a member of the American Sailing Association. Sailing lessons are available for both adults and children. Instruction is offered on 23-foot Sonars, Rhodes 19s, and cruising sloops with wheel steering, roller furling sails, and diesel auxiliary engines. All private and group sailing lessons are designed to accommodate an individual's unique learning style.

The Port Sailing School in Port Washington (516-767-7245, www.portsailing.com) offers a variety of age-appropriate private and group sailing lessons for kids, teens, and adults.

SUFFOLK COUNTY

The kid-friendly attractions and activities in Suffolk Country are mostly seasonal, and many involve the outdoors. You'll discover that several historical sites in Suffolk County also host special kid-oriented programs.

Families with kids can enjoy an afternoon visiting one of the region's local farms that offer seasonal "pick-your-own" activities. For example, at Davis Peach Farm (561 Hulse Landing Rd., Wading River; 631-929-1115; http://davispeachfarm.com), guests can pick peaches, nectarines, and apples between 9 a.m. and 5 p.m. daily (weather permitting) for only $1 per pound. At Hank's Pumpkintown (240 Montauk Hwy., Water Mill; 631-726-4667; http://hankspumpkintown.com) in Sept and Oct, guests can pick their own pumpkins and apples, take a hayride, or run around in vast corn mazes. Lewin Farms (Fresh Pond Ave., Calverton; 631-929-4327; http://lewinfarms.com) offers seasonal pick-your-own apples, strawberries, peaches, peppers, and tomatoes. In the fall you'll find a massive, four-acre corn maze here for kids and teens.

ADVENTURELAND AMUSEMENT PARK
2245 Broadhollow Rd. (Rte. 110), Farmingdale
(631) 694-6868
www.adventureland.us/themepark

Open seasonally between Apr and Nov, Adventureland is Suffolk County's largest and most impressive amusement park. Here you'll find a fun-filled carnival atmosphere, complete with rides, shows, games, and attractions. Some of the popular rides for teens and adults include a roller coaster, log flume, haunted house, Ferris wheel, and bumper cars. There is also a bunch of kiddie rides, plus an arcade and on-site dining opportunities.

A season pass for Adventureland is priced at just under $100. If you plan to visit several times throughout the summer and fall, it's an excellent deal compared to the regular daily admission fee of $24.99 for adults. The park is open seven days a week, but hours vary throughout the season. Check the Web site or call for details. Special events and shows are presented throughout the summer season. If you're visiting with kids, plan on spending at least a full day here. This is a great place to host a child's birthday party.

ANIMAL FARM PETTING ZOO
Wading River Rd., Manorville (exit 69 off the Long Island Expwy.)
(631) 878-1785
www.afpz.org

As you approach the parking lot for the Animal Farm Petting Zoo, it's impossible to tell that what

Meet Barbara Albach, owner of the Animal Farm Petting Zoo

Since 1981 Barbara Albach and her family have been operating the Animal Farm Petting Zoo & Family Park in Manorville. This 10-acre zoo and park attracts more than 30,000 visitors per year. What's unique about the Animal Farm is that it's a family-owned, nonprofit operation that's dedicated to caring for, rehabilitating, and sheltering unwanted farm and exotic animals. Unlike other zoos on Long Island, this one is noncommercial and very laid-back, and offers an unique experience that includes direct interaction with a wide range of friendly animals, plus the chance to see many exotic animals up close.

All of the money raised from admission charges goes directly to the care and feeding of the animals, and the maintenance of their cages and living areas. While operating the petting zoo has become more than a full-time job for Barbara Albach and her family, it's something they do motivated by their passion for the animals.

"Before we opened the petting zoo to the public, we were sheltering, raising, and rehabilitating animals here. We opened to the public because we wanted people to be able to see and learn from their own animal interactions, and see firsthand why people should not adopt animals they can't care for, or abuse animals they no longer want. We also needed the financial support to be able to take in and care for the animals," said Albach.

In addition to the admission charges, the petting zoo relies on donations of money, building supplies, landscaping supplies, fencing, and other resources to care for its animals. "We build and maintain all of our own cages and habitats for the animals," explained Albach. "We're always in need of equipment, but we manage to feed, water, and care for all of the animals every single day, regardless of the weather."

The zoo continually takes in unwanted and abused animals of all kinds that the local animal shelters are not capable of caring for. This includes farm animals, circus animals, and exotic pets ranging from snakes, rabbits, pigs, goats, and alligators to lion cubs and even a camel.

At any given time, the Animal Farm Petting Zoo cares for at least 300 animals, almost all of which can be seen by guests during their visit. "We take in a lot of ducks, rabbits, chickens, parrots, monkeys, deer, and pigs, but also a lot of more exotic animals, like lamas, miniature horses, and lion cubs. Often we'll take in animals until we can find better or more suitable homes for them," said Albach. "Among my favorite animals are the miniature African pigmy goats and the baby bunnies, but over the years I've learned to not get too attached to individual animals."

lies behind the main ticket office and modest gift shop is really a very large, extremely impressive, privately owned-and-operated interactive zoo that people of all ages will enjoy. Open seasonally, between Apr and Oct, the Animal Farm Petting Zoo is an outdoor attraction that allows visitors to see a wide range of exotic animals up close. Because the zoo adopts unwanted animals from zoos and circuses, as well as private individuals who can no longer support their exotic pets, new animals are constantly being added.

On any given day you're guaranteed to see parrots, a camel, an ostrich, kangaroos, monkeys, llamas, and reptiles, plus more traditional farm animals. The zoo has also been known to shelter lions and tigers until permanent homes can be found for them. Visitors are able to pet and feed some of the more friendly animals,

The zoo takes in unwanted animals and exotic pets, but not cats and dogs. "In addition to providing safe and comfortable homes for the animals we take in, we try to make it so visitors can see them. If the animals are friendly, we offer interaction with them. For example, guests can pet and feed some of the farm animals and bottle-feed the camel," she said.

One of the biggest challenges Albach faces when it comes to keeping the Animal Farm Petting Zoo operational is finding reliable and dedicated employees during the peak season when the park is open to guests (Apr through Oct). During this time of year, she manages between 10 and 12 employees. During the off-season, when the park is closed, just her immediate family members take care of the animals,.

"I have a love for animals, which is what keeps me motivated year after year to keep the Animal Farm Petting Zoo & Family Park going. There really is nowhere else in the region for unwanted or abused animals to go. The local shelters typically only accept cats and dogs. Over the years we've had all kinds of requests from people to take their unwanted exotic pets," said Albach.

In addition to allowing guests to see the animals up close and to pet some of them, Animal Farm offers kid-friendly activities almost every day, like puppet shows and kiddie rides. "The African pigmy goats love to interact with the kids. Our younger guests also love the free pony rides and the playgrounds we've set up. For parents, we offer a very relaxing atmosphere, and seldom have crowds," added Albach. "What we offer that's unique is the close contact with the animals, and the ability to hand or bottle-feed the friendly ones."

For Albach, in addition to being close to the animals, what she finds the most rewarding about operating the Animal Farm Petting Zoo & Family Park is watching the young children visit. "It's amazing to see a four-year-old's face who has never seen or touched a pony or goat before. They have this joy and excitement in their eyes that's incredible to see. That's a reward onto itself. The sense of reward and achievement I receive from the animals, however, is the true highlight of my life and work. The animals are truly happy here," she said.

If there's one thing that Albach would like people to know about Animal Farm, it's that the complex is really much bigger and more exciting than it looks from the outside. "Thousands of people drive by here every day, including a lot of local residents, but they have no clue whatsoever about what we offer here. From the outside, our facility looks very small. But we cover a full 10 acres, and we fully utilize this space. There is an awful lot to see and do here, and people don't realize it. We don't have an advertising budget like the other zoos in the region, for example. We rely on word of mouth," said Albach.

"I urge people of all ages to visit the Animal Farm Petting Zoo & Family Park. I truly believe it's a hidden gem on Long Island," she added.

like the baby pigs, cows, goats, and lambs. Pony rides are included with admission. During busier times, puppet shows and live animal shows are presented.

The Animal Farm Petting Zoo offers an extremely fun and impressive, but laid-back and noncommercial, parklike atmosphere. Plan on spending at least several hours here. It's also a wonderful place to celebrate a child's birthday. The zoo is a nonprofit organization that's been in operation since 1981. It is open to public Apr through Oct from 10 a.m. to 5 p.m. on weekdays, to 6 p.m. on weekends. The admission fee of $13.50 per adult and $11.50 per child goes directly to the care and feeding of the animals, and additional donations are always welcome.

ATLANTIS MARINE WORLD

413 East Main St., Riverhead
(631) 208-9200
www.atlantismarineworld.com

Themed around the lost city of Atlantis, Atlantis Marine World is an indoor/outdoor aquarium that's open year-round. The more than 100 exhibits blend science and nature with myth in order to create an informative, memorable, and entertaining environment for visitors of all ages. Live shows, interactive exhibits, and plenty of exotic marine life are on display. Admission is $21.50 for adults and $18.50 for children; however, discount coupons are available online and from various tourism guides distributed free at hotels, tourist attractions, and the chamber of commerce offices throughout Long Island.

Plan on spending at least a full day here. If you're visiting the region for the summer, season passes (annual memberships) allow for unlimited visits and are an excellent deal. The aquarium is open year-round every day except Christmas. In addition to the shows, attractions, and exhibits included as part of the standard admission, the aquarium offers a handful of special programs, such as a Pirate Snorkel Adventure, Shark Dive, Animal Trainer program, the Atlantis Explorer Boat Tour, the Scientist for a Day program, Summer Adventure Days, Winter Adventure Days, and Member Sleepovers, which can be experienced for an additional fee.

i One of the more popular exhibits at Atlantis Marine World is the 120,000-gallon Lost City of Atlantis Shark Tank. You'll also discover North America's largest all-living coral reef, which is beautiful, plus the penguin pavilion, where you'll see more than one hundred adorable penguins frolicking around. The daily sea lion show is also highly entertaining.

BAY STREET THEATRE

Bay St. (Long Wharf), Sag Harbor
(631) 725-9500
www.baystreet.org

In addition to offering an ongoing lineup of musicals and shows targeted to families and adults, as well as an adults-only comedy club, Bay Street Theatre has an ongoing children's program called KidStreet, which includes movies, live shows, and concerts. Bay Street also hosts a theater camp for kids in Feb, Apr, and Aug in conjunction with school vacations (see www.baystreet.org/camps). Check the Web site for a listing of kid- and family-oriented shows and performances.

BOOMERS FAMILY FUN CENTER

655 Long Island Ave., Medford
(631) 475-1771
www.boomersparks.com/park/medford/index.html

This is an indoor/outdoor family entertainment complex, complete with restaurant, miniature golf, go-karts, bumper boats, kiddie rides, batting cages, a train ride, video arcade, and other activities. The indoor rides and activities are open throughout the year, while the outdoor rides and activities close during the off-season and reopen in Apr. During the spring and summer, Boomers is open seven days a week, sometimes until 10 p.m. However, during the off-peak season, the complex is only open on weekends and offers more limited hours.

Boomers is a fun and exciting place to visit with kids and teens, and a great place to host a child's birthday party. Plan on spending at least several hours here during each visit. There's a separate charge, between $1 and $6, for each ride or activity you participate in, though money-saving packages are available.

CHILDREN'S MUSEUM OF EAST END

376 Bridgehampton/Sag Harbor Tnpk., Bridgehampton
(631) 537-8250
www.cmee.org

This kid-friendly museum offers a variety of fun and educational hands-on exhibits and activities that focus on several different themes, including agriculture, nature, fishing, and history. Some of the exhibits are permanent, while others change with the season. The 10,000-square-foot museum is open daily except Tues, typically from 9 a.m. to 5 p.m. Visiting the Children's Museum of East End is a perfect rainy day activity, or a great way to spend an afternoon enjoying quality time with your kids. In addition to the popular indoor activities and exhibits, visitors are encouraged to explore the museum's outdoor attractions, which include extensive, people-size mazes and gardens. Workshops, special performances, and unique events are hosted here throughout the year. General admission is $7 for anyone over the age of one, or free with an annual membership.

i For toddlers, the Children's Museum of East End offers ongoing art, music, and movement classes with MoonSoup, as well as Mommy & Me classes (for parents and children together) and gymnastics classes taught in the Hamptons Tumblebus (a custom-modified bus). Kid-specific cooking classes and Sandpiper music programs are also held throughout the year. There are fees associated with each of these classes and workshops. For more information or to register by phone, call (631) 537-8250, or visit www.cmee.org/classes.asp. Space is limited, and classes are kept small.

COLD SPRING HARBOR FISH HATCHERY & AQUARIUM

Rte. 25A and Rte. 108, Cold Spring Harbor (on the Nassau/Suffolk border)
(516) 692-6768
www.cshfha.org

While not originally designed to be a tourist attraction, the Cold Spring Harbor Fish Hatchery & Aquarium has evolved into a popular, fun, and educational place for kids and teens to visit. This fish hatchery has been in existence since 1883, when the first brown trout were important to America. The hatchery has now become an environmental education center, as well as a working fish hatchery and aquarium.

Within the aquarium exhibits is the largest collection of freshwater fish in New York State. You'll also see reptiles and amphibians on display, plus view firsthand how a working fish hatchery operates. Visitors can typically see and feed newly hatched trout. The Cold Spring Harbor Fish Hatchery & Aquarium is open year-round. A $6 per adult and $4 per child admission fee applies. Plan on spending at least several hours here to see the exhibits and demonstrations. Special events are also held throughout the year. Visit www.cshfha.org/events.html for a complete listing of events.

DEEP HOLLOW RANCH

Montauk Hwy., Montauk
(631) 688-2744
www.deephollowranch.com

This working ranch offers a variety of fun and educational activities for kids and families alike. In addition to horseback-riding lessons, pony rides for young kids, and horse-drawn wagon tours for everyone, a theatrical narrative featuring actors portraying famous historical figures is presented. Cattle drive and sheep-herding demonstrations are also offered. Deep Hollow Ranch is America's oldest cattle ranch. It has been in operation since the 1800s, and is guaranteed to provide unique and memorable entertainment for everyone.

HARBOR TOURS ABOARD *AMERICAN BEAUTY II*

Sag Harbor
(631) 725-0397
www.americanbeautycruises.com

With so much beautiful water surrounding Long Island, one of the best ways to experience it is by taking a sightseeing cruise. Captain Don Heckman and his boat, the *American Beauty II,* is just one of your many options if you're looking to experience a 90-minute narrated sightseeing cruise or two-hour sunset cruise in and around Sag Harbor. The boat's capacity is 38 passengers. Tour prices start at $23 for adults and $13 for children. *American Beauty II* operates seasonally from Sag Harbor in Suffolk County.

i In Montauk, one of the companies that offer sightseeing cruises, as well as fishing excursions, is Vikings of Montauk (631-688-5700, www.vikingfleet.com). The half-day fishing expeditions, for example, are designed for people of all ages, including kids and teens. If you want to experience a sightseeing cruise while visiting Nassau County, contact Lady Liberty Cruises in Port Washington (516-486-3057) or *Nautical Queen* and *Nautical Princess* in Freeport (516-623-5712).

HOLTSVILLE ECOLOGY SITE & PARK
249 Buckley Rd., Holtsville
(631) 758-9664

Open throughout the year, this small, kid-friendly zoo features an assortment of animals, including goats, sheep, mountain lions, bobcats, bald eagles, and deer. Many of the animals here are being rehabilitated, or were injured and for some reason cannot be returned to the wild.

LONG ISLAND DUCKS
CitiBank Park, Islip
(613) 940-DUCK
www.liducks.com

The 6,000-seat Citibank Park is home to the Long Island Duck minor-league baseball team. Home games are played between May and Oct, with tickets going on sale beginning in Mar. The tickets are affordable, and many games offer special kid-friendly programs and activities, including fireworks shows and a "Kids Club Day." This is a wonderful, family-friendly activity, particularly for baseball fans. Throughout the season you can sign your kids up for baseball clinics, which are taught by the players and coaches. For $25 per year, children can also register for the official Long Island Ducks Kids' Club, which has a variety of perks and benefits.

LONG ISLAND GAME FARM WILDLIFE PARK & CHILDREN'S ZOO
Chapman Blvd., Manorville (exit 70 off the Long Island Expwy.)
(631) 878-6644
www.longislandgamefarm.com

Open between Apr and Oct, the Long Island Game Farm Wildlife Park & Children's Zoo offers a more traditional and commercial, zoolike experience than the Animal Farm Petting Zoo, though both are well worth visiting with kids. Long Island Game Farm features kangaroos, giraffes, cougars, peacocks, lemurs, and dozens of other animals. The zoo also has its own gift shop and presents animal-feeding shows throughout the day. It has been around for more than 40 years, and continues to expand and improve each year, with new exhibits, shows, and attractions. Kids in particular will enjoy the petting zoo areas, where they can pet, cuddle, and even bottle-feed baby animals, including pigs, chickens, ducks, rabbits, and ponies.

While visiting the zoo, kids can also experience the carnival-style rides, such as the spinning teacups, Rio Grande mini train, and antique carousel. Pony rides are also offered. Long Island Game Farm is open daily from 10 a.m. to 4:30 p.m. on weekdays, and to 5:30 p.m. on weekends. During the peak summer season (late May through early Sept), a one-day admission ticket is priced at $17.45 plus tax for adults, $15.45 plus tax for kids. If you're spending the summer on Long Island, however, a season pass offers a much better deal, as well as additional perks for guests. In addition to the usual day-to-day activities, shows, and exhibits, a variety of special events are held here throughout the summer, including a festive opening-day celebration at the start of the season in April.

PAINTBALL ARENA
400 Patton Ave., West Babylon
(631) 694-2707
www.islandpaintball.net

For more than 20 years, Paintball Arena has been a premier destination on Long Island to experience the thrill and competition of paintball. All of the equipment needed can be rented on the premises. The indoor arena, which is open year-round, is the perfect place to host a birthday party, special event, or friendly competition with friends. The arena is open Tues through Sun, and hours vary by season. The basic package starts at $35 per person per day, and includes admission

Send Your Kids to Camp Zoo for a Week

Of particular interest to kids is the weeklong Camp Zoo programs offered each summer at the Long Island Game Farm Wildlife Park & Children's Zoo. Camp Zoo is a day-camp program for children between the ages of 4 and 11, with sessions that run throughout July and Aug.

During each day of Camp Zoo, participants experience different fully supervised activities within the zoo, including behind-the-scenes tours, close-up animal encounters, nature walks, arts and crafts, sing-alongs, and other zoo- and animal-themed activities. Each day's activities run from 10 a.m. to 3 p.m., with camp sessions held Mon through Fri, rain or shine.

Camp Zoo sessions throughout the summer are targeted to specific age groups. Space is limited, so it's important to register your child early. The "New Camper" rate to participate in Camp Zoo is $445 per week. This includes two snacks per day, water, and juice. Participants should bring their own lunch. Each participant receives an official Camp Zoo T-shirt and a CD containing photos of their weeklong experience.

and equipment rental. Check the Web site for weekly specials.

PUFF & PUTT FAMILY FUN CENTER
Montauk Village, Montauk
(631) 668-4473

This outdoor family-fun complex offers sailboat, pedal boat, Hobie Cat, canoe, and kayak rentals by the hour, as well as a fun and challenging 18-hole miniature golf course. It's open seasonally. This is a great place to take the kids during the day or evening just for fun, or to celebrate a special event such as a birthday party. A family with kids can easily spend between one and three hours here per visit.

RITA'S STABLE
3 West Lake Dr., Montauk
(631) 668-5453

In addition to offering horseback-riding trail excursions and lessons to kids and teens, as well as adults, Rita's Stable also features pony rides for toddlers and a lovely, interactive petting zoo. Fresh free-range farm eggs and organically grown vegetables can also be purchased here. Rita's Stable is open year-round, but some activities and offerings are seasonal.

i Many of the golf courses on Long Island offer private and group lessons specifically for kids, and some offer more formal golf day camps.

SAG HARBOR FIRE DEPARTMENT MUSEUM
Sage St. and Church St., Sag Harbor
(631) 725-0779
www.sagharborfd.com/museum.htm

Open only during July and Aug, this museum showcases the work of the oldest volunteer fire department in the state, and pays tribute to their accomplishments. The fire department was established in 1803, and the building that houses this museum was constructed in 1833. The small museum opened to the public in 1978. On display you'll find firefighting equipment dating back to the 19th century. Hours are 11 a.m. to 4 p.m. every day except Wed. There is a $1 admission fee for adults, 50 cents for children.

SOUTH FORK NATURAL HISTORY MUSEUM & NATURE CENTER
377 Bridgehampton/Sag Harbor Tnpk., Bridgehampton
(631) 537-9735
www.sofo.org

Take a Day Trip to NYC with the Kids

If you're looking for something fun to do with your kids and can't seem to find just the right activity on Long Island, consider taking a day trip to Manhattan, where you'll find literally hundreds of activities and attractions that are suitable for people of all ages.

New York's Central Park (www.centralparknyc.org), for example, offers a kid-oriented zoo, multiple playgrounds, and other activities. You can also purchase tickets for a matinee Broadway show (www.Broadway.com), such as *Disney's The Lion King*, or take a 90-minute, two-hour, or three-hour tour around Manhattan aboard the Circle Line (www.circleline42.com). For kids, the 90-minute tour is recommended, during which you'll see New York's amazing skyline, Ellis Island, and the Statue of Liberty.

There are also several fun bus tours that'll take you around Manhattan and let you hop on and off at your leisure. Check out the tours operated by Gray Line (www.newyorksightseeing.com), for example. Kids and teens, however, will prefer taking a tour with NYC Ducks (888-838-2570, www.coachusa.com/nycducks). These entertaining and lighthearted 75-minute tours operate seasonally and use large amphibious vehicles, created during World War II, that travel both on land and in the water.

A trip to the top of the Empire State Building, where the view of Manhattan is spectacular, is typically a favorite among kids and teens. Or, you can visit Rockefeller Center and take the NBC Experience Tour (www.nbcuniversalstore.com), go ice-skating in the winter, see the Rockefeller Christmas tree during the holiday season, and/or visit the Top of the Rock Observatory (www.topoftherocknyc.com).

While you're in the area, consider seeing a show or concert at Radio City Music Hall (www.radiocity.com). *The Radio City Christmas Spectacular, Featuring The Rockettes,* is a must-see show during the holiday season. Just outside of Manhattan is the Bronx Zoo (www.bronxzoo.com) and the New York Botanical Gardens (www.nybg.org), both of which offer a full-day's worth of entertainment for the entire family.

Open throughout the year, the South Fork Natural History Museum & Nature Center (SoFo) is a state-of-the-art facility that features exhibits, activities, workshops, and special programs for people of all ages, especially for kids. There's also a group of interactive habitats here that feature live animals, such as native reptiles and amphibians. The marine touch tank allows young people to touch local marine wildlife.

SoFo does an excellent job at bringing nature indoors. As guests walk through the museum, it's like taking an interpretive hike through nature. At the start of your journey, you'll be provided with a field guide to help you understand and relate to what you're experiencing at each stop. The displays and exhibits will engage all your senses. You and the kids will feel like naturalists exploring a new territory for the first time. The museum is open seven days a week from 10 a.m. to 4 p.m. A low admission fee is charged for both adults ($7) and kids ($5).

SOUTHAMPTON TOWN RECREATION CENTER
1370A Majors Path, Southampton
(631) 287-1511
www.sysinc.com

Southampton Youth Services, a nonprofit organization, manages the Southampton Town Recreation Center—a 65,000-square-foot facility offering basketball, volleyball, indoor soccer, field hockey, lacrosse, batting cages, a walking track,

Sports fans of all ages will enjoy catching a home game played by the New York Yankees, New York Mets, New York Jets, New York Giants, New York Knicks, or one of the other mega-popular sports teams that call the Big Apple home. See the "Spectator Sports" chapter for information on attending professional sporting events in NYC.

If you'd rather take your kids shopping, there's the world's largest Toys "R" Us store in Times Square (www2.toysrus.com/TimesSquare), as well as the world-famous FAO Schwartz toy store (767 Fifth Ave., www.fao.com) and the popular American Girl Place (609 Fifth Ave., www.americangirl.com). The shops and activities at the South Street Seaport (www.southstreetseaport.com) are also fun, especially when the weather is nice.

New York is also world-famous for its museums. The American Museum of Natural History (www.amnh.org) is a perennial favorite of kids and teens, thanks in part to the massive dinosaur exhibit.

As for dining, New York City is home to plenty of theme restaurants, like Planet Hollywood (www.planethollywood.com) and the Hard Rock Cafe (www.hardrock.com), both located in Times Square. A few blocks from Times Square is Mars 2112 (www.mars2112.com), a family-oriented restaurant with an outer space and space aliens theme. The waiters and waitresses wear detailed alien costumes, and the main dining room resembles a space station on Mars. A wide range of special effects are used to add realism to the very unique dining and entertainment experience.

Also in the Times Square area is Ellen's Stardust Diner (www.ellensstardustdiner.com). This New York–style diner is unique in that all of the waiters and waitresses are also talented singers—in fact, many have performed on Broadway. In between serving guests their meals, the staff performs popular, family-friendly songs throughout the day and evening. This is a great place to bring a family for lunch, dinner, an after-show snack, or dessert. The food is just average, but the entertainment is highly enjoyable and lively.

To avoid dealing with tolls, traffic, and parking in Manhattan, simply take the Long Island Railroad from wherever you're staying on Long Island. It'll take you directly to Penn Station in the heart of New York City within one hour from Nassau County or two hours from Suffolk County.

and a wide range of other activities. Throughout the year, particularly in the summer, many kid-oriented activities and programs are offered. Visit the Web site or call for details.

i In the fall, during harvest time, many of the farms on Long Island's North Fork create interactive corn mazes that are open to the public. These mazes will keep your kids entertained for hours as they run through the corn fields searching for the exit. Look for roadside signs for these mazes, or check out ads in local newspapers and tourist publications.

SPLISH SPLASH ISLAND
2549 Splish Splash Dr., Calverton
(631) 727-3600
www.splishsplashlongisland.com

On hot summer days, if you're looking for an exciting alternative to a day frolicking at the beach, check out the region's largest water park. Splish Splash Island, which celebrated its 20th season in 2010, is open seasonally (late May through early Sept). The family-friendly park encompasses 96 acres and is chock-full of waterslides, rides, and swimming pools. While you'll find small slides and pools for kids, this water park also caters to thrill-seeking teens and adults. For example, one of the park's most recent additions is Dr. VonDark's Tunnel of Terror, a waterslide that ends with an extremely steep 40-foot drop. Hollywood Stunt Rider is a high-speed white-water rafting ride, while Max Trax allows two people to simultaneously race down a steep waterslide with a 50-foot drop.

In addition to the park's water-based activities, Splish Splash Island features an impressive tropical parrot show, *Close Encounters of the Bird Kind*. It's presented several times daily (11 a.m., 1 p.m., 3 p.m., and 5 p.m.) mid-June through early Sept. Daily ticket prices are $36.99 per adult and $27.99 per child. However, if you'll be staying in the area, an annual pass, priced at $69.99 per person, offers a much better deal.

SUFFOLK COUNTY FARM & EDUCATION CENTER
4600 Yaphank Ave., Yaphank
(631) 852-4600
http://ccesuffolk.org

This is a 100-year-old, 300-acre working farm that's open to the public from Apr to late Oct (and limited times during various holiday periods). What you'll discover here are entertaining and informative interactive workshops and demonstrations, plus a petting zoo that features sheep, goats, pigs, cows, and other animals. Developed and operated by Cornell University faculty and local youth-development specialists, visitors can participate in a self-guided tour of the farm and its facilities, plus take part in a variety of educational programs that cover such topics as gardening, landscaping, food, nutrition, and health. The farm also hosts a variety of specialized kid-friendly programs. It is open daily from 9 a.m. to 3 p.m., except for Thanksgiving, Christmas, and Easter. Admission is free. Visit the Web site for a listing of special kid-oriented events and day-camp activities offered during the summer. This is a great place to host a child's birthday party.

i If you're looking for a weeklong day camp for your child in the Southampton area, between mid-June and late Aug, Future Stars Summer Camp (631-287-6707, www.fscamps.com) hosts a variety of specialized camps for kids between the ages of 4 and 16. For example, the organization offers specialized squash, tennis, soccer, basketball, and golf camps.

SUFFOLK COUNTY VANDERBILT MUSEUM (AND PLANETARIUM)
180 Little Neck Rd., Centerport
(631) 854-5555
www.vanderbiltmuseum.org

The state-of-the-art planetarium at the Suffolk County Vanderbilt Museum has ongoing Sky Shows that are both entertaining and educational. It's open year-round and offers a variety of kid-friendly shows and programs. Throughout the summer the main museum also offers special children's programs. During summer 2009, for example, there was a program open to kids between the ages of 6 and 12 called Wizard University. During the month of July, four weeklong sessions were held, with each day's activities lasting from 9 a.m. to 3 p.m. During the month of Aug, instead of weeklong programs, single-day classes and workshops were held. Contact the museum for schedules.

SPECTATOR SPORTS

When it comes to sports, Long Island shares many of its professional teams with all of New York. Though Long Island itself doesn't have many of its own teams, several New York teams have their home on Long Island.

As you'd probably guess, New Yorkers can be pretty passionate about their home teams and favorite athletes, whether they're baseball, football, basketball, hockey, soccer, lacrosse, NASCAR, tennis, golf, swimming, ice-skating, boating, fishing, or equestrian fans. Thus, when it comes to enjoying their free time, these fans can be found attending home games or events, or hanging out at local sports bars watching their favorite team(s) and athlete(s) compete, or they'll have the ultimate home theater setup in order to watch their favorite sports in high-definition with surround sound.

Thanks to the latest mobile phone technology, keeping up with professional sports teams and athletes is easy via the Internet. Plus, coverage of local professional sports is abundant in all forms of New York media—from newspapers and regional magazines to sports-oriented radio stations and sports reports on the local TV news. On the various Long Island and New York cable television systems, there are also local sports television networks, as well as the ESPN networks.

After all, some of the most popular sports teams in the world are based in New York, including the New York Jets and New York Giants NFL teams; New York Yankees and New York Mets MLB teams; New York Knicks NBA team; New York Liberty WNBA team; New York Rangers and New York Islanders NHL teams; New York Red Bulls MLS team; and the Long Island Lizards major-league lacrosse team.

Whatever your favorite sport, chances are you'll be able to watch it live and in person either on Long Island, or by taking a quick trip into Manhattan (home of Madison Square Garden), the Bronx (home of Yankee Stadium), Flushing (home of Mets Stadium), or East Rutherford, New Jersey (home of Meadowlands Stadium, where the New York Giants play until 2012, when their new stadium will be completed).

Most of the professional and college-level spectator sports on Long Island take place in Nassau County. However, Suffolk County does host events such as boating, fishing, bicycling, and golf competitions.

For professionals and amateurs alike, golf is a huge deal on Long Island. In fact, the region is home to some of the most famous golf courses on the East Coast, and is where a handful of major golf tournaments are hosted each year. For example, Bethpage State Park's Black Course (known among golfers simply as "The Black") hosted the PGA's U.S. Open in June 2009 (for the second time in a decade), as well as countless other tournaments. The Red Course at Eisenhower Park is also a popular course for PGA tournaments, including an annual PGA seniors tour event. Golf is one of the most popular pastimes throughout

i The *Long Island Newsday* newspaper features ongoing, extensive coverage of local and regional high school sports, and maintains an online magazine offering up-to-the-minute high school sports coverage, which can be accessed for free at www.newsday.com/sports/high-school.

Sporting Event Tickets

Whether you're a New Yorker, Long Islander, or just visiting, you'll probably want to purchase season or individual tickets to your favorite sporting events and home games well in advance, as they tend to sell out quickly.

Each team has its own ticket office, and many of the teams and events also utilize Ticketmaster (www.ticketmaster.com) for ticket sales. In addition to the general ticket information and ordering phone number, which is (866) 448-7849, Ticketmaster has special phone numbers to purchase tickets for NBA games (800-462-2849), U.S. Open tournaments (866-673-6849), WNBA games (877-962-2849), and New York Yankees games (212-307-1212). Throughout New York, including Long Island, Ticketmaster also has retail locations where tickets can be purchased in person, without having to visit the venue's box office.

Once tickets to an event or game are sold out, you can often purchase tickets through a licensed ticket broker (usually for a hefty premium). When working with a broker, tickets often go for double, triple, or even quadruple the original ticket price, depending on demand. Some ticket brokers will purchase tickets from private sellers unable to utilize them.

Another, less reliable option is to purchase tickets from scalpers (often found outside of stadiums, arenas, and venues) or from private sellers using an online service, such as eBay or Craigslist. When utilizing one of these two methods, however, you never know if the tickets you're buying are authentic until you try to enter the venue.

The following is a partial listing of independent ticket brokers you can contact yourself:

Hallmark Tickets: (800) 910-1225, www.hallmarktickets.com/Venues/Long_Island_University

Online Seats: (866) 999-4518, www.onlineseats.com/college-basketball-tickets/liu-brooklyn/index.asp

Sold Out Tickets: (800) 316-5733, www.soldoutbroadwaytickets.com/long_island_ducks.htm

StubHub: www.stubhub.com/sports-tickets

Ticket Center: (800) 838-9292, www.ticketcenter.com

Ticket City: (800) 880-8886, www.ticketcity.com/long-island-tickets.html

Ticket Liquidator: (800) 456-8499, www.ticketliquidator.com

Tickets of America: (212) 736-2300, www.ticketsofamerica.com

the Hamptons. The Shinnecock Hills Golf Club in Southampton, for example, has been in existence since 1891 and has hosted numerous major golfing events over the years, including the U.S. Open in 1896, 1986, 1995, and 2004.

BASEBALL

LONG ISLAND DUCKS
CitiBank Park, Islip
(613) 940-DUCK
www.liducks.com

The 6,000-seat Citibank Park in Islip is the home of the Long Island Duck minor-league baseball team. Home games are played between May and Oct, with tickets going on sale starting in Mar. The tickets are affordable, and many games offer special family- and kid-friendly programs and activities, including fireworks shows and a "Kids Club Day." This is a wonderful family-friendly activity, particularly for baseball fans.

i In New York State (including Long Island), reselling sporting event tickets for more than face value requires a license from the Department of Consumer Affairs. A licensed ticket broker will display its license number in all advertising, or be happy to reveal this information to you over the telephone. To determine if a ticket broker is licensed, call (212) 487-4436 during business hours.

NEW YORK METS
Citi Field
Roosevelt Ave. at 126th Street, Flushing, Queens
(718) 507-8499 (tickets)
www.mets.com

The New York Mets now play their home games in a state-of-the-art stadium called Citi Field, which replaced Shea Stadium. Completed in 2009, this new stadium has a seating capacity of 41,800, along with 54 luxury suites, an auditorium, a business center, and 6 restaurants. Plenty of parking is available at the stadium (more than 12,000 parking spaces), plus it's easily accessible via New York subway or Long Island Railroad.

The New York Mets are a member of the East Division of Major League Baseball's National League. The team formed in 1962 and won the World Series title in 1969 and again in 1986. The Mets earned their most recent East Division title in 2006. According to research conducted in 1998, Long Islanders are more apt to be Mets fans than Yankees fans.

NEW YORK YANKEES
Yankee Stadium
161st St. and River Ave., The Bronx
(718) 293-6000 (tickets), (718) 579-4531 (tours)
www.yankees.com

As one of Major League Baseball's most popular teams, and probably the most famous baseball team in the world, in 2009 the New York Yankees moved into their brand-new, state-of-the-art stadium. The very first game played there was against the Boston Red Sox in front of more than 74,200 spectators. The new stadium has a capacity of 52,325 (including standing room) and includes 56 private luxury suites, 410 party suites, 272 permanent concession stands, 172 portable concession stands, and 12 unique dining options, including full-service restaurants, several bars/lounges, and a food court. The original Yankee Stadium had been in use since 1923. The final game played in the historic stadium took place on Sept 21, 2008, against the Baltimore Orioles. To commemorate the stadium's final season, the 2008 Major League All-Star Game was hosted at the now former Yankee Stadium.

The New York Yankees were founded in 1903, when the defunct Baltimore franchise of the American League was purchased for just $18,000 and moved to New York. Since then this team and its individual players have continued to make history. In 1920, for example, the Yankees purchased the contract of Babe Ruth from the Boston Red Sox. In 1921 the team clenched the American League pennant and construction began on the now former Yankee Stadium. Over the decades dozens of the sport's most famous players have worn a Yankees uniform, including Mickey Mantle, Lou Gehrig, Joe DiMaggio, Phil Rizzuto, Don Mattingly, Reggie Jackson, and Yogi Berra.

As soon as the Yankees settled into their new home, the team quickly set a new major-league record by playing 18 consecutive error-free games, between May 14 and June 1, 2009. Throughout its history, the team has won the World Series 27 times, most recently in 2009. The 2010 season is slated to begin and end with games against the team's longtime rival, the Boston Red Sox.

i The scoreboard at the new Yankee Stadium is 59 feet high by 101 feet wide. It shows video in True HD.

BASKETBALL

NEW YORK KNICKS
Madison Square Garden
Seventh Ave. between 31st St. and 33rd St., New York
(212) 465-6471 (tickets)
www.nba.com/knicks

Madison Square Garden (www.thegarden.com) is home to the New York Knicks, New York Liberty, and New York Rangers. This is a massive indoor stadium/arena located in the heart of Manhattan, directly above Penn Station. Long Islanders can simply hop on the Long Island Railroad to Penn Station, go up a few escalators (or elevators), and find themselves courtside (or rinkside).

Because of the New York Knicks' popularity, it's common to see celebrities and local politicians at their home games. Games take place between Nov and Apr. The team was founded in 1946 as a founding member of the Basketball Association of America (BAA), and was originally known as the New York Knickerbockers. It later became part of the NBA when the BAA merged with the NBA. During its history, the team has won two championships (1970 and 1973), eight conference titles (most recently in 1999), and nine division titles (most recently in 1994).

NEW YORK LIBERTY
Madison Square Garden
Seventh Ave. between 31st St. and 33rd St., New York
(212) 564-WNBA (tickets)
www.wnba.com/liberty

This popular, professional women's basketball team also plays at Madison Square Garden. The league's season runs from May through Sept. The Liberty was established in Oct 1996, when the WNBA was launched. It was one of just eight charter teams. Among the first players to join the now famous team were Rebecca Lobo and Teresa Weatherspoon.

During the 2008 season, the players on the team averaged just 24.2 years old, the youngest average age in the WNBA. Yet, the team scored 105 points for the first time in franchise history when hosting the defending WNBA champion Phoenix Mercury, back in June 2008. Pat Coyle coached the team's first 19-win season since 2001, wrapping the regular season with a 19-15 record. The team then made its fifth appearance in the Eastern Conference Finals.

COLLEGE SPORTS

College-level sports also continue to be popular among sports fans of all ages, and Long Island hosts its share of major college sporting events. For example, throughout the year there's sure to be some type of athletic competition (such as a college basketball game) happening at Hofstra University's David S. Mack Sports and Exhibition Complex in Hempstead, or at the university's massive stadium, which is where the New York Jets practice.

C. W. Post in Brookville has both men's and women's teams that perform well season after season in football, basketball, soccer, and lacrosse, while the teams associated with Nassau Community College and Adelphi University in Garden City participate in no less than 21 intercollegiate sports.

HOFSTRA UNIVERSITY
Hempstead
www.hofstra.edu/Athletics, www.goHofstra.com

As New York's largest private college, Hofstra University actively participates in 17 intercollegiate sports that compete at the NCAA Division I level. All games, tournaments, and sporting events are open to spectators. For people living in Nassau County who follow college sports, chances are it's the Hofstra teams they're rooting for.

If you're interested in watching baseball, field hockey, softball, wrestling, volleyball, or men's or women's basketball, cross-country, golf, lacrosse, soccer, or tennis, you'll find the competition to be fierce, and the team spirit to be high, at Hofstra

University. Tickets for events can be purchased online, starting as low as $8 each.

FOOTBALL

NEW YORK GIANTS

Giants Stadium
East Rutherford, NJ
(201) 935-8111 (tickets)
www.giants.com

In Aug 2010 the New York Giants are scheduled to move into a brand-new stadium that's currently being constructed (www.nyg2010.com). They'll share the stadium with the New York Jets. The Giants's previous stadium (located right next to the new one) was the team's home in East Rutherford, New Jersey, since 1976.

At a cost of $1.6 billion, the new stadium will offer 82,500 seats, 9,300 "club seats," a 130,00-square-foot Club Lounge area, 4 scoreboards, more than 800 concession stands, and 27,500 parking spaces. Throughout the stadium will be 2,500 high-definition monitors showcasing the on-field action. There will also be four massive, 40-by-100-foot high-definition video screens—one in each corner of the stadium. In addition to numerous restaurants and bars, the new stadium will also feature 20,000 square feet of retail space. There will be direct train service to the new stadium from Penn Station, which is where Long Islanders wind up if they take the Long Island Railroad into Manhattan.

Within the NFL, the New York Giants are part of the Eastern Division of the National Football Conference. The team joined the NFL in 1925, and over the years has earned seven NFL titles, including three Super Bowl championships, in 1986, 1990, and 2007. Giants team members have included 15 Hall of Fame players, including as Mel Hein, Frank Gifford, and Lawrence Taylor.

NEW YORK JETS

Meadowlands Sports Complex
50 Rte. 120, East Rutherford, NJ
(516) 560-8200 (tickets)
www.newyorkjets.com

For the 2010–11 season the New York Jets will move into their new stadium, a 700,000-square-foot complex located slightly north and slightly east of the old stadium (where the former no. 3, 4, 6, 7, and 8 parking lots were located). The new stadium will offer a wide range of improvements, including 82,500 wider, cushioned seats, a variety of new restaurants and bars, and a state-of-the-art sound system. Thanks to a new train station near the complex, getting to the new stadium is easy from anywhere on Long Island. Simply take the Long Island Railroad to Penn Station, then hop on the new direct train to the stadium and enjoy the 20-minute trip.

The New York Jets are members of the Eastern Division of the NFL's American Football Conference. The team was established in 1960 and was originally called the New York Titans. In 1963 the team joined the NFL (when it merged with the AFL), and the name was changed to the New York Jets. The Jets have made their way into the playoffs a total of 13 times in their history, most recently during the 2009 season. One of the most famous team members was Joe Namath, though other players, such as Dan Marino, Ken O'Brien, Art Monk, and Brett Favre, have made football history playing for the Jets. In Jan 2009 the team welcomed Rex Ryan as its newest head coach.

GOLF

On Long Island, golf is both a participatory sport and a wildly popular spectator sport. A wide range of amateur, charity, and professional tournaments are held at the various Long Island golf courses during the warmer months. In fact, you can pretty much find some type of tournament to attend almost every weekend between early May and late Oct at one of the region's popular golf courses.

For a listing of golf tournaments and events taking place on Long Island, contact the Long Island Golf Association at (516) 746-1015 or visit www.longislandgolf.org. Among the members of the not-for-profit Long Island Golf Association are 81 private and public clubs. The organization hosts 15 championships for its members, plus manages a team of Long Island's best amateurs who compete annually in the Stoddard Trophy against teams from Westchester, New Jersey, and Connecticut.

The following golf courses host ongoing tournaments and are among the island's most popular.

BETHPAGE STATE PARK'S BLACK COURSE
99 Quaker Meetinghouse Rd., Farmingdale
(516) 249-0700
www.nysparks.state.ny.us/golf-courses/11/details.aspx

In addition to the internationally known Black Course, Bethpage State Park is home to four other 18-hole golf courses (the Red, Blue, Green, and Yellow), which are open to the public. The Black Course was designed by A. W. Tillinghast, and was home to the U.S. Open in 2002 and 2009. Approximately 300,000 rounds of golf are played annually, plus these courses regularly host tournaments.

EISENHOWER PARK GOLF COURSES
Stewart Ave. and Merrick Ave., East Meadow
(516) 572-0327
www.nassaucountyny.gov/agencies/Parks/Golf/18hole.html

Eisenhower Park is home to three 18-hole championship golf courses, the Red, White, and Blue courses, each of which regularly hosts amateur, charity, and professional tournaments during the warmer months of the year. To discover what tournaments or events are being held at any given time, call or visit the Web site.

The Red Course was designed by Devereux Emmet and constructed in 1914. It was originally part of the Salisbury Golf Club, and it hosted the PGA Championship in 1926. The course was taken over by Nassau County in 1944, and in 1969 was rededicated as Eisenhower Park. More recently, the course has hosted the PGA's Champions Tour. In 2007 *Newsday* ranked it number 4 on its list of top-10 Long Island golf courses. The White Course was designed in 1950 by Robert Trent Jones. Like the Blue Course, which was also designed by Jones (in 1951), it is open year-round, weather permitting. The Red Course closes altogether during the winter months.

THE SHINNECOCK HILLS GOLF CLUB
200 Tuckahoe Rd., Southampton
(631) 283-1310

As a private club, the Shinnecock Hills Golf Club is not open to the public for playing, but the public is often invited to be spectators for major tournaments and golfing events held here. This is the oldest formal golf club in the United States (founded in 1891), and was the first to admit women. The club's 18-hole course has hosted the U.S. Open four times, in 1896, 1986, 1995, and 2004.

i **Long Island is home to more than 100 scenic and championship golf courses that are open to the public.**

HOCKEY

NEW YORK ISLANDERS
Nassau Veterans Memorial Coliseum
1255 Hempstead Tnpk., Uniondale
(800) 882-ISLES
www.newyorkislanders.com, http://islanders.nhl.com

Out of all the professional sports teams based in New York, the Islanders are definitely the most popular on Long Island, in part because this NHL team is based here and plays its home games at the Nassau Veterans Memorial Coliseum. The team is part of the Atlantic Division of the Eastern Conference of the NHL, and is one of three NHL teams in the Tri-State area (the New York Rangers and the New Jersey Devils are the other two).

The Islanders were founded in 1972 and won four consecutive Stanley Cup championships between 1980 and 1984. Over the years a handful of Islanders team members, including Al Arbour, Mike Bossy, Clark Gillies, Denis Potvin, Billy Smith, Bryan Trottier, Bill Torrey, and Pat LaFontaine have been inducted into the Hockey Hall of Fame. Between 2000 and 2006 the Islanders had a change in ownership, but along with that came a return appearance in the playoffs. For the 2007–8 season, the team redesigned their well-known royal blue, white, and orange striped jerseys. To help draw crowds, in addition to offering the high-speed action the NHL is known for, during television breaks the beautiful Ice Girls perform.

Young fans of the Islanders can join the official Kid's Club by visiting http://islanders.nhl.com/club/page.htm?id=43391. Membership is free, but there's also a Slap Shot membership package that has an annual fee of $39, and a Hat Trick package with an annual fee of $99. The Hat Trick membership includes four tickets to an Islanders game, a team photo, a yearbook, an Islanders calendar, and an Islanders practice jersey, along with a bunch of other perks.

The regular NHL season runs from late Sept to mid-Apr. On game days, you're sure to find massive crowds at sports bars throughout Long Island as they cheer on their true home team. Home games are broadcast on MSG+, a Long Island–based sports television cable network. You can listen to evening games on 94.3 WMJC and 90.3 WKRB. All afternoon games can be heard on WHLI 1100 AM.

i Want to receive the latest New York Islanders news right on your cell phone? Sign up for free text alerts at www.txtstationcontrol.com/promotionengine/public/txtalerts/Islanders.aspx.

NEW YORK RANGERS
Madison Square Garden
Seventh Ave. between 31st St. and 33rd St., New York
(212) 465-6040 (tickets)
http://rangers.nhl.com

When it comes to NHL hockey, Long Islanders have a choice: They can support their true home team, the New York Islanders, or they can support the New York Rangers, which plays its home games at Madison Square Garden in Manhattan.

Since 1926 the New York Rangers have been the pride of New York as they've entertained fans with some of the most action-packed and memorable games in NHL history. During the team's first 16 seasons in existence, it only missed participating in the playoffs once. The Rangers continue to draw sold-out crowds, which include celebrities and local politicians among the New Yorkers and hockey fans from around the globe.

i When not hosting a basketball or hockey game, Madison Square Garden transforms into a popular venue for big-name concerts and traveling live shows, such as *Ringling Bros. and Barnum & Bailey Circus* and *Disney on Ice*. It's also the venue where the world-famous Westminster Kennel Club Dog Show is hosted each year in mid-Feb.

HORSE RACING

AQUEDUCT RACETRACK
110th St. and Rockaway Blvd., Jamaica
(718) 641-4700 (tickets)
www.nyra.com

Aqueduct Racetrack, one of New York's major racetracks for thoroughbred racing, opened on Sept 27, 1894. Prior to its opening the property was owned by the Brooklyn Water Works, which transported water to New York City from the Hempstead Plain, hence the name "Aqueduct Racetrack." The track occupies about 210 acres and is located in Queens, which geographically is part of Long Island. It's situated just 8 miles from its sister track, Belmont Park. Aqueduct Racetrack underwent massive renovations in the mid to late 1980s. Aqueduct attracted its highest attendance ever for a single event on May 31, 1965, when 783,425 spectators visited the track.

BELMONT PARK
2150 Hempstead Tnpk., Elmont
(516) 488-6000 (tickets)
www.nyra.com/index_belmont.html

This 430-acre racetrack in Elmont, close to the border of Queens and Nassau County, is where you can experience thoroughbred racing at its best. Each year there are two race meetings at Belmont Park, including the 64-day spring/summer meeting (held between Apr and July) and the Fall Championship meeting (held between mid-Sept and late Oct). The most celebrated race held here each year is the Belmont Stakes (www.belmontstakes.com) in early June—the final jewel of racing's Triple Crown. Since 1919, when Sir Barton was the first to sweep the Kentucky Derby, the Preakness, and the Belmont Stakes, the "Test of the Champion" has crowned just 11 winners of racing's most prestigious prize.

Belmont Park is now part of the New York Racing Association. However, it started as a racetrack back in 1905, after a group headed by August Belmont II and former Secretary of the Navy William C. Whitney purchased land on Long Island to build what was then the most elaborate racetrack in America, modeled after the famous racetracks in Europe. On Belmont Park's opening day, May 4, 1905, Long Island experienced its very first traffic jam as more than 40,000 people attended the event. Long Islanders have since grown accustomed to traffic.

The New York Racing Association was created more than a half century ago, so that New York State could share in the revenues generated from this popular sport. In 2008 this association was granted the exclusive right to conduct racing at Belmont, Aqueduct, and Saratoga until 2033. Currently, thoroughbred racing contributes more than $2 billion annually to New York State's economy. Since its inception in 1955, the New York Racing Association has paid more than $3 billion in direct revenue to the state of New York.

LACROSSE

LONG ISLAND LIZARDS
James M. Stuart Stadium
Hofstra University, Hempstead
(866) LIZARD-1
www.longislandlizards.com

Opened in 1963, the 15,000-seat Stuart Stadium is the largest outdoor stadium on Long Island. In addition to hosting a wide range of collegiate sporting events, the stadium is home to the Long Island Lizards lacrosse team. Their season takes place between May and Aug.

It was in 1998 that Jake Steinfeld, best known for his "Body By Jake" videos, came up with the idea to start an outdoor lacrosse league. A few years later, after taking on several business partners, the Major League Lacrosse League was launched in 2001. The league is comprised of six teams—located in Boston, Chicago, Denver, Long Island, Toronto, and Washington—containing 240 of the best lacrosse players in the world. In 2009 the Major League Lacrosse season consisted of a total of 36 regular games. Many games are broadcast on ESPN or ESPN2. For more information about Major League Lacrosse, visit www.majorleaguelacrosse.com.

RUNNING

LONG ISLAND MARATHON
(516) 986-5537, (516) 572-0248
www.thelimarathon.com

For almost 40 years the Long Island Marathon has been the premier competitive running event on the island. The main event is a grueling 26.2-mile run. In the 1980s, however, a second Half Marathon race was added, along with a 10K, 5K, 1-mile, and Kidz Fun Run, which collectively have become knows as the RXR Long Island Marathon Festival of Races.

The main event starts at 8 a.m. sharp on the first Sun in May. The starting location is Charles Lindbergh Blvd. in Uniondale (adjacent to the Nassau Veterans Memorial Coliseum), and the finish line is in Eisenhower Park. A full-color course map can be downloaded from the official Long Island Marathon Web site. Spectators are encouraged to watch the marathon and sister races from the start or finish line areas, as well as from various view points along the route. There is no charge for spectators.

i The Long Island Marathon is always recruiting volunteers. If you're interested, visit www.thelimarathon.com/index.php?t=volunteer. No previous experience is necessary, and a wide range of pre-race and day-of-race volunteer positions are available.

SOCCER

NEW YORK RED BULLS
Red Bull Arena
Harrison, NJ
(201) 583-7000
www.newyorkredbulls.com

When the New York Red Bulls, the region's only Major League Soccer (MLS) team, kicked off its 2010 season, it was in its new stadium, Red Bull Arena, located in Harrison, New Jersey. This state-of-the-art arena was designed from the ground up to be a premiere North American soccer venue. The overall seating capacity for soccer matches at the arena is 25,189, including 30 luxury suites (20 lower level and 10 upper level) and 1,116 club seats. Other amenities include three stadium clubs and two retail stores.

It was in 1994 that Major League Soccer announced its formation and stated that New York would be one of the cities to have a team. Originally the team played at Giants Stadium and was called the MetroStars. In Mar 2006, however, the team was purchased and renamed. The MLS season runs from Mar to Oct.

STOCK CAR RACING (NASCAR)

RIVERHEAD RACEWAY
Rte. 58, Riverhead (exit 73 off the Long Island Expwy.)
(631) 842-RACE, (631) 727-0010
www.riverheadraceway.com

In addition to being the only track in the New York area where you can experience NASCAR and stock car racing, Riverhead Raceway hosts a wide range of other events, including demolition derbies, monster truck events, and enduro races. The raceway also hosts a major July 4 fireworks display that has become famous throughout Long Island. At Riverhead Raceway, the racing and event season kicks off in mid-Apr with warm-ups and officially begins in May. The final events of the season are held in late Sept. The raceway itself is one of the oldest stock car racetracks in the country. It was built in 1949 and is a quarter-mile asphalt, high-banked oval, which includes a figure-eight course.

The raceway is located 1 mile east of the last exit on the Long Island Expwy. (I-495) at exit 73, where the North and South Forks of Long Island begin. Thus, the raceway is located just minutes away from the Hamptons and Long Island's wine country. The raceway is part of the NASCAR Whelen All-American Series circuit, and has been part of NASCAR for most of its existence. The track hosts five or six racing divisions every Sat night, with an average count of 150 cars in the pits. Throughout the racing season, Riverhead Raceway hosts a wide range of family-friendly and special kid-oriented events, all of which are extremely affordable. Admission for kids between the ages of 6 and 12 to any race is just $5. Adult ticket prices vary by event.

TENNIS

U.S. OPEN TENNIS CHAMPIONSHIP
USTA Billie Jean King National Tennis Center
Flushing Meadows Corona Park, Flushing
(718) 760-6200 (tickets)
www.usta.com

Every year the biggest names in professional tennis gather at the USTA Billie Jean King National Tennis Center for a two-week-long competition known around the world as the U.S. Open Tennis Tournament. In 2008 the U.S. Open kicked off with a celebration that included a parade of champions commemorating the 40th anniversary of Open Tennis in New York. The event wrapped up with Robert Federer winning his fifth consecutive men's singles title. In 2008 Serena Williams was also a champion and returned to the winner's circle nine years after winning her first title and six

i In addition to following the U.S. Open on TV and online, you can access the official Facebook page (www.facebook.com/pages/US-Open-Tennis-Championships-Official/96832392186) or Twitter feed (http://twitter.com/usopen) throughout the year, plus add the official widget to your Facebook page, MySpace page, or blog by visiting www.usopen.org/en_US/widgets/index.html.

Other Spectator Sports on Long Island

The following amateur, collegiate, and professional spectator sports are also held on and around Long Island.

Equestrian (Horseback Riding) Events: The United States Equestrian Federation (859-258-2472, www.usef.org) is composed of equestrian competitors, leisure riders, coaches, fans, and enthusiasts. This organization serves as the national governing body for equestrian sport. Since its inception in 1917, the federation has been dedicated to pursuing excellence and promoting growth, all while providing and maintaining a safe and level playing field for both its equine and human athletes. A local calendar of equestrian competitions and events can be found at the Long Island Equine Web site (www.liequine.com/events.cfm) or by contacting the Nassau-Suffolk Horsemen's Association (631-423-0290, www.nshaonline.org).

Fishing: If you're interested in fishing tournaments held around Long Island, visit the Long Island Fishing Reports Web site (www.lifishingreports.com/forums/calendar.aspx) for a calendar of events.

Rowing: Rowing is a popular water-based sport on Long Island. For details about various rowing associations and competitions at the high school, college, and professional level, visit www.longisland.com/sports/rowing.php.

Sailing: The Yacht Racing Association of Long Island Sound (516-767-9240, www.yralis.org) is a prime source of information about sailboat races held around Long Island. The organization has been in existence for more than 100 years and is dedicated to promoting safe, fair, and challenging sailboat racing throughout western Long Island Sound. Currently more than 65 member clubs and over 1,000 individual members (with over 700 boats) are registered with the organization.

Swimming and Diving: Eisenhower Park's Nassau County Aquatic Center is open year-round and hosts a wide range of high school, college, and professional swimming and diving competitions. To access a schedule of events, visit www.nassaucountyny.gov/agencies/Parks/WheretoGo/recreation/aquatic/Schedules.html.

years after earning her second title. She beat her sister, Venus, in the quarterfinals.

Also during the 2008 U.S. Open, an attendance record was set for the second consecutive year. More than 720,000 spectators passed through the turnstiles during the event. In 2010 the event is scheduled to take place between Aug 30 and Sept 12. In addition to tennis fans from all walks of life, celebrities can often be seen attending the U.S. Open.

i **The Nassau County Rifle and Pistol Range at the Mitchel Athletic Complex in Uniondale (516-572-0420, www.nassaucountyny.gov/agencies/Parks/WheretoGo/recreation/NC_rifle_range.html) hosts a variety of shooting competitions throughout the year.**

PARKS AND RECREATION

Anytime you hear someone talk about all that Long Island has to offer, or you read something about Long Island tourism, one of the very first things mentioned are the beaches, followed by the unusually high number of well-equipped and extremely well-managed state, county, and local parks. Long Island is a unique region because the island is long, narrow, and surrounded by water (Long Island Sound, Atlantic Ocean, or a series of sheltered bays). As a result, a majority of the towns and villages on Long Island are located right on the water—one major reason why Long Island has become such a popular summer tourist destination.

From an economic standpoint, much of Long Island's resident population (as well as the visitors) are pretty affluent and civic minded. Thus, many of the regions have taken tremendous steps to protect their land with strict zoning laws and conservation efforts. On a state, county, and local level, a lot of emphasis has been put on creating and maintaining parks, beaches, and the overall environment. What's offered at the various parks and beaches, however, goes well beyond just natural resources. Many offer full services and amenities for visitors, as well as activities and organized programs designed to help people truly experience and enjoy the amazing outdoor environments Long Island has become famous for.

This section focuses on the state, county, and local parks, as well as the public beaches and golf courses, that are in abundance throughout Long Island. As you'll discover, there's often a tremendous overlap in these areas, as many county and state parks, for example, contain beaches, public swimming pools, golf courses, ice-skating rinks, tennis courts, and a wide range of other amenities that are available to the general public.

So if you enjoy spending time outdoors, and you're looking for the best places to sunbathe, surf, hike, jog, walk, bicycle, Rollerblade, or participate in your favorite sport or water-based activity (such as swimming, sailing, or jet skiing), this is the section of the *Insiders' Guide to Long Island* that you'll want to read carefully.

EXPLORING THE GREAT OUTDOORS IN NASSAU COUNTY

Much of Nassau County is located along the water. The northern part of the county, referred to as the North Shore, overlooks the Long Island Sound, while the southern side of the island, referred to as the South Shore, also offers a lot of waterfront real estate. The waterfront along the South Shore, however, is mostly sheltered bay areas that ultimately connect to the Atlantic Ocean.

The South Shore is where you'll find some of Nassau County's most famous beaches. Plus, just off the South Shore's mainland is Fire Island, which is also lined with gorgeous sandy beaches. Nassau County's North Shore also has its share of beautiful beaches, but these open out directly onto the Long Island Sound, not sheltered bays. The experiences beachgoers will have will be vastly different depending on whether they visit the North Shore or South Shore. With the widest point between the north and south sides of Long Island being just 23 miles across, it's relatively easy for beachgoers to travel between beaches by car or by using Long Island's bus services.

In Nassau County alone there are more than 70 county-managed parks, preserves, museums, athletic facilities, and historic properties, which encompass more than 6,000 acres combined. In total, there are more than 30 parks. The entire county is composed of 183,680 acres, meaning a generous amount of land is dedicated to county parks, beaches, and outdoor recreation available to residents and visitors alike. (And these figures do not include state or local parks, only county parks.) One of the largest parks in Nassau County is the 930-acre Eisenhower Park in East Meadow.

i To access an up-to-date listing of special events happening at the various parks and beaches in Nassau County, visit www.nassaucountyny.gov/agencies/Parks/events.html. To view and print out free detailed maps of Nassau County's most popular parks, go to www.nassaucountyny.gov/agencies/Parks/Maps/index.html.

As you'll discover, the parks in Nassau County fit into one of two main categories—active or passive. Active parks are large, heavily used outdoor areas that offer activities, amenities, and services with a strong focus on recreation. These parks also have a full-time staff working at each of them. Long Island's passive parks tend to be smaller and are usually kept all natural, with few or no services and amenities. These parks tend to be great for walking, hiking, or jogging.

Eisenhower Park is the perfect example of an active park because it's massive and offers a wide range of recreational activities, such as the Nassau County Aquatic Center, an 18-hole golf course, the Harry Chapin Lakeside Theatre (where you can catch concerts, movies, and other seasonal performances), and a variety of other sports and recreation facilities, including tennis courts and athletic fields. Of course, Eisenhower Park also offers plenty of wooded areas and grassy fields, which is what most people envision when they hear the words "county park."

Cantiague Park is another example of an active park in Nassau County. One of its amenities is a popular indoor ice-skating rink. Other parks, like Christopher Morley and Grant Park, have outdoor ice skating rinks, open seasonally.)

Active Parks in Nassau County

The following is a summary of the services, amenities, and activities offered within each active park in Nassau County. Almost all of the parks are open daily, typically between sunrise and sunset, but this varies based on the season and the activities offered. Parks that feature nighttime events, activities, and concerts, for example, are obviously open well past sunset.

North Shore

The following are the active parks available within the North Shore region of Nassau County. These parks have a low admission fee, usually between $5 and $20, depending on whether or not the guest is a Long Island resident and has an annual park "Leisure Pass."

CANTIAGUE PARK
Hicksville
(516) 571-7056
www.nassaucountyny.gov/agencies/Parks/WhereToGo/active/cantiague.html

This 127-acre park, located in Central Nassau, is also open year-round. It is considered one of the county's premier active parks. In addition to its massive swimming pool complex, this park is known for its indoor ice-skating rink, which has hosted a variety of Olympic skaters over the years. Cantiague Park is located in Hicksville on Cantiague Rock Rd., just off the Southern State Pkwy. To reach it by car, take the Southern State Pkwy. to exit 29 north (the Hicksville Rd. exit) and proceed less than 5 miles into Hicksville. Turn left onto West John St., and you'll find the entrance to Cantiague Park on your right. The park can also be reached via the Long Island Expwy. Use

i Nassau County is serious about maintaining its parks and offering the best outdoor recreational experiences possible. In fact, the operating budget for the county parks system was $18 million in 2009, which equates to just below 1 percent of overall county expenditures for the year.

Google Maps or MapQuest to determine the best route from your starting location.

Cantiague Park opened in 1961. There is a small fee to participate in some of the activities and use some of the facilities. Some of the park's activities include:

- 5 lighted tennis courts
- 6 lighted handball/paddleball courts
- 3 lighted basketball courts
- Several lighted athletic fields for soccer, football, lacrosse, and rugby
- A lighted artificial-turf field that accommodates football, soccer, and lacrosse
- An 18-hole miniature golf course
- A children's playground
- 2 separate picnic areas
- A 9-hole, par-30 golf course
- A lighted golf driving range
- An indoor ice-skating rink (often referred to as the best on Long Island), where skating lessons are available
- A massive swimming pool complex (with locker room facilities)

CHRISTOPHER MORLEY PARK

Roslyn–North Hills
(631) 571-8113
www.nassaucountyny.gov/agencies/Parks/WhereToGo/active/morley.html

On the North Shore, Christopher Morley Park is located in Roslyn–North Hills, along Searingtown Rd. (north of the Long Island Expwy.). If arriving by car, take the LIE to exit 36 (Searingtown Rd.) and travel north on Searingtown until you reach the park entrance, which is about 200 yards from the LIE's exit. The park was named after Christopher Morley, a famous 20th-century writer whose works include plays, novels, poetry, and essays. After Morley's death, his property became a county park in 1966.

This park has a year-round, full-time staff and is comprised of 98 acres. Here, you'll find a wide range of activities, including:

- A 9-hole, par-30 golf course
- 5 tennis courts
- 4 lighted handball/paddleball courts
- 2 paddle-tennis courts
- 3 baseball fields
- Volleyball courts
- A children's playground
- A 140-by-300-foot boat basin created for model boats
- Picnic areas
- A 1-mile fitness trail with 20 different workout stations
- A dog run
- An outdoor ice skating rink (open early Dec through mid-Mar)
- An outdoor swimming pool complex (with locker room facilities)
- More than 30 acres of wooded nature trails
- A weekly farmers' market June through late Nov on Wed from 7 a.m. to 1 p.m.

This park, like all of Nassau's county parks, is open to both residents and visitors. However, there is a small fee to participate in some of the activities and use some of the facilities, like the golf course, swimming pool, and ice-skating rink, for example.

EISENHOWER PARK

East Meadow
(516) 572-0348
www.nassaucountyny.gov/agencies/Parks/WhereToGo/active/eisenhower.html

Often referred to as the "jewel" of Nassau County's impressive park system, Eisenhower Park encompasses 930 acres and is the largest public park space in New York's entire metropolitan area—yes, even larger than New York City's Central Park. In addition to vast wooded spaces and plush lawns, the park offers a wide range of outdoor activities for athletes and families alike. It was officially dedicated in Oct 1949, but rededicated as the Dwight D. Eisenhower Memorial Park in Oct 1969.

Eisenhower Park is located in East Meadow, along Merrick Ave. and Stewart Ave. To reach the park by car, take the Meadowbrook Pkwy. North to exit M3 (East/Stewart Ave.). Turn right onto Stewart Ave. and follow it until you reach the park's main entrance. If you're approaching from the Meadowbrook Pkwy. South, take exit M3 (Stewart Ave.). As you exit, turn left onto Stewart Ave. and follow it until you reach the park's main entrance.

There is a small fee to participate in some of the activities and use some of the facilities, many of which are available throughout the entire year. Eisenhower Park offers a wide range of activities, services, and amenities, including:

- 16 lighted tennis courts
- Multiple lighted athletic fields, including 17 baseball fields, 4 soccer fields, and 3 football fields
- A full-court basketball court, complete with fiberglass backboards
- A batting cage with 9 batting areas
- The famous Nassau County Aquatic Center (featuring a massive pool for swimming, water polo, and diving)
- A 2-mile fitness trail with 20 workout stations
- 3 separate 18-hole golf courses—the Red Course, White Course, and Blue Course, which are ranked amongst the best public courses on Long Island
- A lighted golf driving range
- An 18-hole miniature gold course
- 3 children's playground areas
- Several picnic areas
- The Harry Chapin Lakeside Theatre, with seasonal outdoor entertainment in the form of concerts, movies, and theatrical performances
- Several jogging paths
- A popular sledding hill (seasonal)

Eisenhower Park also has its own restaurant, called Carlton on the Park. It's a privately operated dining establishment that also offers a full-service bar. For reservations, call (516) 542-0700.

i **In Oct 2009 plans were announced to create a pedestrian walkway and bike path that will connect New York State's existing bike path along the Hempstead Tnpk. and lead directly to Eisenhower Park. The additional path will be about 10 miles in length and will cost approximately $5 million. It's expected to be completed sometime in 2010.**

Also within Eisenhower Park you'll discover the Veterans Memorial and Wall of Honor, as well as a 9/11 memorial that honors the 344 Nassau County residents who were killed during the Sept 11, 2001, terrorist attack on the World Trade Center in Manhattan. There are also two memorials dedicated to Nassau County firefighters who have died in the line of duty.

South Shore

Along Nassau County's South Shore, you'll discover 10 additional active parks, although none offer as much in the way of activities, services, and amenities as Eisenhower Park, for example. There is a small fee to participate in some of the activities and use some of the facilities, many of which are available throughout the entire year.

BAY PARK
East Rockaway
(516) 571-7245
www.nassaucountyny.gov/agencies/Parks/WhereToGo/active/bay.html

This is a beautiful, 96-acre park that offers two lighted tennis courts, two lighted basketball courts, and several athletic fields, along with bicycle and walking paths. There's also an outdoor roller-skating rink, several picnic areas, a large children's playground, a dog run, a boccie court, and a fishing dock that features a sailboat and slip boat ramp. This park is located off the Southern State Pkwy.'s exit 17.

CEDAR PARK
Seaford
(516) 571-7470
www.nassaucountyny.gov/agencies/Parks/WhereToGo/active/cedarcreek.html

Since 1975 this 259-acre county park has offered residents and visitors alike a wide range of activities, such as eight tennis courts, eight handball/paddleball courts, multiple athletic fields, a 1.5-mile walking/jogging path, a separate 1-mile walking/jogging/bicycle path, a children's playground, a large picnic area, an outdoor roller-skating rink, multiple sledding hills (seasonal), a dog run, an archery range, a field designed for flying radio-controlled model airplanes, and a tether-car racetrack. The park is located off the Southern State Pkwy.'s exit 27 South.

CENTENNIAL PARK
Roosevelt
(516) 571-8695
www.nassaucountyny.gov/agencies/Parks/WhereToGo/active/centennial.html

This is one of the smaller county-operated parks. It encompasses just 2 acres and features a children's playground, 12 basketball hoops, and 2 tennis courts. The park is located off the Southern State Pkwy.'s exit 21 South. Centennial Park's claim to fame is that basketball superstar Julius Erving (aka Doctor J) grew up in the area and played basketball at the park as a child.

Residents: Don't Forget Your Nassau County Leisure Pass

Many of the activities, services, and amenities at the various county parks have a small admission or usage fee for the swimming pools, golf courses, tennis courts, beaches, marinas, ice-skating rinks, or roller-skating rinks, for example. To receive a discount on park admission, in some cases visitors to the park must also possess a Nassau County Leisure Pass, which identifies the holder as a local resident. Guests (non-residents) are welcome, however, to visit the park. Cardholders receive admission and fee discounts when using the fee-based services, activities, and amenities within the parks.

The annual fee for a Nassau County Leisure Pass is $25. The passes can be obtained at several of the active county parks, as well as online (www.nassaucountyny.gov/agencies/Parks/leisure.html).

COW MEADOW PARK & PRESERVE
Freeport
(516) 571-8685
www.nassaucountyny.gov/agencies/Parks/WhereToGo/active/cowmeadow.html

This 150-acre park is both a traditional active park (with activities, services, and amenities) and a nature preserve that showcases Long Island's marine wetlands, salt marshes, mud flaps, and tidal creek habitats. With more than 150 species of birds in the area, this park is ideal for bird-watching along the quarter-mile nature trail that winds through a variety of natural habitats. Other offerings at the park include a lighted baseball field, four lighted basketball courts, six lighted tennis courts, four lighted handball courts, and a large athletic field. There's also a large children's playground and picnic area, a popular fishing pier, and a marina with about 30 boat slips. The park is located off exit M9 West of the Meadowbrook Pkwy.

GRANT PARK
Hewlett
(516) 571-7821
www.nassaucountyny.gov/agencies/Parks/WhereToGo/active/grant.html

This 35-acre park has been a part of the county's park system since 1955. Its offerings include three basketball courts, four tennis courts, four handball/paddleball courts, several jogging/biking/walking paths, a children's playground, a large picnic area, an outdoor roller-skating rink that in the winter is transformed into an ice-skating rink, and a sledding hill. There's also a lake that's open for fishing. The park is located off the Southern State Pkwy.'s exit 19 South.

INWOOD PARK
Inwood
(516) 571-7894
www.nassaucountyny.gov/agencies/Parks/WhereToGo/active/inwood.html

Here you'll find a somewhat small, 16-acre park that is surrounded by water. It offers a lighted baseball field (which can also be used for football), two basketball courts, two tennis courts, a walking/jogging path around the park's perimeter, a children's playground, and a lighted roller-skating rink. There's also a boat launch ramp and a waterfront area that offers fishing and crabbing. The park is located in the middle of Inwood, a short distance from Rockaway Tnpk.

NICKERSON BEACH PARK
Lido
(516) 571-7700
www.nassaucountyny.gov/agencies/Parks/WhereToGo/active/nickerson.html

One of the unique aspects of this park is that it offers a campground with 74 RV and 12 tent sites, in addition to 2 basketball courts, 2 tennis courts, a skateboard park, a children's playground, picnic areas, 2 swimming pools, and a dog run. There's also a restaurant located within the park, Nathan's at Nickerson (516-870-4381), which offers the restaurant chain's famous hog dogs, fries, and other fast-food favorites. This park is located less than a half mile from Nassau Beach, just off the Loop Pkwy.

NORTH WOODMERE PARK
North Woodmere
(516) 571-7801
www.nassaucountyny.gov/agencies/Parks/WhereToGo/active/nwoodmere.html

Located in the southwest part of Nassau County, this 150-acre park offers an impressive assortment of activities, services, and amenities, including 10 lighted tennis courts, 6 lighted handball/paddleball courts, several athletic fields, paths suitable for cross-county skiing (seasonal), a children's playground, a picnic area, a 9-hole (par 30) golf course, an outdoor swimming complex (with locker room facilities), and a shorefront where fishing and crabbing is permitted. The park is located off Branch Blvd.

REV. ARTHUR MACKEY SR. PARK
Roosevelt
(516) 571-8692
www.nassaucountyny.gov/agencies/Parks/WhereToGo/active/mackey.html

This park is located close to the Roosevelt Preserve and is situated around a gorgeous lake. It's one of the newer parks in the county's park system, having been added in 1984. It offers two tennis courts, two handball/paddleball courts, two full-size basketball courts, four basketball half-courts, a baseball field, a children's playground, and a picnic area. Walking and jogging paths can be found around the lake. The park is located off the Southern State Pkwy. East, exit 23.

WANTAGH PARK
Wantagh
(516) 571-7460
www.nassaucountyny.gov/agencies/Parks/WhereToGo/active/wantagh.html

This is a 111-acre park located on the waterfront. In addition to providing a handful of activities, it also offers an amazing view. At this park you'll find five lighted tennis courts, a basketball court, several athletic fields, a 1-mile walking/jogging/bicycle path, and a separate 2-mile walking/jogging/bicycle path. There's also a fitness trail with 20 workout stations, a children's playground, a picnic area, an outdoor swimming pool complex (with locker room facilities), a boat launch and boat slips, a dog run, and a fishing pier. The park is located off the Southern State Pkwy.'s exit 27 South.

ENJOYING OUTDOOR ACTIVITIES IN SUFFOLK COUNTY

Suffolk County has 23 county parks and marinas, in addition to a handful of state parks and literally dozens of town/community parks. From Huntington to Montauk, Suffolk County Parks manages over 46,000 acres of parkland. As you'd expect, many of these parks take full advantage of the local geography and terrain. Some of the parks feature camping sites, horseback-riding trails, beaches, children's playgrounds, picnic areas, hiking/walking/jogging trails, fishing, boating, and historical landmarks.

Suffolk County's park system, and what it offers in each park, is vastly different from Nassau County's. Many of the county parks in Suffolk are less developed and don't offer amenities like

Nassau County's Passive Parks: Nature That's All Natural and Often Undeveloped

In addition to the popular active parks, Nassau County offers over a dozen passive parks that are maintained by the Nassau County Park system. There are also dozens of additional parks maintained by local towns and communities throughout the county, plus many that are privately owned and operated, like Old Westbury Gardens in Old Westbury.

The county's passive parks tend to be between 1 and 14 acres, and offer little more than open grassy areas, wooded areas, and paths for walking or hiking. Most are totally undeveloped. Unless otherwise posted, these parks are open year-round from sunrise to sunset.

For detailed descriptions of each passive park in Nassau County, along with driving directions, visit www.nassaucountyny.gov/agencies/Parks/WhereToGo/passive.html.

The region's passive parks include:

Baxter's Pond/Barbara Johnson Park & Preserve: Port Washington on the North Shore (5 acres)

Camman's Pond Park: Merrick on the South Shore (8 acres)

Doxey Brook Park: North Woodmere on the South Shore (8 acres)

East Gate/West Gate Park: Valley Stream on the South Shore (2 acres)

Hall's Pond Park: West Hempstead in Central Nassau (11 acres)

Herricks Pond Park: Herricks on the North Shore (4 acres)

Lofts Pond Park: Baldwin on the South Shore (14 acres)

Milburn Pond Park: Freeport on the South Shore (8 acres)

Polaris Field: Levittown in Central Nassau (3 acres)

Silver Lake Park: Baldwin on the South Shore (9 acres)

Stannards Brook Park: Port Washington on the North Shore (3 acres)

Tanglewood Park & Preserve: Lakeview on the South Shore (11 acres)

Terrell Avenue Park: Oceanside on the South Shore (1 acre)

Washington Avenue Park: Seaford on the South Shore (4 acres)

swimming pools, tennis courts, or ice-skating rinks. Instead, the parks here rely on their natural surroundings to provide the settings for recreational activities. Also, the parks in Suffolk County are not classified as active or passive. All of the county parks are open year-round, and many offer special events and activities throughout the seasons. To access a schedule of upcoming events or for more information on all of the parks listed below, visit www.suffolkcountyny.gov/Home/departments/parks.aspx.

BLYDENBURGH COUNTY PARK

Smithtown

(631) 854-3713

The main activities offered at this park include hiking, picnicking, camping, freshwater fishing, rowboat rentals, horseback-riding paths, a children's playground, a dog run, and a historic trust area. Located on the property is the Blydenburgh Farm and New Mill Historic District, which contains a historic gristmill (one of several still standing on Long Island). This is a 627-acre park that's open throughout the year. Between mid-May and Labor Day, rowboat rentals are available. For camping information, call (631) 244-7275.

i **Countless freshwater and saltwater fishing spots can be found throughout Suffolk County's parks, including Blydenburgh, Cedar Point, Cupsogue Beach, Lake Ronkonkoma, Sears Bellows, Shinnecock East, Southaven, Smiths Point Beach, and Theodore Roosevelt.**

BROOKSIDE COUNTY PARK
Sayville
(631) 563-7716

Brookside is a relatively small, undeveloped park that's centered around water. It offers a meandering river and plenty of wooded areas. This park was the former estate of architect Isaac H. Green. The main activities here are strolling, hiking, and bird-watching. Guided nature walks are offered seasonally. The Great South Bay Audubon Society hosts guided bird watching tours here throughout the year. Call for details and to make reservations.

CATHEDRAL PINES COUNTY PARK
Middle Island
(631) 852-5500

This park is mainly a campground and nature preserve. It's composed of 320 acres, the majority of which remain totally undeveloped and all natural. Hiking, mountain biking, and picnicking are the main activities here. This park is known for its campground, which includes 10 sites with water and electric hookups for RVs. Adjacent to this park is the Prosser Pines Nature Preserve. Here you'll discover hundreds of white pine trees that were planted in 1812. Both the park and the nature preserve offer gorgeous scenery that is appealing to amateur and professional photographers alike, not to mention hikers.

CEDAR POINT COUNTY PARK
East Hampton
(631) 852-7620

This lovely 607-acre park offers fishing, hiking, a picnic area, camping, a children's playground, rowboat rentals, bike trails, hunting, scuba diving, and outer beach access. Within the park you'll find the historic Cedar Point Lighthouse, which was built in 1860. It was used to help guide ships in and out of Sag Harbor, when this was a major shipping port. Thanks to the hurricane of 1938, it's now possible to walk to this lighthouse, which used to be situated on a small island. This is a popular park for camping and picnicking, plus there's a beach. The Cedar Point General Store and a snack shop can also be found here (631-324-7147). During the summer, free Sat-night movies are presented in the park.

CUPSGOUE BEACH COUNTY PARK
Westhampton
(631) 852-8111

This is a 296-acre park with a beautiful barrier beach. Activities offered here include swimming, fishing, scuba diving, camping, and outer beach access. Beach facilities include restrooms and showers. During the peak summer months, you'll find a lifeguard on duty along the white sandy beach area. There's also a seasonal food concession stand, along with a separate area for RV parking and camping.

DWARF PINES PLANES PRESERVE
Westhampton

This park is known for its unique ecosystem. Guided tours and walking trails are pretty much all that's offered here, although the scenery is stunningly beautiful, especially in the spring, summer, and fall foliage months. The newly constructed walking trail designed to expose visitors to the ecosystem that thrives here is just under 1 mile long and takes about 20 minutes to walk. On the trail you'll encounter rare birds and wildlife, including the black-throated green warbler, American kestrels, and marsh hawks. Several species of owls can also be found here, but they're nocturnal, so they're more apt to be seen at night.

As a general rule, dogs are not allowed within state parks. A few parks offer exceptions, however, at least in certain areas.

GARDINER COUNTY PARK

West Bay Shore

(631) 854-0935

The property this park is situated on was originally owned by the Gardiner family. It later became part of the historic Sagtikos Manor Estate. The park encompasses about 231 acres and is mainly used for hiking along the beautiful nature trails. While much of the park remains totally undeveloped, there are public restrooms here, along with clearly defined hiking trails and a separate fitness trail. The park's main entrance is located south of Montauk Hwy. (Rte. 27A), about a half mile east of the Robert Moses Causeway.

INDIAN ISLAND COUNTY PARK

Riverhead

(631) 852-3232

At this 275-acre park, year-round camping is offered, along with hiking trails, a picnic area, fishing, an athletic field, and a children's playground. This beautiful park is located at the mouth of the Peconic River. It's open year-round and is a popular site for camping. Both tents and RVs can be accommodated here. Restrooms and shower facilities are available.

LAKE RONKONKOMA COUNTY PARK

Lake Ronkonkoma

(631) 854-9699

What you'll find at this beautiful park is a fishing pier, baseball field, several handball and basketball courts, and a picnic area. The fishing pier, which offers a lovely view, is fully wheelchair accessible and is the main attraction at this relatively small park.

LAKELAND COUNTY PARK

Islandia

(631) 853-2727

Nature trails are the main attraction of this park, which also offers basketball courts and a picnic area with a gazebo. People also come here for the fishing. If you're interesting in exploring nature but don't want to get your shoes dirty, this park is equipped with extended boardwalks that allow visitors to explore the wetland areas and tropical vegetation. These boardwalks are fully wheelchair accessible.

MASCHUTT BEACH COUNTY PARK

Hampton Bays

(631) 852-8205

This park features swimming, camping, a children's playground, a nice picnic area, and a seasonal food concession with a dining area called the Beach Hut (631-728-2988, www.thebeachhuts.com). Public restrooms and showers are available. During the summer a variety of special events are regularly held here. Located on Great Peconic Bay, on the east side of the Shinnecock Canal, this is a popular spot for people who want to enjoy a day at the beach. Windsurfing and sailing are also popular activities in the area. The park's campground can accommodate tents, self-contained trailers, and campers.

PINE BARRENS TRAILS

Manorville

(631) 852-3449

In addition to a visitor information center, this park features hiking trails, a seasonal children's museum, and a seasonal environmental education center. The centerpiece of the park and its main attraction are the Pine Barrens. There's a three-quarter-mile long, fully wheelchair-accessible boardwalk here, which allows visitors to see a sampling of the flora and fauna. The Pine Barrens Trail Information Center is open Fri through Mon, between May and Oct.

RAYNOR BEACH COUNTY PARK

Lake Ronkonkoma

(631) 854-9168

In terms of county parks in the area, this one offers a nice assortment of activities, including two children's playgrounds; several basketball, tennis, and handball courts; a soccer field and baseball field; a spacious picnic area; and a variety of walking/hiking/jogging trails.

ROBERT CUSHMAN MURPHY COUNTY PARK
Manorville

Bird-watchers and hikers are among the people who really enjoy this park, which also offers fishing, boating, hunting, and a biological research center, in addition to its 60-acre pond. What you'll find within this park is what naturalists refer to as a "rare coastal plain pond shore habitat." Here you'll find a wide range of fish and wildlife, including largemouth bass, yellow perch, bluegill, bullhead catfish, and pumpkinseed sunfish. To fish in Swan Pond, you must have a New York State fishing license.

SEARS BELLOWS COUNTY PARK
Hampton Bays
(631) 852-8290

Among this park's popular offerings are hiking, camping, picnicking, freshwater fishing, rowboat rentals, hunting, and horseback-riding trails. The park is located within Long Island's Pine Barrens. Campsites are available for both tents and RVs. Daytime-only fishing is probably the most popular activity here, thanks to the abundance of different types of fish that can be found within the waterways.

SHINNECOCK CANAL COUNTY MARINA
Hampton Bays
(631) 854-4952

This county-operated marina has docking space for 50 vessels and offers full facilities, including restrooms, showers, and a sewage pumping station. If you're arriving by boat, reservations for docking space are required. The maximum stay for boats, however, is two weeks. What's most appealing about this marina is that it's located within walking distance of the Meschutt Beach County Park.

SHINNECOCK EAST COUNTY PARK
Southampton
(631) 852-8899

This county park is allocated primarily for outer beach camping, specifically for self-contained RVs (no tents). The park offers 100 campsites. In terms of activities, there's saltwater fishing and areas designated for off-road recreational vehicle use. The park is located along the eastern border of Shinnecock Inlet, where the waterway meets the Atlantic Ocean. As a result, the area offers both ocean and calmer bay beaches.

SMITH POINT COUNTY PARK
Shirley, Fire Island
(631) 852-1313

This is the county's largest waterfront park, so the majority of activities are based around the beach, boating, and fishing. Popular activities include swimming, scuba diving, surfing, saltwater fishing, and camping. Outer beach access, a food concession stand, a children's playground, and restrooms and showers are available. In 2009 this park celebrated its 50th anniversary. It's located at Smith Point (as the name suggests), on the Fire Island barrier beach. Thanks to its pristine white sand, it's an extremely popular beach during the warmer months. Lifeguards are on duty throughout the summer. It's also a popular campground, with water and electric hookups available for RVs. If you get hungry, there's the Smith Point Beach Hut (www.thebeachhut.com), which serves mainly seafood.

i Many of the county parks that offer horseback-riding trails also have county-owned stables, where visitors can participate in horseback tours, even if they don't own a horse. County parks where horseback riding for non–horse owners is available include Blydenburgh, Sears Bellows, Southaven, Smiths Point, Theodore Roosevelt, and West Hills, in addition to the Bohemia Equestrian Center (631-854-4949).

SOUTHAVEN COUNTY PARK

Brookhaven

(631) 854-1414

The gorgeous Carmans River flows directly through this park, which offers hiking, camping, picnicking, freshwater fishing, rowboat rentals, canoeing, and hunting. On the land, you'll find an abundance of pine and oak trees. The park encompasses about 1,356-acres and includes a massive campground facility suitable for both tents and trailers.

THEODORE ROOSEVELT COUNTY PARK

Montauk

(631) 852-7878

Among the activities offered here are horseback riding, hiking, biking, canoeing, picnicking, fishing, and hunting. Outer beach access and RV camping sites are also available, as well as a gift shop. In terms of historical attractions, the park features a Spanish-American War exhibit and the Third House, which was originally occupied by cattle ranchers who worked the region. It was later used as the headquarters for Camp Wikoff during the Spanish-American War. Camp Wikoff is open to the public May through Oct, Wed through Sun, from 10 a.m. to 5 p.m.

TIMBER POINT COUNTY MARINA

Great River

(631) 854-4952

This county-operated marina is situated on the Great South Bay and offers 153 slips, a fuel dock, sewage pump-out station, public restrooms, electric hookups for boats, and fresh water. Transient slips are also available. Reservations for docking must be made in advance by calling (631) 854-0938.

VIETNAM VETERANS MEMORIAL PARK

Farmingville

(631) 854-4949

Located at the very top of Bald Hill, which is among the highest points on Long Island, this monument was constructed with the help of the Suffolk County Vietnam Veterans Memorial Committee back in 1991. The monument was designed to acknowledge the service and sacrifice of all Vietnam veterans, including those who died, those who were wounded, and all of the men and women who served their country during this war.

WEST HILLS COUNTY PARK

Huntington

(631) 854-4423

Visitors enjoy hiking and picnicking at this park. It also features Jayne's Hill, which is Long Island's tallest peak, reaching an elevation of 400 feet. The park is known for its nature trails, including the Walt Whitman Trail. Camping is offered here, but only to organized youth groups. Within the park's main visitor center, called Sweet Hollow Hall, organized children's activities are offered. There's also a playground, meeting hall, horseback-riding paths, and a dog run.

LONG ISLAND'S COUNTY-OPERATED GOLF COURSES

In all, more than 100 golf courses, both public and private, can be found on Long Island. In addition to the numerous privately owned-and-operated golf courses and golf clubs, Nassau County and Suffolk County both operate several public courses.

Nassau County Public Golf Courses

The following is a listing of public golf courses in Nassau County. No membership is required, however, fees do apply. Call each course to reserve tee times and determine rates.

Bay Park Golf Club: East Rockaway, (516) 571-7242

Bethpage State Park Golf Course: Farmingdale, (516) 249-0701

Cantiague Park Golf Course: Hicksville, (516) 571-7061

Christopher Morley Golf Course: North Hills, (516) 571-8120

Eisenhower Park Golf Club: East Meadow, (516) 572-0327

Glen Cove Golf Course: Glen Cove, (516) 671-0033

Long Island's State Parks

As if the abundant natural resources and activities offered within Long Island's county park system weren't enough, you'll find on the island no fewer than 26 state parks, which include some of the area's most popular attractions and activities. Jones Beach State Park is probably the most popular state park on Long Island, followed by Montauk Point State Park and Orient Beach State Park.

Many of the state parks on Long Island offer extremely popular beaches and water-based activities, in addition to a wide range of land-based activities. Some are also where you'll find historic landmarks, such as the Montauk Point Lighthouse, a very beautiful and popular tourist attraction. A few of the state parks, such as Bethpage State Park and Montauk Downs State Park, are known for their world-class golf courses that are open to the public. Jones Beach State Park is where you'll find the Nikon at Jones Beach outdoor amphitheater, which offers a seemingly endless lineup of musical entertainment by big-name artists and music groups throughout the summer.

While not all of the state beaches on Long Island have world-famous amphitheaters, most of them do have gorgeous beaches (with locker room facilities), on-site restaurants or concessions, picnic areas, children's playgrounds, swimming pools, organized recreational programs, athletic fields, tennis courts, and hiking/jogging/biking trails. Some also offer fishing, museums, some type of performing arts center, and gift shops.

The state parks are open year-round, but hours of operation vary by season or are based on what's offered within each park. Admission to the parks is free; however, a parking fee or admission fee to a museum or historic attraction may apply.

You can learn more about each of these state parks, including what special events and activities are being held at them throughout the year, by visiting http://nysparks.state.ny.us/parks and choosing which park you're interested in.

Throughout Long Island, the state parks include:

Argyle Lake Park: Babylon, (631) 444-0273, www.longislandexchange.com/parks/argyle lake-statepark.html

Bayard Cutting Arboretum State Park: East Islip, (631) 581-1002, http://nysparks.state.ny.us/parks/95/details.aspx

Belmont Lake State Park: North Babylon, (631) 667-5055, http://nysparks.state.ny.us/parks/88/details.aspx

Bethpage Lake State Park: Farmingdale, (516) 249-0701, http://nysparks.state.ny.us/parks/108/details.aspx

Caleb Smith State Park: Smithtown, (516) 265-1054, http://nysparks.state.ny.us/parks/124/details.aspx

Camp Hero State Park: Montauk, (631) 668-3781, http://nysparks.state.ny.us/parks/97/details.aspx

Captree State Park: Babylon, (631) 669-0449, http://nysparks.state.ny.us/parks/65/details.aspx

Caumsett State Historic Park: Lloyd Neck, (631) 423-1770, http://nysparks.state.ny.us/parks/23/details.aspx

Cold Spring Harbor State Park: Cold Spring Harbor, (631) 423-1770, http://nysparks.state.ny.us/parks/115/details.aspx

Connetguot River State Park: Oakdale, (631) 581-1005, http://nysparks.state.ny.us/parks/8/details.aspx

Heckscher State Park: East Islip, (631) 581-2100, http://nysparks.state.ny.us/parks/136/details.aspx

Hempstead Lake State Park: West Hempstead, (516) 766-1029, http://nysparks.state.ny.us/parks/31/details.aspx

Hither Hills State Park: Montauk, (631) 668-2554, http://nysparks.state.ny.us/parks/122/details.aspx

Jones Beach State Park: Wantagh, (516) 785-1600, http://nysparks.state.ny.us/parks/10/details.aspx

Montauk Downs State Park: Montauk, (631) 668-3781, http://nysparks.state.ny.us/parks/29/details.aspx

Montauk Point State Park: Montauk, (631) 668-3781, http://nysparks.state.ny.us/parks/61/details.aspx

Nissequogue River State Park: Kings Park, (631) 269-4927, http://nysparks.state.ny.us/parks/110/details.aspx

Orient Point State Park: Orient, (631) 323-2440, http://nysparks.state.ny.us/parks/106/details.aspx

Planting Fields Arboretum: Oyster Bay, (516) 922-9200, www.plantingfields.org

Robert Moses State Park: Fire Island, (631) 669-0470, http://nysparks.state.ny.us/parks/7/details.aspx

Shadmoor State Park: Montauk, (631) 668-3781, http://nysparks.state.ny.us/parks/16/details.aspx

Sunken Meadow State Park: Kings Park, (631) 269-4333, www.longislandexchange.com/parks/sunkenmeadow-statepark.html

Trial View State Park: Woodbury, (631) 423-1770, http://nysparks.state.ny.us/parks/39/details.aspx

Valley Stream State Park: Valley Stream, (516) 825-4128, http://nysparks.state.ny.us/parks/159/details.aspx

Walt Whitman State Park: Huntington Station, (631) 427-5240, www.longislandexchange.com/parks/waltwhitmanbirthplace-statepark.html

Wildwood State Park: Wading River, (631) 929-4314, http://nysparks.state.ny.us/parks/68/details.aspx

Harbor Links Golf Course: Port Washington, (516) 767-4816

Lido Golf Course: Lido Beach, (516) 889-8181

Merrick Road Park Golf Course: Merrick, (516) 868-4650

North Woodmere Golf Course: North Woodmere, (516) 571-7814

Peninsula Golf Course: Massapequa, (516) 798-9776

Town of Oyster Bay Golf Course: Woodbury, (516) 677-5960

i In June 2009 the Bethpage Black Course hosted the U.S. Open. It also hosted the 2002 U.S. Open, as well as a variety of other local, regional, and national tournaments.

Suffolk County Public Golf Courses

Open between mid-Mar and late Dec, Suffolk County operates four different golf courses. Each course has its own pro shop and is staffed by PGA professionals. They all offer a driving range and a practice green, along with a full-service restaurant. Golf cart rentals are available, as are public restrooms.

A centralized phone number (631-244-7275) is available to book tee times at any of the following courses:

Bergen Point Golf Course: West Babylon

Indian Island Golf Course: Riverhead

Timber Point Golf Course: Great River

West Sayville Golf Course: West Sayville

In addition to these public courses, western Suffolk County contains no fewer than 29 other 9-hole or 18-hole golf courses that are open to the public, including Dix Hills Country Club (Dix Hills, 631-271-4788), Timber Point Country Club (Great River, 631-581-2401), Crab Meadow Golf Course (Northport, 631-757-8800), the Links at Shirley (Shirley, 631-395-7272), Bergen Point Golf Course (West Babylon, 631-661-8282), and the Ponds (Lake Grove, 631-737-4649).

The North Fork region has at least nine additional public golf courses, including Island's End Golf Course (Greenport, 631-477-0777), Shelter Island Golf Course (Shelter Island, 631-749-0416), and Green Rock Golf Course (Wading River, 631-929-1200).

On the South Fork, there are three public golf courses: Poxabogue Golf Course (Bridgehampton, 631-537-0025), Montauk Downs State Park Golf Course (Montauk, 631-668-1100), and Sag Harbor Golf Course (Sag Harbor, 631-725-2503). Of course, in and around the Hamptons, there are numerous private golf clubs and golf courses.

i For the latest news about events and tournaments happening at all of the golf courses on Long Island, check out *Long Island Golf News'* Web site at http://longislandgolfnews.com. To access a comprehensive listing of public golf courses and private courses that accept guests, visit http://longislandgolfnews.com/courses.

LONG ISLAND'S PUBLIC BEACHES

Throughout Long Island there are more than 150 public beaches, along with countless private beaches maintained by resorts, hotels, and inns, for example. Listed below are the main public beaches. Details about each of them, including what facilities and amenities are offered (if any) and applicable admission/parking fee(s), can be found online at www.longislandexchange.com/beaches.html or at www.discoverlongisland.com/sub_cats.cfm/ID/24.

Each beach has a very different atmosphere and attraction for swimmers, sunbathers, surfers, etc., based on which body of water a particular beach is situated on. Beaches within sheltered bays, for example, will be very calm, while beaches that open directly to the Atlantic Ocean will potentially have much bigger waves, stronger tides, and a vastly different view.

Not all of these beaches have lifeguards on duty, even during the peak summer season. Near the access to each beach will be posted signs listing beach hours, along with beach rules and regulations.

Starting on page 174 is an alphabetical list of beaches located throughout Nassau County and Suffolk County:

Putting around Long Island

The public golf courses in Nassau County are a huge draw for both residents and tourists who don't want to pay big bucks to play golf at one of the prestigious county clubs or private golf clubs in the region. Being county operated, these golf courses are affordable and well maintained. All offer a pro shop and equipment rentals.

Here's a sampling at what's offered at some of these public golf courses:

The Glen Cove Golf Course, which is located along Lattingtown Rd. in Glen Cove (516-676-0550), is a lovely 18-hole course that is famous for its stunning waterfront view. In addition to the course itself, you'll find a pro shop and driving range here, along with the Soundview Cafe. Also located on the property is Stanco Park, which features tennis courts and a children's playground. Compared to a private golf club, the rates at this course are extremely affordable. For example, 2009 rates for 18 holes were just $24 on weekdays and $30 on weekends. An unlimited annual pass can be purchased for $1,400. Tee times can be reserved up to seven days in advance, and discounts are available for seniors and young adults (age 17 and under).

The Bethpage State Park Golf Course is located at 99 Quaker Meetinghouse Rd. in Farmingdale (516-249-0700). It's really five 18-hole public golf courses at one location. Here, you'll find the world famous Black Course, which has hosted the U.S. Open twice. More than 300,000 rounds of golf are played at these five courses annually. Each course caters to golfers at various skill levels, with the Black Course being the most challenging. At Bethpage you'll find a fully-equipped pro shop, where equipment and electric cart rentals are available. Greens fees at these courses are a bit more expensive than at other public golf courses in Nassau County, ranging from $36 per person on weekdays ($41 on weekends) for the Green, Blue, and Yellow Courses, to $100 per person on weekdays ($120 on weekends) for the Black Course. There's also a reservation fee of $5, but advance reservations are an absolute must, especially for the Black Course.

Over at the **Lido Golf Course,** located at 255 Lido Blvd., Lido Beach (516-889-8181), you'll experience a private golf club setting that's beautiful and very well equipped and maintained. This course was created on land between the Atlantic Ocean and Reynolds Channel, so you're surrounded by incredible beauty as you experience this championship course that stretches over 6,900 yards and plays to a par 72. A pro shop offers equipment and cart rentals. The course was designed by Robert Trent Jones and was named one of the "Best Places to Play" by *Golf Digest* magazine, after earning three and a half stars. Rates for the Lido Golf Course are extremely affordable, starting at $33 for 18 holes of weekday play for residents and $42 for nonresidents. Electric carts cost $33 extra, plus there's a $5 reservation fee. Tee times can be booked by telephone, in person, or online (www.lidogolf.com/proshop_teetimes.htm).

The Harbor Links Golf Course, located at 1 Fairway Drive in Port Washington (516-767-4816, www.harborlinks.com), is another extremely beautiful and popular course in Nassau County. There's an 18-hole championship course here, along with an Executive Course, a separate driving range, and a miniature golf course. Residents pay just $44 for a round of 18 holes on weekdays, and between $72 and $81 on weekends. Nonresident fees are slightly higher. In addition to daytime golf, this course is known for its "twilight golf."

Hitting the Surf on Long Island

With more than 150 public beaches along Long Island's coast, there's no shortage of ways to enjoy the sun, surf, and sand. During the summer months, many of the larger beaches have lifeguards on duty, along with public restrooms, showers, and changing areas, plus plenty of parking. Depending on where you go, some of the beaches tend to be less crowded midweek, but during the summer season in touristy areas, you can count on good-size crowds anytime the sun is shining.

The following is a brief summary of what you'll find at just a few of Long Island's popular public beaches.

Coopers Beach, located along Meadow Ln. and Coppers Neck Ln. in Southampton (631-283-0247), consistently ranks as one of the top 10 beaches in America. Here you'll find gorgeous, white sandy beaches along with a view of the region's historic (and extremely expensive) mansions. You'll also find a concessions stand, public restrooms and showers, and chair and umbrella rentals here. Parking will cost you a whopping $40 per day. During the peak summer season, expect crowds pretty much throughout the week. However, the beach is spacious and beautiful, so it's well worth the visit.

East Hampton Main Beach (631-324-0362) is one of five public beaches located in East Hampton. Like Coopers Beach, it's consistently been ranked among the top 10 beaches in America. The main beach is located along Ocean Ave. and has lifeguards on duty during the

Amagansett

Atlantic Avenue Beach, (631) 324-2417

Big Albert's Landing Beach, (631) 324-2417

Indian Well Beach, (631) 324-2417

Aquebogue

Iron Pier Beach, (631) 727-5744

Asharoken

Asharoken Beach, (631) 261-7574

Babylon

Gilgo Beach, (631) 893-2100

Robert Moses State Park, (631) 669-0470

Bay Shore

Benjamin Beach, (631) 224-5778

Bayville

Charles E. Ransom Beach, (516) 624-6160

Blue Point

Corey Beach, (631) 451-6100

Centerport

Centerport Beach, (631) 261-7574

Fleets Cove Beach, (631) 261-7574

Copiague

Tanner Park, (631) 893-2100

East Hampton

Georgica Beach, (631) 324-4150

Maidstone Park, (631) 324-2417

Main Beach, (631) 324-0074

East Islip

Heckscher State Park, (631) 581-2100

East Rockaway

Hewlett Point Park, (516) 599-4064

Eastons Neck

Hobart Beach, (631) 261-7574

Fire Island

Atlantique Beach, (631) 583-8610

Davis Park, (631) 451-6100

Great Gun, (631) 451-6100

Sailors Haven Beach, (631) 289-4810

Fort Salonga

Callahana Beach, (631) 754-9808

Glen Cove

Crescent Beach, (516) 676-3766

Morgan Memorial Park Beach, (516) 676-3766

Pryibil Beach, (516) 676-3766

Greenport

Norman Klipp Park, (631) 765-5182

Hampton Bays

Ponquogue Beach, (631) 728-8585

Sears Bellows County Park, (631) 852-8290

summer months (10 a.m. to 5 p.m. daily, weather permitting), along with public bathrooms and a seasonal snack bar. As with most public beaches, boating, fishing, and surfboards are not allowed in the posted swimming areas. Dogs are not allowed on Main Beach during daytime hours from the second Sun in May through Sept. At this beach, there's plenty of room to sunbathe on manicured sand as well as swim. Parking costs $20 per day.

Governor Alfred E. Smith Sunken Meadow State Park, located along Sunken Meadow State Pkwy. in Kings Park (631-269-4333), offers a wide range of land- and water-based activities, including a beautiful 3-mile-long beach along the Long Island Sound. Full facilities are offered here, including restrooms and showers. The parking fee ranges between $6 and $8 per day.

Hempstead Harbor Beach Park, located along West Shore Rd. in Port Washington (516-571-7930), offers a 60-acre park with a half mile of pristine beachfront. Walkways run along the entire length of the beach and connect to a nearby fishing pier. So in addition to sunbathing and swimming, this beach provides visitors the opportunity to walk on paved areas along the sand.

If you're staying in Nassau County, the most popular beach in the region is definitely **Jones Beach,** located within Jones Beach State Park, along Ocean Pkwy. in Wantagh (516-785-1600). This park boasts a wide range of daytime and nighttime activities, including 6.5 miles of ocean beach and a half-mile-long bay beach (which offers much calmer waters). You'll also find two swimming pools, plus areas designated for surfing, fishing, and boating. The beach is wheelchair accessible and offers restrooms, showers, changing room facilities, and umbrella rentals. Parking costs between $6 and $8 per day.

Huntington

Crescent Beach, (631) 261-7574

Gold Star Battalion Beach, (631) 261-7574

Islip

Islip Beach, (631) 224-5345

Kings Park

Sunken Meadow State Park, (631) 269-4333

Lake Ronkonkoma

Lake Ronkonkoma Beach, (631) 451-6100

Ronkonkoma Beach, (631) 467-3308

Lido Beach

Eugene Nickerson Beach, (516) 571-7700

Lido Beach, (516) 431-6650

Sands Picnic Beach, (516) 431-3900

Lindenhurst

Venetian Shores, (631) 893-2100

Lloyd Harbor

West Beck Beach, (631) 261-7574

Montauk

Ditch Pines, (631) 324-2417

East Lake Drive Beach, (631) 324-2417

Hither Hills State Park, (631) 668-2554

New Suffolk

New Suffolk Beach, (631) 765-5182

Nissequogue

Long Beach, (631) 584-9684

Short Beach, (631) 360-7654

North Sea

Emma Rose Elliston Park, (631) 728-8585

Northport

Crab Meadow Beach, (631) 261-7574

Orient Point

Orient Beach State Park, (631) 323-2440

Oyster Bay

Centre Island Beaches, (516) 624-6124

Patchogue

Sandspit Beach, (631) 451-6100

Point Lookout

Point Lookout Beach, (516) 431-3900

Port Washington:

Bar Beach Park, (516) 869-6311

Hempstead Harbor Beach Park, (516) 571-7930

Quogue

Tiana Beach, (631) 728-8585

Riverhead

South Jamesport Beach, (631) 727-5744

Sag Harbor

Foster Memorial Beach, (631) 728-8585

Sagaponack
Sagg Main Beach, (631) 728-8585
Shelter Island
Crescent Beach, (631) 749-0291
Wades Beach, (631) 749-0291
Shirley
Shirley Beach, (631) 451-6100
Smith Point County Park, (631) 852-1316
Shoreham
Shoreham Beach, (631) 451-6100
Southold
Southold Town Beach, (631) 765-5182
Stony Brook
Stony Brook Beach, (631) 451-6100
Wading River
Wading River Beach, (631) 727-5744
Wading River: Wildwood State Park, (631) 929-4314
Wantagh
Jones Beach State Park, (516) 785-1600
Water Mill
Flying Point Beach, (631) 728-8585
Mecox Beach, (631) 728-8585
Scott Cameron Beach, (631) 728-8585
West Hampton
Cupsogue Beach County Park, (631) 852-8111
Westhampton Beach
Pikes Beach, (631) 728-8585

WHO'S IN CHARGE ANYWAY? THE PARKS AND RECREATION AUTHORITIES

If you want to learn more about the various state, county, and local parks on Long Island, here are the governing organizations you'll want to contact:

NASSAU COUNTY DEPARTMENT OF PARKS, RECREATION & MUSEUMS

Administrative Building, Eisenhower Park, East Meadow, NY 11554
(516) 572-0200
www.nassaucountyny.gov/agencies/Parks/index.html

The Nassau County Department of Parks, Recreation & Museums manages 70 county-operated parks, preserves, museums, athletic facilities, and historic properties throughout Nassau County. Information about many of the county's historic landmarks and sites can be obtained from the Nassau County Historical Society (516-538-7679, www.nassaucountyhistoricalsociety.org) in Garden City, or from the local historical society within the town or community where a specific historic site or landmark is located.

NEW YORK STATE PARKS, RECREATION AND HISTORIC PRESERVATION

Empire State Plaza, Building 1, Albany, NY 12238
(518) 474-0456
http://nysparks.state.ny.us

This agency manages the more than 25 state parks located throughout Long Island, as well as all of the other state parks in New York. The office also assists communities in identifying, evaluating, preserving, and revitalizing their historic, archaeological, and cultural resources. The office also has a mandate to promote heritage tourism and help build the public's awareness of local park resources and historical sites.

SUFFOLK COUNTY PARKS, RECREATION & CONSERVATION

P.O. Box 144, West Sayville, NY 11796
(631)854-4949
www.co.suffolk.ny.us/departments/parks.aspx

Suffolk County Parks, Recreation & Conservation manages more than 46,000 acres of parkland within Suffolk County, including several beaches, marinas, golf courses, and historic sites. Information about many of the county's historical landmarks and sites can be obtained from the Suffolk County Historical Society (631-727-2881, www.suffolkcountyhistoricalsociety.org) in Riverhead, or from the local historical society within the town or community where a specific historic site or landmark is located.

i To learn about any of the town- or community-managed parks on Long Island, contact the local chamber of commerce for that town or community. You'll find a complete listing of Long Island chamber of commerce offices at www.longislandexchange.com/chambers-commerce.html.

DAY TRIPS AND WEEKEND GETAWAYS

Long Island is a unique destination because it covers a lot of territory and is divided into several very distinct regions. Thus, it's common for people living in Nassau County, for example, to enjoy a day trip or a weekend getaway in the North Fork or South Fork of Suffolk County, or to get away to Fire Island. So, even if you live in one part of Long Island, don't discount the day trip and weekend getaway opportunities that exist elsewhere on the island.

Long Island is also a short trip from Manhattan, which provides for another incredibly memorable day trip or weekend getaway opportunity. Plus, because Long Island is also within a few hundred miles of Connecticut, Rhode Island, Massachusetts, Philadelphia, and Washington, D.C., it's easy and convenient to take road trips to these and other nearby destinations.

If you're not in the mood for a long drive, you'll discover that the Long Island Railroad will take you directly to Penn Station in Manhattan. From there, its easy to hop on the high-speed Amtrak train service (the Acela) and travel from New York City to Boston (with stops in Connecticut and Rhode Island) or down to Philadelphia or Washington, D.C. These train trips take two to four fours, depending on your destination. You can also utilize LaGuardia or JFK Airport and take a quick flight almost anywhere. The flight to Boston; Washington, D.C.; or Philadelphia is under one hour, and several airlines offer hourly shuttle service between these cities.

This section offers a few ideas about how you can enjoy a fun, exciting, educational, or romantic day trip or weekend getaway to a destination that's quick and easy to reach from Long Island.

LOCAL DAY TRIPS AND WEEKEND GETAWAYS

No matter where you're staying or living on Long Island, if you travel to another region of the island, what you'll experience will be vastly different. The following four potential day trips or weekend getaways will keep you on Long Island, but expose you to a totally different environment. If you're looking to experience a one-day getaway or a short weekend trip, this section offers ideas on how to best utilize that limited time, but still have the opportunity to experience firsthand some of what Long Island has to offer.

Long Island's Wine County

If you're living or staying in Nassau County, for example, taking a drive (or a train ride on the Long Island Railroad) to Suffolk County's North Fork to experience the wine country can be an extremely romantic getaway, or simply a fun diversion from day-to-day life. Once you arrive in the North Fork region, participate in a one-day wine tasting tour either by hiring your own limo or by taking a group bus tour. (A list of tour operators is offered in the "Wine Country" chapter.)

During the day you'll visit a handful of wineries and vineyards and have the opportunity to explore the beautiful landscapes, plus taste plenty of locally produced wine. When the tour comes to an end, choose a nearby restaurant for dinner, where you'll enjoy a gourmet, fine-dining experience. During the peak summer months, be sure to make your reservations in advance.

After dinner you can either return home or, preferably, check into a nearby inn or B&B, like the **Barlett House** (631-477-0371, www.bartletthouseinn.com) in Greenport, which is an elegant mansion built in 1905. It has been transformed into a lovely 10-room B&B, where you can enjoy a romantic night with a loved one in a cozy setting. Another option is the **Harborfront Inn** (631-477-0707, www.theharborfrontinn.com) in Greenport. This is an upscale, 35-room boutique hotel that is located right on the water. Each room has a private balcony and comfortable furnishings, and offers a stunning and insanely romantic sunset view of the water.

During day two of your stay in the North Fork region, spend a few hours exploring the lovely shops and boutiques in **Greenport Village** (www.greenportvillage.com). This is a quaint and historic community that's not only beautiful and located on the water, but offers a unique and affordable shopping opportunity featuring a handful of one-of-a-kind shops, cafes, and galleries.

While exploring Greenport Village, you can enjoy a fresh seafood lunch at **Claudio's** (631-477-0627, www.claudios.com), which has been in operation since 1870, and then visit the **Blacksmith Shop** in the center of town for a free, live demonstration. **The Greenport Jail and Police Museum** and the **Railroad Museum of Long Island** are also interesting places to visit in Greenport Village. Or, in the winter months, you can go ice-skating in the center of town, in Mitchell Park. In other words, you can easily spend an entire day just exploring Greenport Village, which is vastly different than any community you'll find in Nassau County or other parts of Suffolk County.

The Hamptons

While the Hamptons are located on Long Island, this is a separate vacation destination unto itself, and one which people come from all over the world to enjoy. It's also a viable and popular day trip or weekend getaway option for people living in or visiting other regions of Long Island.

Each of the villages and communities within the Hamptons offers its own unique vibe and atmosphere, not to mention different types of activities. You can easily spend a day or more in just East Hampton or Southampton, for example, in order to experience the local shopping, dining, museums, galleries, beaches, and golf courses.

You don't have to be rich and famous to enjoy spending a day or two in the Hamptons. **Southampton,** for example, offers a nice mix of one-of-a-kind, upscale, and affordable shops in a quaint, small-town setting. You can easily spend a day shopping here, but take a break for lunch at one of the local cafes or restaurants, such as the **Blue Duck Bakery Cafe** (631-204-1701), which serves freshly baked Danish, pies, cakes, and cookies, along with gourmet coffee. You can also enjoy a full-service lunch or dinner at **75 Main** (631-283-7575, www.75main.com), which serves up all-American cuisine and ultra-fresh seafood.

While in Southampton, you can take part in a historic walking tour around the village (call 631-241-5554 for reservations) or visit the **Pelletreau Silver Shop** (631-283-2494) and see handcrafted jewelry being made by master jeweler Eric Messin, who also offers tours of the historic building (built in 1686), as well as jewelry-making demonstrations. The **Southampton Historical Museum** (631-283-2494) showcases the history of Southampton, while the **Water Mill Museum** is housed within an 18th-century water-powered gristmill that's interesting to explore firsthand.

Over in East Hampton, you can easily spend a day browsing around the upscale shops, or take a self-paced driving tour of the historic mansions and estates in the area. In or near the center of town, you'll find several museums and historic sites worth visiting, such as **Miss Amelia's Cottage** (built in 1725) and the **Hook Mill** (built in 1806). There's also the **East Hampton Town Marine Museum** and the **South End Cemetery,** which dates back to the 17th century.

For overnight accommodations, you'll find dozens of small B&Bs and inns that each offer something unique and special. For example, there's **Blakes Lodging** (631-324-1815), which is an 1810 farmhouse that has been transformed into a B&B. It's located within a five-minute walk from the center of town. The **Mill House Inn** (631-324-9766) is located on the outskirts of town and offers extremely upscale and romantic B&B accommodations. **The Hedges Inn** (631-324-7101) is another option if you're looking for an elegant and romantic B&B within East Hampton.

There are many ways to spend romantic evenings in and around the Hamptons. For example, you can take a sunset cruise (from a service like **Harbor Tours** in Sag Harbor, 631-725-0397, www.americanbeautycruises.com), eat at a fine-dining restaurant, or enjoy a take-out meal while cuddling in front of the fireplace in a private room at a small inn or B&B. You can order a gourmet take-out meal from one of many local restaurants and have the food delivered to your guestroom, using a service like **Hamptons Gourmet** (http://hamptonsgourmet.com/ordertakeoutlive.html).

i The beaches in the Hamptons are vastly different from any of the beaches in Nassau County. So, if you're a beachgoer, you can easily spend a full day at any of the area's beaches and not feel like you're anywhere close to home.

Nassau County's Jones Beach

While Nassau County is more suburban than the rural areas of Suffolk County, it is also where you'll find one of Long Island's most famous beaches—Jones Beach. Not only is this public beach a popular spot for sunbathing and swimming during the summer season, it's also located within **Jones Beach State Park** (http://nysparks.state.ny.us/parks/10/details.aspx), where you can easily spend several days and nights participating in a wide range of activities. At night during the summer season, you'll find a wide range of concerts and live performances on several different stages.

Your day or weekend in Nassau County can also include an overnight stay at one of the many affordable hotels or motels (see the "Accommodations" chapter), or you can plan a more upscale getaway by choosing overnight accommodations at someplace like the **Garden City Hotel** in Garden City (516-747-3000) or the ultra-luxurious **Oheaka Castle Hotel & Estate** in Huntington (631-659-1400), which is probably the most upscale and exclusive resort on Long Island, complete with its own golf course and restaurant.

It's easy to spend a full day shopping at **Roosevelt Field Mall** in Nassau County, or visiting the area's day spas, playing golf, or touring the museums. There are also plenty of fine-dining restaurants to choose from, where you can top off your visit with a memorable meal.

Short Trips to Shelter Island or Fire Island

Shelter Island and Fire Island are technically parts of Long Island, but each is a stand-alone island that can only be reached via boat or ferry. Particularly during the peak summer season (Memorial Day to Labor Day), these islands are each extremely popular vacation destinations, offering lodging, activities, beaches, shopping, golf, fishing, restaurants, bars, and historic attractions. Even if you're already spending the summer vacationing on Long Island (or living here), taking a day trip or weekend getaway to either Shelter or Fire Island is a viable option, and one well worth it since what you'll experience on these islands is once again vastly different from what's offered on other parts of Long Island.

During a summer day on Shelter Island, you can enjoy an outdoor hike in the **Mashomack Preserve,** pick up some gear at **Jack's Marine, Bait and Tackle Shop** (631-749-0114) and go fishing, or view the contemporary art that's on display at the **Boltax Gallery** (631-749-4062). For ultra-fresh seafood, you won't want to miss dining at **Bob's Fish Market** for lunch or dinner (631-749-0830), or experience the dining at the **Chequit Inn** (631-749-0018), which is located in a Victorian inn that was built in 1872.

Shelter Island is a small island that's composed of about 8,000 acres of land. Here you'll find a bunch of farms, beaches, and a few attractions, plus a small assortment of shops, restaurants, and bars and a handful of cozy hotels, inns, and B&Bs. It's mainly a summer resort community. Throughout the year only about 2,500 people live on the island, but the population expands to over 8,000 between Memorial Day and Labor Day. The island is located between Suffolk County's North and South Forks. Depending on where on Long Island you're coming from, the drive to the ferry will be anywhere from a few minutes to

Travel in Style between New York City and the Hamptons

If you'd like to travel between New York City and the Hamptons in style, you have a few options. You can hire a private limousine service to take you door-to-door, charter a private helicopter or small airplane, or ride aboard the Hamptons Luxury Liner (631-567-5100, www.hamptonluxuryliner.com) bus service, which is definitely the most affordable option but still very luxurious compared to a typical bus or driving yourself.

While the Hamptons Jitney offers basic bus transportation to and from various parts of Manhattan and Long Island, the Hamptons Luxury Liner service utilizes ultra-comfortable, custom-designed buses. For less than $40 each way per person (less if you buy a round-trip ticket), passengers experience plush, reclining seats (with more than 15 inches of legroom), complimentary Wi-Fi Internet access, and televisions with free DirectTV movies and TV shows, plus free nonalcoholic drinks and snacks. Each bus is equipped with a restroom and holds up to 44 passengers.

The scheduled Hamptons Luxury Liner bus service travels between Manhattan and the Hamptons several times per day year-round. In Manhattan, stops include 40th St., 47th St., 59th St., 70th St., and 86th St. In the Hamptons, stops include Southampton, Water Mill, Bridgehampton, Wainscott, East Hampton, and Amagansett.

Reservations are required and can be made by phone or online. If you don't want to drive yourself, the Hampton Luxury Liner offers a convenient, comfortable, and reasonably affordable way to travel between Manhattan and the Hamptons in two and a half to three and a half hours, depending on traffic and on your pick-up and drop-off location.

Particularly for day trips, this is a great way to get to the Hamptons from Manhattan, if you leave early in the morning and plan to return late in the evening. By not having to drive yourself, you're free to enjoy all of the wine tastings you desire, and have the option of sleeping comfortably on the bus during your trip home.

three hours. The ferry ride itself takes about five minutes.

Fire Island is considered a barrier island. It's about 31 miles long and 0.25 mile wide, and is located off the south shore of Long Island, within Suffolk County. During any given summer, you'll find more than 820,000 people visiting the Fire Island beaches. Ocean Beach, for example, is the part of the island where most of the restaurants, bars, and shops are located. Cherry Grove and Fire Island Pines attract a large gay population, but are open to everyone. No private cars are allowed on Fire Island. After arriving by boat or ferry, most people get around on foot or by bicycle. There are a handful of small hotels, inns, and B&Bs; however, if you want to stay on the island, particularly between Memorial Day and Labor Day, advance reservations are an absolute must.

One of the best places to enjoy a sunset and some drinks on Fire Island is **The Dock** (631-583-5200), which is a bar as well as a steak and seafood restaurant located right on the water. At **The Out** (631-583-7400) you can also take in the gorgeous waterfront scenery as you dine and listen to live music on weekends throughout the summer. Another popular restaurant, especially if you love seafood, is **Hurricane's Bar & Grill** (631-583-8000). During the peak summer season, there's always a festive crowd, as some of the most tasty food on the island is served here.

Even if your time is limited on Fire Island, you can certainly party. Drinking and dancing, or listening to live musical performances, is a popular evening and nighttime activity here, while during the day, most people hit the beach or partake in various water-based activities, like fishing, swimming, or boating. One of the must-see sights on Fire Island, however, is the **Sunken Forest.** It's one of the last remaining maritime forests on the East Coast, and an absolutely beautiful place to explore. You'll discover trees that have grown and twisted into unique and unusual shapes, plus see a wide assortment of other exotic marshland growth, not to mention local wildlife. The Sunken Forest encompasses about 40 acres, which you can explore on foot by walking along boardwalks. You can continue your day exploring Fire Island with a trip to the Fire Island Lighthouse, which was built in 1857. The lighthouse and grounds are open to the public during the summer between 9:30 a.m. and 5:30 p.m.

DAY OR WEEKEND TRIPS TO NEW YORK CITY

If you're coming from Long Island, you'll find it cheaper and more convenient to leave your car on the island and take the Long Island Railroad or a bus into Manhattan. Having to deal with New York City traffic, finding a place to park, and then paying the outrageously high parking fees (up to $50 per day) can be a bit unnerving for most people. Depending on where on Long Island you're coming from, the train trip will take between 45 minutes and three hours, and cost under $10 each way.

i Travel between New York City and almost anywhere on Long Island is easy via the Long Island Railroad. There are also easily affordable bus services, such as the Hampton Jitney (631-283-4600, www.hamptonjitney.com), that offer inexpensive ongoing service between Manhattan and many regions of Long Island, as well as point-to-point destinations on the island itself.

Once you're in downtown Manhattan, you can get around easily on foot, via taxi, or by taking a subway or bus. For first-timers coming to New York City, if you only have a day or two here, consider taking a bus tour around the city so you can see the main sights and tourist attractions (Times Square, the Statue of Liberty, Wall Street, Ground Zero, Central Park, South Street Seaport, Empire State Building, Rockefeller Center, Radio City Music Hall, Fifth Avenue, Madison Avenue, Greenwich Village, etc.) in the least amount of time possible. Two bus tour operators that'll take you to New York's must-see attractions are **Gray Line Double Decker Bus Tours** (800-669-0051, www.newyorksightseeing.com) and **CitySights New York Bus Tours** (212-812-2700, www.citysightsny.com).

Beyond taking a bus tour, if your time is limited in Manhattan, consider experiencing a Broadway show and dining at one of the city's most famous restaurants. While the shows are always changing on Broadway, *The Lion King, Wicked,* and *Mama Mia* are long-running favorites that are well worth seeing. You can learn which Broadway shows are playing by visiting www.broadway.com, or stopping by the TKTS Booth in person (it's located in the heart of Times Square).

In the Times Square area alone, you'll find literally hundreds of restaurants, from **Sardi's** (a fine-dining restaurant just off Broadway in Times Square that is famous for its celebrity clientele) to **The Olive Garden** (where from the dining room you can enjoy a stunning view of Times Square). There's also a **Planet Hollywood, ESPN Zone,** and **Hard Rock Cafe** in Times Square, which offer memorable theme-dining opportunities.

If you're spending a night or two in Manhattan, choose a hotel in the downtown area, such as the **London NYC** (866-690-2029) or **Marriott Marquis** (212-398-1900) in the Times Square area, or stay on the outskirts of Central Park, at **The Ritz-Carlton** (212-308-9100), for example. If you're looking for a trendy, boutique-style hotel, **W Hotels** (212-755-1200) offers several locations in Manhattan, while more affordable accommodations can be found at the various **Holiday Inn Express** (212-695-7200) locations, which have all been recently remodeled.

If time permits, consider visiting one or more of New York City's famous museums and other tourist attractions. A walk or horse-drawn carriage ride through Central Park and a few hours visiting the shops and sights in Times Square should definitely be part of your itinerary. And if shopping is your thing, you'll easily be able to fill one or two entire days just on Fifth Avenue and Madison Avenue alone.

If you're planning to spend the night in New York City, be prepared to spend top dollar for comfortable, albeit basic accommodations. An average, three-star hotel guestroom in Manhattan will cost at least $300 to $500 per night, and you'll pay considerably more for a four-star, luxury hotel. You can sometimes find good deals by shopping online, using a service like Hotels.com, Hotwire, Travelocity, or Kayak. Any hotel costing less than $250 to $300 per night in Manhattan will probably be substandard, in a lousy location, or offer a not-so-clean or comfortable room. You may find it more cost-effective to stay on Long Island at night and take day trips into the city.

OTHER POPULAR WEEKEND GETAWAYS

Beyond New York City, people visiting or living on Long Island can venture out and explore the city's other boroughs, like Queens, the Bronx, and Staten Island. In the Bronx, for example, there's the New York Botanical Gardens and the Bronx Zoo, which offer at least a full day's worth of activities and which people come from all over the world to experience.

If you're willing to take a car trip, train trip, or a short flight away from Long Island, you can easily visit Boston, Connecticut, Philadelphia, and Washington, D.C.—either for a day or for a weekend.

Boston

From New York City, Boston is just over 200 miles away. It's easy to reach by car; however, regular train and bus service is also offered, as is an hourly shuttle from LaGuardia Airport on US Airways and Delta Airlines. From Suffolk County, it's easier to take the Cross Island Ferry from Orient Point. In 80 minutes you'll be in New London, Connecticut, and then you can drive along I-95 for less than two hours to reach downtown Boston. From Nassau County, it's easier to drive along I-95 for the entire trip, which takes about three and a half to four hours.

Boston is a historic city in the heart of New England, and a wonderful place to visit year-round. During a weekend Boston getaway, you can easily take a drive to Cape Cod, Maine, Vermont, or New Hampshire, for example. Cape Cod is a popular summertime destination (very much like Suffolk County on Long Island), while Maine, Vermont, and New Hampshire offer amazingly beautiful fall foliage and excellent skiing in the winter.

You'll find a bunch of popular hotels in the downtown area, like the **Fairmont in Copley Plaza** (617-267-5300) or the new **W Hotel** (617-261-8700), which is located in Boston's theater district. The **Boston Harbor Hotel** (617-439-7000) is located right on the water on the outskirts of the city, and is within walking distance of several popular attractions, like the New England Aquarium and the historic North End.

For shopping, some of the places you'll want to visit in Boston include **Newbury Street, Faneuil Hall, Copley Place,** and the **Prudential Center.** However, what Boston is really known for is its culture, arts, and history. If you're a history buff, be sure to explore Boston's **Freedom Trail** (www.thefreedomtrail.org). It's a self-paced, 2.5-mile walking tour that'll take you to 16 historic locations, including the State House, Faneuil Hall, Paul Revere's house, the Bunker Hill monument, and the site of the Boston Massacre. As for museums, you won't want to miss the **Boston Tea Party Ship & Museum** (617-338-1773) along with the famous **Museum of Fine Arts** (617-267-9300, www.mfa.org). **Boston's Symphony Hall** (617-266-2378, www.bso.org) is where you can see a performance of the Boston Pops or the Boston Symphony Orchestra, as well as other musical performances throughout the year.

While there are many fine-dining as well as affordable restaurants in Boston, out-of-towners mainly come for the fresh seafood. Be sure to dine at any of the popular **Legal Sea Foods** locations in and around Boston. Within Faneuil Hall, you'll also find a handful of restaurants, including **Durgin Park** (617-227-2038, www.arkrestaurants.com/durgin_park.html), which is a historic, family-oriented restaurant. It's been around since 1742, and the waiters here are famous for their attitude. For the ultimate in authentic Italian dining, the likes of which you'd typically find only in Italy, be sure to take a stroll around Boston's **North End** and drop in at one of the small, family-operated restaurants you'll discover along the narrow and winding streets. Each of these restaurants offers its own Italian specialties, utilizing imported ingredients and recipes passed down through several generations, to ensure authenticity. Not only is the food amazing, but the historic atmosphere and the adorable little restaurants make for a memorable experience.

Once you're in downtown Boston, you can get around easily on foot, via taxi, or by using the subway system (called the "T"). For more information about visiting Boston, visit the Greater Boston Convention and Visitors Bureau official tourism Web site at www.bostonusa.com/visit. You can also call (888) SEE-BOSTON.

Connecticut Casinos

One thing Long Island doesn't offer is casinos and resorts that feature Las Vegas–style shows and entertainment. If you want that, short of traveling to Atlantic City or Las Vegas, you can drive from Long Island to the casinos in Connecticut. Between the gambling, restaurants, golf courses, shops, day spa, shows, and on-site attractions, visiting any of the three major casinos in Connecticut can easily provide a weekend's worth of entertainment and fun.

FOXWOODS RESORT & CASINO
350 Trolley Line Blvd., Mashantucket, CT
(860) 885-3000
www.foxwoods.com

This resort and casino offers everything you could possibly want from a weekend getaway, all under one roof. Here you'll find fine-dining restaurants, a world-class spa, live entertainment, nightclubs, six massive casinos, and luxury accommodations. Combined, the casinos within Foxwoods feature 6,200 slot machines and 380 gaming tables (featuring 17 different table games). If poker is your game, you'll find 100 poker tables here, plus a high-tech Race Book and the world's largest bingo hall.

Special events and concerts are held here throughout the year. Oh, and when you get hungry, there are 30 restaurants available to serve you, many of which are open 24 hours a day. Foxwoods, like the other casinos in the area, offers a true Las Vegas–style experience.

To get to Foxwoods Casino or MGM-Grand at Foxwoods from Long Island by car, travel toward New York City and then take I-95 North to exit 92 in Connecticut, past New London. Turn left onto Rte. 2 West. Foxwoods Casino is 8 miles west on Rte. 2. The drive time is about three hours from Nassau County.

MGM-GRAND AT FOXWOODS
240 MGM Grand Dr., Mashantucket, CT
(860) 312-3000
www.mgmatfoxwoods.com

A recent addition to the Foxwoods Casino complex is the MGM-Grand, a massive stand-alone casino/resort. It too offers everything you'd want in a single building, so once you arrive, there's really no reason to leave until you're ready to head home. Here you'll find 1,400 slot machines and 60 gaming tables, plus a handful of world-class restaurants and several large theaters that present live shows, sporting events, and concerts almost nightly. There's also a luxurious day spa, plus two on-site golf courses. In terms of accommodations, the MGM-Grand offers 825 guestrooms and suites, all featuring ultra-modern and extremely comfortable furnishings and decor.

MOHEGAN SUN
1 Mohegan Sun Blvd., Uncasville, CT
(888) 777-7922
www.mohegansun.com/gateway/index.html

Established in 1996 by the Mohegan Indian tribe of Connecticut, Mohegan Sun is the region's most established casino/resort complex. It features 30 restaurants, luxurious hotel accommodations, live entertainment, shopping, and more than 300,000 square feet of casino space, which includes nonsmoking areas. One highlight of Mohegan Sun is the Casino In The Sky, located at the top of the 34-story hotel tower. There's also a gorgeous 55-foot indoor waterfall and a 10,000-seat indoor arena where shows, concerts, and sporting events are held.

For directions to Mohegan Sun using public transportation or your own car, visit www.mohegansun.com/getting-here.

i Bus service is available to the Connecticut casinos from Manhattan; however, most people find it easier and more convenient to drive from Long Island. It's particularly convenient from Suffolk County if you take the ferry to New London, Connecticut, and then drive directly to the casino of your choice.

Philadelphia

Like Boston, Philadelphia is a historic city, and one that provides plenty to see, do, and experience during a weekend or several-day visit. It's also a city that'll appeal to people of all ages. Getting to Philadelphia is relatively easy by car, bus, train (via traditional or high-speed Amtrak service), or plane. In fact, it's one of the few non-Florida cities you can fly to directly (nonstop) from Long Island MacArthur Airport, which is more convenient than getting to and from LaGuardia or JFK Airports from Long Island.

One of the most fun ways to see Philadelphia during warm-weather months is via a **Ride the Ducks tour** (877-88-QUACK). These tours utilize amphibious vehicles that travel on land and in the water, providing a 70-minute overview of the city's historic district, South Street area, Old City, and the Delaware River.

Within the historic district of Philadelphia, you can make many stops. For example, there's the **Betsy Ross House** (215-686-1252), where you can see the home built in 1740 that was once occupied by Betsy Ross and learn about the creation of the first American flag. Experiencing the **Constitutional Walking Tour of Philadelphia** offers a nice overview of Independence National Historic Park and 20 historic sites. This is a 75-minute, 1.25-mile guided tour that departs from the Independence Visitor Center (Sixth St. and Market St.) spring through fall. Self-paced tours are also available. You can use your cell phone to experience the audio portion of your private tour (call 215-229-8687).

Philadelphia is chock-full of chain hotels, from Hiltons to Sheratons, and everything in between. The new **Aloft Philadelphia Airport Hotel** (267-298-1700) offers ultra-trendy and affordable accommodations created by the folks behind the W Hotels.

When it comes to dining, Philadelphia is a major city, and contains hundreds of restaurants in all price ranges. The **Water Works Restaurant and Lounge** (215-236-9000), for example, is housed in a 140-year-old waterworks building that was the engine room for Philadelphia's water department back in the day. Today it is an upscale restaurant located close to the Philadelphia Museum of Art. Because it's on the water, the setting is extremely romantic. The menu offers all-American cuisine with a Mediterranean influence.

A much less formal, but equally memorable, place to eat is **H & J McNally's Tavern** (215-247-9736), which is a friendly and extremely popular bar and restaurant that attracts locals and tourists alike. This tavern has been a Philadelphia landmark since 1921, and it's now operated by the original owner's great-granddaughters. Featured on the extensive pub menu is the Schmitter, which is a signature dish here. It's a Philadelphia cheesesteak sandwich that's simply mouthwatering. Another of the city's more famous restaurants is **Georges'** (610-964-2588). It offers a casual yet sophisticated dining atmosphere and an affordable menu featuring contemporary French cuisine.

At night, if you're a beer drinker, you'll want to drop into **Triumph Brewing Company** (215-625-0855), which is a popular hangout among locals. This establishment has its own microbrewery and serves up a selection of award-winning beers and ales.

To learn more about the vacation and weekend getaway options available in Philadelphia, visit the Web site for the Greater Philadelphia Tourism office at www.gophila.com or call (800) 537-7676 during normal business hours.

Washington, D.C.

As the nation's capital, Washington, D.C., offers plenty to do in a single weekend, from visiting the monuments and museums to seeing national landmarks like the White House and U.S. Capitol. From Long Island, you can fly to Washington from LaGuardia Airport or JFK Airport, or drive. The driving distance is about 250 miles. Regularly scheduled bus service, as well as traditional or high-speed train service (through Amtrak), is available from Manhattan. Between driving to and from airports and the approximately 60-minute flight time, it is possible to travel to DC for a single day, leaving early morning and returning at night, but you'll have a much more leisurely and enjoyable time if you can spend a weekend or longer in the area.

While you'll need to plan way ahead and jump through some hoops to take a tour of the **White House** (www.whitehouse.gov/about/tours-and-events), anyone can easily spend several days visiting the various Smithsonian museums (www.si.edu/museums) in the DC area. For example, there's the **Air and Space Museum, Museum of American History,** and **Museum of African Art,** along with about a dozen others—all offering free admission. A more lighthearted but extremely informative museum well worth visiting is the **International Spy Museum** (202-EYE-SPY-U, http://spymuseum.org). While you'll pay an admission fee, you'll spend several hours learning how international spies operate. The **National Zoo** (http://nationalzoo.si.edu/) is also a fun destination, and it's where you can see more than 2,000 animals, including the famous giant pandas.

Of course, the DC area is also famous for its monuments, not to mention **Arlington National Cemetery.** If your time is limited, consider taking one of many narrated bus tours that offer an overview of these monuments in less than two or three hours. Otherwise, you could easily spend several hours exploring the **National Mall** and each monument, such as the **Lincoln Memorial, Washington Monument, Jefferson Memorial,** and **Vietnam Veterans Memorial,** at your own pace.

The DC area is home to several hundred hotels. Some are famous and historical, while others offer more of a run-of-the-mill chain hotel experience. **The Ritz-Carlton** (202-835-0500) offers plush accommodations, but for a truly historic experience, you should consider staying across the street from the White House at the famous **Willard Intercontinental Hotel** (202-628-9100, www.washington.intercontinental.com/washa/index.shtml). This hotel was built in 1850, and is where numerous U.S. presidents, including Lincoln, and countless world leaders have stayed.

To learn about the vacation and weekend getaway options available in Washington, D.C. and surrounding areas, visit the official Destination DC tourism Web site at http://washington.org or call (800) 422-8644 during normal business hours.

Appendix

LIVING HERE

In this section we feature specific information for residents or those planning to relocate here. Topics include real estate, education, health care, and much more.

RELOCATION

Most people hate change, so the concept of moving to a new area, a new state, or a new part of the country, and potentially taking on a new job, represents a life-changing experience that often invokes feelings of fear and trepidation. Whether you're interested in relocating to Long Island to start a family, retire, potentially improve your quality of life, experience a change of surroundings in terms of your living situation, or pursue a new job, for example, the actions you're about to take will require you to make many important decisions. And, what you ultimately decide and the actions you take will, no doubt, have long-term implications on many aspects of your life (and the lives of your family members).

The best way to go about making life-altering decisions that involve relocating, and ultimately choosing the very best place to live on Long Island (based on your budget, lifestyle, needs, desires, and unique circumstances), is to do plenty of research *before* making any firm commitments.

This section of the *Insiders' Guide to Long Island* will guide you through the relocation process, help you choose the best place on Long Island to live, and help you determine whether your financial situation will allow you to maintain or improve your current standard of living—especially during these unpredictable economic times.

As you already know, Long Island is a very diverse region. While real estate prices across America have been extremely unstable in recent years, the negative impact of the nation's economy has had a somewhat lesser impact on Long Island, so real estate prices have remained strong. This is mainly because of the region's overall affluence and close proximity to New York City.

However, just like everywhere else, economic conditions have resulted in sometimes significant increases in cost-of-living expenditures and moving costs, all of which you'll need to calculate into your budget. In fact, the biggest complaints among Long Islanders are the high costs of their property tax and utilities (primarily gas and electricity) and the shortage of affordable apartments, condos, and single-family homes on the island. Affordable rental properties (apartments and homes) are also in high demand and short supply.

The following steps will help guide you through the relocation process as you establish a new life on Long Island.

STEP ONE: CHOOSE WHERE TO LIVE BASED ON YOUR UNIQUE NEEDS

Now that you've learned a bit about the various regions of Long Island, first choose an area where you might want to live. This decision should be based on a wide range of factors, including but not limited to:

- Your budget
- Local real estate costs
- The type of home (single-family house, condo, apartment, etc.) you're looking to purchase or rent
- Ongoing real estate taxes and insurance costs
- Whether your relocation is for a seasonal or year-round residence
- The area's proximity to New York City, and what commuting options are readily available
- The area's distance from your job and the ongoing cost to commute
- The quality and reputation of the local public school system, or the proximity to suitable private schools for your children

- Local crime statistics
- Local climate
- Demographic makeup of the community
- Traffic congestion in the area
- How well the area fits your lifestyle
- Current economic condition of the community or region, and whether the local economy is projected to improve or decline in the immediate future and over the long term
- Whether the costs associated with living in the selected area will reduce, maintain, or improve your quality of living, based on your income versus anticipated living expenses. You'll want to utilize, among other tools, a cost-of-living calculator for this.
- Determine the average salary for someone with your experience, job title, and qualifications who currently works in the region. Whether you're currently working or seeking new employment, you'll want to use tools like Salary.com or the Salary Calculator at Fairhome.com. If you're moving from out of state, this will be particularly helpful if you haven't yet lined up employment, to determine your earning potential.

Property Taxes

In addition to buying a home, and then paying for utilities and upkeep, one of the significant ongoing expenses you'll incur are the property taxes you're required to pay. The following resources will help you calculate property taxes for the specific area of Long Island you're interested in moving to. Your real estate broker will also be able to provide this information.

Nassau County

To learn about property tax rates in Nassau County, contact the Nassau County Department of Assessment office at (516) 571-1500 or visit the agency's Web site at www.nassaucountyny.gov/mynassau property/main.jsp. From this Web site you can gain free access to almost all information maintained by the Department of Assessment, including: assessment roll data, district information, tax maps, property photographs, past taxes, tax rates, exemptions with amounts, and comparable sales.

Suffolk County

The following are assessment offices within Suffolk County from which you can learn about local property taxes and related information:

- Babylon Department of Assessment: (631) 957-3014, www.townofbabylon.com/departments/details.cfm?did=4
- Brookhaven Town Assessor: (631) 451-6300, www.brookhaven.org/Assessor/Assessor/tabid/183/Default.aspx
- Huntington Assessor: (631) 351-3226, http://town.huntington.ny.us/department_details.cfm?ID=26
- Smithtown Assessor: (631) 360-7560, www.smithtowninfo.com/Assessor'sOffice
- Southampton Assessment: (631) 283-6000, www.town.southampton.ny.us/listing.ihtml?cat=Assessment&id=3
- Southold Board of Assessors: (631) 765-1937, http://southoldtown.northfork.net/assessors.htm

i The Suffolk County government directory can be found online at www.co.suffolk.ny.us.

Commuting to and from Manhattan

One reason why people who work in Manhattan opt to live on Long Island is because of the lovely suburban neighborhoods and the small-town lifestyle available. In order to live on Long Island and work in Manhattan, however, a daily commute is required.

While plenty of people opt to drive to and from work, and incur toll and parking charges on a daily basis, a more convenient, often faster, and less expensive option is to commute via the Long Island Railroad (LIRR) between various train stations throughout Long Island and Penn Station in Manhattan. How much you'll pay for your commute will depend on the distance you live from Manhattan. The farther away you are, the more expensive your rail ticket will be. Nassau County is where the majority of people who work in Manhattan opt to live.

As you calculate your cost-of-living expenses and salary requirements, you'll need to budget for your monthly commuting expenses, which will probably be several hundred dollars per month.

LIRR Fare Zones (Effective June 17, 2009)

The LIRR divides Long Island into zones, which are based on distance from Penn Station in Manhattan (located in Zone 1). Full-fare monthly tickets for 2009 on the LIRR are as follows (zones do not go in numerical order):

Within Zone 1: $149
Between Zone 1 and Zone 3: $177
Between Zone 1 and Zone 4: $204
Between Zone 1 and Zone 7: $232
Between Zone 1 and Zone 9: $274
Between Zone 1 and Zone 10: $306
Between Zone 1 and Zone 12: $362
Between Zone 1 and Zone 14: $392

i To access, download, and print a Long Island Railroad fare chart, which displays monthly ticket prices, visit http://mta.info/lirr/pubs/LIRRFares.pdf. To save money on monthly tickets, LIRR passengers have two options: Mail & Ride (800-649-NYNY, www.mailandride.com) and Web Ticket (www.lirrticket.com/webticket/Cart/Welcome), both offering a 2 percent discount. Major credit cards are accepted.

STEP TWO: CHOOSE A REPUTABLE REALTOR TO HELP EDUCATE YOU ABOUT THE AREA

If you need assistance pinpointing regions of Long Island that might be suitable, or you're ready to begin looking at real estate or housing options, after doing your own preliminary research, start working with a reputable and experienced Realtor who is familiar with the region(s) of Long Island you're interested in exploring.

All real estate agents are not the same. Thus, when it comes to finding a suitable place to live, it's essential that you work with someone who is reputable, experienced, knowledgeable about the region, and trained to offer the personalized assistance a real estate buyer needs to make intelligent and cost-effective decisions. The term "Realtor" is not generic, like "real estate agent." According to the National Association of Realtors (www.realtor.com), "All real estate licensees are not the same. Only real estate licensees who are members of the National Association of Realtors are properly called 'Realtors.'"

These real estate professionals display the Realtor® logo on their business cards and other marketing and sales literature. Members of this organization subscribe to a strict and well-documented code of ethics, and maintain a higher level of knowledge pertaining to the entire process of buying and selling real estate. You can find a nationwide directory of Realtors at the Realtors.com Web site, which also contains a free detailed document (www.realtor.com/basics/allabout/realtors/why.asp) explaining all of the reasons why a buyer should consider working with a Realtor versus a generic real estate agent.

Not only will a Realtor be able to help you choose the ideal community in Long Island that's best suited to your budget, wants, and needs, he or she will be able to tell you all about each community and then show you specific properties that are currently for sale. Many Realtors also handle rental properties.

i Even if you plan on renting, at least initially when you relocate to Long Island, you can work with a real estate agent to help you find the perfect place to live.

STEP THREE: GET YOUR FINANCES IN ORDER

As you work with a Realtor (or other well-qualified real estate agent) to help you determine where on Long Island you'd like to live, and you begin actually shopping around for a home, you'll probably need to begin working with a mortgage broker or lender to start the mortgage prequalification or preapproval process.

These days getting approved for a mortgage is more difficult than ever—even for people with an above average or excellent credit rating. Before you begin filling out mortgage applications, invest some time to obtain free copies of your own credit reports from Experian, Equifax, and TransUnion (call 877-322-8228 or visit www.annualcreditreport.com), and be prepared to purchase your related credit scores. By examining your credit reports and scores, you can quickly obtain an overview of your credit rating, which directly impacts your ability to qualify for and get approved for a mortgage. Ideally, you want to go into the home-buying process with an above average or excellent credit rating, with as little preexisting debt as possible.

If you notice your credit rating isn't as strong as it should be, start taking steps immediately to improve the situation, starting six months before you begin shopping for a mortgage (and your new home). The following tips will help you improve your credit rating:

- Pay all of your bills on time, especially your existing mortgage. For at least a 12-month period, it is essential that no late payments are reported related to your current mortgage (if applicable). If any of the credit-reporting agencies are reporting even one late mortgage payment within a 12-month period, you will find it extremely difficult to get approved for a new mortgage in today's tough economic situation, since lenders are being much stricter about mortgage application approvals. Also, avoid having any accounts transferred to a collections agency, having credit card companies "charge off" your accounts due to nonpayment, or having an automobile lender repossess your vehicle.
- Keep your credit card balances low (below 35 percent of your available credit line for each card). By doing this, you'll notice your credit scores will improve within one to three months. Pay off as much of your credit card debt as possible, before applying for a mortgage.
- Keep unused but positive accounts with lenders and creditors open. Part of your credit score is calculated based on the duration of your positive relationships with your existing creditors and lenders.
- In the months leading up to applying for a mortgage, refrain from applying for new credit cards, car loans, or other types of credit.
- If you're planning on getting a divorce or are recently divorced, make sure all of your preexisting joint accounts are closed, or that your name is removed from them. Do this even if as part of the divorce settlement the judge mandated that your former spouse is responsible for the old debt or loans. As far as creditors, lenders, and the credit-reporting agencies are concerned, as long as your name appears on an account, you will be penalized for late or missed payments made by your former spouse for as long as the account remains open or there's an outstanding balance associated with the joint account.
- As you review your credit reports, check each one carefully for errors. It's important to request and review the credit reports from Experian, Equifax, and TransUnion separately. Never assume that the information on all three reports is identical. In fact, it's common to see significant differences in the information being reported on each report. However, it's your responsibility to ensure all of the information is factually correct. (Keep in mind that there's a difference between information that is factually correct and positive.)
- Avoid having excessive hard inquiries from creditors and lenders added to your credit report for at least six months prior to applying for a mortgage. Every time you apply for a credit card or loan, a hard inquiry will be placed on your credit report. Having more than two or three hard inquiries on a credit report within a three- to six-month period will result in a temporary drop in your credit score, regardless of whether or not your applications were approved.
- Avoid bankruptcy. In years past it was much easier to get approved for a mortgage, even with a bankruptcy in your financial past. This information remains on your credit reports

(and negatively impacts your credit rating) for up to 10 years. Mortgage lenders do not look favorably on past bankruptcies.

- If possible, avoid consolidating your credit card balances onto a single credit card. While you might save money in interest charges and fees by doing this, it will readjust your credit utilization percentages, which negatively impacts your credit score.
- If any negative but accurate information currently appears on your credit reports, contact those creditors and lenders directly and negotiate for the information to be reported in a more favorable way. To accomplish this, you'll need to pay off or settle outstanding debts; however, doing this will improve your credit rating, thus making it easier to get approved for a mortgage.
- Pay your unpaid medical bills, or while disputing them, negotiate a payment plan so that they don't go to a collections agency and thus appear negatively on your credit reports. Unpaid medical bills are one of the biggest causes for significant drops in someone's credit score. In fact, any unpaid bill that is turned over to a collections agency will have an immediate and long-term negative impact on your credit scores and overall credit rating for up to seven years. This includes unpaid utility bills, cell phone bills, credit card bills, or unpaid student loans that have been turned over to an agency.
- If there is, in your opinion, too much negative information currently listed on your credit reports, or your credit scores are too low for you to qualify for competitive mortgage rates, work closely with an accountant, personal financial planner, or credit counselor, in addition to your Realtor and a reputable mortgage broker, to help you devise a plan for improving your situation. Keep in mind that this could take several months to several years, depending on the severity of the situation and how relevant your specific credit-related problems are in relation to what mortgage brokers and lenders deem important in their approval process.

Due to the shortage of affordable housing on Long Island, someone with a below-average credit rating will be at a strong disadvantage when trying to relocate to this part of New York State. This applies even if you're simply trying to rent an apartment. In addition to charging first and last month's rent, and a deposit to move into a rental property, landlords always check prospective tenants' credit ratings before allowing them to move in. Because of the shortage of available rental properties, landlords can pick and choose which tenants they allow to move in, in part based on their credit rating, which is an indicator of their ability to pay their rent.

STEP FOUR: FIND A MORTGAGE BROKER

Applying for and getting approved for a mortgage is a time-consuming and complex process. To assist you in this ordeal, you'll definitely want to work with a mortgage broker or lender who is experienced, knowledgeable, able and willing to offer you personalized service, and most important, honest and reputable.

Seek out referrals from friends, relatives, and your Realtor, for example. Shop around and do your research before settling on the mortgage broker you opt to work with. Yes, finding the most competitive and affordable mortgage rates is essential, and choosing a broker/lender with the lowest possible fees is a must; however, it's important that you feel comfortable working with the broker or lender you choose, and that you trust him or her.

Once you choose a mortgage broker or lender to work with, start the prequalification or preapproval process as you're shopping around for a new home, and begin gathering the paperwork and financial documents you'll need to complete a mortgage application. As you do this, based on your unique situation, you may want to start the process of putting your existing home on the market.

STEP FIVE: PURCHASE YOUR NEW HOME ON LONG ISLAND

Separate from the mortgage application and approval process is the actual home-buying process, where you work with your real estate agent and the seller to negotiate the price of the home you'd like to purchase, negotiate the conditions of the sale, and then make the actual purchase. This too is a complex and often confusing and time-consuming process. However, having a qualified and reputable team of experts working on your side, including a real estate agent, lawyer, and mortgage broker, will make the process that much easier, faster, and smoother.

i In addition to obtaining personal referrals, you can read consumer/client reviews of Long Island's real estate agents and Realtors at www.topagentquest.com.

Long Island–Area Realtors

The following is a partial listing of residential real estate agents that service all or parts of Long Island. Because each region of Long Island is totally different, once you pinpoint where you're interested in living, you'll want to work with a broker who is familiar with the area, as well as experienced and reputable.

Coldwell Banker Nassau County: (631) 343-3815, www.coldwellbankermoves.com/realtors/New_York/Nassau/Nassau_county.htm

Coldwell Banker Suffolk County, (631) 343-3815, www.coldwellbankermoves.com/realtors/New_York/Suffolk/Suffolk_county.htm

Century 21: (866) 732-6139, www.century21.com/search/purchase_realestate_local/landingpage.jsp

Corcoran Group: (516) 380-0538, www.myhamptonhomes.com

Herricks Realty: (516) 294-8040, www.herricksrealty.com

MLS Long Island: www.mlsli.com

Prudential Douglas Elliman Real Estate: (800) 355-4626, www.prudentialelliman.com/LI.aspx

Re/Max Unlimited: (516) 822-7362, www.remaxunlimitedny.com

i To view interactive maps of Long Island that can help you pinpoint a specific neighborhood, and then find a Realtor who specializes in that geographic area, go to www.realtor.com/longisland/nbregion.asp.

STEP SIX: PLAN YOUR MOVE

Safely packing up all of your belongings and then having them transported to your new home on Long Island is another time-consuming and detail-oriented process. Depending on your budget, you can opt to handle everything yourself (including the packing and then renting and driving your own moving truck), or you can hire professional, licensed, insured/bonded movers to help make the process easier.

The more comprehensive the services you request, the higher your moving expenses will be. The distance of the move, the time of year, and what's involved in the move itself will also determine costs. There are moving companies that will come into your existing home, professionally pack everything up for you, transport your belongings to your new home, and even unpack for you. However, this is the most expensive option.

To hire a mover, follow these basic steps:

- Determine your exact needs.
- Determine when and where you'll be moving, along with the distance from your existing residence (the exact mileage is important).
- Determine the level of service you want from the mover.
- Obtain written "binding" quotes from several moving companies.
- Hire your moving company.
- Make sure you have home owner's insurance for your new home in place before your move, and make sure your belongings are

LIVING HERE

fully covered while in transit. If you'll be renting an apartment or house, obtain renter's insurance and make sure it's active before your move.

- Execute your move.

There are many Web services you can use to help you find movers, choose the moving services you want or need, plan a budget for your move, and then plan your move. For example, there's the American Moving and Storage Association (www.moving.org), which in addition to offering online tools, offers a free, downloadable moving guide called *Consumer Handbook: A Practical Guide to Interstate Moving.*

i The Moving.com, National Association of Realtors (www.realtor.com), and U-Haul (www.uhaul.com) Web sites offer an abundance of free online tools and services useful for planning a move.

10 Tips for Packing before a Move

There are many steps involved in packing up all of your furniture and belongings, and then preparing for the move to your new Long Island residence. The following steps will help keep this process organized and more manageable:

1. Pack one room at a time. Be sure to label each box with a description of its contents. The more detailed you are with your descriptions, the easier it'll be to unpack and organize everything in your new home.
2. Determine what furniture or belongings you'll need immediately when you reach your new home, and if possible, pack those items or boxes last so they're easily accessible from your car or moving truck.
3. Be sure to fill up each box. If it's not totally filled to capacity, it is more likely to get crushed. However, it's equally important not to overfill a box to the point where it'll break or fall apart when moved or lifted.
4. Keep the weight of each box within your ability to lift it, especially if you'll be handling the packing and unpacking yourself. Put heavier items in smaller boxes to make them easier to carry. However, when moving any heavy boxes, use the appropriate equipment, such as a dolly and/or a back brace.
5. Be sure to add plenty of cushioning around fragile items. Crumpled paper, polystyrene foam, or biodegradable packing peanuts tend to work best as filler in boxes.
6. For bulky items like clothing, linens, blankets, and towels, use airtight Space Bag storage packs (www.spacebag.com) to reduce the amount of space they take up and to keep your items clean and undamaged during transit and when being stored.
7. Get rid of everything you don't need before the move. Eliminate as much clutter as possible. This will reduce your moving costs, make the unpacking process faster and easier, and potentially earn you some extra money if you sell your unwanted stuff at a tag sale, garage sale, or on eBay, for example, before the move.
8. When packing lots of small items, wrap them in brightly colored tissue paper and make sure everything is properly marked. Keep small items together so you don't accidently throw them out with the garbage.
9. Instead of using newspaper as a packing tool, use unprinted newsprint paper. You don't want the ink from the newspapers transferring to your belongings and damaging them.
10. Don't reuse boxes that look like they've been heavily worn or show signs of wear and tear. Each box should be sturdy, capable of being stacked, and be able to withstand getting crushed.

Even if you plan to hire a professional moving company to handle some or all of your packing and moving, some of the useful items you'll want on hand as you prepare for your move include a dolly, furniture pads (and/or blankets), plenty of boxes (in different shapes and sizes), specialty boxes for storing/moving specific or unusually shaped items, packing materials (crumpled paper, polystyrene foam, bubble wrap, and/or biodegradable packing peanuts), box labels and markers, dish dividers, plastic mattress and sofa covers, garment boxes or bags for your nice clothing, a tape gun/dispenser, and strong packing tape (at least 2 inches wide).

i Companies like U-Haul offer a large selection of boxes and moving supplies. To keep your belongings safe during a move, don't try to cut corners. You're better off buying the right size and shaped boxes and related packing materials to do the job. Otherwise, you could wind up with damaged items when you arrive at your new home and begin the unpacking process.

STEP SEVEN: NOTIFY EVERYONE NECESSARY ABOUT YOUR CHANGE OF ADDRESS

As soon as you know when and where you'll be moving, contact all of the local utilities. Plan to have your old services discontinued and your new services activated. This includes contacting the following companies:

- Cable TV company
- Electric company
- Gas company
- Home alarm company
- Internet provider
- Phone company (for local and/or long-distance service)

Ideally, this should be done two to four weeks prior to your move, to ensure everything will be turned on and fully activated when you step foot into your new Long Island home. When contacting your existing utility companies, be sure to have at least one old bill on hand so you can reference your account numbers easily. The appropriate phone number to call to discontinue services will also be on your old bills. Your real estate agent or the person you're purchasing your home from should be able to provide you with contact numbers for the utility companies on Long Island that service where you're moving to.

At the same time you do this, you'll want to contact the U.S. Post Office and initiate a formal change of address. This can be done at the local post office where you currently live or where you'll be moving, or online at www.usps.com. For details about changing your address, call (800) ASK-USPS.

i Be sure to notify the IRS about your change of address by calling (800) 829-3676 or visiting the Web site to obtain a Form 8822, Change of Address (www.irs.gov/pub/irs-pdf/f8822.pdf).

Some of the other companies or individuals you'll probably want to send change of address notifications to include:

- Accountant/CPA/financial planner
- Airline frequent flier accounts
- Attorney
- Bank(s) and other financial institutions you do business with
- Cell phone service provider(s)
- Charities you're active with
- Clubs or associations you participate in
- Credit card companies
- Department of motor vehicles (update your driver's license and vehicle registration)
- Doctor, dentist, optician, and other medical professionals
- Dry cleaners
- Financial companies that manage your investments and your retirement account
- Health club
- Insurance companies
- Landscaper
- Library
- Newspaper and magazine subscriptions
- Religious organizations
- Social Security Administration
- Union
- Veterinarian
- Voter registration office

The trick to a successful relocation is proper research and planning, so allow plenty of time to do everything that's necessary and be sure to line up a reliable and reputable team to help you (real estate agent, lawyer, moving company, mortgage broker, etc.).

CHILD CARE

Things have changed over the past few decades. The cost of living has risen dramatically, so families need more money just to maintain their standard of living and make ends meet. In addition, more and more couples are getting married and having kids but wind up getting divorced. Meanwhile, it's become totally accepted within our culture for single people to have and raise kids without being married.

For those couples that do get married (and stay that way), a significantly higher percentage of parents are both entering the workforce. As a result of these and other situations, the days of stay-at-home moms (or dads) are fading fast.

With both parents employed, the need for day care or child care for infants and toddlers is on the rise, as is the need for after-school day care for children who are in elementary and perhaps middle school. Even on Long Island, where the average median family income is significantly higher than in other parts of the country, the need for high-quality, reliable, and affordable child care or day care is a common one.

For many parents, finding the best possible child-care or day-care solution is one of the biggest challenges they'll face. After all, it's a tough decision to leave your child in the care of someone else. The day-care or child-care solution you select needs to be affordable yet give you peace of mind that your child is in the absolute best possible care whenever you're not around.

A "quality" child-care option is one that offers:

- Programs and activities that help children learn and develop
- A warm, safe, and friendly setting
- Reliable supervision
- The space, resources, and materials to properly care for the children in a safe environment (both indoors and outdoors, when appropriate)
- A service that's fully licensed by the state and insured

Although the terms are used somewhat interchangeably, for the purposes of this chapter, "day care" refers to the care and supervision of a child during the day (including before and after school for school-age children), when a parent can't be home to watch their kids. "Child care" is a broader term that also includes live-in care, as well as care during the nighttime, weekends, and potentially holidays.

TYPES OF CHILD-CARE PROGRAMS

Before selecting any type of day-care or child-care solution, it's essential that you do your homework and investigate all of your options. According to the New York State Office of Child and Family Services–Child Care Services Division, the following types of child-care programs can be licensed within New York State:

Day-Care Centers

These are commercial businesses that care for more than six children at a time and are not operating from a personal residence. They include the franchise day-care centers, like KinderCare (888-525-2780, www.kindercare.com).

Small Day-Care Centers

These are small day-care operators that care for no more than six children at a time, but also do not operate from a personal residence.

Family Day-Care Homes

These services provide day care for three to six children at a time and operate from within a personal residence. How many children one of these services can care for simultaneously depends on the ages of the children and the number of infants in the agency's care.

Group Family Day-Care Homes

These services are allowed to care for between 7 and 12 children simultaneously within a personal residence. A provider, however, must have an assistant when more than six children are being watched. How many children one of these services can care for simultaneously depends on the ages of the children and the number of infants in the agency's care at any given time.

School-Age Child-Care Programs

These services offer child care for more than six children who are enrolled in school, between kindergarten and age 12. They operate during non-school hours, as well as during school vacation periods and on some holidays. Their primary goal is to provide day-care services before and after school, while parents are at work.

Nursery Schools

These services provide care for three hours a day or less. They can voluntarily register with the State Education Department (SED).

Pre-Kindergartens

These services are typically located within public schools, but some private schools or child-care centers offer them as well. They are supervised by the State Education Department and usually have an educational or child-development element to them in terms of how the participants spend their time.

Head Start Centers

Targeted to pre-school-age children, these are day-care centers and services offered to low-income families. It's a federally funded program. The facilities are licensed as day-care centers within the state.

Legally Exempt Care

This type of child care or day care refers to providers who care for only one or two children at a time, unusually within their home. This type of service is not required to register with the state.

In addition to these options for out-of-home day care, families have the option to hire an in-home nanny, au pair, or babysitter. These people provide very personalized and exclusive care for children, usually within the family's own home. In addition to the potentially high cost associated with in-home child care, if the nanny or au pair will be live-in, the host family must provide room and board and literally bring a stranger in to live in their home on a long-term basis to care for the kids.

i Recent statistics show that approximately 13 million infants, toddlers, and preschool children are regularly in non-parental care in the United States, including 45 percent of children younger than one year.

MATCHING YOUR OPTIONS WITH YOUR NEEDS

Of these many child-care and day-care options, there's no perfect solution for everyone. Each family needs to determine what works best for its unique situation, schedule, and budget, and then carefully weigh the pros and cons, do the necessary background research, select their child-care or day-care option, and ultimately keep close tabs on their children once they're in whatever solution that's selected.

As you investigate these options, some of the things to consider include:

- Your ability as a parent to drop into the day-care or child-care facility unannounced at any time to check on your child and observe the program.
- The ratio of adult care-givers to children. State regulated programs limit the number of chil-

dren a single adult care-giver can handle, based on the age of the children and other criteria. These standards are used to help insure each child receives ample supervision and care. Obviously, you should seek out a facility that offers a low adult care-giver to child ratio.

- Consider the training and experience of the care-givers(s). Licensed care-givers must have at least a minimum level of training, plus receive ongoing training in specific areas, including safety, nutrition, and child abuse prevention.
- Make sure the program is licensed, registered, and regulated through the State Office of Child and Family Services. Be sure that you ask to see the license or registration certificate and check out the service directly with Child and Family Services.
- Check to determine when the service was last inspected by Child and Family Services. For most licensed services, an inspection takes place whenever their license comes up for renewal; however, at least 50 percent of the registered child-care services are inspected annually. Ask to see a copy of the inspection report or the official results of the inspection.

There are more than one 1,000 licensed day-care centers and other child-care options available on Long Island. These are spread throughout the various communities, towns, and villages, so regardless of where you live, chances are you'll have at least a handful of viable options to choose from. The trick, of course, is finding a solution that meets your needs and is affordable.

For many families, just as a mortgage and car payment account for a specific percentage of their overall income, in many cases, the same is true for child care or day care. Depending on the type of care you choose, the costs can be significant.

i Some employers offer on-site day-care services. In these situations, the employer typically subcontracts out the operation to a licensed day-care company or service provider. For many parents of infants, toddlers, and pre-kindergarten-age children, on-site day care where they work is a welcome benefit and perk.

USEFUL CHILD-CARE AND DAY-CARE RESOURCES AND REFERRAL SERVICES

For families wanting to learn about child-care or day-care options on Long Island and in their own city, town, or community, there is a variety of government-operated and private agencies available to help. Following are some of these agencies.

CHILD CARE COUNCIL OF SUFFOLK COUNTY

(631) 462-0303

www.childcaresuffolk.org

This organization gathers and maintains detailed information about child-care and day-care services, including child-care centers, state registered and licensed family day-care homes, in-home nanny agencies, and school-age programs offered in Suffolk County. The council has offices in Commack, Riverhead, and Southampton and offers the following services:

- Assistance in locating providers in your area (within Suffolk County) that will meet your family's specific needs
- General information and tips for finding quality care for children
- Checklists to assist you on visits to specific child-care programs when evaluating them
- Information about how to locate and hire in-home caregivers

LONG ISLAND HEAD START

(631) 758-5200

www.liheadstart.org

Head Start is a federally funded program for preschool children from low-income families. In addition to day care, many participants are also eligible for free medical and dental care, as well as healthy meals and snacks. On Long Island there are two Head Start organizations: Children's Community Head Start (631-585-3131, www.childrenscommunityhs.org), which has facilities in Ronkonkoma and Port Jefferson, and Long Island Head Start. Long Island Head Start operates 15 centers in towns and communities throughout the island, including Amityville, Bay Shore, Bellport, Bridgehampton, Central Islip, North Fork, Riverside, and Southampton.

NATIONAL ASSOCIATION FOR THE EDUCATION OF YOUNG CHILDREN
www.naeyc.org
This organization literally sets the standards for what's required of a licensed child-care facility or service. It works in conjunction with the New York State Department of Social Services and New York State Office of Child and Family Services. The National Association for the Education of Young Children is a good resource for learning about the standards that day-care and child-care facilities must meet and adhere to.

i To report child abuse or neglect, contact the New York State Office of Child and Family Service's Child Abuse or Neglect Hotline at (800) 342-3720. To file a complaint about a child-care service or agency, call (800) 732-5207.

NEW YORK STATE OFFICE OF CHILD AND FAMILY SERVICES
Child Care Services Division
(800) 345-KIDS
www.ocfs.state.ny.us/main/childcare/default.asp
While many people think of this as the agency to turn to when neglect, abuse, or endangerment issues are facing a child (which it certainly is), it's also a valuable resource for finding and researching state-licensed day-care and child-care providers within New York State (including all of Long Island). It also maintains a database of public schools that offer low-cost before- and after-school programs for school-age children. To research a licensed day-care or child-care facility in New York State, visit http://it.ocfs.ny.gov/ccfs_facilitysearch.

HIRING A NANNY OR AU PAIR

Aside from the traditional child-care and day-care options already discussed, you also have the option of hiring a part-time or full-time nanny or au pair. In some cases the person you hire would actually live in your home; otherwise, they'd simply come to your house during the times their service is needed in order to provide in-home care for your children.

You can find a nanny or au pair through a referral, privately (where you hire the care provider directly), or by working through a licensed agency. When hiring a nanny, you'll need to determine in advance if they'll work full-time (more than 20 hours per week) or part-time (less than 20 hours per week), and whether or not you'll provide food and board for the nanny (live-in versus live-out).

How much you'll be required to pay a nanny varies greatly, based on a number of factors, including your location, the experience of the care-giver, the age and number of children requiring care, the nanny's education, and whether or not you'll be expecting the nanny to handle additional household duties, such as cleaning, food shopping, or laundry. The number of hours of work per week and whether or not work will be required in the evenings, on weekends, and/or during holidays will also be factors in determining salary.

Live-in nannies are offered housing (a separate and private bedroom with a separate bathroom, and use of the common spaces within the home). It is not mandated by law that benefits be provided to a full-time or part-time nanny. However, at an additional expense (above and beyond salary), families can choose to offer health and dental insurance, as well as a handful of other perks and benefits including:

- Use of a family car or transportation
- Paid vacations
- Paid sick leave
- 401K
- Paid travel and expenses when they participate in family vacations
- A continuing education allowance for child-care-related education

i If you're planning to hire a nanny or au pair who will be spending considerable time alone with your children, insist that the person you hire be CPR and first-aid certified. If she is not, consider paying for her certification before she starts spending time with your children.

What Is an Au Pair, Anyway?

Unlike a nanny who is typically an adult who lives full-time within the United States and who has some type of child-care background or education, an au pair is a young adult who comes from a foreign country and who lives with an American family. In exchange for room and board, as well as a small salary, which is typically much lower than what you'd pay a live-in nanny, the au pair provides live-in child care to the family for a period of at least one or two years at a time.

Au pairs are part of an international program that within the United States is sponsored by the U.S. Department of State. When you agree to bring an au pair into your home, you're not hiring an employee. While your au pair will be responsible for providing up to 45 hours per week of in-home child care, the concept behind this program is that the au pair becomes an extended member of their host family. Thus, the au pair participates in family meals and activities and goes along on family trips, for example.

In addition to providing the child care you need, the goal of the au pair program is for everyone—the parents, the children, and the au pair—to benefit from a long-term cultural exchange. Just as the host family will share its American customs and lifestyle, the au pair will share her customs and experiences from her home country.

An au pair who operates within the United States must follow the strict guidelines and meet the criteria that's outlined by the Department of State. The au pair must be sponsored by a State Department–approved program. Some of the criteria the au pair must meet includes being between the age of 18 and 26, able to speak English, and willing to commit to at least 12 months to two years with a single host family. He or she must also have at least 200 hours of preexisting and documented child-care experience (if caring for a child under the age of two) and receive specialized training in child safety and development that meets the Department of State's requirements. Furthermore, an au pair who wants to work in the United States must possess an international driver's license and complete at least six hours of academic credit during his or her time in the United States.

Families can hire an au pair through a licensed referral and placement service. It's the responsibility of these services to pre-screen and interview all au pair applicants and ensure they meet (or exceed) and then adhere to the requirements mandated by the Department of State. A thorough placement service will also carefully evaluate a prospective au pair's character, personality, disposition, work experience, and educational background and take steps to ensure the au pair will integrate nicely and smoothly into the host family's home, while being able to provide top-quality, loving, attentive, and patient care for the children.

i Long Island University's C. W. Post Campus offers a university program for au pairs. Contact the school (516-299-2359, www.liu.edu/CWIS/cwp/aupair) for referrals to recent graduates and alumni in the Long Island area.

Nanny and Au Pair Referral/ Placement Services

The following is just a sampling of Long Island or New York State resources that can help you find a responsible, experienced, and caring nanny or au pair:

ABSOLUTE BEST CARE
(516) 802-3780 (Nassau County)
(631) 486-4594 (Suffolk County)
www.absolutebestcare.com
This is a placement agency that offers experienced nannies, baby nurses, babysitters, and

housekeepers throughout New York State, including Long Island.

FAMILY HELPERS
(914)674-8535
www.familyhelpers.net
This service serves as a placement agency for nannies throughout New York State, including Long Island.

INTEREXCHANGE
(800) 287-2477
www.interexchange.org/content/2/en/Au%20Pair%20USA.htmlny-new-york/suffolk-nassau-long-island.htm
This is one of several au pair referral and placement agencies that service Long Island.

NANNY LOCATORS
www.nannylocators.com/longisland.htm
This Web site lists classified-style ads directly from nannies who are available for immediate hire directly. You are responsible for checking their references, conducing the interview, performing a background check, etc.

NANNY ON THE NET
(631) 418-8536
www.anannyonthenet.com/longisland.html
The nannies this agency works with have at least three years' experience and are considered "career nannies." This is a placement agency that has been in business since 1991. It receives a one-time fee for its placement and nanny match-up services. According to the agency, it conducts a thorough interview with each of its nannies and verifies their references. The organization also performs a background check, All nannies are CPR and first-aid certified before they are placed with a family.

NEW YORK STATE DEPARTMENT OF LABOR
(212) 352-6079
If you're thinking about hiring a nanny or au pair, this state-run agency handles the licenses and regulates all private employment agencies, including all nanny and au pair agencies that operate within New York State (including Long Island). The New York State Department of Labor can be helpful when trying to locate legitimate, licensed agencies and also for researching specific agencies.

i If you need to hire a babysitter, try seeking out a referral or hiring a responsible teenager from your community who comes from a family you know well. Another option is to use a babysitter referral service, like SitterCity (888-SIT-CITY, www.sittercity.com).

HEALTH CARE

Whether you live or work on Long Island, or you're just planning a visit, hopefully you'll remain healthy and never have the need to visit a hospital or walk-in medical clinic, or have to deal with any type of medical emergency. Unfortunately, however, that's not always realistic. At some point, you or a loved one might get sick or become injured and require more elaborate, immediate, or specialized medical attention than a typical physician can offer from their office or local practice.

This section offers information about the major hospitals and walk-in clinics on Long Island, as well as provides a directory of emergency and health-related resources you can access by phone or the Internet.

When seeking out medical experts, don't forget that New York City (and its boroughs) is home to many of the most respected and renowned hospitals and medical facilities in the world, and working at these facilities are top-notch doctors and medical specialists. So, in addition to the vast medical resources available on Long Island, consider researching what options are available to you in and around New York City.

MAJOR LONG ISLAND HOSPITALS

The following is a listing of major hospitals on Long Island. Each is dedicated to serving the community or region where it's based, and each has a 24-hour emergency room, along with a full range of other services and specialties.

Nassau County (listed alphabetically by town)

NEW ISLAND HOSPITAL
4295 Hempstead Tnpk., Bethpage
(516) 579-6000
www.newislandhospital.org

This full-service, community-oriented hospital is affiliated with the North Shore Long Island Jewish Health System. It was established in May 1999. Currently the emergency department cares for more than 37,000 patients per year. A full range of other medical and surgical services are offered, including an ambulatory surgery unit, the Center for Sleep Medicine, hyperbaric medicine and wound healing, critical care, and an endoscopy unit. New Island Hospital is part of the Long Island Health Network, which is a network of 10 hospitals that work together to provide better and lower-cost care for patients.

NASSAU UNIVERSITY MEDICAL CENTER (NUHEALTH)
2201 Hempstead Tnpk., East Meadow
(516) 572-0123
www.ncmc.edu

With 1,200 beds, this is one of the largest hospitals in the region. It includes a 530-bed tertiary-care teaching hospital and a 589-bed skilled nursing facility. The hospital treats more than 80,000 people per year in the emergency department and more than 200,000 per year in its 80-plus specialized clinics. Since it opened in 1935, this hospital has helped literally millions of patients, allowing them to receive coordinated medical care at every stage of life. Within the hospital's main 19-story tower (which is Nassau County's tallest building) are 12 operating suites, more than 80 outpatient clinics, a burn center, a stroke center, an extensive laboratory, and an imaging and research facility, plus a wide range of other facilities designed for teaching and providing the highest medical care.

As a teaching and research hospital, Nassau University Medical Center is academically affiliated with the Health Sciences Center of the State University of New York at Stony Brook, the New York College of Osteopathic Medicine, the New York College of Podiatric Medicine, the American University of the Caribbean School of Medicine, and the soon-to-open Hofstra University School of Medicine.

GLEN COVE HOSPITAL

101 St. Andrews Ln., Glen Cove
(516) 674-7300
www.northshorelij.com

This 265-bed, full-service hospital offers a wide range of medical and surgical procedures that cater to the needs of its patients. It is home to the internationally recognized Orthopedic & Rehabilitation Institute, which features state-of-the-art programs in joint replacement and an all-inclusive spine program. The emergency department was recently ranked one of the best in the nation, and the hospital regularly receives outstanding scores in patient satisfaction. Glen Cove Hospital is also known for its Family Practice Residency Program, which trains physicians from across America.

LONG BEACH MEDICAL CENTER

455 East Bay Dr., Long Beach
(516) 897-1000
www.lbmc.org

This is a 203-bed hospital and 200-bed skilled nursing facility specializing in rehabilitation medicine. Long Beach Medical Center is a full-service, family-oriented hospital that caters to the needs of patients primarily from Long Beach, Lido Beach, Atlantic Beach, Point Lookout, and Island Park. The hospital was founded in 1922. While serving the routine health-care needs of its patients, it also handles a wide range of advanced medical procedures and offers cutting-edge treatments in many specialized areas of medicine. The hospital's staff is composed of physician specialists in family practice, pediatrics, obstetrics, gynecology, cardiology, and general surgery, among many others.

NORTH SHORE UNIVERSITY HOSPITAL

300 Community Dr., Manhasset
(516) 562-0100
www.northshorelij.com

This is a tertiary-care facility as well as an academic campus for the New York University School of Medicine. It's a 731-bed facility that was very highly ranked by AARP's *Modern Maturity* magazine. On staff at this hospital are more than 2,700 medical specialists and subspecialist physicians. Specialties include open-heart surgery, neurosurgery, urology, and maternal-fetal medicine. North Shore University Hospital also specializes in intensive-care treatment for medical, surgical, newborn, and pediatric patients. The Schwartz Ambulatory Surgery Center performs more than 10,000 procedures each year, while the hospital itself offers more than 65 specialty clinics in-house.

WINTHROP UNIVERSITY HOSPITAL

259 First St., Mineola
(516) 663-0333
www.winthrop.org

This 591-bed hospital offers a full complement of inpatient and outpatient services, plus has a strong focus as an educational and research facility. The goal of this hospital, which has been in existence for more than 100 years, is to provide top-notch care specifically to the residents of the region.

LONG ISLAND JEWISH MEDICAL CENTER

270-05 76th Ave., New Hyde Park
(516) 470-7000
www.northshorelij.com

This is an 827-bed, not-for-profit teaching hospital that is part of the North Shore Long Island Jewish Health System. More than 500 full-time physicians work here. The hospital is situated on a 48-acre campus located about 15 miles east of Manhattan (on the border of Queens and Nassau County). The medical center consists of three main hospitals, including the Long Island Jewish Hospital, Schneider Children's Hospital, and the Zucker Hillside Hospital.

SCHNEIDER CHILDREN'S HOSPITAL
269-01 76th Ave., New Hyde Park
(516) 470-3000
www.schneiderchildrenshospital.org

This modern hospital focuses on the medical needs of children—from premature babies to adolescents. The ratio of patients to personnel is extremely high. Since the hospital is designed exclusively to handle the care of children, each patient room is equipped so parents can stay comfortably with their child day and night, in a warm and comfortable setting. In fact, parents and siblings are encouraged to be part of the overall healing process of the young patients. While top-notch medical care is offered, the hospital also caters to its patients' emotional needs, offering several playrooms chock-full of toys and games, plus a schoolroom. The five acres this hospital is situated on are dedicated to providing both inpatient and outpatient services.

SOUTH NASSAU COMMUNITY HOSPITAL
2445 Oceanside Rd., Oceanside
(516) 632-3000
www.southnassau.org

This full-service hospital offers a wide range of general and specialized medical services, ranging from ambulatory surgery and behavioral health to a cancer center, cardiac-care center, state-of-the-art emergency room, a GI endoscopy unit, and a pain-management clinic. The hospital also offers a pediatric unit, prenatal care, physical rehabilitation, and a sports medicine clinic, along with psychiatric services, a sleep center, a stroke center, a substance abuse clinic, and a weight and life-management center.

PLAINVIEW HOSPITAL
888 Old Country Rd., Plainview
(516) 719-3000
www.northshorelij.com

This 239-bed facility treats patients with a wide range of medical, surgical, pediatric, obstetric, and gynecological conditions. It's known for its highly active same-day surgery program and its busy and well-equipped emergency department, which contains a state-of-the-art chest pain emergency room. Plainview Hospital is a member of the North Shore Long Island Jewish Health System and is designed to be an acute-care community hospital.

MERCY MEDICAL CENTER
1000 North Village Ave., Rockville Centre
(516) 705-2525
http://mercymedicalcenter.chsli.org

This is a 375-bed, not-for-profit hospital best known for its maternal health, oncology, and physical medicine services, as well as its emergency and trauma care. More than 700 physicians and a staff of 1,700 are employed at this hospital, which offers a wide range of medical and surgical services for children and adults alike. The hospital will soon be celebrating its 100th anniversary and is proud to deliver more than 1,500 newborns each year. Mercy Medical Center is home to Memorial Sloan-Kettering Cancer Center in Nassau County and is the region's leader in cancer care.

ST. FRANCIS HOSPITAL
100 Port Washington Blvd., Roslyn
(516) 562-6000
www.stfrancisheartcenter.com

Founded in 1922, this hospital is where you'll find some of the nation's top specialists in interventional cardiology, cardiothoracic surgery, and arrhythmia treatment, though it's very much a full-service hospital. It is proud of its ongoing investment in technology and offers the most cutting-edge treatments possible for a wide range of medical problems and illnesses. For example, within the DeMatteis Center for Cardiac Research, researchers and doctors are utilizing noninvasive imaging technology, such as a 64-slice CT scanner and a three-dimensional echocardiography system, to improve currently used techniques for diagnosing and treating heart disease. Each year the hospital performs more than 1,560 open-heart surgeries and almost 8,800 cardiac catheterizations.

SYOSSET HOSPITAL
221 Jericho Tnpk., Syosset
(516) 496-6500
www.northshorelij.com

This is a full-service community hospital with an inpatient medical-surgical unit and intensive care unit, as well as an active emergency department that continuously receives high patient-satisfaction ratings. Syosset Hospital is known for its Center for Surgical Specialties and employs highly skilled surgeons with a wide range of medical specialties. The hospital specializes in minimally invasive laparoscopic procedures, utilizing the latest laser and other surgical and endoscopic technologies. It also has a 20-bed short-term psychiatric unit.

FRANKLIN HOSPITAL MEDICAL CENTER
900 Franklin Ave., Valley Stream
(516) 256-6000
www.northshorelij.com

This is a 305-bed hospital that offers a comprehensive array of programs and services to patients from Nassau County and southeastern Queens. It offers one of the most advanced emergency departments in the region and a 21-bed psychiatric unit. Franklin Hospital Medical Center is best known for its 120-bed Orzac Center for Extended Care and Rehabilitation, which offers long-term care and rehabilitative medicine.

Suffolk County (listed alphabetically by town)

BRUNSWICK HOSPITAL CENTER
80 Lounden Ave., Amityville
(631) 789-7000
www.brunswickhospital.com

This is a modern, full-service community hospital. It's known for the Center for Behavioral Health & Wellness, which is licensed by the New York State Office of Mental Health. The hospital is situated on a 17-acre campus in Amityville and offers a wide range of adult services, geriatric services, and child and adolescent services through its three primary divisions.

SOUTH OAKS MENTAL HOSPITAL
400 Sunrise Hwy., Amityville
(631) 264-4000
www.south-oaks.org

For more than 100 years this hospital has been offering treatment and recovery programs for people suffering from psychiatric illness and/or various addictions. It is located on the border between Nassau and Suffolk Counties. South Oaks features a Child & Adolescent Center, adult programs, senior adult programs, programs for gambling and chemical dependency, and a wide range of support groups.

SOUTHSIDE HOSPITAL
301 East Main St., Bay Shore
(631) 968-3000
www.northshorelij.com

This is a 371-bed community hospital that offers a wide range of medical, surgical, obstetric, gynecological, and pediatric specialties. It's also known for its physical medicine and rehabilitation programs. Southside Hospital has developed a superior reputation for treating brain injuries through its Regional Center for Brain Injury Rehabilitation, which offers both inpatient and outpatient services. The hospital also offers advanced radiation therapy for outpatients and inpatients through its highly respected Frank Gulden Radiation Oncology Center.

BROOKHAVEN MEMORIAL HOSPITAL MEDICAL CENTER
101 Hospital Rd., East Patchogue
(631) 654-7100
www.brookhavenhospital.org

Brookhaven is a state-of-the-art, 306-bed, acute-care facility that was founded in 1956. It contains a well-equipped Level II trauma center. The goal of the hospital is to serve the medical, surgical, and emergency needs of 28 neighboring communities throughout central Suffolk County. More than 2,000 people are employed at this hospital, which continues to pioneer new surgical procedures in a wide range of medical fields. For help finding a physician in the Suffolk County region, the hospital offers a Find a Physician hotline, which can be reached at (631) 654-7100.

EASTERN LONG ISLAND HOSPITAL
201 Manor Place, Greenport
(631) 477-1000
www.elih.org
This is a smaller, 90-bed, full-service community hospital that was established in 1905. The focus of this hospital is to serve the medical, surgical, and emergency needs of patients from the North Fork and Shelter Island areas. The hospital utilizes the most advanced technology possible, combined with expert, highly personalized, and compassionate care, when catering to the needs of its patients. In addition to emergency care, the hospital offers specialties in geriatrics, ambulatory surgery, pain management, general surgery, women's health, plastic surgery, psychiatry, radiology, men's health, physical therapy, and addiction services.

HUNTINGTON HOSPITAL
270 Park Ave., Huntington
(631) 351-2000
www.hunthosp.org
This is a full-service, not-for-profit community hospital that is a member of the North Shore Long Island Jewish Health System. It provides a full range of inpatient, outpatient, and specialized health-care services. Huntington Hospital was founded in 1916 and currently offers 408 beds.

JOHN T. MATHER MEMORIAL HOSPITAL
75 North Country Rd., Port Jefferson
(631) 473-1320
www.matherhospital.org
As a not-for-profit, 248-bed community hospital, this facility offers a wide range of medical services to the region. When the hospital first opened its doors in 1929, it housed just 54 beds. Today it is situated on a 35-acre campus and provides care to more than 12,000 inpatients and 42,000 emergency room cases annually. John T. Mather Memorial Hospital employs more than 600 doctors, 440 nurses, and a non-medical staff of more than 1,180 people. The Fortunato Breast Health Center provides services to upwards of 15,000 patients per year, while the Mather's Sleep Disorder Center has treated more than 5,000 patients since it was formed in 1997. The hospital is a member of the Mather Hospital family.

ST. CHARLES HOSPITAL & REHABILITATION CENTER
200 Belle Terre Rd., Port Jefferson
(631) 474-6000
http://stcharleshospital.chsli.org
This is a 231-bed, acute-care community hospital that is a member of Catholic Health Services of Long Island. As a not-for-profit hospital, it has served the residents of the Three Village area for more than a century. The hospital has three main centers which focus on maternal/child, orthopedics, and rehabilitation, along with more than 20 specialty clinics for children and adults.

PECONIC BAY MEDICAL CENTER
1300 Roanoke Ave., Riverhead
(631) 548-6000
www.peconicbaymedicalcenter.org
Since 1951 this hospital has been committed to improving the health of nearby communities by providing quality, comprehensive, and compassionate care. The 182-bed facility includes a 60-bed Skilled Nursing and Rehabilitation Center and a certified home-care agency. The medical center is a regional provider of orthopedics through the Hamptons Orthopedic & Rehabilitation Institute, and is home to the Richard Rubenstein MD Center for Bariatric Surgery. Through a partnership with Stony Brook University Hospital, Peconic Bay Medical Center has trauma-trained specialists staffing its emergency center.

ST. CATHERINE OF SIENA MEDICAL CENTER
50 Rte. 25A, Smithtown
(631) 862-3000
http://stcatherines.chsli.org
This medical complex offers a full-service hospital, nursing home, medical office building, and senior village. It is dedicated to providing care to entire families. The hospital's emergency room accepts more than 28,000 patients per year. In all, this is a 311-bed facility that employs more than 1,470 people, including a medical staff of 640 people.

SOUTHAMPTON HOSPITAL

240 Meeting House Ln., Southampton
(631) 726-8200
www.southamptonhospital.org

This hospital serves the Hamptons and is known for providing a full range of high-quality medical services. Southampton Hospital was founded in 1908 and is a relatively small but well-established state-of-the-art facility with a highly skilled medical staff. Among the specialty clinics offered are the Center for Weight Loss Surgery and the Ellen Hermanson Breast Center.

STONY BROOK UNIVERSITY MEDICAL CENTER

Nicholis Rd. and Health Sciences Dr., Stony Brook
(631) 444-4000
www.stonybrookmedicalcenter.org

Established in 1980, this is a large, full-service hospital committed to patient care, research, education, and community service. It is one of the largest and most advanced hospitals in the region, offering a comprehensive array of medical and surgical services while also serving as a teaching hospital and research facility. Stony Brook University Medical contains dozens of clinics and treatment facilities, ranging from the ambulatory surgery center to the Carol M. Baldwin Breast Care Center. There's also the Cody Center for Autism and Developmental Disabilities, a dermatology clinic, a heart center, an imaging center, occupational and physical therapy centers, a pain management center, a radiation oncology center, and a sleep disorder center.

GOOD SAMARITAN HOSPITAL MEDICAL CENTER

1000 Montauk Hwy., West Islip
(631) 376-3000
http://goodsamaritan.chsli.org

This 537-bed facility includes 100 nursing home beds and is a not-for-profit, full-service hospital that caters to the medical needs of the community. It celebrated its 50th anniversary in 2009. Each year the hospital provides about $20 million worth of community service and charity care. In total, the hospital cares for about 30,000 patients annually. Good Samaritan employs 4,400 people, including a medical staff of 830 and a nursing staff of 1,200. In 2008 the hospital treated 95,424 patients in its emergency room and performed almost 15,900 same-day surgeries

DOCTOR & MEDICAL SERVICE REFERRALS AND RESEARCH RESOURCES

The following free online resources are available to help you find a licensed doctor or medical specialist on Long Island or research a specific doctor, medical specialist, or medical facility.

HEALTHGRADES

www.healthgrades.com

HealthGrades is a leading health-care ratings organization, providing ratings and profiles of hospitals, nursing homes, and physicians to consumers, corporations, hospitals, and health plans. Millions of consumers rely on HealthGrades' independent ratings to make health-care decisions based on quality of care.

LONG ISLAND NEWSDAY TOP DOCTORS

www.newsday.com/news/health/doctors

Long Island Newsday, the island's major daily newspaper, maintains a database of top-rated doctors throughout Long Island, categorized by specialty. The doctors whose listings are included in this Top Doctor directory were selected after peer nomination, extensive research, and careful review and screening by a doctor-directed research team. This database lists specialists in more than 60 different medical fields.

i To file a formal complaint against a New York State–licensed doctor, contact the Office of Professional Medical Conduct at (800) 663-6114.

NEW YORK DOCTOR PROFILES

www.nydoctorprofile.com

This Web site allows you to access detailed profiles of doctors who are licensed in New York

State, including Long Island. You must know the first and last name of the doctor.

NEW YORK STATE DEPARTMENT OF HEALTH'S PROFESSIONAL MEDICAL CONDUCT AND PHYSICIAN DISCIPLINE
www.health.state.ny.us/professionals/doctors/conduct
Research a specific doctor using this free online service. The database contains information about complaints issued against physicians, physician assistants, and specialist assistants. It also monitors practitioners who have been placed on probation or disciplined since 1990

PHYSICIAN REPORTS
www.physicianreports.com/directory_search/NY-New-York/more_specialties
This Web site helps you find doctors or medical specialists who are licensed in New York State. The database allows you to quickly search more than 100 medical specialties and fields, and then narrow down result by town, region, or city.

STONY BROOK UNIVERSITY PHYSICIANS
www.stonybrookphysicians.com/primarycare.asp
This Web site offers a comprehensive database of primary-care physicians on Long Island. It includes doctors who practice general medicine, family medicine, OB-GYN, and pediatrics.

VISITING NURSES ASSOCIATION OF LONG ISLAND
(800) 237-0884
www.vnali.org
If you need to hire a private registered nurse, physical therapist, occupational therapist, speech/language pathologist, medical social worker, or nutritionist in the Long Island area, this organization offers referrals who are available 24/7.

WEBMD.COM PHYSICIAN DIRECTORY
http://doctor.webmd.com/physician_finder/home.aspx
This easy-to-use, free service allows you to find a doctor based on his or her name, geographic location, or specialty.

i Do you have a medical question or concern but don't want to track down a doctor or medical specialist right away to get the answer? Check out the free WebMD Web site (www.webmd.com), the Internet's most comprehensive yet easy-to-understand medical resource for everyday people. Medical answers are available 24/7.

HOME HEALTH-CARE SERVICES

In addition to the thousands of doctors and medical specialists working in the region's hospitals, clinics, and medical centers, many Long Island–based agencies offer referral and placement services for home health-care professionals. Some of these resources include:

- Aides at Home: (631) 447-1480, www.aidesathome.com
- Gurwin Home Care Agency: (631) 493-1282, www.gurwin.org
- Home Companion Services: (631) 473-0700, www.homecompanionservices.com
- Interim Healthcare: (631) 689-8920, www.interimhealthcare.com
- Right at Home: (631) 207-2626, www.rightathome.net
- Senior Solutions of Long Island: (631) 979-8730, www.seniorsolutionsofli.com

LONG ISLAND NURSING HOMES

There are no fewer than 420 public and private, licensed nursing homes and assisted living facilities throughout Long Island. For a partial listing of Long Island nursing homes, including addresses and phone numbers, visit www.longislandbrowser.com/health_medical/nursing_homes/index.shtml. The Intercounty Health Facilities Association (IHFA), for example, is an organization of more than 50 health-care facilities on Long Island that care for over 15,000 residents and patients (516-627-3131, www.intercountyhealth.com). For a more comprehensive listing of nursing homes, which are vastly different from assisted living facilities in terms of the level of care and services offered, visit these Web sites:

- Nursing homes in Nassau County: http://nursinghomes.nyhealth.gov/browse_search.php?form=COUNTY&rt=nassau
- Nursing homes in Suffolk County: http://nursinghomes.nyhealth.gov/browse_search.php?form=COUNTY&rt=Suffolk

After working with a doctor or hospital to determine a patient's need for a nursing home, the next step is to research the various facilities that are available, based on the patient's unique needs and budget. As you evaluate a nursing home, another important consideration should relate to the facility's location, and how close it is to the elderly person's family and friends. The services the facility offers to the potential resident is also important, in terms of the quality of life that will be provided on a day-to-day basis. In addition to the medical care, the selection and frequency of activities and resources offered are essential. Make sure that the services offered at the facility are in line with the needs of the potential resident. Some of the region's nursing homes have areas of expertise or cater to the needs of seniors with certain limitations or ailments, while others offer more general services.

i You can download a free, detailed, and highly informative 32-page guide called *Selecting a Nursing Home in New York State* at www.nyhealth.gov/facilities/nursing/select_nh/docs/select_nh.pdf. It's published by the New York State Department of Health.

When touring a facility, don't just focus on the facility itself (although it should be well-equipped, clean, comfortable, and sanitary)—also focus on the current residents. Do they seem happy, comfortable, well cared for, well groomed, and highly engaged in the available activities? Does the staff treat the residents in a friendly, personalized, and caring manner that is also respectful and helpful?

The ongoing costs should also be a consideration. Make sure you understand what's included in the base monthly cost, and what additional fees you can expect. Keep in mind that it is possible to negotiate rates at many private nursing homes and assisted living facilities. This has become a highly competitive business, and one that has been impacted heavily by the economy in terms of elderly people able to afford long-term care and housing. If a private facility has several empty beds, that gives you more leverage when negotiating rates and fees.

In addition to the elderly patent's primary-care physician and/or the social worker at a local hospital, depending on the needs of the patient, the following organizations may prove to be helpful resources as you seek a suitable nursing home on Long Island.

A PLACE FOR MOM
(877) 666-3239
www.aplaceformom.com/new-york-senior-care/long-island-metro-area
This is a free elder-care referral service geared toward helping families find resources of every kind. For example, the organization has helped more than 8,360 seniors in the Long Island area find viable senior-care options.

HEALTHGRADES
www.healthgrades.com
HealthGrades is a leading independent health-care-ratings organization, providing ratings and profiles of hospitals, nursing homes, and physicians to consumers, corporations, health plans, and hospitals.

LONG ISLAND ALZHEIMER'S FOUNDATION
(516) 767-6856
www.liaf.org
This organization can be extremely helpful in finding resources and nursing homes capable of caring for people suffering from Alzheimer's disease.

NEW YORK STATE DEPARTMENT OF HEALTH NURSING HOME PROFILES
http://nursinghomes.nyhealth.gov

Long Island Emergency Numbers and Medical Resource Directory

The following is a list of emergency phone numbers useful to anyone living in or visiting Long Island:

Alcoholics Anonymous: (516) 292-3040

Alzheimer's Association (Nassau County): (516) 935-1033

Alzheimer's Association (Suffolk County): (631) 580-5100

Amber Alert (New York State): (518) 464-7134

American Red Cross (Nassau County): (516) 747-3500

American Red Cross (Suffolk County): (631) 924-6700

Crime Stoppers (Nassau County): (516) 573-7236

Crime Victims Program (Nassau County): (516) 573-3330

Drug & Alcohol Addiction Hotline (Nassau County): (516) 481-4000

FBI Tip Line: (866) 483-5139

Federal Emergency Management Agency (FEMA): (800) 621-FEMA

Gamblers Anonymous: (631) 586-7171

HIV Counseling and Testing: (516) 565-4628

Hospice Information and Bereavement Services: (516) 627-6376

KeySpan Gas Leak Emergencies: (800) 490-0045

Long Island Power Authority–Electric Service Emergencies: (800) 490-0025

Long Island Power Authority–Fallen Power Line Hotline: (800) 490-0075

Long Island Railroad Emergency/MTA Police: (516) 733-3900

Mental Health Crisis Hotline (New York State): (800) 273-8255

Missing Persons: (516) 573-5370

Nassau County Department of Health: (516) 571-3410

Nassau County Police Department: (516) 573-7000

National Hurricane Center (Local Office): (631) 924-0517

Pet Safe Coalition (Nassau County): (516) 676-0808

Poison Control Center: (800) 222-1222

Rape Crisis Hotline: (800) 942-6906

Senior Citizens Help Line (Nassau County): (516) 227-8900

Suffolk County Health Department: (631) 853-5593

Suffolk County Health Department Flu Line: (631) 853-3055

Suffolk County Police: (631) 852-6000

Suffolk County Sheriff: (631) 852-2200

Suffolk County Water Authority–Emergencies: (631) 665-0663

Suicide & Crisis Hotline (Nassau County): (516) 679-1111 (available 24/7)

Suicide & Crisis Hotline (Suffolk County): (631) 679-1111 (available 24/7)

Veterans Administration Primary Care Clinic: (516) 694-6008

This free Web site offers detailed descriptions of licensed nursing homes throughout New York State, including Long Island. You can easily utilize the site to gather information about specific nursing homes and the quality of care they provide. Some of the data offered comes from the Centers for Medicare & Medicaid Services.

i To help you select the very best nursing home facility possible, the New York State Department of Health offers a free, comprehensive questionnaire that you should utilize when touring facilities and meeting with representatives from them. You can access this questionnaire online at www.nyhealth.gov/facilities/nursing/select_nh.

HOSPICE CARE

When it comes to caring for the terminally ill, one commonly overlooked resource is hospice care. These public and private facilities typically offer highly personalized attention and a clean, safe, and comfortable place where someone can go to pass away comfortably and with dignity (as opposed to a hospital room or their own home).

Hospice facilities are staffed by compassionate medical professionals who not only support the patients, but are also trained to deal with grieving family members and loved ones. The goal and services offered at hospice centers are vastly different than what's offered within a hospital. These are places where people with a life expectancy of six months or less can go to be cared for. In addition to hospice-care facilities, at-home hospice care can also be arranged, but these services tend to be more limited.

To learn more about what hospice care offers, visit the Hospice Care Network's Web site at www.hospice-care-network.org or call (516) 832-7100. When someone participates in hospice care, it's important to understand that the focus is on caring and pain management, not curing the patient. As a result, the type of care and services offered are vastly different from what's available in a typical hospital. In addition, counseling and other services are offered to family members. Hospice Care Network cares for patients of all ages, religions, races, and illnesses in Nassau, Suffolk, and Queens Counties.

The Hospice & Palliative Care Association of New York State (800-860-9808, www.hpcanys.org) is also an excellent resource for learning about what hospice care can offer to anyone with limited life expectancy. Throughout Nassau and Suffolk Counties there is a handful of private and hospital-affiliated hospices, which the Hospice & Palliative Care Association can refer you to.

EDUCATION

If you're thinking about relocating to Long Island and you have kids (or plan to), one of the most important things you'll need to consider when choosing where to live is the overall quality of the public school system—that is, unless you're planning to send your kids to private school, in which case you want to move within a reasonable distance of potential academic institutions

The good news is that Long Island's public schools—both in Nassau County and in Suffolk County—are incredibly good and far above national standards. Plus, there are about 230 top-quality K–12 private schools on Long Island which may be viable options for your kids, if you're willing to pay the tuition.

In addition to superior public and private elementary, middle, and high schools, Long Island is also home to a handful of prestigious colleges and universities, as well as other educational institutions for pursuing an undergraduate, graduate, or higher-level education. In total, Long Island has 17 colleges and universities that offer four-year degrees, 8 two- or three-year junior colleges, and 5 professional education institutions.

Whether you send your kids to one of Long Island's public, parochial, or private school, you will be giving them a competitive edge in terms of getting them into a college or university, and giving them the chance to receive a high-quality, well-rounded, K–12 education in a safe environment.

As you'll discover, almost every single school in the region scores above the national average in terms of education quality, safety, teaching proficiency, budget, and student academic performance. It's for these reasons that many parents choose to relocate their families to Long Island as opposed to other areas of New York State, including Manhattan and its boroughs.

CHOOSING WHERE TO LIVE BASED ON THE LOCAL PUBLIC SCHOOLS

Parents thinking about moving their family to Long Island will find it pretty difficult to make a truly bad decision. Like most regions throughout the United States, Long Island's schools are comprised of public school systems, parochial schools, and private K–12 schools.

Throughout Long Island (Nassau County and Suffolk County), there are 127 public school districts, which, in total, have an enrollment of more than 476,000 students and employ over 36,000 educators. Most Long Island school districts are composed of at least one elementary, middle, and high school, sometimes more.

What the majority of these 127 public school systems share is their extremely low drop-out rates. In 2008 in Nassau County the drop-out rate was a mere 1.3 percent, and in Suffolk County it was only 2.4 percent. Compare that to the national average of 8.7 percent, according to the U.S. Department of Education, and you can easily see that the Long Island public schools are doing something right when it comes to the K–12 education being provided.

Of the students who graduate from a Long Island public high school, approximately 88 percent go directly to college or pursue some type of higher education. If the public school success statistics don't impress you, there's always the private and parochial school option for K–12, of which there are 230 to choose from. These private institutions enroll more than 53,000 students and employ almost 4,900 educators.

So, if you're thinking about moving to Long Island and you want to choose a city, town, or community that offers the very best public school system, you may want to do a bit of your own research to obtain the very latest report cards and statistics for the school systems and individual schools where you might be sending your kids. Listed in alphabetical order (not order of importance), some of the useful statistics and information worth looking at when evaluating a potential K–12 school system or school include:

- Annual teacher turnover rate
- Average class size
- Average student attendance rate
- Extracurricular activities offered
- Percentage of graduates receiving advanced diplomas
- Percentage of overall school budget spent on education
- Percentage of teachers with permanent certification compared to provisional status
- Reading and math proficiency rates
- Spending per year per student
- Student dropout rate
- Students-to-teacher ratio
- Total student enrollment

While looking at a school system and individual school's statistics and ratings is important, there are other things to consider before deciding where your children should receive their public or private school education. When visiting/touring a prospective public or private school, some of the questions you should obtain answers to include:

- What is the average family makeup within the community?
- What are the main instructional approaches and teaching methods used within the school?
- What are the school's homework and discipline policies?
- How involved are the parents in the education of their kids and in the oversight of the school? How active is the PTA, for example? What volunteer opportunities are available for parents within the school? How available are the teachers for parent/teacher conferences?
- How good are the school's resources and facilities, and what is the school's long-term reputation?
- How up-to-date and new are the school's textbooks, computers, and teaching tools?
- What is the student safety record at the school? What measures are in place to insure each student's safety?
- How ethnically and culturally diverse is the student body and the facility?

i Due to the federal "No Child Left Behind" legislation passed in 2001, public schools are now rated and receive annual report cards that help convey to parents the quality of education students are receiving. While parents can access these report cards from a variety of sources, the National Center for Education Statistics (http://nces.ed.gov) provides free detailed analysis of the report cards, as well as the report cards themselves.

SCHOOL RESOURCES AND WEB SITES

Once you've narrowed down the general area on Long Island where you might want to live, based on suggestions offered in the "Relocation" chapter, consider going to the following Web sites to obtain the very latest reviews and reports for each potential public school system where you might ultimately be sending your kids.

LONG ISLAND EXCHANGE

www.longislandexchange.com/schools/school-districts.html

This Web site offers a summary of each Long Island public school system, as well as overall ratings and scores. It also provides links to each individual school system.

LONG ISLAND SCHOOLS

www.LongIslandSchools.com

This site offers details about every public school system on Long Island, including the latest statistics and review reports from a variety of sources. You can obtain details about the Nassau or Suffolk County school systems in general, or more specifically, about individual public school systems or the individual schools within each public school system. This is a free, extremely up-to-date, and comprehensive online resource.

NASSAU REGIONAL PTA
www.nassaupta.org
In addition to the local PTA organizations in each community, the regional PTA maintains data relating to all of Nassau County's public schools.

i In addition to sending your kids to the best available K–12 school, one way to help ensure the best education possible is to supplement their schooling at home. The New York State Department of Education offers the New York State Parent Web site to help parents get more involved with the education of their kids. This is a free online resource available at www.nysparents.com/nys.

NEW YORK STATE EDUCATION DEPARTMENT
http://usny.nysed.gov/public/
This online resource is useful for learning more about a particular school or even the certification status of an individual teacher working in the public school system.

NEW YORK STATE TESTING AND ACCOUNTABILITY REPORTING
www.nystart.gov
From this state-managed Web site, parents can obtain current information about the performance of public schools in New York State, including school and district report cards (with associated translation guides), statewide report cards, and links to other publicly available data. All of the relevant data for Long Island's public schools can be found on this free online resource. Much of the information distributed on this site is compiled by the Office of Information and Reporting Services, which is responsible for the collection and reporting of enrollment, assessment, school violence, state and "No Child Left Behind" accountability, career and technical education, graduation rate, post-graduation plans, teacher certification, and school staff data for school districts, public schools, charter schools, and nonpublic schools in New York State.

SCHOOL MATTERS
www.schoolmatters.com
This is a free, independently operated Web site that allows visitors to compare information about public schools or public school systems of their choosing, plus obtain statistics and detailed information about individual schools throughout the country, including Long Island's. Thus, this tool can be used to quickly compare the school or school system your child is currently enrolled in with the school or school system on Long Island where you might be placing your child. Basic stats, like school-wide reading and math proficiency, student-to-teacher ratio, total enrollment, breakdown by ethnicity, district's financial info, and extracurricular activities offered can be obtained with a few clicks of the mouse.

THE SCHOOL REPORT EXPRESS
www.homefair.com/real-estate/school-reports/index.asp
This site allows parents to access individual school report cards and information. The database contains detailed information for over 89,000 public and private schools nationwide, from kindergarten through 12th grade. Information on 15,000 school districts and subdistricts nationwide are also offered through this free service.

i While the public and private schools on Long Island are superior, some parents opt to provide their children with an added edge in their academic career by providing them with ongoing private tutoring. There is a variety of private tutoring services available on Long Island for school-age (K–12) children. Kumon Learning Centers (877-586-6673, www.kumon.com), for example, is a franchise-based tutoring service that has dozens of locations throughout Long Island.

Sample Nassau County School District Comparison

Garden City School District

- Average class size: 13.5
- Average spending per student per year: $17,325
- Graduates receiving advanced diplomas: 79%
- Graduates receiving regents diplomas: 95%
- Student drop-out rate: 0%
- Teacher's median years experience teaching: 12

Oyster Bay–East Norwich School District

- Average class size: 10.9
- Average spending per student per year: $21,695
- Graduates receiving advanced diplomas: 60%
- Graduates receiving regents diplomas: 95%
- Student drop-out rate: 1%
- Teacher's median years experience teaching: 14

Westbury School District

- Average class size: 12.7
- Average spending per student per year: $17,368
- Graduates receiving advanced diplomas: 25%
- Graduates receiving regents diplomas: 61%
- Student drop-out rate: 4.5%
- Teacher's median years experience teaching: 12

SUFFOLK REGIONAL PTA
www.suffolkpta.org
In addition to the local PTA organizations in each community, this regional PTA maintains data relating to all of Suffolk County's public schools.

NASSAU COUNTY'S PUBLIC SCHOOL SYSTEM

As of 2008 the public school system in Nassau County had 211,771 students enrolled county-wide and employed almost 16,550 teachers. The overall student-to-teacher ratio was 12.8 to 1, and the average school spending per student was $16,943 per year. The average teacher working in the Nassau Public School system had at least 12 years of teaching experience, and the average salary was $75,284. The student drop-out rate (county-wide) was just 1.3 percent.

As you investigate individual public school systems within Nassau County, these average statistics vary slightly. Selected at random, let's take a quick look at the public school systems in Garden City, Oyster Bay-East Norwich, and Westbury to give you an overview of how they compared based on their recent ratings and statistics. The 2008 data comes from LongIslandSchools.com.

i The HomeFair.com Web site (www.homefair.com/real-estate/school-reports/index.asp) offers free school reports for communities across the country, including Long Island.

SUFFOLK COUNTY'S PUBLIC SCHOOL SYSTEM

As of 2008 the public school system in Suffolk County had 264,322 students enrolled county-wide and employed almost 19,300 teachers. The overall student-to-teacher ratio was 13.7 to 1, and the average school spending per student was $15,004 per year. The average teacher working in the Suffolk Public School system had at least 10 years of teaching experience, and the average salary was $66,087. The student drop-out rate (county-wide) was 2.4 percent.

As you investigate individual public school systems within Suffolk County, these average statistics vary slightly. Selected at random, let's take a quick look at the public school systems in East Hampton, Port Jefferson, and Riverhead to give you an overview of how they compare based on their recent ratings and statistics. The 2008 data comes from LongIslandSchools.com.

A FEW WORDS ABOUT LONG ISLAND'S K–12 PRIVATE SCHOOLS

Throughout Long Island there are 230 private and parochial K–12 schools, which employ about 5,000 teachers and have a total of approximately 53,000 students enrolled. Many of the private K–12 schools on Long Island are either religious or gifted schools.

The region's private schools all strive to maintain academic excellence and small classes. Thus, each has very strict admissions guidelines, a qualification and admission process that's equivalent to a college's or university's, and many

Sample Suffolk County's School District Comparison

East Hampton School District

- Average class size: 11.1
- Average spending per student per year: $19,634
- Graduates receiving advanced diplomas: 42%
- Graduates receiving regents diplomas: 91%
- Student drop-out rate: 2.2%
- Teacher's median years experience teaching: 14

Port Jefferson School District

- Average class size: 14.1
- Average spending per student per year: $22,529
- Graduates receiving advanced diplomas: 52%
- Graduates receiving regents diplomas: 97%
- Student drop-out rate: 0%
- Teacher's median years experience teaching: 11

Riverhead School District

- Average class size: 14
- Average spending per student per year: $14,993
- Graduates receiving advanced diplomas: 41%
- Graduates receiving regents diplomas: 87%
- Student drop-out rate: 3.7%
- Teacher's median years experience teaching: 12

have a long waiting list for acceptance. These private institutions typically also have high tuition charges. The admission guidelines are set by the private schools themselves, with no government intervention. Therefore, there is often much less race, cultural, and economic diversity in the overall student body at private schools.

On Long Island, like everywhere else in the United States, the public schools are run and overseen by the local and state government and are funded by taxpayer dollars. Thus, there is no extra tuition. While the private schools are subject to government-imposed guidelines, they are not funded by taxpayers, so you can expect to pay an annual tuition.

Parochial schools (which are schools with some type of religious affiliation) typically have lower tuitions than private schools that are truly independent. In terms of these independent K–12 private schools, some are day schools, while others are boarding schools, and the annual tuition for each will vary dramatically, from $2,000 per year to well over $50,000 per year.

Unlike public schools, which must follow a state-controlled curriculum and employ only state-certified teachers, individual private schools have much more control over the curriculum that's taught and the faculty members are not required to be licensed or certified by the state or any other organization or association. Private schools might hire an expert in his or her field as opposed to a licensed teacher to teach a specific subject, for example. Like public schools, however, many private schools rely on standardized testing as a measure of their success in educating the students.

One of the main reasons why parents opt to send their children to private school is for the smaller class sizes and increased level of student-teacher interaction. While class sizes are an issue nationwide, within Long Island's public schools, they're typically kept pretty small, so this benefit that private schools offer isn't as relevant.

Parents who have aspirations of sending their kids to Ivy League colleges and universities often turn to private K–12 schools for that added competitive edge. Whether or not your child should receive a private school education is a highly personal decision that parents must make for themselves, based on budgetary considerations, the goals they have for their children, and the faith they have in their local public school system to give their child a quality and well-rounded education.

Parents with strong religious convictions sometimes choose a private parochial school for their children to help them expand and strengthen their own religious ideas and beliefs. Again, the decision about whether or not an education with a strong religious component is suitable for your kids is a highly personal one.

i For a listing of Long Island–area K–12 parochial schools and information about each of them, visit www.longislandexchange.com/schools/parochial-schools.html. A complete listing of private K–12 schools can be found at www.citidexli.com/817.htm#C3530.

COLLEGES AND UNIVERSITIES ON LONG ISLAND

New York City has its fair share of high-profile, well-known colleges and universities; however, if you'd prefer to pursue a college, graduate, or post-graduate degree on Long Island, you have a nice selection of highly reputable schools to choose from.

Four-Year Schools

The following schools offer traditional four-year undergraduate degree programs, and in some cases graduate and post-graduate degrees as well.

ADELPHI UNIVERSITY
1 South Ave., Garden City
(800) 233-5744
www.adelphi.edu

Adelphi University is one of the oldest educational institutions in New York State. The school was founded in 1863 as Adelphi Academy, a private preparatory school in Brooklyn, New York.

However, the school ultimately transformed itself into Adelphi University and became the first private coeducational institution of higher learning on Long Island.

Today Adelphi University is composed of multiple colleges and schools, which offer a wide range of academic paths to pursue. For example, there's the College of Arts and Sciences, the Gordon F. Derner Institute of Advanced Psychological Studies, the Honors College, the School of Business, the Ruth S. Ammon School of Education, School of Nursing, School of Social Work, and University College. As of 2009 more than 8,600 students were enrolled at Adelphi University and participated in classes at the school's main campus in Garden City, as well as its satellite campuses in New York City, Hauppauge, and Poughkeepsie.

i In addition to offering a traditional campus, complete with classrooms, dormitories, etc., Adelphi University offers a complete distance-learning program via the Internet. This program is designed to meet the needs of students who want the quality education that Adelphi and its faculty offer, but who need a very flexible schedule or, for whatever reason, choose not to participate in traditional classes.

HOFSTRA UNIVERSITY
Hempstead
(516) 463-6600
www.hofstra.edu

Hofstra University, a private institution, currently offers a choice of more than 150 undergraduate and 160 graduate programs in liberal arts and sciences, business, communications, education, and health and human services, plus has a well-respected law school. The university boasts a student-to-faculty ratio of 14 to 1 and an average class size of 22 students, as well as all of the state-of-the-art and traditional resources students need to excel. In addition to academics, the school offers a vast selection of social, athletic, and recreational activities to provide for a well-rounded college experience on its 240-acre campus.

Hofstra was founded in 1935 as a private, nonsectarian, coeducational university. Colleges and schools offered as part of Hofstra University include the Hofstra College of Liberal Arts and Sciences, Frank G. Zarb School of Business, School of Communication, School of Education, Health and Human Services, School of Law, School for University Studies, Honors College, Continuing Education, and the proposed Hofstra University School of Medicine in partnership with North Shore Long Island Jewish Health System.

As of 2009 there were 7,327 full-time students enrolled at Hofstra University. The total student body, including part-time undergraduate, graduate, and School of Law, consisted of approximately 12,100 students. The student body in 2009 was 45 percent male and 55 percent female. In total, the school possesses 21 academic accreditations.

LONG ISLAND UNIVERSITY
700 Northern Blvd., Brookville
(800) 548-7526
www.liu.edu/liu_start.html

For more than 90 years Long Island University has been giving its students the opportunity to pursue higher education. What the school offers is a multi-campus, diverse, doctoral institution of higher learning. Long Island University is one of the largest private universities in the country, with approximately 590 undergraduate, graduate, and doctoral degree programs and certificates. It educates over 24,000 students in degree-credit and continuing education programs through its Brooklyn, Brookville (C. W. Post), Brentwood, Riverhead, Rockland, Westchester, and Southampton campuses.

For example, the Arnold & Marie Schwartz College of Pharmacy and Health Sciences helps to prepare students for successful careers in the fields of pharmacy and health care, while the university Global College offers a wide range of study-abroad options at overseas centers in countries like China, Costa Rica, India, Japan, and South Africa. To help foster the educational process, Long Island University has almost 650 full-time faculty members. As of 2009 the university had more than 167,000 alumni who have gone on to pursue careers in many different fields and industries around the world.

LONG ISLAND UNIVERSITY–C. W. POST CAMPUS

720 Northern Blvd., Brookville
(516) 299-2000
www.cwpost.liu.edu/cwis/cwp

The Long Island University–C. W. Post Campus was founded back in 1954 to accommodate the educational needs of World War II veterans living in Nassau County. As of 2009 the school had 5,672 undergraduate and 3,099 graduate students enrolled. The student body is diverse and comes from 38 states and 48 countries. One interesting statistic is that only about 35 percent of the student body attending classes at the university is male.

Along with the full-time students, each year approximately 2,300 additional students enroll in continuing education courses offered at the school. Currently the school offers 104 programs leading to a baccalaureate; 75 programs leading to a master's; 58 programs leading to a dual degree (bachelor's/master's); and 3 academic programs leading to a doctorate. For the full-time undergraduate students, degrees offered at the C. W. Post Campus include Bachelor of Arts, Bachelor of Science, Bachelor of Fine Arts, Bachelor of Music, and Associate in Arts. On the graduate level, degrees offered include Master of Arts, Master of Science, Master of Business Administration, Master of Fine Arts, Master of Public Administration, Master of Science in Education, Master of Science in Library and Information Science, Doctor of Psychology, Master of Social Work, Doctor of Philosophy in Information Studies, and Doctor of Education in Interdisciplinary Educational Studies.

This is a private educational institution that is generally recognized for its quality academic programs, renowned faculty, and cooperative education program, not to mention its beautiful 307.9-acre campus located on Long Island's Gold Coast. In addition to focusing on academics, the school has 15 NCAA men's and women's sports teams, most of which utilize the school's 70 acres of playing fields, and the Pratt Recreation Center, which is a modern athletic facility that's equipped with an eight-lane swimming pool, three-court gymnasium for basketball and volleyball, weight room, fitness center, and multiple dance studios, as well as racquetball courts and an elevated jogging/walking track.

i If you or your kids are thinking about applying to a college or university and will require financial aid or scholarships, a visit to the FAFSA (Free Application for Federal Student Aid) Web site is an absolute must (www.fafsa.ed.gov). You can also call the Federal Student Aid Information Center at (800) 4-FED-AID. Keep in mind that the process for applying for and receiving scholarships and/or financial aid can take several months for approval, so plan accordingly.

MOLLOY COLLEGE

1000 Hempstead Ave., Rockville Centre
(888) 4-MOLLOY
www.molloy.edu

For more than 50 years Molloy College has evolved dramatically in an ongoing effort to meet the demanding needs of its students and prepare them for successful careers. The school currently offers degrees in many areas, including business, education, criminal justice, allied health sciences, and computer information systems. Molloy also offers programs in psychology, theology, philosophy, history, political science, music therapy, and mathematics, plus the school has the fourth-largest nursing program in the country.

Outside of the academics, Molloy College offers a well-rounded lineup of activities, including 40 clubs and honor societies, as well as a well-established athletics program. The school's various athletic teams compete in the New York College Athletic Conference (NYCAC) and the NCAA Division II. Popular teams and sports offered at the college include lacrosse, basketball, baseball, softball, soccer, volleyball, tennis, cross-country, equestrian, and a dance team.

The school's Global Learning Program has recently expanded to include study-abroad opportunities in France, Spain, Italy, Belgium, Japan, India, Australia, and Thailand. Malloy's main objective is to prepare every student "to live and work in a world where their only boundaries are self-imposed."

NEW YORK INSTITUTE OF TECHNOLOGY

Northern Blvd., Old Westbury
(516) 686-1000
300 Carleton Ave., Central Islip
(631) 348-3000
www.nyit.edu

New York Institute of Technology (NYIT) was founded in 1955 and currently offers undergraduate, graduate, and professional degrees in more than 90 fields of study. In addition to the main campus in Old Westbury, NYIT has satellite campuses in Central Islip, New York City, Abu Dhabi, Canada, Jordan, and several other countries. NYIT schools include the School of Architecture and Design, School of Education, School of Engineering and Computing Sciences, School of Health Professions, School of Management, College of Arts and Sciences, and College of Osteopathic Medicine.

NYIT is a nonprofit, independent, private institution of higher education that as of 2009 had more than 15,000 students enrolled and attending classes at its Long Island and Manhattan campuses, as well as online. The school's goal is to provide students with a career-oriented professional education and then assist them in pursuing their career endeavors.

In addition to a wide range of clubs and extracurricular activities, NYIT has the following athletic teams: baseball (NCAA Division I), men's and women's basketball (NCAA Division II), men's and women's cross-country (NCAA Division II), men's lacrosse (NCAA Division II), men's and women's soccer (NCAA Division II), softball (NCAA Division II), and women's volleyball (NCAA Division II).

SUNY COLLEGE AT OLD WESTBURY

Old Westbury
(516) 876-3000
www.oldwestbury.edu

Within its beautiful 604-acre campus that's centrally located on Long Island, the SUNY College at Old Westbury offers a quiet atmosphere dedicated to learning, yet it's just 20 miles from Manhattan. As of 2009 approximately 3,300 students from across America and 20 different countries were enrolled at the college. The school has a 122-person full-time faculty and boasts a 17 to 1 student-to-teacher ratio.

Currently SUNY College at Old Westbury offers 45 undergraduate majors and 16 minors, in both liberal arts and professional fields, along with a graduate program in accounting. Undergraduates can pursue the following four-year degrees: Bachelor of Arts, Bachelor of Science, and Bachelor of Professional Studies. Master of Science in Accounting and Master of Science in Taxation degrees are also offered.

SUNY FARMINGDALE

Farmingdale State College
2350 Broadhollow Rd., Farmingdale
(631) 420-2000
www.farmingdale.edu

Farmingdale State College's roots are as an agricultural college, founded in the early 1900s. Over the years, however, it has transformed into an academic institution focused on applied technology, ground-breaking research, and economic development in a wide range of fields. Today, as Farmingdale State approaches its 100th anniversary and its 15th anniversary as a four-year, baccalaureate institution, it offers 33 degree programs in areas as diverse as aeronautical science, applied economics, and electrical engineering. The coeducational public school has approximately 6,500 students enrolled, and boasts that it has become one of the most important centers of learning and research on Long Island.

Farmingdale State is located on 380 acres in the heart of Long Island, approximately 45 minutes from New York City. Since the 1980s, when the school successfully made the transition from being an agricultural college to a technology college, the campus has continued to focus heavily on preparing students for careers in the workplace, through its Schools of Business,

Arts and Sciences, Engineering Technology, and Health Sciences. Regardless of the area of study a student pursues here, technology is integrated into the coursework, so students are provided cutting-edge instructional techniques that make them attractive recruits for public and private industries. As part of the State University of New York, Farmingdale State offers a top-quality education that is affordable.

U.S. MERCHANT MARINE ACADEMY

300 Steamboat Rd., Kings Point
(516) 773-5000
www.usmma.edu

For more than 50 years young individuals have come to Kings Point to acquire the knowledge, experience, discipline, and skills that strong leadership demands. Graduates of the Merchant Marine Academy go on to serve their country by pursuing highly successful careers in the maritime industry and the armed services. Many students, however, wind up continuing their studies in graduate or professional schools, and some have even become outstanding government and business leaders. Every year the academy selects just 275 young men and women for entry into the "plebe class." These students come from across America and from all walks of life. The academy encourages diversity and welcomes people of all races, colors, creeds, and ethnic backgrounds to apply for admission.

Thousands upon thousands of ships and tankers, owned by U.S. companies and registered and operated under the American flag, are operated by active members of the U.S. Merchant Marine. In times of war or national emergency, the Merchant Marine becomes vital to national security. It represents a "fourth arm of defense." U.S. merchant ships are responsible for delivering military supplies overseas to our forces and allies.

WEBB INSTITUTE

298 Crescent Beach Rd., Glen Cove
(516) 671-2213
www.webb-institute.edu

If you haven't heard about Webb Institute, it's not surprising. Located in Glen Cove (on Long Island Sound), this is a very small academic institution with a student body of just 90 undergraduates and a full-time faculty composed of just 10 professors. The people who attend Webb pursue just one academic option—a double major in naval architecture and marine engineering.

Not surprisingly, Webb Institute is the only full-tuition scholarship, private undergraduate program of its kind in the country. In other words, if you're admitted into the program, you receive a 100 percent four-year scholarship. As a result of its highly specialized curriculum, graduates have a 100 percent job-placement success rate, and many undergraduate students go on to receive graduate school placement. This school has been ranked fifth in the United States as a source of empirical science PhDs.

Two- and Three-Year Junior Colleges

For many people, pursuing a four-year degree on a full-time or even part-time basis simply isn't possible based on their current career, family, or economic situation. For these and other individuals who wish to pursue their education beyond high school, Long Island offers a handful of two- and three-year junior colleges, two of which being Briarcliff College and Nassau Community College.

BRIARCLIFF COLLEGE–BETHPAGE CAMPUS

1055 Stewart Ave., Bethpage
(516) 918-3600
www.bcl.org

Briarcliff College–Bethpage Campus offers a selection of career-targeted programs that are designed to meet the needs of today's business and industry. The Commission on Higher Education of the Middle States Association of Colleges and Schools accredits Briarcliff College. This commission is an institutional accrediting agency recognized by the U.S. Secretary of Education and the Commission on Higher Education Accreditation. The New York State Board of Regents also authorizes Briarcliff to offer diploma, associate's degree, and bachelor's degree programs.

At the Bethpage campus, the school offers associate degree programs in applied science,

Long Island's Professional Schools

The following schools on Long Island offer advanced degrees in specialized fields:

Adelphi University Graduate Programs: 1 South Ave., Garden City; (800) 233-5744; www.adelphi.edu

Hofstra University School of Law: Hempstead; (516) 463-5916; http://law.hofstra.edu/home/index.html

New York College of Health Professionals: 6801 Jericho Tnpk., Syosset; (516) 364-0808; www.nycollege.edu

New York College of Osteopathic Medicine: Northern Boulevard, Old Westbury; (516) 686-3747; http://iris.nyit.edu/nycom

Stony Brook School of Dental Medicine: SUNY at Stony Brook, Stony Brook; (631) 632-8900; www.stonybrookmedicalcenter.org/dental

Stony Brook School of Health, Technology & Management: SUNY at Stony Brook, Health Sciences Center, Stony Brook; (631) 444-2252; www.hsc.stonybrook.edu/shtm

Stony Brook School of Medicine: SUNY at Stony Brook, Stony Brook; (631) 444-2113; www.stonybrookmedicalcenter.org/som

Stony Brook School of Nursing: SUNY at Stony Brook, Stony Brook; (631) 444-3200; www.nursing.stonybrook.edu

Stony Brook School of Social Welfare: SUNY at Stony Brook, Stony Brook; (631) 444-2138; www.stonybrookmedicalcenter.org/ssw

Touro Law Center: 225 Eastview Dr., Central Islip; (631) 761-7000; www.tourolaw.edu

criminal justice, graphic design, networking and computer technology, and paralegal studies. Bachelor's degrees are offered in accounting, information technology, management, marketing, criminal justice, and graphic design. Briarcliff College also has campuses in Patchogue and Queens.

NASSAU COMMUNITY COLLEGE

1 Education Dr., Garden City
(516) 572-7501
www.ncc.edu

As of 2009 more than 22,000 day and evening students, and almost 15,000 continuing and professional students, of all ages and backgrounds were enrolled at Nassau Community College, which offers a 225-acre campus in the center of Long Island. The school is proud of its high academic standards and first-class facilities, as well as a highly distinguished faculty. Nassau Community College offers one of the best teacher-to-student ratios in New York State.

All enrolled students have access to the latest technology in the classroom and laboratory facilities as they pursue more than 60 fields of study, including business; fine, graphic, and performing arts; health-related sciences; liberal arts and sciences; mathematics and computers; natural sciences; engineering technologies; office technologies; and social sciences.

SENIOR SCENE

Between the golf courses, resorts, county clubs, and abundance of cultural activities and restaurants offered on Long Island, the region definitely attracts the 65-and-up crowd—both as a summer vacation spot and as a year-round destination to live. Needless to say, seniors on Long Island typically lead very happy, active, and productive lives, whether they're living totally independently or within a retirement community, assisted living facility, or nursing home.

Many of the retirement-age people living or vacationing on Long Island are considered affluent, or at least upper-middle class, so the prices associated with the various housing options, for example, are mainly in line with that (with a few exceptions, of course). Long Island is known for having a shortage of affordable housing and rental apartments in any price range.

AREA AGENCIES ON AGING AND HELPFUL RESOURCES

The following agencies, organizations, and resources can help Long Island's senior citizens and their families in a wide range of areas.

AARP
(888) 687-2277
www.aarp.org

With more than 40 million members in the United States, AARP is a nonprofit, nonpartisan membership organization that helps people age 50-plus improve the quality of their life. The organization's prime mission is to enhance the quality of life for everyone as they age.

CATHOLIC CHARITIES
www.catholiccharities.cc/ourservices/senior.html

This organization provides a range of services to help Long Island seniors enjoy a high quality of life. It aims to ensure that seniors can live independently, in comfort and safety, while maintaining physical and emotional health. The social activities sponsored by Catholic Charities help seniors to better remain connected with their community. Some of the programs offered include Meals-On-Wheels (Nassau County: 516-377-2691; Suffolk County: 631-842-4123); the operation of Senior Community Centers in Franklin Square (516-481-3322), Massapequa Park (516-797-5357), Oceanside (516-764-9792), and Seaford (516-679-8373); and Caregiver Support (516-348-8010).

MEDICARE RIGHTS CENTER
(800) 333-4114
www.medicarerights.org

This Web site is designed to help seniors understand their rights when it comes to Medicare benefits.

NATIONAL CONSUMER VOICE FOR QUALITY LONG-TERM CARE
(202) 332-2275
http://nccnhr.org

This is a nonprofit consumer-advocacy organization that caters primarily to nursing home residents. It's mandate is to provide information on staffing in nursing homes, details about citizen-advocacy groups, tips on how family members can advocate for good care, and details about government policies, laws, and regulations affecting residents. Additional free resources available from the Web site include fact sheets on malnutrition, neglect, abuse, use of restraints, and resident rights. You'll also discover a nationwide listing of agencies and organizations to contact to file a complaint about poor nursing home care.

NEW YORK FOUNDATION FOR SENIOR CITIZENS
(212) 962-7559
www.nyfsc.org
This is an organization dedicated to assisting New York State's seniors in avoiding the need for premature institutionalization, thus allowing them to be able to more thoroughly enjoy a healthier, safer, productive, and dignified life while remaining in their own homes.

NEW YORK STATE SENIOR CITIZEN RESOURCE GUIDE
(800) 342-9871
www.aging.ny.gov/ResourceGuide/Index.cfm
Published by the New York State Office for the Aging, this Web site is a free consumer's guide relating to information, programs, and services for older New Yorkers, including those living on Long Island.

RIVERHEAD SENIOR CITIZEN DEPARTMENT
(631) 722-4444
www.riverheadli.com/senior-services.html
The town of Riverhead offers a handful of programs, activities, and support services for seniors. Some of the information on this site is relevant to all Long Island seniors, not just those living in Riverhead.

SOCIAL SECURITY ONLINE
(800) 772-1213
www.ssa.gov
This Web site is operated by the U.S. Social Security Administration and is designed to help seniors better understand their benefits and the resources available to them.

SUFFOLK COUNTY OFFICE FOR THE AGING
(631) 853-8200
www.co.suffolk.ny.us/departments/CountyExec/aging.aspx
The Suffolk County Office for the Aging is the designated area agency on aging under the Older Americans Act. This agency oversees or administers a handful of federal, state, and county programs for people over the age of 60.

TOWN OF BROOKHAVEN SENIOR CITIZENS DIVISION
(631) 451-9191
www.451-town.com/OfficeoftheSupervisor/SeniorCitizensDivision/tabid/63/Default.aspx
The Town of Brookhaven offers a range of special services for seniors, including medical and shopping transportation, adult day care, in-home services, home chore and repair services, senior citizen clubs, summertime picnics, sports, and day trips. Some of the information on this site is relevant to all Long Island seniors.

COMMUNITY AND SENIOR CENTERS

Almost every town, village, and community on Long Island offers some type of community center or senior center, as well as organized activities and services for local seniors living in or visiting the area. This translates to several hundred active senior centers on Long Island.

To learn about what's offered in a specific community, visit the local chamber of commerce, town hall, or city hall in your area. For a partial listing of senior centers located in Nassau County, visit www.nassaucountyny.gov/agencies/Seniors/Senior%20Affairs/MultiService.html. For senior centers in Suffolk County, go to www.co.suffolk.ny.us/home/departments/CountyExec/aging.aspx and click on the "Programs and Services Guide" link.

i **In addition to senior centers and community centers, many of Long Island's colleges and universities offer special educational programs for seniors. See the "Education" chapter for a listing of local colleges and universities.**

RETIREMENT COMMUNITIES

Retirement communities are apartments, condos, or gated communities composed of stand-alone houses, for example, where residents must be over a specific age, such as 55 or 65, in order to live there. These communities offer activities such as clubhouses, fitness centers, swimming pools, tennis courts, and golf courses, but are not designed to be assisted living facilities or nursing homes. Residents are 100 percent independent.

Throughout Long Island there are more than 100 retirement communities that offer vastly different resources and amenities. The majority of them require the purchase of real estate, along with the payment of monthly fees, thus the costs relate directly to the real estate market where the properties are located. The best way to learn about these housing communities is to work with a real estate agent (Realtor) who specializes in the senior/retirement market on Long Island. (See the "Relocation" chapter for a partial listing of Long Island–area Realtors.)

The following is just a small sampling of retirement communities on Long Island. Some of these communities are sold out, so the developer no longer directly sells units. However, units or houses may be available on the secondary market through private owners/sellers.

- **Eagles Walk:** East Quogue, (631) 208-9340, http://blueandgoldhomes.com/eagleswalk
- **Eastport Meadows:** Eastport, (631) 801-2769, www.northwindgroup.com/eastport.asp
- **Encore:** Lake Grove, (866) 260-9822, www.encoreatlakegrove.com
- **Fairfield:** St. James, (631) 862-8155
- **The Greens at Half Hollow:** Melville, (631) 271-4500, www.thegreensathalfhollow.com
- **Greenwood Village:** Manorville, (631) 878-3214 or (631) 878-4200
- **Harbor View:** Port Washington, http://harborviewpw.com/outside_home.asp
- **Port Harbor Condominiums:** Port Washington, (516) 944-3595
- **Saddle Lakes:** Riverhead, (631) 727-7935, http://suffolkexperts.com
- **Stoneleigh Woods:** Riverhead, (631) 208-9340 or (845) 225-0639, http://blueandgoldhomes.com/stoneleighwoodsatriverhead
- **Sunken Pond Estates:** Riverhead, http://sunkenpondestatesriverhead.com/condos/Home.aspx
- **Sunrise Village:** Sayville, (631) 589-6161
- **Village Vistas:** Port Jefferson, (631) 582-8300, www.northwindgroup.com/village-vistas.asp

Additional listings for senior citizen housing options and retirement communities in Nassau County can be found at www.longislandexchange.com/nassauseniors.html. For a partial listing of senior citizen housing and retirement communities in Suffolk County, visit www.longislandexchange.com/suffolkseniors.html.

i Be sure to read the "Health Care" chapter for more information about Long Island's more than 420 nursing homes and assisted living facilities.

ASSISTED LIVING FOR SENIORS

An assisted living residence is a housing option in which five or more elderly adults live with non-family members. These residences provide meals, on-site monitoring, and other services for the residents, with the goal of providing a home-like setting. In some cases, funding for this housing option is available through Supplemental Security Income (SSI) and Medicaid programs."

In other words, assisted living facilities offer housing options for seniors where the residents maintain their independence, yet a wide range of services and resources are available to them as they're needed.

To learn more about assisted living residences in a specific Long Island community, contact the Office for the Aging by calling their Senior Hotline at (800) 342-9871 or visit www.aging.state.ny.us. For a listing of senior housing developments and the 100-plus assisted living facilities on Long Island, call (631) 777-4663 or visit www.longislandseniorshousing.com.

MEDIA

Long Island is closely affiliated with the number one media market in the United States—New York City. However, in addition to having access to all of the New York City area's major newspapers, regional magazines, radio stations, television stations, and Web sites with a NYC focus, Long Island also has its own, more localized media outlets.

MAJOR DAILY AND WEEKLY NEWSPAPERS

While many Long Islanders read the *New York Times*, *New York Daily News*, and/or the *New York Post*, the following are the major daily and weekly newspapers published on Long Island and targeted to a local or regional readership.

ANTON NEWS

(516) 747-8282

www.antonnews.com

This newspaper publisher regularly publishes 18 different daily and weekly newspapers, covering 70 communities throughout Nassau County. The individual weekly newspapers are available by subscription (with home delivery via U.S. Mail) for as little as 31 to 35 cents per week when you sign up for a three-year subscription. The newspapers are also sold at local newsstands and retailers. They cover local and regional news and sports, along with national headlines. Each offers its own local columns, calendar of events, obituaries, and ongoing insight into the community it covers.

INDEPENDENT EAST END NEWSPAPER

(631) 324-2500

www.indyeastend.com

This is a print and online publication that covers the Hamptons, including East Hampton, Southampton, Riverhead, Southold, and Shelter Island. It's a general interest, news, and lifestyle publication. The regularly published arts and entertainment section covers all of the ongoing special events taking place within the region, while the real estate section keeps up-to-the-minute tabs on the local real estate market and the impact the economy is having on it. Featuring local columnists, this paper has a very small-town feel and will appeal to local residents and visitors spending time in the region.

LONG ISLAND BUSINESS NEWS

(631) 737-1700

www.libn.com

Available in both print and online formats, this is the region's primarily business-oriented publication covering local industries and businesses throughout Long Island. The printed edition is published weekly and covers local commerce and trends impacting Long Island's more than 120,000 businesses. This is a "must read" publication for anyone doing business on Long Island, or who wants to stay current on how the economy and other trends are impacting the local job market, for example. The classifieds section offers job listings as well as information about local businesses and commercial real estate for sale. Published weekly, a one-year subscription for the print edition of *Long Island Business News* (which includes access to the online edition) is priced at $109.

LONG ISLAND CATHOLIC

(516) 594-1000

www.licatholic.org

This is the official publication of the Catholic Diocese of Rockville Centre. The weekly print edition of the newspaper is priced at $20 per year. Offering a strong religious slant on local, regional, and national events, some of the regularly published columns featured in the newspaper include "From the Pope," "Faith and New Works," "Reading the Signs," "Word of God," "The Church and Prayer," "Faith and Thought," "Harvesting Hope," and "The Catholic Home."

LONG ISLAND NEWSDAY
(800) 639-7329
www.newsday.com
This is Long Island's largest and most respected major daily newspaper. Home delivery of the print edition is available; however, you can also purchase single copies of *Newsday* at newsstands and other retailers throughout Long Island and in New York City. This newspaper covers both Nassau and Suffolk County as a region, with some focus on the smaller communities. However, it also covers national news stories, entertainment, sports, and everything else you'd find in a major daily newspaper, like the *New York Daily News* or *New York Post*. The subscription rate for daily home delivery, seven days a week, is just $4.50 per week.

LONG ISLAND PRESS
(516) 284-3300
www.longislandpress.com
This is Long Island's largest weekly news and entertainment publication. It covers both Nassau and Suffolk County and offers local and regional coverage of news events, arts and entertainment, and sports. It's known for its annual "Best of Long Island" special edition, which rates things like the best restaurants and shopping on the island.

TIMES BEACON RECORD NEWSPAPERS
(631) 751-7744
www.northshoreoflongisland.com
This is a group of newspapers covering northern Suffolk County. Printed and online editions are available. Local news, politics, sports, and arts and entertainment are covered. The calendar publishes information about all types of events happening throughout the year, from fund-raisers and special events to theater and movie listings. The annual subscription rate for the print edition of each local newspaper is $39. Single issues are also available from local newsstands and merchants.

i There are many smaller daily and weekly newspapers published throughout Long Island that cater to individual towns and communities, such as the *East Hampton Star*, *Amityville Report*, *Massapequa Post*, and *Babylon Beacon*. These newspapers are available for home delivery or from local newsstands and retailers.

REGIONAL MAGAZINES

Especially in the tourist areas of Long Island, there is a handful of monthly, bimonthly, quarterly (seasonal), and annual magazines published specifically for tourists. Many of these publications are available from the various chamber of commerce or tourism offices throughout Long Island, and are also distributed for free at hotels, tourist attractions, and some restaurants. The following are just a few of the more popular regional magazines published on Long Island that are of interest to residents and tourists alike.

THE CROSS SOUNDER
(631) 843-2222
www.longislandferry.com
This is the official publication of the Cross Sound Ferry, which serves Long Island and New England riders throughout the year. It's distributed free aboard the ferry. Most of the articles cover news and history about the ferry boats in the fleet, as well as special events happening near Orient Point and New London, Connecticut, where the ferry docks. In a recent issue there was an article about the historic lighthouses along the Long Island Sound, as well as "Top Picks" for what visitors should do on Long Island.

DINING OUT & ENTERTAINING
(631) 287-1500
www.27east.com
Published each season, this publication offers a comprehensive listing of Long Island's restaurants and features news and articles related to

dining out. It's published by the Press Newsgroup, owner of the *East Hampton Press* and the *Southampton Press*. This free publication is a "must read" for anyone who is interested in learning about new restaurants and major changes at existing restaurants, enjoys reading about local chefs, or takes dining out seriously.

LONG ISLAND PULSE
(631) 289-4315
www.lipulse.com
This is a monthly, full-color, glossy lifestyle magazine with a Long Island focus. Local dining, fashion, nightlife, sports, and family life are covered through feature articles and ongoing columns—all written by Long Islanders. The subscription rate for 12 monthly issues is $18.

LONG ISLAND TRAVEL GUIDE
(877)-386-6654
www.discoverlongisland.com
Published by the Long Island Convention & Visitors Bureau and Sports Commission, this is an indispensible, free, full-color resource for people planning a trip to Long Island. It's available from tourism offices, attractions, and local chamber of commerce offices throughout Long Island, or can be mailed to you for free upon request.

LONG ISLAND WINE PRESS
(631) 298-3200
www.liwines.com
This is the official, full-color magazine published by the Long Island Wine Council. It offers comprehensive coverage of Long Island's wine country and the wineries and vineyards found in the region. It's published every six months and available free of charge.

RADIO STATIONS

In addition to dozens of radio stations originating from New York City (and surrounding boroughs) that offer music, news, talk, sports, and a wide range of other programming, Long Island also has a handful of its own radio stations. Some of the more popular Long Island–based stations include:

WALK-FM–97.5: Music and news
WAXQ-FM–104.3: Classic rock
WBAB-FM–102.3: Rock
WBBR-AM–1130: Bloomberg Radio
WBEA–FM-101.7: Today's hottest music ("The Beach")
WBLI-FM-106.1: Hit music
WBZO-FM–103.1: Greatest hits (oldies)
WDRE-FM–105.3: Dance, hip-hop, and R & B
WGBB-AM–1240: News/talk
WHLI-AM–1100: All-time favorites music
WKJY-FM–98.3: Today's hits and yesterday's favorites
WLVG-FM–96.1: "Long Island's Best Mix " music
WRCN-FM–103.9: Classic rock
WRKS-FM–88.7: Hofstra University radio station
WUSB-FM–90.1: Stony Brook University radio station

TELEVISION STATIONS

In addition to the following island-based television stations, Long Island also receives the broadcast signals from New York City television stations, including all of the network TV affiliates. Based on where you are on Long Island, however, a cable TV subscription may be required to receive all of the popular New York City–based channels, as well as an extensive lineup of basic and premium cable TV channels.

NEWS 12 LONG ISLAND
This is Long Island's answer to CNN. It's a local, 24-hour, all-news network that exclusively covers Nassau and Suffolk Counties. It's available to more than 800,000 households through the various Long Island Cablevision cable services that operate on the island.

WLNY-TV (CHANNEL 55)
This is an independent TV station on Long Island that broadcasts a lineup of popular syndicated shows, from *Judge Judy* and *Dr. Phil* to *Wheel of Fortune* and *Jeopardy!*

WVVH-TV (HAMPTONS TELEVISION)

This local television station is dedicated to covering the Hamptons. It broadcasts on UHF channel 50, as well as through many of the region's local cable TV providers (channel number varies). The station covers local news and events, in addition to human interest stories.

NYC TV Affiliates

While channel numbers will vary based on your local cable provider, New York City's network television affiliates and popular non-cable include:

ABC–WABC-TV: Channel 7

CBS–WCBS-TV: Channel 2

NBC–WNBC-TV: Channel 4

The CW–WPIX-TV: Channel 11

FOX–WNEW-TV: Channel 5

PBS–WNET-TV: Channel 13

Telemundo–WNYU-TV: Channel 47

Independent–WOR-TV: Channel 9

LONG ISLAND WEB SITES

The following online magazines and interactive publications offer a wide range of news, sports, entertainment, and lifestyle information of interest to Long Islanders and visitors alike.

i Long Island Cablevision/Optimum (631-267-6900, 516-364-8400, www.cablevision.com) is the primary cable television provider for all of Long Island. However, Verizon's FIOS service (888-881-8161, www.verizon.com) is slowly being made available across Long Island as an all-digital alternative to cable TV. Another alternative to cable TV programming is DirectTV satellite service (888-777-2454, www.directtv.com).

DISCOVER LONG ISLAND

www.discoverlongisland.com

This is the official Web site of the Long Island Convention & Visitors Bureau and Sports Commission (877-FUN-ON-LI). It's an excellent resource for anyone looking to vacation on Long Island, with information on accommodations, restaurants, activities, attractions, special events, and the history of Long Island. The site is updated regularly with articles and information about what there is to see and do on the island throughout each season.

EXPLORE LONG ISLAND

www.exploreli.com

This is a comprehensive online news, lifestyle, and entertainment magazine operated by the *Long Island Newsday* staff. If you're looking for a great place to eat, for example, this site maintains a complete listing of all Long Island restaurants, plus offers featured reviews of new restaurants. You'll also find a detailed events listing here. Another useful resource is the online edition of *Long Island Newsday* (www.newsday.com/long-island).

HAMPTONS.COM

www.hamptons.com

Targeted to residents and visitors to the Hamptons, this online magazine and directory offers everything you want and need to know about the region, including a listing of current events, profiles of local merchants, reviews of local restaurants, and information about top tourist attractions.

LONGISLAND.COM

www.longisland.com

This site combines the resources of an online-based newsmagazine with a comprehensive directory of events, services, activities, and other resources on Long Island. From hotel and restaurant listings to a detailed events calendar covering all of Long Island, you'll find it here.

LONGISLANDPRESS.COM

www.longislandpress.com

This is the online edition of the *Long Island Press,* which is one of the largest weekly newspapers in the United States. It caters exclusively to Long Island residents and visitors.

NASSAU COUNTY GOVERNMENT WEB SITE

www.nassaucountyny.gov

This site offers a wide range of information about Nassau County, including news and lifestyle information of interest to residents and tourists alike. It's of more interest to people living and working in Nassau County, and covers local politics and other issues. You can also read about local elected officials and obtain their contact information.

NEWS 12 ONLINE

www.news12.com

This is the interactive news and information Web site operated by News 12 Long Island, the 24-hour local news service dedicated to covering the counties of Nassau and Suffolk. The cable TV–exclusive service currently reaches nearly 800,000 households through the Long Island Cablevision system.

NORTHFORK.COM

www.northfork.com

This is an informative and entertaining online magazine covering Long Island's North Fork region (wine country). It covers news and events at the local vineyards, as well as provides details about local lodging, events, dining, attractions, shopping, recreation, real estate, local services, and the weather forecast. There's also a local classified ads section and a map section on the site. Most of what's on the site is in the form of links, as opposed to original articles and editorial coverage, but it's a great resource for someone planning a trip to this region.

SUFFOLK COUNTY GOVERNMENT WEB SITE

www.co.suffolk.ny.us

This site offers a wide range of information about Suffolk County, including news and lifestyle information of interest to residents and tourists alike. It is of particular interest to anyone living or working in Suffolk County, since it covers local politics and provides information about local government programs and issues. The site also provides information about local elected officials, along with their contact information.

INDEX

INSIDERS' GUIDE®

The acclaimed travel series that has sold more than 2 million copies!

Pointing You in the Right Direction

Santa Barbara
Including Channel Islands National Park

Glacier National Park

Columbus

Now with a fresh new look!

Written by locals and true insiders, each guide is packed with information about places to stay, restaurants, shopping, attractions, fun things for the kids, day trips, relocation tips, and local history. For over twenty years, travelers have relied on ***Insiders' Guides*** for practical and personal travel and relocation information.

To order call **800-243-0495**
or visit www.InsidersGuides.com